BIG-CITY
POLICE

BIG-CITY POLICE

Robert M. Fogelson

AN URBAN INSTITUTE STUDY

HARVARD UNIVERSITY PRESS
Cambridge, Massachusetts, and
London, England

Job H-84

Copyright© 1977 by the President and Fellows of Harvard College
All rights reserved
Printed in the United States of America
Third printing 1979
Library of Congress Cataloging in Publication Data

Fogelson, Robert M.
    Big-city police.

    (An Urban Institute study)
    Includes bibliographical references and index.
    1. Police—United States—History. I. Title.
II. Series: Urban Institute. An Urban Institute study.
HV8138.F55   363.2'0973   77-5096
ISBN 0-674-07281-2 (cloth)
ISBN 0-674-07295-2 (paper)

mmmmmmmmmmmmmmmmmmmmmmmmmmmmmm

To Oscar Handlin
and the memory
of Mary Handlin

Foreword

Because of the wall that by the late 1960s had grown up between citizens and government agencies, the twin issues of citizen participation and citizen control were early targets for investigation by the Urban Institute. The police were a case in point. Tense racial problems and mounting violence frequently found the police in the middle. Often they did not appear to be accountable to mayors and city managers. The loss of public faith was demonstrated by the popular questioning of the tradition of local autonomy. People took their fears and concerns to the national government, where members of Congress and the President repeatedly promised to "do something" about lawlessness in the streets, the schools, and the marketplace.

Patrick V. Murphy, the Institute's first director of public safety research, brought from his police experience the highly unconventional view that it might make sense to return to some of the features of late nineteenth and early twentieth century police systems. He favored experimentation with restoring authority at the precinct or beat level, assigning officers in ways to assure they would get to know the people and problems of the neighborhood, and reinstating foot patrols. These proposals were conceived not as gimmicks but as a major reversal of the modern, motorized, highly centralized police force that had lost touch with the community. Pursuing this philosophy, the Institute launched research into what is known as neighborhood team policing.

Yet historical questions about the relationship between police and citizens loomed large. If certain past practices hold answers to today's problems, why had they been largely abandoned? If bureaucratication and professionalism, which had been posed as correctives to the corruption and abuses of previous eras, were now the focus of complaints of police coldness, how could the old pitfalls be avoided once the police and community were brought closer together? Joseph H. Lewis, then director of the Institute's urban governance research, was trying to find a way to unravel these questions when he learned of Robert Fogelson's interest in the evolution of big-city police. As a social historian, Fogelson had already undertaken a probing study of urban riots and violence. Moreover, his interest did not focus narrowly on the police developments of the 1890s or 1930s for their own sake; rather, he was trying to see what light these past eras could shed on contemporary problems.

Fogelson has here provided a historical view of big-city police, with emphasis on the changes wrought by the reform movement. Future debates over residency and other entrance requirements for police work will not easily ignore his findings that the reform movement inadvertently led to the exclusion of blacks and other minorities from the police forces. His views about police pension systems are especially pertinent, first as they relate to the pressures that mounting pension costs have placed on city fiscal affairs, and second as they relate to the incentives for experienced officers to retire when they still have many productive years to offer.

Local political and community leaders have much to learn from Fogelson's analysis of the dynamics of change in urban society and government. Although substantial segments of the urban community felt alienated from the police during the 1950s and 1960s, he found that for a far longer period the majority of the police have felt isolated and alienated from the community. His insights will help people to understand how the institution of policing came to be conceived as a bulwark *against* society, and also how it might be reshaped into an institution that cooperates *with* society in the maintenance of order and justice.

WILLIAM GORHAM

The Urban Institute
Washington, D.C.

Preface

Several years ago I wrote a book about riots and ghettos, one chapter of which dealt with the big-city police. As the chapter focused largely on the recent past, I did only a little research on the history of policing. But on the basis of that research I was struck by how much the big-city police had changed since the late nineteenth century. I began to wonder just what had happened to policing in the first two-thirds of the twentieth century. Many questions came to mind. How much had the big-city police changed? In what ways? If the changes were deliberate, which groups brought them about? What did they hope to accomplish? How well did they succeed? What impact did the changes have on big-city policing? And what impact did they have on the process of mobility, the distribution of power, and the struggle for a status in urban America? To find the answers, I looked at the files of police departments, went through the archives of presidential commissions, poured over the transcripts of investigative committees, read innumerable newspaper articles, and even watched a few Keystone Cops movies. It took much longer than anticipated. But gradually a story began to unfold, a story that reveals as much about the process of institutional change in urban America as about the history of big-city policing in the twentieth century. *Big-City Police* tells that story.

I incurred a good many obligations in the course of writing this book. The Urban Institute provided the funds to launch the study, helped open the door to several police departments, and waited patiently for me to complete the manuscript. For their support I would like to thank William Gorham, president of the Institute, Harold W. Guthrie, vice-president for research, B. J. Stiles, director of publications, and Joseph H. Lewis, then director of the Institute's program on urban governance and now director of evaluation at the Police Foundation. I would also like to thank Alan A. Altshuler, who first brought my study to the Institutes's attention. I am grateful to the Social Science Research Council, which gave me a fellowship to study American policing, and to the John Simon Guggenheim Memorial Foundation, which awarded me a fellowship to analyze police unions. Some of the research was done under the auspices of a project on innovative resource planning, housed at MIT's Operations Research Center, which was sponsored by the Division of Social Systems and Human Resources of the National Science Foundation. Thanks are due Richard C. Larson, head of the project. Other research was carried on as part of a study of municipal employee unions, housed at the Harvard-MIT Joint Center for Urban Studies, which was supported by the Center for Studies of Metropolitan Problems of the National Institute of Mental Health. Thanks are also due Elliot Liebow, director of the Center for Studies of Metropolitan Problems.

Chief Herbert T. Jenkins allowed me to go through the files of the Atlanta Police Department and otherwise made a trip to Atlanta one of the high points of the study. Chief Jerry V. Wilson gave me access to the files of the Washington, D.C., police, which reveal a good deal not only about the Washington force but about other big-city departments as well. Harvey N. Johnson let me examine the files of the Chicago Crime Commission, which are a mine of information about the Chicago Police Department. Royce Givens was kind enough to permit me to look at the files of the International Conference of Police Associations, one of the two major organizations of rank-and-file groups. Thomas A. Mela put at my disposal the files of the Massachusetts Law Reform Institute. Anthony M. Platt was good enough to let me go through his files on the struggle for community control of the police. And Patrick Sheehan introduced me to the remarkable resources of the Motion Picture Section of the Library of Congress. I am grateful to all these people. I am also grateful to the staffs of the Harvard College Library, Library of Congress, Bancroft Library, MIT Libraries, National Archives, Federal Records Center, New York City Municipal Archives, Los Angeles Municipal Records Center, Los Angeles City Clerk's Office, Atlanta City Clerk's Office, and San Francisco Board of Supervisors' Office.

I have learned much about big-city policing from other historians and social scientists, most of whom are mentioned in the footnotes. My thanks go especially to Joseph G. Woods, whose doctoral dissertation has a wealth of detail about police reform in Los Angeles and, so far as I know, is the only full-scale history of a big-city police department in the twentieth century. I have also learned much about police unions from former and current students, most of whom are also referred to in the notes. My thanks go particularly to Margaret A. Levi, whose doctoral dissertation helped me to figure out the process by which the patrolmen's associations were transformed from pressure groups into de facto labor unions. Margaret E. Dewar, Mark H. Furstenberg, Oscar Handlin, Richard C. Larson, Joseph H. Lewis, Gary T. Marx, David J. Rothman, Lloyd L. Weinreb, and James Q. Wilson read and commented on all or parts of an earlier version of the manuscript. I am grateful to them, as well as to Aida DiPace Donald and Virginia LaPlante, my editors at the Harvard University Press. At every stage of this work I have been able to draw upon Oscar Handlin for the special sort of inspiration and counsel that only his former students can fully appreciate.

ROBERT M. FOGELSON

Contents

BIG-CITY
POLICE

Prologue

On February 14, 1892, the Reverend Charles H. Parkhurst, minister of the Madison Square Presbyterian Church and president of the Society for the Prevention of Crime, delivered the first of several sermons decrying the corruption and incompetence of the New York City Police Department. The sermons generated a furor. But aside from spurring a few grand jury investigations and departmental trials, Parkhurst made little headway in his crusade to clean up the police force and overthrow Tammany Hall, the Democratic machine that ran New York City. In the midst of this crusade the Republicans gained control of the New York State legislature. In an effort to increase the party's influence over the city police, Thomas Platt, the Republican leader—about whom a rival once quipped, "when he took snuff they [the Republicans] all sneezed"—proposed a bill putting the police department under a bipartisan commission. While the legislators deliberated, Gustav H. Schwab and several other prominent business and civic leaders who had been aroused by Parkhurst's crusade prevailed on the New York Chamber of Commerce to call for a full-scale investigation of the police force. Assuming that an investigation would enhance their bill's prospects, the Republicans backed the chamber's proposal. On January 30, 1894, the New York State Senate appointed a special committee, consisting of five Republicans and two Democrats and chaired by Senator Clarence Lexow of Rockland County, to look into the Reverend Parkhurst's charges against the New York City Police Department.[1]

Many New Yorkers viewed the Lexow Committee, which arrived in the city on February 1, with skepticism. Previous legislative committees — including a special assembly committee chaired by Theodore Roosevelt, which had probed the police department in 1884, and a regular senate committee chaired by J. Sloat Fassett, which had examined the municipal government in 1890 — had accomplished little. If the Lexow Committee stuck to the terms of the enabling resolution, which required that the report be submitted by February 20, it could do nothing more than hold a few weeks of hearings, which would probably be designed merely to stir up support for Platt's bipartisan commission. Parkhurst, Schwab, and their allies moved swiftly to prevent a whitewash. They persuaded the committee to appoint John W. Goff, an indefatigable and tenacious Irishman and a Republican to boot, as counsel and then prevailed on the legislature to enlarge the committee's jurisdiction, extend its deadline, and even more important, appropriate $25,000 for its expenses. Governor Roswell P. Flower, a loyal Democrat, vetoed the appropriation on the grounds that the investigation was an unwarranted interference in local affairs and a Republican stratagem to embarrass a Democratic administration, which was not far from the truth. But the Chamber of Commerce advanced the committee enough money to cover its anticipated costs in the months ahead.[2]

The committee began its hearings in the New York County Courthouse in Manhattan on March 9. For five weeks Republican ballot clerks, poll watchers, and election inspectors told how the police had threatened Republican voters, ignored Democratic repeaters, tampered with ballot boxes, and committed or permitted, in the committee's words, "almost every conceivable crime against the elective franchise." Up to this point the investigation attracted modest attention. Not only was its approach flagrantly partisan, as Police Counsel Delancy Nicoll and Democratic Senator Jacob Cantor charged, but in a community where elections had often triggered sporadic violence, its revelations were common knowledge. The situation changed abruptly on May 21 when the committee resumed its hearings and widened the scope of its inquiry. Under Goff's direction it now subpoenaed not only patrolmen, detectives, captains, and inspectors but also judges, politicians, saloon keepers, policy bankers, con men, gamblers, prostitutes, peddlers, storekeepers, and scores of citizens of every class whose daily lives brought them into close touch with the police department.[3] For a while many police officials and local politicians attempted to undermine the investigation. Some defied subpoenas; others intimidated witnesses; and at least one, the Tammany Hall leader Richard Croker, took a trip to Europe. But gradually it became clear that the Lexow Committee could not be stopped.

Coaxed, prodded, and sometimes bullied by Goff, the witnesses told a shocking story. According to them, the police secured appointments and won promotions through political influence and cash payments. In return for regular payoffs they protected gambling, prostitution, and other illicit enterprises. Officers extorted money from peddlers, storekeepers, and other legitimate businessmen who were hard pressed to abide by municipal ordinances. Detectives allowed con men, pickpockets, and thieves to go about their business in return for a share of the proceeds. Officers also assaulted ordinary citizens with impunity. As Captain Max Schmittberger, a twenty-two-year veteran whose testimony was the high point of the investigation, charged, the department was "corrupt to the core." On December 29, 1894, the committee adjourned, having issued fully 3,000 subpoenas, heard almost 700 witnesses, and taken more than 10,000 pages of testimony. Front-page news for months, the committee's hearings commanded widespread interest throughout the United States and even parts of Western Europe, an accomplishment well beyond the expectations of Senator Lexow and his fellow legislators. If not "the most important political event of the year and probably the decade," as one journal wrote, the Lexow Committee investigation was at least the most thorough probe of its kind in the nation's history.[4]

The report, which came out on January 18, 1895, was anticlimactic. After briefly describing the origins and activities of the committee, Senator Lexow and all but one of his colleagues came up with four main conclusions. First, the police behaved at the polls not "as guardians of the public peace," trying to maintain order, but rather "as agents of Tammany Hall," seeking to influence elections. Second, far from suppressing gambling, prostitution, and the numbers racket, the officers regularly and systematically licensed vice in return for a share of the proceeds. Third, the detectives looked for stolen property only if the owner offered a reward and agreed to repay the pawnbroker the money advanced to the thieves. Fourth, the police frequently intimidated, harassed, and otherwise oppressed the defenseless and law-abiding citizens whose protection was their central duty.[5] The committee blamed these outrageous practices not on the patrolmen, who were "true, reliable, and incorruptible," if perhaps a trifle quick with a club, but on the superior officers. It attributed the scandalous conditions in general to Tammany Hall's pervasive influence over the police department and the other parts of the criminal justice system.

The committee's recommendations were highly partisan, as Senator Cantor pointed out in a minority report. To the amazement of Parkhurst and many other New Yorkers, the committee rejected a proposal to replace the current board of police commissioners, which had long been dominated by Tammany Hall, with a single commissioner or chief of police. The committee recommended instead that the police department should be headed by a bipartisan board of two Republicans and two Democrats, an arrangement that was devised to give the Republican party a fair share of the patronage and an equal voice in policy making. Despite pressure from Parkhurst and others, the committee also turned down a proposal to set up a board of elections independent of the police department and another proposal to put the department under the city's civil service system. The committee recommended instead that the police department should retain the responsibility to supervise elections and that the bipartisan commission should set up a board of high-ranking officers to review all applications for appointment. On other less controversial issues the committee called on the authorities to change the pension system in ways that would enhance the commission's power to remove superannuated officers and also to revise the accounting procedures in ways that would subject the department to the same outside auditing as other municipal agencies. In concluding, the committee urged the commissioners to reorganize the police department along these lines and to commence a thorough purge of incompetent officers.[6]

The Lexow Committee investigation did not have much impact

on the New York City police. The commissioners removed several officers, some of whom were also convicted of criminal offenses; but the courts reversed the convictions, and the department reinstated the officers. In the meantime, Parkhurst and Tammany's other foes joined forces with the Republicans to elect William L. Strong as the fusion candidate in the 1894 mayoral election. Mayor Strong soon made two controversial decisions. Despite the vigorous and virtually unanimous opposition of Parkhurst and his supporters, Strong gave his approval to the so-called Lexow Committee bills, which were passed by the state legislature in 1895. To head the bipartisan board, the mayor then selected Theodore Roosevelt, a long-time critic of the force, who promptly started a campaign to reform the department, which sputtered along until Roosevelt resigned to become assistant secretary of the navy two years later. But neither decision mattered much in the end. In 1898, not long after the Democrats regained power, a new board chose as police chief William S. Devery, a close friend of Richard Croker and a staunch supporter of Tammany Hall, who held court every night from about nine to three in front of a saloon on West Twenty-eighth Street. And in 1901, in the wake of another official investigation of the New York City police, the state legislature replaced the bipartisan board with a single commissioner and created an independent board of elections.[7]

The Lexow investigation nevertheless had a profound impact on the big-city police. For decades it served as the model for probes of police departments in other cities, and for years a "Lexow investigation" was virtually synonymous with a police investigation. It also supplied an endless store of scandals that was subsequently tapped to inspire and justify police reform elsewhere in urban America. What is more, the Lexow Committee sharply revealed how vulnerable a Democratic machine could be when the Republican party dominated the state legislature. Henceforth the Republicans would make increasing use of investigative committees in their struggles with the Democrats in New York, Illinois, Missouri, and other states. During the mid-1890s it was conceivable that the Lexow Committee's revelations were unique to New York City; after all, no other American metropolis had so large a police force, so powerful a political machine, so infamous a criminal element, and so heterogeneous a populace. By the end of the century, however, a series of similar investigations in Atlanta, Philadelphia, Kansas City, Baltimore, Chicago, Los Angeles, San Francisco, and other cities made it clear that most police departments carried on in much the same way virtually everywhere in urban America.

In January 1895, a month after the Lexow Committee adjourned its hearings, the Atlanta City Council suspended three detectives who, it was alleged, had falsely accused a local saloon keeper of harboring criminals and receiving stolen property. The police commission responded by charging the detectives with failing to prosecute known criminals, extorting money from the victims, mutilating official records, and protecting illegal businesses. To review the charges, the commission held, in the Atlanta *Constitution*'s words, "the longest and most sensational investigation" in the city's history. Although few witnesses admitted making payoffs, many others — including a saloon keeper who believed that "one good turn deserved another" and therefore allowed detectives free access to the bar in return for advance warning of raids — testified to an intimate relation between the detectives and the underworld. In their defense the detectives pointed out not only that their work brought them into close touch with disreputable people and disagreeable places but also that the charges came about as the result of a recent crackdown on gambling in downtown Atlanta. Finding evidence of dubious judgment but not of criminal behavior or official misconduct, the commission exonerated one detective, cautioned another, and reprimanded a third.[8]

Two months later the Citizens' Municipal Association of Philadelphia, a bipartisan and upper-middle-class reform group, petitioned the Pennsylvania Senate to appoint a special committee to look into charges of malfeasance in the city government. After the association pledged to underwrite the costs, the Senate agreed to set up the committee, which was known after its chairman, Senator William H. Andrews of Crawford County, as the Andrews Committee. The Committee held extended hearings, which touched not only on policing but also on public works and a wide range of other official activities, and then submitted a report in May 1897. According to witnesses, the police acted as the political agent of the various factions of the Republican party, which dominated Philadelphia as completely as the Democratic party dominated New York. Policemen not only labored hard at the nominating conventions but also hindered voters, discarded ballots, and otherwise violated the law at the Republican primaries, which were the crucial elections. By utilizing their political influence, well-connected officers even evaded departmental discipline and thereby escaped punishment for engaging in brutality and harassment or for protecting gambling and prostitution.[9] No one strongly disputed the Andrews Committee's conclusions. Even the public safety director, who freely admitted that the police force had long been entangled in Philadelphia politics, could only promise to deal with the problem in the not-too-distant future.

Early in 1895, at about the same time that the Andrews Committee began its investigation, a few Kansas City politicians prevailed on the governor of Missouri to name a new board of police commissioners more in sympathy with the local Democratic organization. Shortly thereafter the board removed the police chief, made wholesale changes in personnel, and adopted a liberal approach to gambling. The Republican party, the American Protective Association (an anti-Catholic outfit), and the Civic Federation (a nonpartisan reform group), protested so strongly that in January 1897 the Missouri Senate voted to investigate the Kansas City Police Department. The Missouri House, which was heavily Democratic, attempted to undermine the inquiry by creating its own committee, but after a few days of complicated maneuvering the Senate Committee opened hearings. For about a week witnesses testified that the police board had replaced native-American Republicans with Irish-American Democrats, many of whom were physically and mentally unfit for police work. Witnesses also explained that the patrolmen were expected to protect Ed Findley, a well-known gambler who operated out of Alderman Jim Pendergast's saloon, and to arrest his competitors. The Senate Committee submitted its report in March 1897.[10] An innocuous document, bordering on a whitewash, it found that the department permitted gambling, denied that it behaved as a political faction, and recommended a general reorganization without, however, providing specific guidelines.

Three months later the Baltimore Reform League, a group that had been formed by the business and social elites in 1895 and which sometimes collaborated with the Society for the Suppression of Vice, accused the police department of failing to enforce the laws against the numbers racket. The board of police commissioners—which had shifted from Democratic to Republican control for the first time in thirty years as a result of a major upset in the 1895 municipal election—responded by bringing charges against one captain and two sergeants. For two weeks the board held hearings. The league's counsel charged that the police, far from trying to eradicate the numbers racket, had staged fake raids and employed other improper practices which permitted the runners to operate in the central district and spread throughout the city. The police replied that they had done their utmost to suppress the racket, but that their efforts had been stymied because the grand juries were reluctant to indict the numbers bankers and the petit juries were unwilling to convict them. Two weeks later, without warning, the board dismissed not only the captain and one of the sergeants, both of whom were Democrats, but also Marshal Jacob Frey, another Democrat and a thirty-year veteran who had headed the force since 1885.[11] Frey protested that the board had fired him for political reasons, which was probably true, but to little avail.

A few days after the Baltimore police commission started its hearings, Superintendent Joseph Kipley of Chicago, an appointee of Carter H. Harrison, the recently elected Democratic mayor, removed, demoted, or transferred scores of Republican police officers for strictly partisan reasons. His actions angered not only the Civic Federation and other nonpartisan groups, which had worked hard to extend the civil service rules to the police department, but also the governor of Illinois and other Republicans, who feared the political consequences of Democratic control of the police force. The governor responded by proposing a bill to place the Chicago police under state supervision, and to enhance the bill's prospects, the Illinois Senate authorized a committee to inquire into the conduct of the force. The committee, which was known after its chairman, Senator O. F. Berry of Hancock County, as the Berry Committee, held hearings in January 1898 and released its report in February. The senators came up with four main conclusions. First, the Harrison administration had completely ignored the civil service rules in making appointments and removals. Second, it had operated the pension system not to aid policemen and their families but to replace Republicans with Democrats. Third, in return for regular payoffs, Chicago's patrolmen protected gambling parlors, poolrooms, opium dens, and other joints. And fourth, rather than enforcing laws and protecting lives and property, the police force licensed vice and served the Democratic organization.[12] The Senate later adopted the report, but the legislature ultimately rejected the bill.

Two years later several prominent Los Angeles businessmen and professionals, alarmed by the rise in crime and the calls for vigilante activity, organized a Committee of Safety to improve the police force. At first the committee urged the city council to remove the entire police board for reasons of incompetence and inefficiency, but the council refused to do so. The committee then hired a few detectives, purchased a saloon, and thereby tried to gather evidence of incompetence and corruption which would strengthen the case for police reform. The Committee of Safety published the results of its investigation in November 1900. According to its report, the police board granted the city's Chinese gamblers immunity from prosecution and, in return for payoffs and other favors, sometimes even transferred honest patrolmen and staged fake raids. For a price the board also issued licenses to operate saloons and allowed the saloon keepers to stay open on Sundays or at night in violation of the municipal liquor laws. Moreover, most policemen gained their appointments through political influence, and many of them were overage, undersized, debt-ridden, immoral, and otherwise unfit for a position of responsibility. Tracing these abuses to the injection of partisan politics into local government, the committee called on the citizens to turn the city council over to "honest men," regardless of party affiliation.[13]

Three months later the San Francisco *Examiner* charged that Mayor James D. Phelan and Chief of Police William P. Sullivan, Jr., had worked out an agreement with the underworld by which gambling and prostitution would be licensed in Chinatown. The story created such an outcry that the California Assembly appointed a committee to investigate the charges, which was known after its sponsor, Assemblyman Arthur G. Fisk of San Francisco, as the Fisk Committee. For about two weeks the committee grilled the mayor, the chief, and scores of other witnesses whose testimony fully corroborated the *Examiner*'s story and greatly aroused the city's middle and upper middle classes. The witnesses also implicated the district attorney, the police commissioners, and the captain of the Chinatown precinct, who had apparently come up with the idea of licensing vice. In their defense the mayor and the chief explained that gambling and prostitution were necessary evils and that, by strictly regulating these practices, the administration had rendered them less offensive. The Fisk Committee's report, which appeared in February 1901, criticized the corruption and incompetence of the police department and denounced the scandalous conditions in Chinatown. It recommended that if the police department and the district attorney did not enforce the laws, a grand jury should institute de facto impeachment proceedings against the officials involved.[14] For the time being the municipal authorities were forced to clamp down on vice in Chinatown.

Many other agencies looked into the big-city police during these years. A special committee of the New York State Assembly found in 1899 that the New York City Police Department had, if anything, changed for the worse since the Lexow Committee investigation. The Denver Board of Fire and Police Commissioners charged in 1901 that in return for a share of the proceeds policemen were protecting gambling and otherwise failing to enforce the vice laws. A special committee of the Atlanta Board of Police Commissioners reported in 1901 that the police department was profoundly demoralized for months before the municipal elections because the officers had no assurance that the new administration would reappoint them.[15] Other inquiries were held shortly thereafter in Chicago, Philadelphia, and St. Louis. Henceforth they occurred in one city after another, reaching one peak in the mid-1910s, another in the late 1920s and early 1930s, and still another in the early 1950s. But the later investigations only confirmed what the earlier ones had already revealed. That is, by the turn of the century, many Americans were no longer willing to put up with the customary policies and practices of the big-city police.

Other probes had taken place in Baltimore and St. Louis in the 1860s, Washington, D.C., in the 1870s, and Boston and Milwaukee in the 1880s.[16] But these probes were overshadowed by the outburst of investigations in the 1890s. Never before had so many committees been appointed in so few years; never before had they held hearings in so many cities, attracted so much attention throughout the nation, and demonstrated so convincingly that corruption and incompetence were endemic to the big-city police. Never before had the investigators gained the support of so many citizens who had the wealth, power, and prestige to carry on a long-term political battle; and never before had they dug up so many sordid and incriminating details about the everyday activities of the police forces. By the end of the nineteenth century the investigations had placed all big-city departments "under suspicion," to quote one observer prone to understatement. As a former New York City police commissioner put it, nowhere in urban America were even the most outrageous accusations against high-ranking officers "received with incredulity."[17] Even more important, these investigations turned policing into a political issue of such magnitude and intensity that for roughly two generations thereafter it provoked widespread controversy just about everywhere in urban America.

With hindsight it is clear that these investigations marked the beginning of a movement for police reform which transformed the big-city police over the next two generations. This movement had two distinct, if overlapping, phases. In the first phase, which ran from about 1890 to 1930, the movement was led by commercial, civic, and religious groups, which based their reforms on a military analogy. In the second phase, which went from about 1930 to 1970, the movement was headed by the law enforcement community, which derived their reforms from a professional model. Notwithstanding these differences, the reform movement altered the structure, personnel, and function of the big-city police. The police departments did not change in the same way, at the same time, to the same degree, or even for the same reason; nor did they end up the same. The process differed somewhat from city to city; and so did the outcome.[18] Nonetheless, for two generations the reform movement proceeded along similar lines and with similar results in so many different communities that it stands among the foremost examples of institutional change in urban America.

The reform movement can be viewed in several ways. For one, it marked the end of one era of policing, which went back to the middle of the nineteenth century, and the start of another, which ran through the second third of the twentieth century.[19] For another, it reflected the struggle between the Progressive elites and the political machines or between the upper-middle- and upper-class native Americans and the lower- and lower-middle-class first- and second-generation newcomers.[20] For yet another, it triggered many of the changes in the structure, personnel, and function of the big-city police which, with modifications, would be recognizable as the hallmarks of American policing two generations later. These changes had an impact on more than just the quality of law enforcement and criminal justice in urban America. For the big-city police have always done more than just enforce the law, keep the peace, and·serve the public. They have also decided, or at least helped to decide, which laws to enforce, whose peace to keep, and which public to serve. Hence the changes in policing had an impact on the process of mobility, the distribution of power, and the struggle for status in urban America.

During the 1960s many Americans began to have second thoughts about the course of police reform. Some were concerned because the reformers had not wiped out corruption, incompetence, and lawlessness in the police, much less stamped out crime in the streets. Pointing to the rising costs of police salaries and the mounting deficits of police pensions, others were troubled by the fiscal consequences of the reform effort. Still others believed that the reformers had made the police forces more responsive to the bureaucrats who ran them than to the citizens who dealt with them. And still others thought that the reform campaign had changed the entrance requirements in ways which barred blacks and other minorities from the big-city police. These reservations shattered the reform coalition and brought the reform movement to a standstill. They even prompted a few Americans to attempt to reverse the course of police reform in the name of community.[21] The questions that were raised remain today as some of the most pressing issues to face the nation's cities. It would be rash to predict how these issues will be resolved. But it is safe to assume that the outcome will have a great impact on urban America in the years ahead.

1. Adjunct of the Machine

Addressing the Third Annual Convention of the National (later International) Association of Chiefs of Police, held in Atlanta in 1896, Superintendent W. J. McKelvey of Brooklyn boasted about how much police work had advanced since he had begun as a patrolman thirty years before. His fellow chiefs, who ordered the speech published, were also impressed by the advances. Many, especially the older men, remembered how a series of riots, disturbances, and other threats to public order had prompted the authorities to organize the first police departments in the 1830s, 1840s, and 1850s. Many others, including the younger men, also recalled how the departments had gradually established themselves as integral features of urban life in the 1860s, 1870s, and 1880s.[1] Thus when the chiefs compared their own well-established departments with their precarious predecessors, they found abundant evidence of progress. Yet what was noteworthy about the American police in the 1890s was not how much but how little they had changed since the mid-nineteenth century. For by then most American cities had more or less resolved the cardinal issues of policing in ways that were not only consistent with the country's traditions and ideology but also incipient in the institution's origins and early development.

From the outset most Americans had a firm belief that the police should be controlled by local officials and organized along municipal lines. For them, a national police, like the Italian *carabinieri,* was inconceivable; a state police, like the German *polizei,* was undesirable; and a ward police, which had been tried earlier in Philadelphia and New Orleans, was impractical. By the mid-nineteenth century, however, it was plain that in most police departments local control meant Democratic control. Hence the Republican leaders, who generally spoke for the upper middle and upper classes, demanded state control, arguing that it would remove the police from partisan politics and improve the quality of law enforcement. Their Democratic opponents countered that state control would merely shift the focus of political interference and plainly violate the principal of self-government. The issue erupted in one city after another, with the Republicans usually getting their way. They imposed state control of the police in New York City in 1857, Detroit in 1865, Cleveland in 1866, New Orleans in 1868, Cincinnati in 1877, Boston in 1885, and Omaha in 1887. They also established metropolitan police departments, with jurisdiction over the central city and adjacent territory, in New York in 1857, Albany in 1865, and a few other places thereafter.[2]

Under these arrangements the state authorities appointed a board to manage, or at any rate to oversee, the big-city police. But the states did not contribute anything toward the upkeep of the police departments; nor, except in a few cases, did they authorize them to operate in the metropolitan area, much less throughout the entire state. Not until the early twentieth century did Pennsylvania, New York, and a few other states form statewide constabularies; and these forces, which patrolled mainly in small towns and rural districts, supplemented rather than supplanted the municipal police. Thus despite these changes, the American police remained decentralized to a degree unheard of anywhere in Western Europe. By the late nineteenth century, moreover, state control was well on the wane. The Democrats attacked it at every opportunity; and in the face of mounting evidence that the state boards had neither removed the police from partisan politics nor improved the quality of law enforcement, the Republicans were hard pressed to defend it. The issue was soon resolved, usually when the Democrats took office. The state authorities not only abolished metropolitan policing in New York and Albany in 1870 but also reestablished local control in Cleveland in 1868, New York in 1870, New Orleans in 1877, Cincinnati in 1880, Detroit in 1891, and Omaha in 1897.[3] By 1900 the big-city police were controlled by local officials and organized along municipal lines everywhere in urban America except for Boston, Baltimore, St. Louis, Kansas City, and a few other places.

From the start most Americans had a strong conviction that the police should have an essentially civilian orientation too. They believed that a military force, like the Irish constabulary, the Italian *carabinieri,* and the Spanish *guardia civil,* or even a paramilitary force, like the French *police* and the German *polizei,* posed a grave threat to their civil liberties and political rights. But after a while they realized that a strictly civilian force, which was dressed in ordinary clothes, armed with only a badge, and spread out all over the city, could not suppress riots and other disorders nor be easily recognized by citizens and criminals. So from the mid-century on, the authorities in one city after another worked out a compromise. Following the lead of New York City, which in the 1850s had introduced uniforms over the strenuous objections of the rank-and-file, the cities required all officers to wear uniforms while on duty. Shortly thereafter they authorized the patrolmen to carry clubs and then revolvers. They also built station houses, usually one in each precinct, where most patrolmen not only gathered before their tours but also ate, slept, and otherwise passed the time while on reserve.[4] By the 1890s most policemen were uniformed, armed, and readily available virtually everywhere in urban America.

Despite these changes, most departments retained an essentially civilian orientation. Unlike the Austrian and Hungarian police, the American police did not recruit the patrolmen from the army; nor, unlike the French and German police, did they draw their superiors from the commissioned officers. Save for the sergeants and captains, few American policemen held military ranks; the rank-and-file were called patrolmen rather than privates in most cities, and their immediate superiors were commonly known as roundsmen, a position long since abolished. The American police carried more weapons than the English police, who walked the beat without firearms, but fewer than the German police, who, one American scholar wrote, were "armed as if for war." They lived not in isolated barracks, like the Irish constabulary, but in station houses or private homes in communities where in all probability they had worked, voted, and perhaps even grown up before joining the force. Few Europeans would have mistaken the American police for soldiers; and few Americans would have expected them to. The civilian orientation had lost some of its appeal in the late nineteenth century. But it retained enough of a hold in the mid-1880s that a year or so after the Minneapolis city council had reorganized the police department along quasi-military lines, the Minneapolis police commission rescinded the reorganization.[5]

From the outset most Americans had only a few vague ideas about what the police should do besides maintain public order. They did not expect the police, like the German *polizei,* to fight fires, prevent epidemics, operate prisons, manage charities, and otherwise oversee the administration of most essential municipal services. Nor did they want them, like the French *police,* to employ professional detectives or even ordinary civilians to keep citizens, especially disaffected citizens, under surveillance. Neither did most Americans trust the police to draft regulations, prosecute suspects, and sentence offenders, a common practice in the tightly coordinated criminal justice system of Germany.[6] Few Americans were sure whether the police forces or the detective squads, which were originally distinct agencies in Philadelphia, Washington, D.C., and other cities, should be authorized to deal with crime. Nor were they sure whether the responsibility for health and welfare should be given to the police department or to separate departments of sanitation, charities, and street cleaning. Feeling more strongly about what the police should not do than about what they should, most Americans therefore left the authorities a great deal of leeway in their attempt to define, and if need be redefine, the police function.

In the absence of other specialized public bureaucracies, the authorities found the temptation almost irresistible to transform the police departments into catchall health, welfare, and law enforcement agencies. Hence the police cleaned streets and inspected boilers in New York, distributed supplies to the poor in Baltimore, accommodated the homeless in Philadelphia, investigated vegetable markets in St. Louis, operated emergency ambulances in Boston, and attempted to curb crime in all these cities. By the end of the century most departments engaged in a wide range of activities other than keeping the peace. But under-lying these diverse activities was one common principle: the big-city police were a responsive, as opposed to a preventive, force. They would answer complaints or requests for assistance, but except under extraordinary conditions, they would not actively seek out infractions. The police should enforce the law, a Boston councilman pointed out in 1887, but they should not employ spies, resort to entrapment, or otherwise let their determination to stamp out crime carry them beyond the point "at which decent and honorable men must stop."[7] Thus by the end of the century most departments operated as catchall and essentially responsive agencies virtually everywhere in urban America.

Yet what set the American police apart from the French, German, and British police was not so much their commitment to local control, a civilian orientation, and a responsive style as their relationship with the political machine.[8] The machine was urban America's outstanding contribution to the art of municipal government. Exemplified by Tammany Hall, it emerged in New York, Philadelphia, and other eastern cities in the early and middle nineteenth century and in Chicago, Kansas City, San Francisco, and other western cities not long after. A highly decentralized outfit, the machine was an association of loosely affiliated and largely autonomous ward organizations whose power depended on their ability to get out the vote on election day. Whether allied with the Democrats, as in New York, the Republicans, as in Philadelphia, or neither party, as for a while in San Francisco, the ward bosses operated in much the same way in most American cities. They gave out contracts to local businessmen, found and if need be created jobs for recent immi-grants, provided opportunities for aspiring politicians, and otherwise exchanged material inducements for political loyalty. In return for delivering the vote, the ward bosses demanded a good deal to say not only about the policies of the mayor's offices and city councils but also about the operations of the police departments and other municipal agencies.

For the political machine the police, fire, and sanitation departments, the schools and courts, and the other municipal agencies were as much the stakes of urban politics as the mayor's office and the common council. It was to gain control of these agencies that politicians went to the trouble of doing favors, rounding up voters, and carrying out the countless other chores essential to winning power in urban America. An exchange in 1899 between Richard Croker and Frank Moss, formerly assistant counsel to the Lexow Committee and deputy police commissioner in New York City and at the time counsel to the Mazet Committee, another legislative investigating committee, nicely illustrates this point. To the victor belong the spoils, Croker told Moss. To make the record clear, Moss asked whether Croker meant that the machine should hold "all the offices in every department." "Yes, sir," Croker answered. "Judicial, executive, administrative and everything?" Moss went on. "Yes, sir," Croker replied, "that is what I believe the people voted our ticket for."[9] Few machine politicians—not Isaac Rasin of Baltimore, John Fitzpatrick of New Orleans, Jim Pendergast of Kansas City, and certainly not John Coughlin and Michael Kenna of Chicago—felt much differently. They all realized that unless the organization controlled the police departments and other municipal agencies, it could not hold onto the patronage, contracts, and favors indispensable to its hegemony.

By the 1890s the police departments were more important than ever to the machine politicians. During the middle and late nineteenth century millions of impoverished, illiterate, and unskilled Irishmen, Germans, Scandinavians, Italians, and other Europeans emigrated to the United States.[10] Settling in New York City, Buffalo, Chicago, and the other large cities, they soon found that the private sector did not supply enough jobs to sustain them, much less to raise them up into the middle class. For a full generation, and sometimes longer, they remained underemployed and underpaid, taking menial jobs whenever and wherever available and looking for other work that would provide a decent salary and minimal security. In nearly all the ethnic ghettos a few persons resorted to gambling and prostitution; some worked as pickpockets, strong-arm men, petty thieves, con men, and racketeers; others operated as suppliers, fences, pawnbrokers, bondsmen, and other quasi-legitimate entrepreneurs. But many newcomers sought jobs instead in the fire, police, water, and sanitation departments, the courts and schools, and the other burgeoning government bureaucracies. By the end of the century thousands of first- and second-generation Americans counted on these municipal agencies for their livelihood.

The big-city police had more than a little to say about how

these jobs were distributed. After all, they provided employment for roughly 3,300 men in New York City, 1,600 in Philadelphia and Chicago, 800 in Baltimore and Boston, 600 in St. Louis, and 400 in Cincinnati and San Francisco. These jobs were quite attractive. Patrolmen earned from $600 in Kansas City to $1,200 in San Francisco, more than laborers, weavers, miners, and factory workers and about as much as painters, carpenters, teamsters, blacksmiths, and street railway conductors. Sergeants and detectives received slightly more, captains about twice as much, and deputy chiefs and chiefs most of all. Many policemen also received free medical treatment, modest disability pensions, and other fringe benefits that were not yet available to most other Americans. So long as their party remained in power, most officers also enjoyed a fair degree of job security. Little wonder that in the late nineteenth century four or more men applied for each position on the force in Atlanta and Los Angeles. "If the policemen's clubs were made of gold instead of locust or hickory," Chief Francis O'Neill of Chicago told his fellow chiefs in 1904, "competition for them could be scarcely more strenuous."[11]

During the middle and late nineteenth century riots and other forms of violence often broke out at the polls and in the streets of urban America. What with the enormous influx of foreign immigrants, the high rate of residential mobility, and the deep-seated commitment to universal suffrage, the elections generated much confusion and controversy. In the absence of a spirit of partisan accommodation and a tradition of electoral honesty, these disagreements often developed into minor brawls or even major disorders. So dangerous was the situation that one prudent St. Louis resident told a state investigating committee in the late 1860s that he never went out on election day "except to vote." What with the sharp antagonism between natives and ethnics, Protestants and Catholics, whites and blacks, conservatives and radicals, and employers and workers, the streets were scarcely more secure at other times. In the absence of rigid class distinctions, fixed neighborhood boundaries, and an inclusive sense of community, many groups regarded each other as serious threats to their well-being. For some groups violence was a common, if not legitimate, means of protest, which was designed not to change basic social values but to keep competing groups in their place.[12]

The big-city police also had a lot to say about how these disorders were handled. Empowered to preserve order at the polls, the patrolmen decided whether or not to eject repeaters from the lines, protect voters from the thugs, and respond to complaints by poll watchers and ballot clerks. If the officers abused their authority, the citizens had little or no recourse: the local judges were usually in sympathy with the organization, and by the time the state legislators had received a complaint, the election was long over.[13] Whoever dominated the police could assign to the polls hundreds of tough, well-armed, if not necessarily well-disciplined men, whose jobs, the politicians reminded them, depended on the outcome. Empowered to maintain order in the streets, the police decided whether or not to permit agitators to speak, protestors to march, and laborers to picket, and if so, judged whether or not the protests remained orderly. They also determined whether or not to intervene in racial, ethnic, and religious clashes, and if so, at what point, on whose side, with how many men, and with how much force. Whoever controlled the police possessed an enviable flexibility to respond to confrontations and crises in ways consistent with their own political objectives, which was a tremendous advantage in a society so prone to group conflict.

During the last third of the nineteenth century many upper-middle- and upper-class native Americans were deeply upset by the prevailing life-style and underlying morality of the lower- and lower-middle-class first- and second-generation immigrants. They feared that urban America was literally going to the devil. Following a long tradition of missionary activities in China, Hawaii, and other exotic places, they launched a reform campaign to purify not only their own neighborhoods, which were essentially free of commercial vice, but also the ethnic communities. In time they prevailed on many state legislators, who shared their aspirations, to prohibit gambling, regulate saloons, curtail Sunday business, and otherwise impose their life style on other groups. These laws won widespread support in upper-middle- and upper-class enclaves, which had little need for them, but not in lower- and lower-middle-class communities, which regarded the laws as unreasonable, inequitable, and unenforceable. To the dismay of the reformers, many immigrants continued to gamble, drink, and do business on Sunday; and so, for that matter, did many native Americans. By the turn of the century the issue was clearly drawn. Whether or not these laws were enforced would henceforth shape the prevailing life-styles and underlying morality in urban America and thereby influence the relative standing of its social classes and ethnic groups.[14]

The big-city police had a good deal to say about how this issue was resolved. Notwithstanding the laws, the officers decided whether to tolerate gambling, prostitution, drinking, and other vices, and if so, in which neighborhoods, at whose joints, and under what conditions. Whoever dominated the police not only shared in the underworld's payoffs and earned its political support, but also adjudicated the ethnic and class battles over moral and cultural issues. Under pressure from the native Americans, the politicians kept vice out of the upper-middle- and upper-class communities and occasionally staged a fake raid elsewhere to give the impression of vigorous law enforcement. Under cross-pressure from the first- and second-generation immigrants — who, as one man reminded the New York police, would, no matter what, drink their beer, "bathe in it — swim in it" — they also promised business as usual most of the time.[15] And in the interests of everyone involved, they encouraged the gamblers and prostitutes to carry on in an honest way and the saloons to operate in an orderly fashion. In other words, those who controlled the police had the opportunity to implement a policy about vice consistent with the prevailing life-style and underlying morality of their constituents. As the moral and cultural conflict between the natives and the ethnics intensified, many politicians found this opportunity a heavy burden, but not one that they dared turn over to anyone else.

To control the police, or at any rate to influence departmental policy, was therefore among the principal objectives of the ward bosses. If they succeeded, they could hand out scores of attractive jobs to their supporters and shape law enforcement practices in ways that would help their organization come election day. If they failed, other politicians would exploit the force in the same ways. At issue during the nineteenth century was not whether the police departments would be operated in someone's interests, a point firmly settled, but in whose interests they would be operated. The Republicans, as well as the upper middle and upper classes in general, regularly denounced the machine's hold over the police and exploited it to rationalize state control of the force in New York, Detroit, Boston, and other cities. By the end of the nineteenth century, however, the political machines had more influence over the big-city police than ever before and, though few suspected it, more than they would ever have again. And they exerted their influence in ways that had a profound impact on the structure, personnel, and function of policing in urban America.

The police departments were supposed to be highly centralized. According to the organizational charts, formal authority corresponded closely with actual power. The chiefs were superior to the captains, the captains to the sergeants, the sergeants to the roundsmen, the roundsmen to the patrolmen, and among the patrolmen the veterans to the recruits. From the chief down to the greenest recruit, the officers derived their prerogatives and influence from their official positions in the departments, and from these positions alone. Here was a presumably rigid and self-contained hierarchy. According to the organizational charts, formal organization corresponded closely with actual operation too. The chiefs and their aides made departmental policy at headquarters, translated it into general orders or other directives, and held their subordinates responsible for its implementation. The captains, who managed the precincts, the sergeants, who supervised the special details, and the chief of detectives brought these directives to the attention of the patrolmen and the detectives. Conversely, the rank-and-file carried out departmental policy or answered to the sergeants, who reported to the captains, and so on up to the chiefs and their aides.[16] Here was a presumably tight and effective chain of command.

But as the Lexow and other investigations demonstrated, the organizational charts were misleading. Formal authority corresponded poorly, if at all, with actual power. With a few notable exceptions, most chiefs had little if any control over the captains, who were, in the words of one state investigative committee, "absolute monarchs" in their districts. The captain's wardman, a patrolman who collected the payoffs in the precinct, had more influence than many sergeants and roundsmen; and so did veteran patrolmen who were well regarded by local politicians. As every recruit who survived for long learned, most officers derived their prerogatives and influence as much from their political connections as from their official positions. Formal organization also corresponded poorly, if at all, with actual operation. The chiefs could not possibly know what went on outside headquarters; and their assistants, who owed their positions to the political organizations, would rarely tell them. The captains, who got their jobs through the ward bosses, felt no compunction about ignoring departmental instructions inconsistent with the injunctions of the local machines.[17] And the detectives and patrolmen carried out official policy only if so ordered by the captains and the politicians; and even then they did not always do so.

The disparity between theory and practice reflected the pervasive influence of the political machines. To begin with, the machines had a powerful and often decisive voice in the selection of the police chiefs, whether they were appointed by mayors, as in Philadelphia, or by local boards, as in Los Angeles. Not surprisingly, the bosses strongly favored candidates like William S. Devery of New York, Joseph Kipley of Chicago, and William P. Sullivan, Jr., of San Francisco, who had long shown concern for the organization's interests. By accepting the patronage of the machines, the chiefs not only lost their autonomy but also found themselves in a precarious position. For once the other party took office, it usually fired the incumbents. Following a change in administration, the Kansas City Democrats dismissed Chief Thomas Speers in 1895 and the Baltimore Republicans removed Marshal Jacob Frey in 1897. In Cleveland, San Francisco, and a few other cities that enjoyed, or from another perspective suffered, political stability, the chiefs held office for a decade or more. But in most cities they turned over with astonishing frequency. Cincinnati went through seven chiefs between 1878 and 1886; Buffalo tried eight between 1879 and 1894; Chicago saw nine come and go between 1879 and 1897; and Los Angeles changed heads thirteen times between 1879 and 1889.[18] Given this rate of turnover, the chiefs did not have the time to wrest control over their departments from the machines.

Nor had they the power. The machine's influence extended beyond the departments to most of the other institutions that fixed the course of local politics and criminal justice in America's cities. It reached the civil service commission, which evaluated candidates for appointment and promotion; the police board, which retained ultimate authority over the department's policies; the city council, which voted its appropriation and defined its jurisdiction; and the mayor's office, which formulated the administration's long-range goals. It also reached the prosecutor's office, which decided whether, when, where, and how to press charges against suspects, and the local courts, which not only ruled on procedure, evidence, and other matters affecting the outcome of these trials but also heard appeals from departmental disciplinary decisions. Since, as Croker pointed out to a New York state investigating committee, these institutions owed their cardinal loyalty to the machine, a police chief who refused to go along with the machine's wishes soon found the entire apparatus of local politics and criminal justice aligned against him.[19] So extensive was the machine's influence over the police department's personnel and finances and so formidable was its capacity to nullify departmental policies and practices that most police chiefs usually settled for nominal authority over their forces.

Although the chiefs had the authority, the captains had the power. It was they who ran the checks on applicants to the department, handed out assignments to the recruits, looked into complaints against the patrolmen, and made most of the other decisions that vitally affected the careers of the rank-and-file. Thus it was they, along with the ward leaders, who decided which laws to enforce, whose peace to keep, and which public to serve. The authorities further enhanced the captains' influence by treating every precinct like a small department. Unlike, say, the Germans, the Americans entrusted not only patrolling but, with the sporadic exception of detection, all other police functions to ordinary patrolmen attached to the precinct instead of to special squads assigned to headquarters under the close supervision of the chief and his assistants. So long as the captains enjoyed the machine's support, they were virtually invulnerable. Appearing before a special committee of the New York Chamber of Commerce in 1905, a former New York City police commissioner testified that he spent years attempting to break corrupt captains, that he succeeded in very few cases, and that in the end, overwhelmed by the strain, he packed a satchel and went to recuperate in Colorado.[20] He was an object lesson in the striking disparity between position and influence in the big-city police departments.

But as Captain Max Schmittberger told the Lexow Committee, most captains deferred to the ward leaders: they protected their cronies, harassed their enemies, favored their appointees, contributed to their campaigns, and in innumerable other ways acknowledged their leadership. The captains had no choice. Since the mid-nineteenth century most cities had drawn the precinct boundaries to coincide closely with the ward lines, and a generation later most politicians still operated according to the principle that whoever controlled the ward vote was entitled to name the precinct captain. The ward leaders not only exerted tremendous and often irresistible pressure on the commissions and boards to appoint their candidates, but also staunchly defended the captains against their chiefs, provided that the captains went along with the organization's position. Referring to Captain Michael Ryan, an allegedly corrupt and incompetent officer known as the police chief of Chicago's first ward, who had long defied his superiors' efforts to remove him, the *Tribune* wrote: "The 'Hink' [Alderman Michael Kenna] put him there. And the 'Hink' and the 'Bath' [Alderman John Coughlin] keep him there."[21] The relationship between the ward boss and the precinct captain was a splendid example of the extreme decentralization of urban politics in the late nineteenth and early twentieth centuries.

Most patrolmen who survived for any length of time quickly discovered the disparity between rank and power. They learned that a patrolman placed his career in jeopardy more by alienating his captain than by disobeying his chief and more by defying his wardman, who regulated vice in the precinct, than by ignoring either his sergeant, who inspected the lineup, or his roundsman, who checked up on the beats. If a patrolman followed his captain's orders, stayed out of the wardman's way, and befriended his sergeant and his roundsman, he could normally keep out of trouble; and if he forgot his place once or twice, he could usually count on the superior officers to protect him. But a patrolman could expect no help from his superiors, or for that matter from anyone else, if he offended the politicians in whose bailiwick his precinct was located.[22] If he did so, he would probably be transferred from his post, shifted from his precinct, or perhaps even dismissed from the force; for so grave a lapse no excuse was acceptable, and unless other politicians intervened, which was highly unlikely, no recourse was available. For the patrolmen who shared the machine's attitudes about crime, morals, and law enforcement the conflict between their official responsibilities and their political obligations created an occasional but by no means intolerable strain.

Many patrolmen also commanded political resources of their own. For one thing, they belonged to assorted fraternal and benevolent associations. Although these associations, which were organized in the late nineteenth century, mainly helped the patrolmen and their families in the event of illness and death, they sometimes took part in political struggles. In Chicago they fought against civil service in 1895; in Philadelphia they lobbied for salary increases in 1897; and in New York they campaigned for an eight-hour day in the early 1900s. Though far from a major power in municipal affairs, these associations won more than a few notable victories in disputes over salaries, pensions, and other bread-and-butter issues. For another thing, many patrolmen belonged to the political clubs that dominated the wards, numbered district leaders among their friends and relatives, and above all worked hard for the political machines. At elections the patrolmen contributed to the organization's treasury and rounded up its supporters; and as every politician knew, they and their families formed a large and reliable block of voters.[23] To the machine, and not to the department or the association, the rank-and-file gave their primary loyalty; in return, they expected choice assignments, rapid promotion, and if caught violating departmental rules, adequate protection. They did not want charity, only recompense for doing their job.

The police departments were also supposed to be completely impervious to political influence. According to the police manuals, the departments required each applicant to take stiff physical and medical tests, know how to read and write English, and in cities that had set up a civil service system, pass a rudimentary competitive exam. They turned away any candidate, no matter how strong his political connections, who failed to meet these requirements or who lived outside the city, had a criminal record, drank to excess, and refused to pay his outstanding debts. The chiefs assigned a recruit to a precinct and transferred him to another precinct or shifted him to a special detail according to his personal skills and the organization's priorities. They also promoted a veteran to sergeant or even captain on the basis of his official performance, as evaluated by his superior officers and, in cities where the civil service rules applied, by his test score. If the chiefs thought a patrolman had broken an official regulation, they could transfer him to and from precincts, in and out of details, or from plainclothes to uniform without an explanation. If the chiefs considered the violation serious enough to warrant suspension, demotion, or dismissal, they could file charges with the police board, the city council, or the civil service commission.[24]

But as the investigative committees discovered, the police manuals were deceptive. Most politicians, including the Democrats who paid lip service to the concept of an apolitical police and the Republicans who criticized their opponents for interfering with the department, viewed control of the force as a prerogative of the party in power. They agreed with James J. Martin, a Tammany Hall district leader and New York City police commissioner, who told the Lexow Committee that on personnel matters, "All things being equal"—which of course they rarely were—"I accept the recommendation of political friends." Most politicians also operated like Matthew A. Frye and Frank G. Johnson, two Democratic stalwarts from Kansas City, who, upon being appointed to the police commission in the mid-1890s, summarily dismissed sixteen members of the force, all of whom were Repubicans.[25] How the politicians exercised this prerogative differed from one city to another and from one year to the next. The differences reflected the organizational structure of the department, the political balance in the city, the ethnic distribution of the population, and the political influence of the chief or commissioners. But these differences only underscored how extensively the politicians intervened in just about all the big-city departments and how strongly they influenced the appointment, assignment, promotion, and discipline of their personnel.

For appointment to the force, political affiliation was the overriding consideration. When the Republicans won the Los Angeles municipal election in 1889 and gained a three-to-two majority on the police board, the commissioners reached an understanding whereby the Republicans named three-fifths of the force and the Democrats two-fifths. But two months later the Republican majority, under intense pressure from their party for more patronage, changed their mind, demanded three-quarters of the positions, and over the Democratic minority's objections replaced twenty Democrats with Republicans. Similar, if less explicit, arrangements prevailed in many other cities. To secure an appointment, most candidates went not to the police commissioners or the police chiefs but straight to the New York district leaders, the Philadelphia ward leaders, the Chicago aldermen, and other influential politicians. Some politicians demanded a payoff: in the 1890s the going rate for a patrolman was $300 in New York City and $400 in San Francisco, according to investigating committees. But most politicians preferred evidence that the candidate and his friends or relatives had been helpful to the party in the past and could be counted on by the organization in the future.[26]

For applicants who had the machine's backing, the official requirements were no problem. Neither the medical examiners, who gave the physical tests, nor the police officials, who made the character checks, were inclined to stand in the way of an influential politician, because they too were political appointees. Small wonder that within a few days many applicants grew several inches taller and years younger, learned to read and write, and like the pilgrims who traveled to holy places, recovered from serious and even chronic ailments. Hence some recruits were overweight, undersize, and overage; others were illiterate, alcoholic, and syphilitic; still others had outstanding debts and criminal records; and one Kansas City patrolman had a wooden leg.[27] For applicants who had the organization's support, the civil service exams were no problem either. The commissioners, who wrote the questions, graded the answers, ranked the candidates, and prepared the lists, were also political appointees and even more vulnerable than the medical examiners to political retaliation. With their compliance and at times their active cooperation, applicants found substitutes to take the tests in Philadelphia, secured advance copies of the exams in Chicago, and circumvented the rules in other ways in other cities. Rarely did the civil service prevent a candidate endorsed by the machine, no matter how low he scored on the tests, from being appointed to the force.

To the recruits nothing was more important than their assignment. On it depended not only whether they walked to work in a few minutes or rode the streetcar for an hour, patrolled among friendly or hostile residents, and shared in the payoffs or managed on their salaries alone, but even more important, whether they ended up in the precincts or on special details. These details, which consisted of ordinary patrolmen on temporary assignment to the courts, docks, theaters, railway stations, and other public places, were among the least taxing and most remunerative positions on the force. They were particularly attractive to veteran officers who were tired of pounding the beat. Contrary to official regulations, the politicians exerted tremendous influence over most assignments. Sometimes they did so to reward loyal officers, as a New York justice and Tammany Hall district leader who had just prevailed on the commissioners to shift sergeants in his neighborhood testified to the Lexow Committee: "Whenever a friend of mine or organization man asks me to do a favor I try to do it." Or as the patrolmen who were transferred for raiding well-connected gamblers in Kansas City and Los Angeles found out, sometimes they did so to punish uncooperative officers. As an intransigent New York City officer told a state investigating committee, "I have been transferred so continuously that I keep my goods packed ready to go at a minute's notice."[28]

To the veterans, nothing was more important than their promotion. The sergeants and the captains earned higher salaries, exercised more authority, and if so inclined, found greater opportunities for graft than the patrolmen. The detectives enjoyed greater freedom, prestige, and prospects for rewards than the uniformed officers. More so than most patrolmen, these officers also gained the confidence of politicians, the deference of criminals and disreputable businessmen, and the admiration, if not necessarily affection, of ordinary citizens. Notwithstanding formal procedures, the politicians also exerted a good deal of influence over promotions. Sometimes they sold them to the highest bidder. In the 1890s, as Captain Schmittberger and other witnesses told the Lexow Committee, the going rate in New York was $1,600 for sergeants and $12,000-$15,000 for captains. And the job was well worth the price. More often the party leaders gave promotions to political favorites. Asked by a state investigating committee whether he preferred Democrats to Republicans, a Democratic civil service commissioner answered, "Every day in the week and every hour in the day."[29] If any of the roughly one out of six policemen who made it to detective, sergeant, lieutenant, or captain forgot his obligation to the organization, he often found himself demoted and once again walking the beat.

Politics permeated discipline as well, rendering some policemen extremely exposed and others nearly invulnerable. The Philadelphia police department discharged one patrolman, who was affiliated with the wrong faction of the Republican party, for having left his post for a few minutes one night even though his doctor testified at a departmental trial that he had been too ill to stay on duty. Yet it levied a mere $25 fine on another patrolman, the associate of a powerful ward leader, who, as his vindictive ex-mistress told a state investigating committee, had been carrying on an affair while on duty for an hour or so about three times a week. This disparity between the gravity of the infraction and the severity of the punishment was not unique to Philadelphia, nor was the assumption that influential politicians should have a voice in disciplinary proceedings. Reviewing the long and bitter trial which resulted in the abrupt dismissal of Marshal Frey and himself, a Baltimore captain criticized not so much the decision as the procedure: "Had the two commissioners said to me, 'We have a republican for your place and would like to have your resignation,' I would have resigned promptly and without question."[30] As most patrolmen soon learned, the sympathetic concern of an influential politician was far better protection than the procedural safeguards of a departmental hearing.

But few politicians, no matter how influential, could protect the patrolmen against a turnover in municipal government. When a new administration came to power in 1897, Superintendent Kipley of Chicago demoted or dismissed hundreds of Republican police officers. By the time he had finished, the *Tribune* complained, "there was not a Republican holding a place higher than desk sergeant, and so few of them they would not figure in a village census."[31] The Democrats on the Los Angeles police did not fare much better after the administration changed hands in 1889, nor did the Republicans on the Kansas City force in 1895 or the Democrats on the Baltimore force in 1897. The ward leaders had little choice in the matter. If they did not compel the authorities to demote or dismiss the opposition's policemen, they could not get appointments for their candidates and promotions for their protégés. If the ward leaders did not handpick the rank-and-file and their superiors, the machines could not retain their hold over the police departments. Nor in the long run could they maintain their hegemony in urban America. In other words, the ward bosses could not reward their friends unless they were prepared to punish their enemies. And with so many candidates clamoring for each opening, the bosses could not afford to let these opportunities pass by.

According to the conventional wisdom, the police departments enforced the law, kept the peace, and served the public; they suppressed vice and eradicated crime, preserved order at the polls and in the streets, and aided citizens in distress.[32] Underlying this notion were two assumptions. One was that most policemen did their job. The patrolmen, who were assigned to the precincts, walked the beat looking for a complaint or a call for help and alternately waited in the station house as reserves in case of emergency. The detectives, who had been brought into the departments under the authority of the chiefs late in the nineteenth century, investigated serious crimes and watched well-known criminals. And the special details maintained order at the courts, theaters, docks, railway stations, and other public places. The other assumption was that most policemen used little or no discretion. Ever since the mid-nineteenth century Americans had generally assumed that the entire population, or in any event the entire urban population, could be neatly divided into two classes, the dangerous or criminal and the respectable or non-criminal. From this assumption they drew the conclusion that in their everyday activity the police should arrest the one class and protect the other and that in the process they should be guided only by the language of the law and the constraints of a policed society.

These assumptions were untenable, however. According to a survey of hundreds of Chicago policemen in 1904, they spent most of their time not on the streets but in saloons, restaurants, barbershops, bowling alleys, pool halls, and bootblack stands. They were everywhere save on the beat. While prostitutes solicited clients and wagons blocked the streets, the officers passed the day eating, drinking, smoking, chatting, and doing all sorts of things other than patrolling. Most of them broke departmental regulations with impunity because neither the sergeants nor the captains nor even the chiefs took their own responsibilities more seriously. These practices were by no means confined to Chicago. According to the Lexow and other investigative committees, the police also exercised a good deal of discretion. Whether in Baltimore, New York, Kansas City, or San Francisco, they raided some gambling houses and spared others, picked up some criminals and ignored others, protected some voters and harassed others, assisted some citizens and clobbered others, suppressed riots under one set of conditions and joined them under others.[33] Although the police usually exercised their discretion in ways that were spelled out by the ward leaders or other politicians, they had something to say about which laws were enforced, whose peace was kept, and which public was served.

Contrary to the conventional wisdom, the police did not suppress vice; they licensed it. From New York's Tenderloin to San Francisco's Barbary Coast and from Chicago's Levee to New Orleans' French Quarter, they permitted gamblers, prostitutes, and saloon keepers to do business under certain well-understood conditions. These entrepreneurs were required to make regular payoffs, which ranged, according to the enterprise and the community, from a few dollars to a few hundred dollars per month, and to stay inside the lower- and lower-middle-class neighborhoods, which had no strenuous objection to gambling, drinking, and other victimless crimes. These operators were also expected to run their business in an orderly fashion. If they did so — or if they reached their own agreements with the politicians, as Ed Findley did with Jim Pendergast — the police would leave them alone and sometimes even raid their competitors. If they did not, a New York madam explained in 1894, the police would raise the ante or, as a last resort, close the enterprise.[34] Most policemen justified this policy, which reflected the position of the political machine, on the grounds that vice was inevitable, that the sumptuary laws were unenforceable, and that segregation was therefore the only sensible approach. But many of them were well aware that an officer who disregarded these arrangements would probably be transferred from his precinct forthwith and possibly removed from the force later on.

Nor did the police eradicate crime; they regulated it. Here the detectives, a small group of policemen who were assigned to either a precinct or a special squad and worked out of uniform without much supervision, played the crucial role. Operating out of saloons and dives on the edge of the underworld — and not, as they reminded their critics, out of Sunday schools — the detectives were, in the view of one deputy police commissioner, hard to tell from the criminals. In return for a share of the proceeds they allowed the con men, pickpockets, burglars, and other thieves to go about their business; and when the opportunity arose, they took a cut from the pawnbrokers and, in the form of a reward, from the victims. The detectives usually split the take with the politicians, who might otherwise have used their power to get them reduced to uniform or even thrown off the force. These arrangements sometimes broke down. After a rash of bank robberies near Wall Street in 1880, Chief of Detectives Thomas Byrnes ordered his men to arrest on sight all professional thieves found south of Fulton Street. During the Atlanta Cotton States International Exposition of 1895 Chief of Police A. B. Connolly instructed his men to arrest all pickpockets and other disreputable types or simply run them out of town.[35] But these aberrations only temporarily disrupted the symbiotic relationship between the criminals and the detectives.

The police did not preserve order at the polls at the expense of their party either. The Chicago police looked on in 1894 as Democrats in the first ward obstructed the polls, invaded the booths, and as the *Tribune* complained, assaulted or intimidated everyone "who wore a clean collar." In the sixteenth ward, moreover, they arrested, or more accurately kidnapped, twenty-five prominent Polish Republicans the day before the election and held them incommunicado until the day after. Under instruction from the politicians the police committed similar, if less blatant, abuses in many other cities. They harassed scores of reform voters in Baltimore in 1875, sided with the Democrats in an election day riot in Kansas City in 1894, solicited votes in Republican primaries in Philadelphia during the mid-1890s, and encouraged Democratic repeaters in New York City from time immemorial. The Young Men's Democratic Association, a reform organization, had so little confidence in the New Orleans police force, which was completely controlled by the local Democratic machine, that it surrounded the polls with companies of riflemen during the 1888 election.[36] In the absence of such drastic measures, however, the political machine could normally count on the police department to do its bidding at most municipal elections.

Nor did the police maintain order in the streets with much objectivity and consistency. Conventional in their economic, political, and social outlooks, most policemen felt a sharp antagonism to labor unions, radical groups, and racial minorities. By virtue of their mandate to preserve order, they also developed a deep antipathy to strikes, pickets, demonstrations, and other protests against the status quo. As a result they sometimes served as a private force for employers, deprived dissenters of their civil liberties, and joined the assaults on blacks and other racial minorities. Yet the police occasionally rose above their personal and occupational prejudices, especially when the conflict threatened to engulf the entire city or to discredit the political machine. Despite the many first- and second-generation Irish-Americans on the force, the New York City police protected Protestant picnickers from Catholic troublemakers at the annual Orangemen festivities in the early 1870s. Notwithstanding vigorous protests from many of the city's leading manufacturers, the Chicago police also behaved with exemplary impartiality during the great machine trades strikes of the early 1900s.[37]

The police sometimes helped and protected the citizenry. Now and then a courageous patrolman saved someone by stopping a runaway carriage, jumping into a freezing river, rushing into a burning building, or otherwise risking his life.[38] Even ordinary patrolmen periodically found a lost child or dog, took an elderly woman across the street, issued directions to a stranger, or gave first aid to an injured man. But many officers usually stayed off their posts or out of sight; if found, they often ignored requests for help and occasionally drove the supplicants away with their clubs. Now and then an alert patrolman caught a man committing or about to commit a serious offense and thereby rescued a citizen from robbery, assault, rape, or murder. And perhaps the ordinary patrolman who walked the beat and otherwise conveyed his presence discouraged muggers, robbers, or other criminals from molesting passersby. But as the police rarely captured criminals either in the act or afterward, their protection was probably worth little. Hence most citizens, especially but not exclusively the lower- and lower-middle-class newcomers, called on the police only as a last resort, and often not even then. Anyone who was obliged to rely on the police was in an unenviable position indeed.

The police served themselves and the machines a lot better than the citizens. They drew an adequate salary; if they put in a full day, which was highly unusual, they worked no harder and no longer than other Americans; and they enjoyed greater security.[39] They also supplemented their salaries with payoffs; most patrolmen preferred taking graft to raiding gamblers and most detectives preferred collecting rewards to arresting criminals. For most policemen, as indeed for most judges, teachers, and other municipal employees, public service was first and foremost a livelihood, and a relatively accessible one at that. Whether licensing vice, regulating crime, preserving order, or helping the citizenry, the police usually kept the interests and concerns of the machines uppermost in their minds. Not only did they realize that their positions were controlled by the ward bosses, but they also understood that their careers were inextricably bound up with the organization's fortunes. For most policemen, as indeed for most firemen, sanitationmen, and other public employees, personal aspirations and organizational imperatives were virtually synonymous. From their perspective, which was shared by most lower- and lower-middle-class immigrants, the police best served the public by first serving themselves and the machines.

To measure the social impact of the big-city police precisely is probably impossible. To begin with, the institution carried out a wide range of functions, which not only differed very much in theory and practice but also affected the various social classes and ethnic groups in quite different ways. It is hard to identify these functions, and as the available statistics are exceedingly unreliable, it is harder still to figure out what impact each of these functions had on each of these groups. It is even harder to come up with criteria by which to evaluate the consequences that would have been acceptable to most Americans in the late nineteenth century. No single standard or set of standards would have satisfied the Crokers and Parkhursts, the ward bosses and reformers, and the lower and upper classes. These groups may have shared a common interest in the prevention and detection of violent crime; but through no fault of their own the police were hard pressed to do much about it. Despite these difficulties it is still possible to draw a few tentative conclusions about the impact of the big-city police on urban America in the late nineteenth century.

To begin with, the big-city police enlarged the employment opportunities that were available in the late nineteenth century. The job of patrolman was just about tailor-made for the new-comers. The candidate needed no education, no capital, no skills, and only minimal literacy and tolerable health; if endorsed by the ward boss, the applicant could circumvent these require-ments if need be. In return for an endorsement the newcomers had only to pledge steadfast devotion to the political machine and, if called upon, to offer a modest bribe to the ward leaders. What the politicians gave they could of course take away. When the Republicans defeated the Democrats in Los Angeles in 1889, the police commission removed virtually all the Spanish-Americans on the force. When the Democrats clobbered the Republicans in Chicago in 1897, Superintendent Kipley replaced scores of native Americans with first- and second-generation Irish-Americans.[40] Similar purges took place in Baltimore, Kansas City, and many other places. But despite these purges the police departments and for that matter the other municipal bureaucracies remained particularly attractive sources of em-ployment for the lower- and lower-middle-class newcomers.

By making appointments on the basis of political considera-tions rather than personal qualifications, the .big-city police ensured the newcomers a disproportionately large share of the available jobs. In so doing, they enhanced the newcomers' mobility. According to the 1890 census, roughly one policeman out of two was born abroad in Chicago, Minneapolis, New York, Cleveland, Milwaukee, and San Francisco, and around one out of three in Boston, Cincinnati, Buffalo, New Orleans, and Pittsburgh. If the officers whose parents were born abroad are included, the newcomers filled about three out of four jobs in St. Louis, four out of five in Chicago, five out of six in New York, and nine out of ten in Milwaukee. The Irish-Americans secured by far the largest share: they made up around one-fifth of the force in St. Paul, Pittsburgh, and Cleveland, one-fourth in Chicago, St. Louis, and San Francisco, and one-third in New York. But others gained a fair share too: the German-Americans held about one-fifth of the jobs in Cleveland and one-third in

Milwaukee, and the Scandinavian-Americans filled roughly one-fifth of the slots in Minneapolis.[41] For most policemen, who according to scattered information about the St. Louis and St. Paul police forces had previously worked as clerks, painters, guards, grocers, carpenters, lumbermen, and laborers, a place on the force was plainly a step up.

The big-city police also reinforced the political decentralization that was characteristic of nineteenth century America. The precincts rather than headquarters carried out most essential police functions; the captains or ward bosses rather than the chiefs or commissioners made most vital departmental decisions. And the ward bosses enjoyed so much control over appointments, assignments, promotions, and discipline that the rank-and-file were more responsive to their instructions than to their superiors' orders. The police departments labored under important constraints. In the event of serious disturbances, like the draft riots of the 1860s, the railroad strikes of the 1870s, and the great industrial disputes of the 1880s, which threatened an entire city, the central authorities usually took charge. They often did so when vice or crime broke out of the lower- and lower-middle-class neighborhoods and, by enraging the upper-middle- and upper-class Americans, endangered the political machines. But provided that the precincts maintained public order and contained vice and crime, the big-city police operated mainly as adjuncts of the ward organizations.[42]

By giving the ward leaders a good deal of leverage over the local gamblers, peddlers, storekeepers, saloon owners, and other businessmen, the big-city police strengthened the political machines.[43] By strengthening the machines, they increased the power of the lower- and lower-middle-class newcomers. Unlike the native Americans, who lived all over the city, commanded most of its wealth, and controlled most of its civic and commercial clubs, newspapers, and magazines, the newcomers derived their influence almost exclusively from the political organizations in the ethnic ghettos. Without these organizations they were virtually powerless. To the newcomers political decentralization offered an opportunity to mobilize local resources, negotiate with other politicians, and in the process win a fair share of the city's bounty, a practice that most native Americans, who enjoyed greater access to the more centralized municipal and state agencies, denounced as inimical to the public interest. Although the ward leaders and ethnic minorities sometimes found themselves at odds, both usually agreed that their interests were well served by the police forces and other municipal departments which encouraged decision-making at the ward level and undermined it at the city-wide level.

The big-city police also promoted the cultural pluralism that characterized urban America in the late nineteenth century. Most policemen, who were recruited mainly from the lower and lower middle classes, had little or no inclination to impose the morality of the upper middle and upper classes on the ethnic ghettos. And most politicians, who were closely affiliated with the gamblers, saloon keepers, and other entrepreneurs of dubious legality, would not permit the police to strictly enforce the vice laws.[44] Here too the police departments operated under serious constraints. They were obliged not only to confine drinking, gambling, and other vices to the lower- and lower-middle-class communities but also to ensure that these businesses functioned with a minimum of decorum. Otherwise the upper middle and upper classes might well launch a crusade against the political machine. Through the nineteenth century, however, most police departments pretty much geared their policy on drinking, gambling, and other forms of vice that bitterly divided the nation to the life styles of the neighborhoods.

By refusing to enforce the laws against drinking among the Irish and Germans, against gambling among the Italians and Chinese, and against Sunday business among the Jews, the big-city police sanctioned the life styles of the lower- and lower-middle-class immigrants. And by sanctioning these life styles, the police enhanced their standing. From the perspective of the upper-middle- and upper-class Americans, who realized that notwithstanding the scores of sumptuary laws already on the books the police would not impose their morality on the rest of society, it seemed painfully clear that the immigrants were gaining control not only of urban America's jobs and votes, which was bad enough, but of its soul, which was worse. But from the perspective of the newcomers, who realized that no matter how much they deviated from the native Americans' attitudes toward drinking, gambling, and other controversial activities, the police would allow them to pursue a life style consistent with their own values and customs, it seemed equally clear that their morality was a legitimate expression of the nation's culture. Although the ethnic minorities were obliged to make regular payoffs to perpetuate their culture in America's cities, this was a modest price to pay in a society where ever since the Civil War, if not earlier, many of the sharpest conflicts had erupted over moral issues.[45]

2. The Military Analogy

None of the Lexow Committee's witnesses told a more poignant story than did Ceala Urchittel. A Jewish widow with three children who ran a cigar store on the Lower East Side, she was blackmailed by a precinct detective who falsely accused her of keeping a disorderly house. Unable to raise the money, she was arrested, convicted, and fined; as a result she lost her business, home, health, and children.[1] On the basis of this sort of evidence the committee concluded that lower- and lower-middle-class first- and second-generation newcomers were the chief victims of police malpractice and inadequate law enforcement. Other investigating committees arrived at similar findings. Yet the demand for police reform, which started in the 1890s, gathered momentum in the next two decades, and continued into the 1920s, came not so much from the newcomers as from the upper-middle- and upper-class native Americans. In other words, it came from the very groups whose families were least likely to be assaulted and harassed by the police and whose neighborhoods were least likely to be overrun by saloons, gambling dens, and disorderly houses. To understand why these Americans were in the vanguard of the reform campaign, it is necessary to bear in mind that so far as most people were concerned, the demand for police reform was not a narrow effort to improve law enforcement but part of a broader movement to transform urban America.

For some people, police reform was an essential feature of a moral crusade to preserve the sanctity of upper-middle-class Protestant values at a time of a vast influx of lower-class Catholic immigrants. To carry out this crusade, the reformers created societies for the suppression of vice, associations for the maintenance of law and order, and other quasi-religious organizations at the turn of the century. These groups lobbied in state capitols and city halls, formed vice commissions, and otherwise pressed elected officials to prohibit drinking, gambling, prostitution, and Sunday business and to suppress cabarets, dance halls, and movie theaters. The reformers were uncompromising. To arguments that vice should be confined to certain neighborhoods and regulated by the police they responded that it should be eliminated forthwith everywhere in the city. To claims that some kinds of vice were less noxious than others they answered that each kind encouraged the victim to indulge in other kinds and thereby weakened his resistance to temptation. To inquiries about the plight of prostitutes evicted from disorderly houses the Reverend Parkhurst replied, "I do not care whether they starve or freeze on the streets as long as they are starved and frozen into a healthier way of thinking and living."[2] From the reformers' perspective nothing less than the morality of urban American was at stake.

But as the reformers learned, it was one thing for the authorities to pass sumptuary laws and quite another for the citizens to obey them. Mayor Brand Whitlock of Toledo, Justice William J. Gaynor of New York, and other public officials argued that in view of the prevailing attitudes toward drinking, gambling, and other vices many of the sumptuary laws were unenforceable and should be amended or rescinded. George T. O'Haver of Memphis, William Copelan of Cincinnati, and other police chiefs agreed; so did F. J. Zeehandelaar of the Los Angeles Merchants and Manufacturers Association, George McAneny of the New York Chamber of Commerce, and other commercial and civic leaders. The reformers, however, denied that the sumptuary laws were misconceived and, pointing to the Lexow and other investigations, insisted that the problem was rather that the police departments were unwilling to enforce the law. Once the departments were removed from political influence, the reformers claimed, the police could easily close down illegal saloons, gambling dens, and disorderly houses.[3] From around 1900 the reformers saw police reform as a prerequisite for moral purification, a means by which they could impose upper-middle- and upper-class American morality on the lower- and lower-middle-class immigrants.

For other people, police reform was an integral component of a political campaign to increase the influence of the native Americans at the expense of the newcomers. To get this campaign underway, the reformers established municipal leagues, city clubs, good government associations, ad hoc citizens' committees, and other nonpartisan organizations early in the twentieth century. These groups drafted and sponsored charter amendments, nominated and financed candidates, badgered elected and appointed officeholders, and otherwise tried to redistribute political power by destroying the big-city machines. The reformers mounted a many-sided attack. Committed to the concepts of an underlying social harmony and an overriding public interest, they labored to replace ward with at-large councils, strengthen the mayor's office, and thereby eliminate the pervasive localism of urban politics. Convinced that city government should be divorced from politics and that its administration should be entrusted to professionals and experts, they struggled to extend civil service, introduce nonpartisan elections, and appoint nonpolitical commissions. Confident in the electoral majority yet distrustful of its elected representatives, they attempted to establish the initiative, referendum, recall, and other forms of direct legislation.[4] From the reformers' point of view nothing less than the autonomy of urban America was at stake.

But as reformers realized, the machines derived a tremendous advantage in this struggle from their control over the police. Mindful that the ward leaders had a good deal to say about appointments, promotions, and other vital matters, most police officers were quite prepared to contribute to the the organization's war chest, support its candidates, and encourage their friends to do so. They were more than willing to enforce municipal ordinances and state laws in ways that put the storekeepers, bartenders, and other businessmen whose activities bordered on the illegal in debt to the ward leaders. As the election day scandals in St. Louis, Philadelphia, Chicago, and other cities revealed, the rank-and-file were even ready to exploit their position at the polls in order to enhance the prospects of the organization's candidates. Unless the police were rendered neutral, the reformers believed, the chances for change were nil. So far as the reformers were concerned, police reform was not a campaign, in the words of *Harper's Weekly,* "against the police force," but against "Richard Croker and his kind" and against the system of municipal politics that gave rise to the bosses and their cronies.[5] It was a means of political regeneration, a device whereby the upper middle and upper classes could weaken the hand of the lower and lower middle classes.

For still other people, police reform was an integral feature of a long-standing effort to improve sanitation, education, transportation, public safety, and other urban services vital to the commercial and financial elites. To launch this effort, the reformers organized civil service leagues, municipal budget commissions, and state and local crime commissions, which were particularly active in Michigan, Missouri, New York, Chicago, Cleveland, and Los Angeles. These groups monitored vital urban institutions, called attention to their defects, drew up policy recommendations, and lobbied for their proposals in city halls and state capitols. The reformers disagreed about what things other than the influx of foreign immigrants and their reluctance to adopt traditional American values and attitudes accounted for the filthy streets, fires, crimes, and traffic jams that plagued the major cities. But they agreed that these conditions were an outgrowth of the maladministration of the vital urban institutions and that, by raising the level of municipal administration, they could improve the quality of urban services.[6] From the reformers' viewpoint nothing less than the prosperity, and in the long run the viability, of urban America hung in the balance.

But as the reformers discovered, the police departments and other urban institutions were less interested in providing services to the elites than in supplying jobs to the newcomers. And as the Lexow Committee and other investigative agencies revealed, the jobs usually went to candidates who had no qualifications other than long and faithful service to the ward leaders. This arrangement infuriated the reformers not only because it lowered the quality of urban services but also because it raised their costs and thus increased property taxes, insurance premiums, and other business expenses.[7] It was bad enough to put up with filthy streets, fires, crimes, and traffic jams, but it was even worse to pay for the institutions whose ineptness was partly responsible for these conditions. It was still worse to know that sooner or later the reformers' money went to unscrupulous politicians who used it to buy votes, intimidate citizens, and otherwise tighten their stranglehold on municipal government. From 1910 on the reformers regarded police reform as essential for administrative efficiency, a device by which they could convert the police departments and other urban institutions from troughs for the riffraff to bulwarks for the elites.

An offshoot of the efforts to transform urban America, police reform started out as part of the Progressive movement. This movement, which began at the turn of the century and thrived for the next two decades, sought to shore up the position of the upper middle and upper classes by reforming the courts, schools, and other urban institutions. It attempted to reorganize their structure, upgrade their personnel, and redefine their function in ways that would once and for all destroy the system of machine politics which had developed in the middle and late nineteenth century. Police reform subsequently gathered momentum as part of the so-called war on crime.[8] This effort, which got underway soon after World War I and continued through the 1920s, was designed to eliminate, or at any rate to reduce, criminal activity, especially when it was controlled by ethnic minorities. The war on crime drew its support from the many Americans who feared that, if crime were left unchecked, it not only would make life and limb precarious but would also weaken traditional morality, reinforce machine politics, and undermine administrative efficiency. So far as these citizens were concerned, the big-city police would have to be completely transformed in order to win the war on crime. To understand the reform crusade, it is therefore necessary to examine the class and ethnic backgrounds of the reformers and to explore their underlying assumptions about urban America.

In view of the striking heterogeneity of American society in the early twentieth century, the reformers were a remarkably homogeneous group. Well-to-do merchants, realtors, lawyers, bankers, investors, executives, industrialists, professors, ministers, and social workers, they came largely from the upper middle and upper classes. They controlled urban America's banks, corporations, law firms, and investment houses, its universities, churches, and charities, and its chambers of commerce, municipal leagues, bar associations, and vice commissions. These commercial and civic organizations stood firmly in the vanguard of the movement for police reform in most big cities. The Chamber of Commerce helped finance one police investigation in New York in 1894; the Citizens' Municipal Association contributed to another in Philadelphia in 1895; and the Committee of Safety underwrote yet another in Los Angeles in 1900. The Illinois, Cleveland, and Missouri bar associations sponsored crime surveys, which were funded, respectively, by the Industrial Club of Chicago, the Cleveland Foundation, and a utility company executive and other wealthy citizens. The Association of Commerce formed the Chicago Crime Commission in 1919, which was supported largely by local banks, and the Community Development Association founded the Los Angeles Crime Commission in 1922, which was underwritten mainly by local businessmen.[9]

With a few notable exceptions—among them John W. Goff, counsel to the Lexow Committee, Jacob H. Schiff of the New York Chamber of Commerce, the Reverend James F. Callaghan of the Chicago Vice Commission, and Professor Felix Frankfurter, a codirector, with Roscoe Pound, of the Cleveland crime survey—the reformers came largely from native-American Protestant families. Among them were Elihu Root of the New York Chamber of Commerce, Harry Chandler of the Los Angeles Crime Commission, and other well-known social figures as well as Charles F. Wyman of the New England Watch and Ward Society, George M. Boynton of the Atlanta Vice Commission, and other prominent Protestant laymen. Many Protestant ministers led or joined the campaign for police reform. They organized the New York Society for the Prevention of Crime, which triggered the Lexow Committee investigation, and the Baltimore Society for the Suppression of Vice, which prompted an inquiry in the Maryland capital. They sat on vice commissions in New York, Chicago, Philadelphia, Minneapolis, and Grand Rapids, and formed similar commissions of their own in several other cities. The Protestant ministers supported a crusade for police reform in Atlanta in the early 1900s, and led by the Reverend R. P. Shuler, they launched another campaign in Los Angeles a decade later.[10]

The similarities among the reformers and their organizations should not be exaggerated. The vice commissions, antisaloon leagues, and other agencies of moral purification recruited largely among clergymen and — whenever prostitution, commonly known as the social evil, was under discussion — among doctors and social workers. The municipal leagues, city clubs, good government associations, and other advocates of political regeneration appealed principally to lawyers, professors, and prominent businessmen. The crime commissions, criminal justice organizations, and other sponsors of crime control attracted contributors mainly among the banks, utilities, insurance companies, and other mainstays of the commercial and financial establishment. In Los Angeles and other cities, moreover, the leaders of the municipal leagues and city clubs often considered the members of the crime commissions, who were by their own statements quite conservative, antagonistic to government reform. Indeed, the Los Angeles Crime Commission broke apart in the late 1920s over the construction of Boulder Dam, the provision of hydroelectric power, and other controversial issues extraneous to law enforcement and criminal justice. Henry B. Chamberlin, the first operating director of the Chicago Crime Commission, repeatedly pointed out that, far from being a reform group, the commission was just a consortium of businessmen bent on wiping out organized crime.[11]

But the similarities among the reformers and their organizations should not be underestimated either. By virtue of their common class and ethnicity, most reformers shared a wide range of experiences which not only linked them together but also set them apart from the lower- and lower-middle-class immigrants. Most of them had grown up in the country, gone to high school and college, entered into business and professions, and joined one another in commercial and financial ventures far removed from the day-to-day struggle for subsistence. They lived in fashionable residential neighborhoods far distant from the crowded central city ghettos and mingled at prominent commercial outfits and exclusive men's clubs located in upper-middle- and upper-class enclaves. If the reformers dealt with the newcomers at all, it was as their superiors or adversaries. With the exception of the Missouri Bar Association, which invited the Order of Railway Conductors and the Association of Master Plumbers to the conference that set up the Missouri Association for Criminal Justice, the reformers did not solicit the support of the trade unions.[12]

From their common background and experience the reformers derived a common outlook, at the core of which were three distinct yet closely related assumptions about American society. First, they believed that social mobility was an economic, private, and individual process, as opposed to a political, public, and collective one, and that success was a result of industry, frugality, integrity, and occasional good luck. Second, they held that political legitimacy was a function of the public interest, the common objectives of the entire community, and not of the parochial interests of particular neighborhoods, ethnic groups, and social classes. And third, they thought that American morality was based on a commitment to abstinence and respectability, an abhorrence of self-indulgence and deviance, and a willingness to employ the criminal sanction to distinguish the one from the other. These assumptions, which were implicit in countless municipal league pamphlets, vice commission reports, and crime commission publications, reflected the deep-seated anxieties of the upper-middle- and upper-class Americans in the late nineteenth and early twentieth centuries. And they ran counter to the convictions of the lower- and lower-middle-class newcomers that public service was a means of social mobility, local control was a source of political legitimacy, and ethnic life-styles were an expression of American culture.

From the perspective of the native Americans, the newcomers' convictions did more than just challenge their cardinal assumptions about American society. Forming, as they did, the ideological underpinning for the spoils systems, the ward organizations, and the saloons, gambling dens, and red-light districts, these convictions also threatened the elite's economic, political, and moral ascendancy. Convinced that their ascendancy was the only hope for a prosperous and righteous society, many native Americans launched a wide-ranging campaign to curb these abuses in the late nineteenth century. A few attempted to impose limits on universal suffrage in the 1880s and 1890s; some tried to establish settlement houses to uplift the newcomers and assimilate their children at the turn of the century; still others labored to impose restrictions on immigration in the 1910s and 1920s.[13] Even more important, a good many mounted a nationwide crusade to transform the police departments, schools, courts, and other urban institutions in ways that would strengthen the position of the upper-middle- and upper-class Americans at the expense of the lower- and lower-middle-class newcomers.

The reformers often disagreed sharply about priorities. In 1905 the Reverend Charles H. Parkhurst took issue with banker Isaac N. Seligman and other members of a special committee of the New York Chamber of Commerce who favored repealing sumptuary laws in order to reduce police corruption. For the reverend and other moral reformers, compromise with vice was inconceivable. A few years later the reformers divided over Chief Fred Kohler's controversial "golden rule" policy, whereby the Cleveland police department, instead of arresting juveniles, alcoholics, and first offenders, gave them a warning and took them home. Kohler's scheme generated heated debate at the IACP's annual meetings in 1908 and 1909. In 1923 the Merchants and Manufacturers Association, the Advertising Council, and other champions of the Los Angeles Crime Commission fought with the Reverend Shuler and other evangelical ministers over whether the police department should enforce sumptuary laws against a charitable circus. For the Los Angeles and other crime commissions, vice was a much less severe problem than crime. Through the early twentieth century these and similar controversies, reflecting important differences over the relative importance of vice suppression, crime control, and political reform, split the reformers in one city after another.[14]

But most reformers agreed completely on one vital point: whatever the problem, the police could and should handle it. The ministerial associations insisted that if the police were purged of corruption, they would have no trouble closing illegal saloons, gambling joints, and disorderly houses and thereby wiping out vice. The associations refused to consider the possibility that sizable segments of the populace did not share their objection to drinking, gambling, and other vices or their enthusiasm for sumptuary legislation. The municipal leagues contended that if the police were insulated from political interference, they would be more responsive to the Progressive view of the public interest. These groups failed to grasp that the machine spoke for a substantial and sorely underrepresented constituency, with a different and yet equally plausible political morality. The crime commissions held that if the police, as well as the prosecutors, courts, and correctional institutions, were made more efficient they would have no problem stamping out criminal activity. These outfits overlooked the possibility that organized crime thrived because many newcomers found the legitimate avenues to economic success severely obstructed. In view of the record of the big-city police in the early twentieth century, the reformers' confidence was based on an extremely shaky foundation.

To construct a strong base for their campaign, the reformers attempted to account for the disparities between the theory and practice of policing in urban America. From the turn of the century through the 1920s they launched investigations, organized conferences, employed detectives, and otherwise sponsored probes of the nation's police forces. Out of these efforts emerged a vast array of speeches, articles, books, reports, and legislative schemes which embodied a fairly consistent diagnosis of the country's police problems. According to most reformers, the corruption, incompetence, and inefficiency of the big-city police departments was fundamentally a function of political involvement in departmental affairs. "Politics is the curse of our free institutions," a New York magistrate told a special committee of the Chamber of Commerce in 1905, "and no where is it more clearly shown than in the Police Department."[15] His remarks were anything but judicious, but other judges in New York seconded them, as did newspaper publishers in Atlanta, investment bankers in Chicago, and evangelical ministers in Los Angeles. So long as the police forces were entangled in local politics, the reformers insisted, they were doomed to machine control.

According to the reformers, the structure of the departments violated several cardinal principles of municipal government. In principle, the police force was, as the St. Louis Civic League put it, an administrative rather than a legislative body; the preservation of order, protection of property, and enforcement of law were not policy issues. In practice, most departments denied their chiefs tenure and otherwise subjected them to the tribulations of political appointees. In principle, the police force required a high degree of administrative centralization and departmental coordination. In practice, most departments permitted the local precincts to operate as semi-, if not wholly, autonomous police forces within their respective wards. In principle, the police force needed a good deal of expertise and specialization to handle its complex and diverse functions. In practice, most departments entrusted not only everyday patrolling but also vice control, internal investigation, record-keeping, and most other critical chores to ordinary patrolmen operating, under little supervision, out of the precincts.[16] Little wonder, most reformers concluded, that few police departments could long withstand the enormous pressure of the political machine.

Nor, under the circumstances, could many departments do their work properly. So long as the chief lacked tenure, one police official remarked, he was "a mere bird of passage, usually flying so fast that the men under him hardly have time to determine his species." No sooner was the chief appointed, another official observed, than everyone began speculating "how long he will remain" and "who will be his successor."[17] By the time that the chief selected his subordinates, molded the rank-and-file, collected the pertinent information, analyzed the available options, and otherwise gained the know-how and experience to manage so complex an organization, the politicians usually demanded his resignation or removal. So long as most police departments were widely decentralized, highly unspecialized, and closely aligned with the local wards, the reformers contended, effective power inevitably gravitated from city-wide officials to ward leaders and from police commissioners to precinct captains. This process, which at once reflected and reinforced the prevailing localism of municipal politics, undermined the already loose chain-of-command in most police departments and subverted the integrity and efficiency of commanding officers and rank-and-file alike. Given so defective a structure, the reformers reasoned, not even well-qualified personnel could properly serve the American people.

Nor were most personnel well qualified, the reformers emphasized. Notwithstanding the legendary bravery and customary generosity of the rank-and-file, which even their sharpest critics acknowledged, many policemen—perhaps as many as nine out of ten, according to some observers—were thoroughly corrupt and incompetent.[18] The reformers did not entirely agree on the reason. The majority, which included Commissioner Theodore A. Bingham of New York and District Attorney William Travers Jerome of Manhattan, claimed that most officers started out physically, mentally, and morally superior to the average citizen, but that as a result of the pressure of constant temptation, the duplicity of commanding officers, and the absence of effective discipline they soon went downhill. This view prevailed through World War I and persisted into the 1920s. A minority, which included Raymond B. Fosdick, an authority on European and American policing, and August Vollmer, chief of the Berkeley police, disagreed. Pointing out that most policemen did not finish high school, scored below average on intelligence tests, received little or no training, earned inadequate salaries, and continued working into their sixties, seventies, and eighties, these reformers argued that the rank-and-file were largely unqualified at the outset and remained so thereafter.[19] This view emerged after World War I and gained considerable support in the 1920s. Whether the reformers sided with the majority or the minority, however, most of them agreed that this situation profoundly demoralized the big-city police.

In the absence of strict discipline, strong leadership, and qualified personnel, most officers followed the paths of least resistance laid out by the ward bosses and precinct captains. Now and then, when pressure from reformers built up, they raided a joint or arrested a crook; but most of the time they kept out of sight and away from trouble. If they ran into a jam, they asked the ward leaders for help. They pocketed a decent salary, supplemented it with modest payoffs, hoped for a transfer to a special detail or a promotion to sergeant or captain, and as the years passed, waited for a soft spot indoors or, where available, a pension. As the patrolmen well knew or soon found out, they were no match for an influential gambler, liquor dealer, or other disreputable businessman, let alone a well-organized, highly mobile, fully armed gang of criminals closely allied with the ward leader.[20] Little wonder, most reformers concluded, that vice continued unabated in the red-light districts, election scandals erupted in the immigrant quarters, and crime spread throughout the nation's leading cities. So long as most police officers remained under the thumb of the ward bosses, the police departments could not mount an effective assault against lawlessness in urban America.

Nor, most reformers charged, did the departments try to do so. Under pressure from the big-city machines and other political interests, most police forces spent much of their time supervising elections, censoring movies, operating lodging homes and emergency ambulances, inspecting boilers, tenements, markets, or factories, and carrying out other nonpolice functions. In the reformers' view these functions should have been handled by the health, building, elections, welfare, and other municipal departments. At the insistence of many influential private and public outfits, which thought that the presence of uniformed officers would help preserve order and expedite business, most police forces also assigned much of their manpower to jails, courthouses, theaters, circuses, sports arenas, docks, railway stations, and other quasi-public facilities. In the reformers' eyes, these facilities should have hired private guards. Some reformers, who carried this position a step further, insisted that vice control was not, strictly speaking, a proper police function, and one or two, including Chief Vollmer, applied this argument to traffic regulation; but very few of their associates were prepared to go quite so far, at any rate not in public.[21] In light of the spread of vice and crime in urban America, most reformers concluded that the catchall tradition of American policing was completely anachronistic.

As the reformers saw it, this tradition demoralized the big-city police for several reasons other than that it exposed ordinary patrolmen to virtually irresistible financial and personal temptations. For one, the extraneous functions consumed anywhere from one-tenth to one-third of the department's manpower and thereby undermined its capacity to maintain order, prevent crime, and enforce the law. For another reason, the special details were in such strong demand that they generated jealousy among the patrolmen and intensified their dependence on the ward leaders who handed out these assignments. For still another reason, these details placed the policemen at the disposal of special interests, sometimes for months or years on end, and thereby blurred their sense of responsibility to the general public.[22] So many policemen were tied up in nonpolice functions or tied down on special details, the reformers pointed out, that many citizens often found it hard, if not impossible, to locate an officer. The failure to draw a sharp line between police and nonpolice functions and between public and private interests therefore cost the big-city police a good deal of support among the law-abiding citizenry. No wonder, the reformers concluded, that law enforcement and criminal justice remained a national scandal well into the twentieth century.

The reformers' diagnosis was an impressive political achievement. It not only offered a resounding and widely praised indictment of the structure, personnel, and function of the big-city police; it also presented a coherent theory of police action, a plausible rationale for police reform, and an implicit ordering of reform priorities. Even more important, the reformers' diagnosis challenged the underlying assumption, which had prevailed since the nineteenth century, that the police force was an essential component of city politics and that its structure, personnel, and function should be conceived of accordingly. As the reformers saw it, this assumption not only violated the principle that the police, courts, schools, and other urban institutions were administrative not legislative bodies, which implemented rather than formulated policies. It also increased the likelihood that the political machines would dominate the police departments. To complete the ideological foundation for police reform, the reformers were therefore obliged not only to figure out a compelling diagnosis of the problem but also to come up with an alternative model of the police, one that would inspire and inform efforts to reconstruct the big-city departments in the years ahead.

The reformers were strongly attracted to the corporate model that had dominated Progressive thinking about the schools and other urban institutions since the turn of the century. As Raymond Callahan, Samuel Haber, and other scholars have pointed out, this model was inspired by an admiration for large-scale enterprise, a fascination with scientific management, and an enthusiasm for corporate organization. According to its advocates, the American city was essentially a business corporation: the citizens were its stockholders, the elected officials its board of directors, and the appointed officials its managers and employees. As such, the city should be run according to sound business principles. From time to time Fosdick and other reformers applied the corporate model to the big-city police; so did the New York Bureau of Municipal Research, the Cleveland Foundation, and the Chicago Crime Commission. They evaluated police practices, reviewed departmental problems, and devised policy recommendations about recruitment, training, discipline, and all sorts of other critical issues according to what they thought were the principles of large-scale business enterprise.[23] With few exceptions, however, most reformers adopted a military analogy instead of a corporate model.

According to this analogy, the American police were a military body or, in the words of Commissioner Theodore Roosevelt, Captain Alexander R. Piper, and Major Frederick H. Ebstein, respectively, a "half-military," "semi-military," and "quasi-military" body. Whether regarded as a "municipal army," to quote a New York City alderman, or a "standing army," to cite a Colorado senator, the police served the city in much the same way that the military served the nation. To Commissioner William McAdoo of New York City the police chief was like the commander-in-chief; to Frank L. Moss, counsel to the Mazet Committee, he was like the secretary of war; and to Leonhard F. Fuld, author of a classic text on police administration, he was like a general. The policeman was a soldier in Fuld's judgment, a quasi-soldier in McAdoo's opinion, and an "absent sentry" when off-duty, to quote from the New York City Police Department's annual report for 1919. The departments were divided, Commissioner McAdoo wrote, into "two great armies": the uniformed force and the detective division. But every officer had the sacred obligation of a soldier, President Woodrow Wilson declared. Governor Calvin Coolidge of Massachusetts agreed; so did Senator Lawrence Y. Sherman of Illinois, Representative Burton L. French of Idaho, and Commissioner Grover Whalen of New York City, who kept a bronze figurine of Napoleon on his desk in police headquarters.[24]

According to this analogy, the American police were engaged in a war on crime which, the reformers pointed out, raged day and night, extended from the Atlantic to the Pacific, and was no less terrifying for being a domestic affair. The implications were staggering. If crime was warfare, as Commissioner Whalen and others reasoned, criminals were the enemy, lawyers were their diplomats, policemen were the main line of defense, and civilians were combatants in the struggle. All of urban America was a battlefield. In this case, one journalist observed, no holds were barred, no tactics ruled out, no rights respected, and no mercy tendered; nothing less than complete victory, presumably the total annihilation of the enemy, was acceptable. From the end of the nineteenth century through World War I the military analogy gained in favor not only among police reformers but also among police administrators. At one IACP annual convention after another the speakers told the chiefs that they were "soldiers of peace," to cite a San Francisco police chief, or "home guard soldiers," to quote a Detroit police chief, waging a never-ending struggle for law and order in urban America.[25] By the 1920s the military analogy was the conventional wisdom of most upper-middle- and upper-class Americans too.

Not everyone concurred. After noting that the police had a far greater impact than the military on the everyday life of the American people, the Lexow Committee concluded that "no true analogy exists." After showing that the military and the police operate according to different principles, Fosdick pointed out that "the analogy is largely fallacious." Judge Daniel E. Finn of New York and Chief James L. Beavers of Atlanta expressed strong reservations. Justice Gaynor, probably the most articulate spokesman for a civilian orientation at the time, contended that advocates of the military analogy had little knowledge of the police and less understanding of democracy.[26] The dissenters were very much in the minority, however, and when speaking or writing about the police, even they sometimes referred to soldiers, enemies, and battles or otherwise resorted to martial rhetoric. More often than not they did so unconsciously, revealing just how deeply the military analogy had penetrated into the commonplace discourse about the big-city police.

In view of the long-standing civilian orientation of the American police, it is hard to tell precisely why the reformers who adopted a corporate model for schools, city councils, and other urban institutions chose a military analogy for the police. They probably did not do so because the police wore martial uniforms, carried guns and other weapons, used force if need be, and gave military ranks to the superior officers. For in their dress, demeanor, and everyday activity the police bore only a superficial resemblance to the military. Few Americans mistook policemen for soldiers; and very few Europeans who visited the United States in these years were struck by the martial bearing of the big-city police. Nor did the reformers choose the military analogy because McAdoo, Fosdick, and other prominent figures who had recently traveled to Europe compared the continental police, which had a strong military bent, favorably to the American police. For these authorities also compared the English police, which had a more pervasive civilian orientation, favorably not only to the American police but also in a few cases to the French, German, and Italian police.[27] On the basis of these experts' accounts, the reformers could have chosen any of several different models.

Rather, the reformers adopted a military analogy largely because it fit so neatly their cardinal assumptions about the police problem. Most reformers were convinced that the ward bosses as well as their allies in the underworld and on the police forces were out to destroy the prosperity, the security, and indeed the very soul of urban America. If this was not warfare, the reformers reasoned, nothing was. If the United States could go to war to liberate Cuba from Spain and to save democracy in Europe, it could do no less to free America from vice and to restore democracy in its own cities. By any measure Johnny Torrio, Al Capone, Jack Zelig, Herman Rosenthal, and other gangsters were as severe a threat to the American way of life as the Spanish king or the German kaiser. Since the reformers were ready to enlist in the struggle, they could demand at least as much of the police. The military analogy was particularly appealing to the many reformers who were convinced that the Italian-Americans and other recent immigrants were responsible for the shocking increase of vice and crime in urban America. Their receptivity was probably heightened by the sharp rise in murders, bombings, and other gangland tactics that culminated in the St. Valentine's Day Massacre of 1929, in which seven members of the O'Banion gang were gunned down in a Chicago warehouse.[28]

Apart from offering an alternative model for the big-city police and completing the ideological foundation for police reform, the military analogy served the reformers in several other ways. To begin with, the analogy had profound emotional connotations. With its repeated emphasis on soldiers, enemies, battles, fronts, strategies, discipline, and other martial terms the analogy conveyed a tremendous sense of urgency or even emergency and an absolute contempt for temporizing and procrastination. It underlined the appeals for all-out commitment and total mobilization, transformed existing conditions into a national as opposed to a local scandal, and raised police reform well up on the Progressive agenda. At the time of the Spanish American and first world wars, of the victories at Manila Bay and Belleau Wood and the heroics of Admiral Dewey and General Pershing, the analogy also played upon the widespread admiration for the navy and army. It set the corruption, incompetence, and buffoonery of the police, which to the dismay of the chiefs was being highlighted during the 1910s in the misadventures of the Keystone Cops, against the alleged integrity, efficiency, and dignity of the military.[29]

What is more, the analogy had far-reaching practical implications. In view of the long-standing and much-heralded separation of the military and the politicians, which had sharply distinguished the United States from most of Western Europe and Latin America in the nineteenth century, it followed that the police should be as free of partisan interference as the army and the navy. And in view of the common conception of the military as a rigidly authoritarian and strictly hierarchical organization, it followed that the police chief — preferably a retired army officer, a West Point graduate, or a successful businessman — should be entrusted with virtually absolute power over the everyday operations of the department.[30] In other words, the military analogy implied that the American police should be controlled not by the politicians, especially not by the ward bosses, but by the police chiefs, who by virtue of their responsibility to the mayor, police commission, or other city-wide body would probably be more amenable to the reformers and their organizations. Not without reason were the reformers confident that they could eliminate the disparities between policing in theory and in practice if the big-city police were conceived of as a military rather than a political outfit.

The reformers were not sure just how far to extend the military analogy. At one extreme stood a few who in their enthusiasm for the paramilitary constabularies organized in Pennsylvania, New York, and other states shortly after the turn of the century spoke in favor of transforming the local forces into branches of the state police. At the other extreme stood some who in their preference for a corporate or other civilian model argued against applying martial principles to any police activities other than perhaps marching in parades and controlling crowds. Most reformers fell somewhere in between. A special committee of the Los Angeles City Council, which in the process of fixing police salaries recommended in 1918 that the police department be reorganized "along more strictly military lines," was typical of this group. So was a Milwaukee alderman who in the course of a search for a new police chief suggested in 1921 that the city give priority to a military officer, preferably one who had served under either Colonel Roosevelt or General Pershing.[31] For these reformers the military analogy was the source of the principles and criteria by which to formulate and evaluate policies for changing the structure, personnel, and function of the big-city police. The analogy was, in other words, the base of their prescription for police reform.

Applying this analogy, the reformers arrived at three distinct yet closely related recommendations: the departments should be centralized, their personnel should be upgraded, and their function should be narrowed. To centralize the departments, the reformers proposed that the chiefs be given as secure a tenure and as capable a staff as military commanders. They debated whether the chiefs should hold office for five years, ten years, or life, should serve at the pleasure of the authorities or by virtue of good behavior, and should answer to the mayor, the governor, or the courts. But most agreed that the chiefs should be appointed for a far longer term and provided with far better aides; and some recommended that they should, in Chief Vollmer's phrase, "be surrounded with every protective civil service device imaginable." The reformers made two other proposals to centralize the police departments. First, pointing to the common reliance on patrol cars, the costly upkeep of station houses, the purported shortage of patrol forces, and the corrupt influence of ward leaders, they urged that the precincts be consolidated or closed down wherever possible. And second, pointing to the importance of specialization in police work, they proposed that vice control, record-keeping, internal investigation, crime detection, and other vital functions be transferred from ordinary patrolmen attached to the precincts to special squads assigned to headquarters.[32]

Once the police chiefs were secure in their positions, they would not only be insulated from the political pressure that had long demoralized their departments but also be assured a chance to ponder their problems, choose their subordinates, mold the rank-and-file, and thereby impose their will on the force. By so doing, they would provide the vigorous leadership hitherto lacking in the police forces, reduce the long-standing disparities between formal authority and actual power, and perhaps even ensure that orders formulated at headquarters were implemented on the beats. Once the station houses were consolidated or closed down and the special squads established, the locus of power would gradually though inexorably shift from patrolmen to specialists, captains to chiefs, and precincts to headquarters. In this process the district leaders would lose access to policy makers, control over police practices, and most important of all, support in ethnic neighborhoods. Besides enhancing the quality of law enforcement, the centralization of the police forces would also undermine the localism of urban politics and, by implication, the foundation of machine government.[33]

From the start the reformers proposed to upgrade the rank-and-file by shielding them from political interference, placing them under martial discipline, removing them from temptation, and generally treating them as soldiers. To this end the reformers recommended that all officers up to or even including the chief be provided civil service status and perhaps be assigned military rank; that internal discipline be modeled along the lines of a court-martial, with appeal to the courts severely limited or abolished outright; that patrolmen be removed from vice duty, which would be handled by special squads, and be forbidden to accept, much less to solicit, rewards; and that all officers be obliged to give exclusive loyalty to their departments. Soon after World War I, however, the few reformers who regarded the rank-and-file less favorably called for more far-reaching changes. To weed out incompetents, they demanded that the physical and mental exams be properly graded and be supplemented by tough intelligence tests, thorough character checks, and other imposing hurdles. To attract applicants, they insisted that salaries be raised and residency requirements eliminated. To supply recruits with the equivalent of basic training, they urged that police academies be established. And to enhance the prospects of retaining experienced officers at their peak and of retiring superannuated policemen afterward, they pressed for adequate service pensions.[34]

As soon as appointments, assignments, promotion. and discipline depended on personal ability instead of political influence, the rank-and-file would no longer be subservient to the ward leaders and obliged to enforce the laws to their benefit. Henceforth they would follow departmental orders to the letter, not only out of fear of the chiefs and their subordinates, but also out of a sense of self-respect, a commitment to the force, and a concern for the public interest. Once credentials were stiffened, salaries raised, training extended, and service pensions established, the police force would attract and retain dedicated officers capable of dealing with complex matters honestly and efficiently. By virtue of this commitment and competence, the public's estimation of the police would rise, as would the cooperation of the community and the status of the occupation. As a result the departments would recruit so many qualified men that, in the view of a small but growing group of reformers, policing would eventually emerge as a profession.[35] In addition to improving service and eradicating corruption, the upgrading of personnel would subvert the force's dependence on the machine and, by implication, the machine's control over the city.

To narrow the police function, the reformers proposed that the departments give up all activities unrelated to the war on crime. Turn the polls over to an election bureau, they urged, the markets and tenements over to the health department, the ambulances over to the municipal hospital, the pool rooms and billiard parlors over to a licensing authority, and the lodging houses, bread lines, and motion picture censors over to the welfare department. Tell the courts, railways, shipping companies, theater owners, and other public and quasi-public outfits to hire their own guards; and wherever possible, employ civilians instead of sworn officers to handle clerical, technical, and other vital but not strictly police tasks. Smedley D. Butler of Philadelphia and other reformers justified this position on the grounds that crime prevention was the principal function of the American police; so did Fosdick and other reformers less taken by the military analogy. Most police chiefs accepted this position too. But when Chief Vollmer and a few others called on the departments to give up vice control and traffic regulation as well, most reformers refused to go along on the grounds, first, that vice and crime were, if not one and the same, at least inextricable and, second, that highway safety was a source of legitimate concern to the force.[36] Apparently they would follow the military analogy only so far.

As soon as the superfluous functions were given up and the

temporary details abolished, the police chiefs would be able not only to release many officers for patrol duty and thus enhance public safety but also to reduce the opportunity for outside interference and so improve departmental morale. In the meantime the chiefs could organize the force's squads, concentrate its energies, develop its expertise, refine its technology, galvanize its supporters, and sustained by a grateful populace, bring the war against crime to a successful conclusion. Nor were these the only advantages of reform. As soon as crime prevention was accepted as the principal function of the police, the departments would have, for the first time since the mid-nineteenth century, a clear criterion by which to judge whether something was or was not a proper police activity. Henceforth virtually every policy, from Cleveland's "golden rule" to New York's third degree, and every innovation, from juvenile officers to police athletic leagues, would have to be rationalized in terms of crime prevention.[37] Other than increasing the efficacy of criminal justice in the cities, the narrowing of the police function would also decrease the force's usefulness to the machine and, by implication, weaken the machine's influence over its constituents.

The reformers' prescription was a formidable ideological accomplishment. It did more than just offer policies that would supposedly suppress vice, eradicate crime, emasculate the machine, and separate politics and policing. By embracing the military analogy and employing it to formulate policy, the prescription overrode the civilian orientation that had heretofore distinguished American policemen from French, German, and Italian gendarmes. And by defining crime prevention as the quintessential function of police departments and using it to evaluate the propriety of other police activities, the prescription violated the long-standing catchall and responsive tradition. Indeed, only in the reluctance to consolidate local police forces along metropolitan, state, and national lines, a practice that was already underway in England, did the reformers show much regard for nineteenth century traditions. Finally, the projected changes in the structure, personnel, and function of the big-city police were bound to have an uneven impact on the well-being of urban America's many social classes and ethnic groups. For this reason, if for no other, a full-scale struggle over police reform was inevitable in the early twentieth century.

The reformers were, to say the least, well prepared for this struggle. Rooted in the upper middle and upper classes, they had lots of money and, through their business corporations, commercial associations, and civic organizations, access to lots more. And they were willing to spend it. The reformers underwrote investigations of the New York City, Philadelphia, and Los Angeles police forces, employed detectives to infiltrate gambling and prostitution in Baltimore and Chicago, and sponsored commissions to study vice in Hartford. They financed the Chicago and Los Angeles crime commissions, subsidized the Cleveland, Missouri, and Illinois crime surveys, and funded Fosdick's books on the American and European police. Through the San Francisco Realty Board, the Colorado Tax Payers Protective League, and anonymous private donors, they hired the Bureau of Municipal Research to make thorough analyses of the San Francisco, Denver, and New York City police departments respectively.[38] As if all this were not enough, the reformers contributed funds to political candidates pledged to police reform on not only the municipal level but also the state and national levels.

Drawn from the native American Protestant elite and thus endowed with a long pedigree, a proper education, and occasionally a feeling of noblesse oblige, the reformers had a special standing in the community and a strong inclination to exploit it. This gave them a moral edge in political controversy. No one honed that edge more finely than Judge Samuel Seabury of New York and Southampton, a descendant of America's first Episcopal bishop and a former justice of the Court of Appeals, who in 1930 exposed an extortion ring running out of the New York police department's vice squad. Few observers had much trouble deciding whether Judge Seabury or Meyer Slutsky, James Quinlivian, Peter Pfiefer, and the other gang members embodied the American ideal.[39] The reformers gained another moral edge because they faithfully reflected the anxieties and aspirations of the millions of middle-class Protestants who lived in small towns and rural villages. The reformers articulated this group's concern about gambling, drinking, prostitution, and white slavery, its enthusiasm for using the criminal sanction to impose conventional morality, and its determination to wrest power from the immigrants and the machines. By speaking for so many Americans outside the cities, and thus by serving as rural America's spokesmen in urban America, the reformers enhanced their already commanding position.

Besides the church federations, municipal leagues, and chambers of commerce, the reformers could usually count on the support of the newspapers, universities, and research institutes. William R. Nelson's *Star* launched the assault that triggered the Kansas City investigation in 1897; and William R. Hearst's *Examiner* exposed the arrangements between the police and the gamblers which brought about the San Francisco inquiry in 1901. Many major newspapers gave the reform crusade such extensive and sympathetic coverage that some critics blamed the press for generating the crime waves. Social scientists at the University of Chicago and Northwestern University carried out statistical and psychological studies for the city council's crime committee, which was chaired by Professor Charles E. Merriam, alderman from ward five. Chicago and Berkeley established professorships in police science. Under the supervision of Bruce Smith, Leonard Harrison, and other well-known authorities, the Bureau of Municipal Research (later the Institute of Public Administration) and other research outfits conducted surveys of police departments all over the country.[40] By applying a veneer of scientific objectivity to the reformers' assumptions, these surveys considerably increased the credibility of their diagnosis and prescription.

Except when the bosses or their allies dominated the state house as well as city hall, the reformers could generally count on the backing of the state authorities. Their backing was important for two reasons. First, the state authorities were empowered to appoint investigative committees and otherwise to probe most municipal agencies. At the prodding of the reformers, the states authorized full-scale inquiries into the New York City, Philadelphia, Chicago, and Kansas City police forces in the 1890s. Later on they organized vice commissions, crime commissions, and other official agencies which strengthened the campaign for police reform.[41] Second, the state authorities were empowered to legislate on a wide variety of matters that profoundly influenced the structure, personnel, and function of the big-city police. Many municipalities needed the state's approval to establish a civil service system, set up service pensions, and apply the criminal sanction to gambling and other consensual crimes. Many municipalities also needed its permission to put into practice nonpartisan elections, at-large councils, the initiative, referendum, and recall, and other Progressive proposals.

The state's influence varied sharply from city to city, largely depending on the degree of home rule, but ordinarily it greatly strengthened the reformers' already powerful position.

The reformers could not expect much cooperation from the police because many of the chiefs and most of the rank-and-file opposed reform. But they could hope for occasional assistance from a small but rapidly growing, highly articulate, and as the years went by, increasingly influential group of high-level police administrators. The group included not only Commissioner Theodore Roosevelt of New York, Deputy Commissioner Metellus L. C. Funkhouser of Chicago, Public Safety Director Smedley D. Butler of Philadelphia, Chief James W. Everington of Los Angeles, and other officials who were appointed from the outside at the behest of the reformers. It also included Richard Sylvester of Washington, James L. Beavers of Atlanta, and other chiefs who had worked their way up the ranks. Many of these officials came from the same background as the reformers. But unlike the reformers, they objected to the current system less on the grounds that it failed to eliminate vice, eradicate crime, and undermine the machines than on the grounds that it rendered them vulnerable to political pressure and susceptible to public criticism. Convinced that in the absence of radical change their position would remain painfully insecure and their status embarrassingly low, these officials responded favorably to the campaign for police reform.

If the annual proceedings of the IACP were indicative, many police officials felt extremely vulnerable to political pressure. In one speech after another they complained about political figures who constantly badgered them to appoint incompetent applicants, promote inefficient patrolmen, release suspected felons, and take other actions inconsistent with their duty. These demands posed a severe threat to the conscientious chief, as the high turnover of the IACP membership revealed. Indeed, so many police chiefs lost their jobs in 1900 because of turnovers in municipal administration that at the next year's annual meeting the association unanimously approved a resolution condemning the dismissal of police chiefs for political reasons and calling for a total separation of policing and politics.[42] Superintendent Sylvester, who presided over the IACP through the 1900s, and his colleagues regularly protested that political interference inhibited effective law enforcement and endangered democratic government. But their protests were generated not so much by professional or ideological considerations as by strong resentment of the politicians, intense dissatisfaction with their own weakness, and above all chronic fear of abrupt removal.

Many police chiefs also felt extremely susceptible to public criticism. At one IACP meeting after another they lamented that the police were not only the victims of widespread popular antipathy and indiscriminate fault-finding, but also the butts of everyday jokes, newspaper cartoons, and after 1900, Keystone studio comedies. The chiefs pointed out that the mass media, particularly the movies, often portrayed policemen at best as well-meaning imbeciles, incapable of carrying out the simplest order, and at worst as out-and-out grafters, ready to fleece everybody in sight. The chiefs were so concerned that the motion pictures were downgrading the police and glorifying the criminals that at their annual meeting in 1913 they passed a resolution pledging to do everything possible to stop this misrepresentation.[43] Superintendent Sylvester and his associates repeatedly complained that the tendency to ridicule and criticize the officers subverted the morale of the police force and thereby decreased the efficiency of the criminal justice system. But these complaints were generated not so much by occupational considerations as by the conviction that this attitude precluded a rise in the status of the American police, which was at the top of the IACP's agenda.

Hence a few ranking police officials responded favorably to the campaign for police reform out of a desire to diminish their vulnerability to political pressure and their susceptibility to public criticism, or in other words, to increase their security and elevate their status. By so doing, they manifested an incipient occupational identity, a commitment to policing and the department, as opposed to politics and the machine, which had tremendous implications for the future. These officials frequently disagreed with the reformers, but for the time being they willingly submerged their differences in a common antagonism to the political machine. If need be, they could work out problems later. Such accommodation was critical because the impetus to police reform came from outside the departments and from ethnic groups and social classes alien to their personnel. The reformers could not carry out their programs over the unequivocal opposition of the superior officers and the rank-and-file. Self-confidence and self-righteousness would bring them just so far. Only with the occasional assistance of high-level officials could the reformers possibly overcome the force's boundless capacity for obstruction. By virtue of this accommodation the reformers rounded out a formidable coalition to carry on the upcoming struggle for control of the big-city police.

3. The First Wave of Reform

Tammany Hall launched a vigorous counterattack shortly after the Lexow Committee began its hearings in 1894. Unscrupulous patrolmen intimidated and, as a lesson to others, framed prospective witnesses; and to the committee's astonishment, the police commissioners suspended a particularly candid captain. Tammany agents gave $1,700 to a well-known madam, who was under subpoena by the committee and sent her, with an escort, to Montreal and Chicago; they offered a local confidence man $50 to leave for Philadelphia and $20 a week to stay there. According to a low-level clerk in the comptroller's office, a municipal employee forfeited his job and even risked his life by appearing before the committee.[1] Similar investigations prompted much the same response in Chicago and other cities. For the politicians' power depended heavily on control of the police force and other municipal agencies. In the face of so explicit a challenge as a legislative investigation, it was natural for them to band together and defend the organization and the policemen who faithfully served it. And when the crusade for police reform was extended to the polls, precincts, city halls, and state capitols, it was logical for the politicians to use whatever tactics necessary to silence their critics. The machines would not lose the struggle for lack of will.

Nor would they lose it for want of power. By dint of thorough organization, inspired leadership, and remarkable sensitivity to the immigrants, the machines usually did very well in municipal elections. If the outcome was in question, and often even if it was not, the ward bosses were prepared to bribe voters, round up repeaters, and use other fraudulent means to improve their showing. If need be, they were ready to send in hoodlums to keep the opposition away from the polls and to order policemen to help the thugs out or at least to mind their own business. By virtue of these efforts, the machines arrived at their heyday around the end of the century. Tammany Hall ruled in New York, as did the Republican machine in Philadelphia. Abe Ruef and his cronies would soon govern San Francisco, though not for long; Jim Pendergast and his organization would shortly take over Kansas City.[2] Even when the machines lost city-wide elections, they usually retained power in New York's Lower East Side, Chicago's first ward, and the other lower- and lower-middle-class immigrant communities that were the prime source of their strength. By so doing, they were able to withstand reform attacks in New York and other cities during the late 1880s and early 1890s; by the turn of the century they felt confident that they would be able to withstand them in the years ahead.

The machines had several other reasons for their confidence. Apart from the police forces, they controlled most of the municipal institutions that were capable of sidetracking, sabotaging, or otherwise obstructing reform campaigns. It would serve no purpose to enforce the law more strictly if, as evidence from Philadelphia and Washington, D.C., showed, very few prosecutors ever won a conviction, much less a prison sentence, against gamblers, bartenders, or prostitutes. It would do no good to tighten departmental disciplinary proceedings if some judges reinstated incompetent and corrupt policemen on legal technicalities. It would not be useful to establish a civil service system if, as reports from New York and Chicago revealed, few commissioners were able and willing to stand up to the pressure of the ward bosses. And it would be pointless to extend a police chief's term of office and otherwise reinforce his position if the machines picked the mayors who appointed him.[3] The organizations did not, of course, expect things to go so far. As investigative committees discovered in New York City and Philadelphia, the machines required every

officeholder to give enough time and money to ensure that the reformers got no chance to implement their proposals.

The machines also spoke for millions of lower- and lower-middle-class newcomers whose opposition to reform aspirations
formed an imposing obstacle to the upcoming campaign. Many
immigrants sympathized with the Chicago alderman who
expressed his antagonism to sumptuary legislation by proposing
the establishment of a "Bureau of Don'ts." Let it be selected by
the "popular or unpopular vote of reformers, hypocrites, bigots
[and] assorted nincompoops," he suggested, and be authorized to
regulate "the right to live, die, breathe, laugh, cry, eat, sleep,
love, hate [and] dance." Many immigrants also agreed with G.
W. Plunkitt, a Tammany district leader, who criticized the civil
service, direct primary, and other reform measures on the
grounds that they deprived the organization of its source of jobs
and its members of their reason for political action. "When the
people elected Tammany, they knew just what they were doin',"
he observed. "We stood as we have always stood for rewardin' the
men that won the victory." Many immigrants even approved of
Al Capone, the Chicago gangster who regarded himself as a
public benefactor. "I've given the people the light pleasures,
shown them a good time," he argued. "Some call it bootlegging.
Some call it racketeering. I call it a business." "They talk about
me not being on the legitimate," he once told a reporter, "Why,
lady, nobody's on the legit."[4]

As if all this were not enough, the machines dominated most
police forces, whose capacity to impede reform was virtually
boundless. As investigators learned in one city after another, the
ward leaders influenced appointments, assignments, and
promotions; and as many policemen who fought the system discovered, they arranged suspensions and dismissals. Well aware
that there were several candidates ready and willing to take their
places and that there were few jobs so attractive in the private
sector, most officers realized that they had much to lose and little
to gain by defying the organization. But the machine's hold over
the police did not depend exclusively on even primarily on insecurity or intimidation. Most officers were linked to the politicians by strong personal, familial, class, and ethnic bonds.[5] They
also regarded public office as a major avenue of mobility and the
machine as the only vehicle available to them. Now that many of

their fellow officers and political associates were being subpoenaed by investigative committees, castigated by newspapers, denounced by state legislators, and otherwise roasted by reformers, few policemen had any doubts where their loyalty lay. For the time being a means of support, a style of life, and a form of organization were fused in their minds.

Most policemen were skeptical of the reformers' aspirations as well. On the basis of their everyday experiences with the seamier sides of urban life, many officers reached the conclusion that not even the most competent and the least corrupt police forces could eradicate vice and crime in the cities. With some exceptions they viewed gambling and drinking as ingrained and irrepressible instincts, prostitution as a degrading but necessary evil, blue laws as unreasonable infringements on personal liberties, and criminal activity as a deplorable but chronic condition. Chief Francis O'Neill of Chicago summed up these sentiments in an address to the IACP in 1904. On the assumption that immorality and dishonesty could never be completely abolished, he claimed that any police department deserved the public's wholehearted support if it faithfully carried out the following duties and nothing more: suppressing gambling only where known to the police, regulating saloons according to the law, wiping out vice only in communities that found it objectionable, and handling all criminals in an impartial and nonpolitical manner.[6]

Most policemen were also suspicious of the reformers' schemes. Priding themselves on their experience, common sense, and understanding of human nature, these officers distrusted the moralists, idealists, and other do-gooders who presumed to offer alternative conceptions of law enforcement and criminal justice. On the basis of their own involvement in the nitty-gritty of municipal politics and their admiration for the efficiency of the political machines, many officers came to the conclusion that even well-meaning reformers left the cities no better off than before and often much worse. Chief W. J. Peterson of Oakland revealed these anxieties in a speech to the IACP in 1916. From time to time, he pointed out, an hysterical reform wave, stirred up by demagogues and women's clubs, sweeps over the country, leaving in its wake unreasonable expectations and a new police chief. For a while the chief tightens the lid, enforcing old ordinances and proposing new ones. But as the citizens soon find out, the statutes do not improve morality: gambling dens and disorderly houses reopen elsewhere, and with the demoralization of the police, criminal activity thrives. Whereupon the reform wave recedes, leaving in its wake frustration and resentment.[7]

For the ward bosses and their followers, compromise was unthinkable. They regarded the existing system of policing as fundamentally sound, a sensible arrangement that was reflective of popular attitudes, sensitive to political pressures, and consistent with the country's traditions. They considered the campaign for police reform an unwarranted, malicious, and self-serving attack on policemen and politicians, which was misguided in its goals, misleading in its means, and inimical to the community's long-term interests. If the reformers succeeded in their crusade to sever the long-standing connections between policing and politics, they would deprive the organization of its valuable mine of jobs and favors. Even worse, by applying the same logic and similar tactics, the reformers might eventually take over the courts, schools, and other municipal institutions that governed day-to-day life in urban America. Hence the machines joined the issue against the reformers on both principled and pragmatic grounds. On the outcome would hinge the course of law enforcement, criminal justice, and urban politics in the years ahead.

At the turn of the century it was hard to tell whether the reformers or the machines enjoyed an edge in the upcoming struggle. Both had ample financial and political resources, good friends in high places, committed leaders and enthusiastic followers, and enormous confidence in their prospects. Both had an abiding faith in their own rectitude, a thorough distrust of the opposition's motives, and a moderately sophisticated appreciation of the stakes. But as the years passed, it was plain that the machines labored under a tremendous and perhaps insuperable handicap: the extraordinary decentralization of their organization. For the machines were essentially associations of loosely affiliated and largely independent ward organizations. So long as the bosses brought out the vote and otherwise dominated their wards, no one, not even the Crokers, could control them. In the absence of effective discipline, many politicians often pursued their short-term goals in ways that were inconsistent with the organization's long-term interests, and so did many of their associates on the police force and in the underworld. Or to put it another way, many politicians, policemen, and gangsters often attempted to enrich themselves and increase their power in such reprehensible ways that they aroused their enemies, disconcerted their friends, and thereby discredited their organization.

A few flagrant but not atypical incidents showed the variety and audacity of their efforts. In 1909 Mayor Arthur Harper, Chief Edward Kern, and a prominent pimp formed a syndicate that attempted to monopolize prostitution in Los Angeles by instructing the police department to enforce the law and harass the prostitutes everywhere except in the vicinity of a few houses recently purchased by the syndicate. Three years later several gunmen, who were allegedly acting for Lieutenant Charles Becker, head of one of the New York City Police Department's vice squads, shot and killed Herman Rosenthal, a professional gambler who had just charged the force with protecting gambling and was scheduled to appear before the district attorney to substantiate his charges. A major scandal broke out in San Francisco in 1913 when the press reported that Frank Esola, Louis Droulette, and nearly a dozen other detectives had recruited a gang of swindlers and, in return for 15 percent of the estimated gross of $300,000 a year, protected its members from the rest of the police department. An even worse scandal erupted in Chicago a year or so later when several members of the underworld who operated out of the Twenty-second Street Levee tried to cripple Major Metellus L. C. Funkhouser's morals squad by threatening his deputy's life, stabbing one officer, and shooting another.[8]

Things were much the same in other cities. During a primary contest in 1917 Councilman Isaac Deutsch and other Philadelphia Republicans imported several thugs from New York who intimidated their opponents, assaulted a well-known politician on election day, and murdered a special officer who rushed to his defense. From 1922 to 1925 scores of Cincinnati policemen and federal agents sold confiscated liquor to bootleggers, gave them advance warning of raids, arrested them at their convenience, and in return for a substantial share of the profits, later reduced or dropped the charges. Other offenders included a California assemblyman who offered spots on the San Francisco Police Department for $400 apiece in 1891, the Chicago gangsters who killed an assistant state's attorney in 1926 and a well-known reporter in 1930, and the New York City officers who protected gambling in local Democratic clubs in the late 1920s.[9] In short, by virtue of their extraordinary decentralization the machines could not as a rule compel the politicians, policemen, gangsters, and other members to ponder the organization's long-term interests before pursuing their own short-run opportunities.

Nor could the machines prevent the reformers from making the most of these scandals. After Mayor Harper of Los Angeles transferred Chief Kern from the police department to the board of public works, which was about to start building a $23 million aqueduct, the most important public works project in the city's history, the reformers launched a recall campaign which not only forced Harper to retire from politics but also replaced him with the city's first Progressive administration. In the wake of Rosenthal's murder, the reformers prevailed on New York City's Board of Aldermen to set up an investigative committee — commonly known after its chairman, Henry H. Curran, as the Curran Committee — which gathered five volumes of testimony, sponsored another volume of reports, and for months subjected the police force to its worst probe since the Lexow Committee hearings. Following the killings of the morals squad officers, the Illinois state's attorney empaneled a grand jury which exposed the relationship between vice and politics in Chicago's first ward and, though failing to gain any convictions, provided ample ammunition for subsequent onslaughts against the machine. In response to the exposé of the swindlers' ring in San Francisco, a grand jury undertook a searching examination of the police force, indicted most of the detectives involved, and prompted Mayor James R. Rolph to order a major shake-up and make other changes in departmental personnel and policies.[10]

Events took a similar turn in other cities. In the aftermath of the killings in Philadelphia, the district attorney charged Councilman Deutsch, Mayor Thomas B. Smith, and other Republicans with conspiracy to commit murder, an ex-police commissioner urged formation of a metropolitan bureau along the lines of the state constabulary, and a grand jury called for removal of the mayor and public safety director. After the Cincinnati grand jury issued its indictments, the Justice Department brought suits which not only sent dozens of officers to prison but also sparked a full-fledged shake-up of the department and laid the groundwork for a subsequent full-scale reorganization. To these examples may be added a Philadelphia grand jury's inquiry into vice control in 1905, a Chicago Civil Service Commission's investigation of police corruption in 1912, an Atlanta aldermanic committee's report on bunco games in 1921, and the Seabury Committee's probe of police malfeasance in the early 1930s.[11] In some instances the reformers exploited the revelations of the grand juries and investigative committees so effectively that they managed not only to discredit the political machine but also to gain control of city hall and police headquarters.

Nowhere did the reformers do so more frequently than in New York City. In the wake of the Lexow Committee investigation, the reformers joined the Republicans to elect a fusion candidate, Mayor William L. Strong, who named to the bipartisan police commission one inactive Democrat, one anti-Tammany Democrat who was a West Point graduate, one regular Republican who was also a West Point graduate, and Theodore Roosevelt. In the aftermath of the Mazet Committee revelations, which shattered Tammany a few years later, the voters selected another fusion nominee, Mayor Seth Low, who appointed Colonel John N. Partridge, a former Brooklyn police chief, as his first commissioner and General Francis V. Greene, a West Point graduate, career officer, and prominent businessman, as his second. After the Curran Committee investigation, the reformers and Republicans joined again to elect a fusion nominee, Mayor John Purroy Mitchel, who chose as police commissioner Major Arthur Woods, a Progressive who went to Harvard, headed Groton, and later emerged, next to August Vollmer, as America's most articulate police chief. And following the Seabury Committee probe, which forced Mayor Jimmy Walker to resign, the voters picked still another fusion candidate, Mayor Fiorello H. La Guardia, who selected General John F. O'Ryan, a former army officer and sometime public servant, as his first police commissioner and Lewis J. Valentine, an anti-Tammany police officer, as his second.[12]

The reformers came to power in several other cities, though not necessarily by the same route. They had a good deal to say in Chicago under Chief Charles C. Fitzmorris in the early 1920s and in Philadelphia under Public Safety Director Smedley D. Butler in the mid-1920s. The reformers had some clout in Cleveland under Chief Fred Kohler in the late 1900s and in Detroit under

Commissioner Frank Croul in the early 1910s. They carried a good deal of weight in Atlanta under Chief James L. Beavers in the early 1910s and in Los Angeles under Chief August Vollmer in the mid-1920s. Thus, outside of Kansas City and a few other places where the machines were too well entrenched, the reformers had a number of opportunities to change the structure, personnel, and function of the big-city police in ways that were consistent with the Progressive assumptions about social mobility, political legitimacy, and American culture. They seized these opportunities, determined not only to transform the big-city police but also to improve the public service, destroy the political machine, and eliminate deviant behavior.

In accord with their prescription, the reformers first attempted to centralize the big-city police. They exerted constant pressure on the authorities to delegate complete responsibility to the chiefs, commissioners, superintendents, or public safety directors, as opposed to the bipartisan boards or commissions, and to provide the chiefs with a large, capable, and committed staff to help handle this responsibility. Here the reformers were fairly successful. From 1900 on they persuaded the state legislatures to replace the police boards with police commissioners in New York City, Detroit, Boston, Cleveland, Cincinnati, Birmingham, Omaha, Buffalo, and so many other cities that by World War I individual administrators headed the police forces in roughly three out of every four cities with more than 100,000 residents.[13] At the same time the reformers prevailed on the municipal authorities to establish deputy chiefs, inspectors, and other ranks above captain and to permit the chiefs to fill these positions with men of their own choice, a change that was supposed to enlarge the influence of headquarters by facilitating the flow of information, raising the quality of advice, and easing the everyday work-load.

The reformers also brought strong pressure on the authorities to enhance the chief's tenure. But here they were less successful. Much as the reformers favored removing the police from politics, some of them objected to placing the chief beyond the control of elected officials on the ground that the municipal administration could then disclaim all responsibility for the misconduct of the police force. With the reformers ambivalent and the ward bosses opposed, the authorities were generally reluctant to extend the chief's term very much, if at all. Hence the chiefs remained vulnerable in Detroit, where Croul was removed by Mayor Oscar B. Marx in 1913, and in New York City, where Woods was discharged by Mayor John F. Hylan in 1917. Nor did the chiefs fare much better in Los Angeles and the handful of other cities where the reformers followed their prescription to its logical conclusion and put them under civil service. The Los Angeles City Council drove Chief Vollmer to resign in 1924, only one year after the Crime Commission had talked him into taking the job, by delaying action on his proposed reorganization of the police department. Notwithstanding strenuous opposition by several Los Angeles civic groups, Mayor John F. Porter's incoming administration compelled Chief James E. Davis to step down five years later by threatening to bring charges which, if sustained, would probably have cost him his service pension.[14]

For their part the reform chiefs devised various tactics to increase their control. With the support of the reformers they organized confidential or, in the departmental argot, "shoe-fly" squads which kept watch over the patrolmen and reported directly to headquarters. These squads aroused a lot of resentment among the rank-and-file, especially in Washington, D.C., where they were referred to as the "Gestapo."[15] Some chiefs also pried supplemental appropriations, commonly known as "secret service funds," out of the city councils, which enabled them not only to check on radicals and criminals but also, as no accounting was required, to underwrite the undercover activities of officers who felt greater loyalty to headquarters than to their fellow officers. With the support of the reformers the chiefs also extended their influence over assignment; but as a result of the expansion of the civil service system, they did not gain control over appointments, promotions, or under most circumstances discipline. Thus none of the reform chiefs — not even General Bingham of New York, Colonel Everington of Los Angeles, or General Butler of Philadelphia, to mention a few of the many military officers who were appointed police chief — held anything remotely resembling the formidable authority of a military commander.

Except in a few cities like Atlanta, where the patrolmen had always operated out of headquarters, or like Los Angeles, where the Progressives had already abolished the wards and established an at-large council, the reformers also sought to weaken the ward leader's position by consolidating or closing down the precincts wherever possible. The authorities closed a few station houses in New York in the mid-1920s, but the ward leaders thwarted similar schemes in Chicago, Philadelphia, and several other cities. The issue erupted in Chicago in 1912 when a council committee, to which a recent Civil Service Commission investigation of the police department had been referred, recommended that the city reduce the number of precincts from forty-four to twenty-five. Shortly afterward the reform councilmen incorporated this recommendation into a projected reorganization of the force. In response Alderman Edward ("Smooth Eddy") Cullerton, an organization stalwart, proposed an amendment, which carried by a majority of nearly two to one, fixing the number of precincts at no fewer than forty-four and requiring council authorization for any reduction.[16] By so doing, Cullerton and his allies blocked the reform effort to sever the connection between the wards and the precincts for the foreseeable future.

The stuggle in Philadelphia got underway late in 1923 when Mayor W. Freeland Kendrick, under terrific pressure from the reformers to clean up the police department, appointed General Butler of the Marine Corps as public safety director. A vigorous advocate of the war on crime, Butler promptly ordered raids on gambling dens and other dives, pressed charges against corrupt and incompetent policemen, and launched a thorough shake-up of the force. The Republican organization complained but took no action. Butler then proceeded to reduce the number of precincts from forty-two to twenty-two and to wipe out the ward lines, having been assured by the city solicitor that council authorization was unnecessary. Whereupon the ward leaders demanded his resignation. The reformers rallied to the general's defense, and the mayor, caught between these cross-pressures, wavered for a while; but when President Calvin Coolidge extended Butler's leave from the Marines for another year, Kendrick allowed him to go ahead with the reorganization. Butler's triumph was short-lived, however. Late in 1925 the ward leaders forced Kendrick to request Butler's resignation. Two years later the voters chose a new mayor, an organization candidate named Harry A. Mackey who was committed to restoring the traditional arrangement between the precinct captains and ward bosses. Shortly after taking office Mackey picked a new public safety director, who reopened all but one of the closed precincts, reestablished the old ward lines, and for the time being reimposed the status quo.[17]

The reformers also tried to overcome the widespread decentralization of the big-city police by transferring vice control and other crucial functions from ordinary patrolmen attached to the precincts to special squads assigned to headquarters. Here they encountered less resistance. One reason was that the proposal attracted strong support from the many citizens who thought that vice control created too great a temptation for most officers and that police work required a high degree of expertise and specialization. Another reason was that it generated keen enthusiasm among the rank-and-file, who found plainclothes duty more satisfying and prestigious than uniform work and regarded it as a lateral, if not vertical, promotion — with a gloss of professionalism. Still another reason was that it appealed strongly to the chiefs and other superior officers, who could at least convey a sense of concern by forming one or another type of squad in the event of public clamor. Not all citizens, not even all policemen or all reformers, approved of special squads. "We don't need beer squads and champagne squads and cocaine and murder squads," declared General Butler, who abolished Philadelphia's vice squad in the mid-1920s. "Hell! We don't want any pussyfooting squads around."[18] But Butler, who created his own special enforcement and confidential squads, spoke for a small and, as the years passed, a dwindling minority.

In the absence of effective opposition by the machines, which did not fully appreciate the long-run implications, the special squads proliferated beyond all expectations. Most police forces organized not only vice, morals, or according to their critics, purity squads but also alcohol, narcotics, and gambling squads; not only detective squads but also homicide, robbery, stolen auto, missing persons, and bomb squads; not only traffic squads but also bicycle, motorcycle, and accident prevention squads; not only crime prevention squads but also women, juvenile, and following Scotland Yard's lead, so-called "flying" or mobile crime squads. Many police forces also established undercover squads, typified by Inspector Dan Costigan's shoe-fly squad in New York and Lieutenant William F. Hynes's Red squad in Los Angeles, to keep tabs on corrupt officers and left-wing groups; ethnic squads, epitomized by New York's Italian squad, to watch over the teeming ghettos; and miscellaneous squads to deal with personnel, records, statistics, complaints, and other internal matters.[19] A few special squads replaced temporary details, a change that had little impact on the police forces. But most special squads assumed responsibility for functions which had heretofore been vested in precincts and entrusted to the patrolmen, a change that had a profound and lasting impact on the big-city police.

Early in 1928 Harry Davis, a career policeman who had recently been appointed public safety director in Philadelphia and would soon be compelled to resign in the wake of a major scandal, announced that "from now on there will be no special squads." A few plainclothes details might be necessary, he stated, but not the many squads "organized for this or that purpose, making a big noise, dragging in thousands of prisoners, resulting in few convictions in court." A reflection of a deep-seated nostalgia for the traditional style of policing, this announcement revealed a mind-boggling naiveté; coming from the ranking police officer of a major American city, it bordered on the incomprehensible. By 1920, or at the latest by 1930, the trend toward special squads was irreversible. So was the move toward functionally, as opposed to territorially, organized police departments, a move that was inspired by Chief Vollmer's proposed reorganization of the Los Angeles police in 1924.[20] Indeed by 1930 the proliferation of special squads assigned to headquarters and the subordination of uniformed officers attached to the precincts led some observers to conclude that the reformers had effectively centralized the big-city police.

The reformers also attempted to upgrade the police personnel. A majority, which believed that the rank-and-file were demoralized by the system, exerted pressure on the authorities to protect the officers from political interference, keep them from temptation, place them under military discipline, and otherwise treat them like soldiers. The response was mixed. Over the objections of many politicians and policemen the authorities, or by referendum the voters, put police departments under civil service in New York City in 1884, Chicago in 1895, Los Angeles in 1902, and Atlanta in 1906. With a few exceptions, among them Kansas City and Birmingham, the other big cities followed suit by 1920. The basic principles of civil service were twofold:

first, the officers should be selected and promoted on merit, as measured by a competitive exam; and second, they should hold office on good behavior, removable only for cause. How these principles were applied varied from city to city. Competitive exams were used for appointments only in Atlanta and for promotions up to lieutenant in Pittsburgh, up to captain in New York, and up to and including chief in Los Angeles. Disciplinary authority was vested in the civil service commission in Chicago, the city council in Atlanta, and the police commissioner in New York.[21] These variations notwithstanding, civil service was a major step toward shifting control over personnel from political bodies tied to the spoils system to administrative agencies committed to the public service.

To deal with the problem of temptation, the reformers did more than just call on the elected officials and police administrators to transfer responsibility for vice control from ordinary patrolmen attached to the precincts to special squads assigned to headquarters. They also pressed these officials to regulate the policemen's occupational practices and personal lives in unprecedented ways. Claiming that the police should serve the public without fear or favor, guided only by their oath and the law, the reformers urged the authorities to forbid officers to accept rewards or to require them to turn rewards over to the departments. Insisting that the police should remain completely independent, free of obligation to local merchants and other special interests, the reformers demanded that the authorities dismiss any officer who failed to pay his outstanding debts. Contending that all policemen should devote full time to their departments, the reformers appealed to the authorities to prohibit officers from taking part-time jobs while off duty, a practice commonly known as "moonlighting." As scattered evidence from Atlanta, Washington, and Los Angeles indicated, however, some cities rejected these demands; and other cities found it difficult, if not impossible, to enforce the regulations.[22]

Inspired by the military analogy, the authorities also gave military ranks to many superior officers. The Missouri legislature designated the St. Louis police chief a colonel and the assistant chief a lieutenant colonel in 1889; eight years later the New York city council promoted the roundsmen to sergeants and the sergeants to lieutenants. Many police chiefs labored to instill a martial spirit in the rank-and-file too. Some appointed a drill-master; others demanded military deportment; many included target practice, physical combat, precision marching, and other martial activities in the curricula of their training academies. In a few cities the authorities even gave in to reform demands for strict military discipline. They modeled the disciplinary proceedings on a court-martial in Pittsburgh, enlarged the public safety director's authority to levy fines and order short-term suspensions in Philadelphia, and delegated ultimate authority over dismissals to the police commissioner in Boston. But in most cities the authorities refused to revise disciplinary proceedings along military lines or, in the face of strenuous opposition by the patrolmen's associations and political machines, to abolish judicial review of departmental discipline.[23]

Arguing that policemen owed the force the same undivided loyalty that soldiers owed the army, the reformers further pressed the authorities to ban the rank-and-file from joining outside organizations in general and labor unions in particular. Prior to World War I the issue was academic because apart from the political machines most policemen belonged only to autonomous benevolent and fraternal associations which only incidentally engaged in political affairs. But the situation changed shortly thereafter when a sharp rise in the cost of living prompted a dozen or so rank-and-file groups to ask the American Federation of Labor (AFL) for charters. Departing from its past policies, the federation agreed, and for a while the police were unionized in Boston, Cincinnati, Washington, and several other cities. The reformers were appalled. Drawing on the military analogy, they pointed out that, as soldiers, policemen should not be allowed to unionize, much less to strike, and should be summarily dismissed for doing so. In conjunction with local politicians and other influential citizens, the reformers fought the fledgling unions and, in the wake of the Boston police strike of 1919, emasculated them.[24] By virtue of these efforts, the rank-and-file were represented only by their fraternal and benevolent groups and their political clubs down through the 1920s.

A minority of the reformers, which believed that most officers were unqualified to begin with, brought pressure on the authorities to weed out incompetent applicants, attract capable recruits, provide proper training, and otherwise improve the caliber of the force. In response to this pressure many police departments and civil service commissions raised the standards for candidates. Besides tightening the height, weight, and other physical requirements, several cities turned away anyone who was more than thirty-five years of age and had not graduated from elementary school; one city even required a high school diploma. Others fingerprinted the candidates, searched the police and court files, conducted background investigations, and thereby attempted to winnow out applicants with prior criminal records, especially felony convictions, and other alleged character defects. Still other cities removed the medical and other examiners as far as possible from everyday politics in an effort to ensure that the civil service tests were fairly graded and impartially administered.[25] Although Chief Vollmer and a few other reformers who wanted to subject the applicants to intelligence tests and psychiatric screening were not fully satisfied, the entrance requirements were a good deal stiffer in the 1920s than in the 1890s.

To attract capable recruits, the reformers argued, it was not enough to raise standards; it was also necessary to increase salaries, improve working conditions, and eliminate residency requirements. Pushed by the reform organizations and the rank-and-file associations, which claimed that prices had risen so much in the 1900s and 1910s that most patrolmen could no longer make ends meet, the authorities granted substantial raises after World War I. Between 1919 and 1929 patrolmen received increments of about 30 percent in Detroit, 50 percent in Chicago, 70 percent in Los Angeles, and 100 percent in Oakland; sergeants, lieutenants, and captains fared nearly as well. On the eve of the Great Depression patrolmen earned annually from a low of $1,500-$1,900 in Cincinnati to a high of $2,100-$2,500 in New York, which left them much better off than most unskilled laborers and about as well off as most skilled workers.[26] In a few cities the authorities also assumed a share of the costs of uniforms, equipment, and other items that were a heavy burden for the rank-and-file; and in many cities they shortened the work day and work week and lengthened sick leaves and annual vacations. But in the face of strenuous objections by the political machines and rank-and-file associations, the authorities retained the residency requirements everywhere except in Berkeley, Washington, and one or two other cities.[27]

Capable recruits were one thing and competent officers another. To turn the one into the other, the reformers argued, it was not enough to give the recruit a badge and a gun, send him out to a precinct, and trust that the veterans would show him the ropes. Nor was it enough to send him for a few weeks to the sort of training school that had been established in New York in 1897 and Detroit in 1911. According to the Bureau of Municipal Research, which did a study in 1912 of the New York City School for Recruits, reputedly the nation's finest training academy, the instruction was inferior, the supervision inadequate, and the curriculum irrelevant. Nothing less than full-fledged institutes, staffed and managed by experts, would suffice to provide a thorough grounding in police work, the reformers insisted. Commissioner Woods reorganized the New York police school along these lines shortly before World War I; and other chiefs followed his lead in Berkeley, Louisville, and Detroit not long after. By 1930 roughly a dozen departments operated large-scale academies, whose survival did not depend on the whim of the chief, and dozens of other departments carried on more limited training programs.[28] Although Chief Vollmer and other reformers who wanted the recruits to attend schools of criminology were not fully satisfied, these academies were plainly an improvement over the training facilities that had been available at the turn of the century.

An appeal for service pensions rounded out this part of the reform agenda. According to the reformers, these pensions would not only help the departments attract capable recruits and retain veteran officers but also enable them to get rid of superannuated officers who had long served the force but could no longer carry their weight. Unlike disability pensions, which were more or less accepted by the 1890s, service pensions generated a good deal of opposition among many officials who deemed it immoral and even un-American to pay an able-bodied man, no matter how deserving, for doing nothing. Under pressure from reform organizations and rank-and-file associations, however, most municipalities adopted service pensions by 1910, which typically provided for retirement at half-pay after twenty or twenty-five years of service and at age fifty or fifty-five. At first the municipalities financed these pensions out of a bewildering variety of sources, including fines against policemen, rewards from citizens, sales of unclaimed property, fees for liquor and dog licenses, salary deductions, and property taxes. But after World War I the reformers, realizing that many pension funds were accumulating a deficit that might eventually lead to bankruptcy, persuaded the authorities to reorganize some of them according to sound actuarial principles. By 1930 the policemen's and firemen's pensions were the envy of the civil service.[29]

The reformers attempted to narrow the police function too. In line with their prescription they urged the authorities to transfer all sorts of health, welfare, and other so-called nonpolice functions from the police departments to other municipal agencies. At the outset the reformers made a good deal of headway. Supported by many New York policemen who objected to the presence of derelicts in the station houses, they prevailed on the state legislature to shift the housing of vagrants to the city's charities department in the mid-1890s. Backed by many New York Republicans, who were fed up with the long history of electoral fraud in the city, the reformers persuaded the state legislature to turn the policing of the polls over to an independent and allegedly nonpartisan elections bureau a few years later.[30] At the insistence of the reformers the authorities also relieved the police forces of Boston, Atlanta, Los Angeles, and other cities of the traditional responsibility to clean streets, inspect markets, distribute free soup, and otherwise serve the community. As a result of these changes, several reform chiefs gained an opportunity to halt, or at any rate slow down, the long-standing and, from the reformers' viewpoint, debilitating proliferation of temporary details.

But after a while the attempt to narrow the police function ran into formidable resistance. Many reformers believed that the enforcement of vice laws subverted the integrity of the police force and depleted the manpower available for the war on crime. Well aware that many upper-middle- and upper-class Americans would vigorously oppose any effort to abolish the vice laws, these reformers came up with two other ways to deal with the problem. One, favored by Seth Low, mayor of New York City in the early 1900s, was to shift vice control from the police department to a morals commission. The other, endorsed by August Vollmer, chief of the Berkeley police in the 1910s and 1920s, was to take vice control away from the police department without specifying where to lodge it. Neither proposal generated much enthusiasm.

In response to the first, critics charged that a morals commission would just be a police department with another name: it too would be plagued by corruption and demoralization. In reply to the second, critics contended that alcohol, gambling, and prostitution were the main sources of criminal activity: the police forces could not wipe out crime without first stamping out vice.[31] With these alternatives eliminated, the police departments had little choice but to retain responsibility for vice control, which was as a rule delegated to special squads assigned to headquarters.

Some reformers also believed that the enforcement of traffic regulations siphoned off scarce resources from the uniformed force and generated resentment among many otherwise law-abiding citizens. As a result the war on crime was severely undermined. Realizing that the proliferation of automobiles would exacerbate highway safety, traffic congestion, and related problems in the years ahead, these reformers called on the authorities to transfer traffic control from the police departments to other municipal agencies. This proposal made no headway, however. Many commercial associations, which were worried about the impact of traffic congestion on retail sales and property values in the central business district, opposed the change. So did many civic clubs, which were troubled by the sharp rise in the number of deaths and injuries on the roads. Most police departments went along with these groups, perhaps believing that if they rendered this service, the municipal authorities would be more receptive to their requests for additional funds and personnel.[32] As a result the big-city police retained responsibility for traffic regulation and, following the prevailing practices, entrusted it to special squads assigned to headquarters.

Meanwhile some police chiefs accepted the reform notion that, by setting up so many temporary details, the departments invited political interference in their affairs, generated jealousy among the rank-and-file, and wasted vital resources on trivial chores. But their efforts to reassign the details to patrol duty bogged down for two main reasons other than the vigorous opposition of many policemen and politicians who had substantial financial and political stakes in the status quo. One reason was that many prominent businessmen did not see why they should hire their own police forces; and in view of their formidable influence, the reformers could not compel them to do so. The reformers could still try to abolish special details for private interests. But as William McAdoo, a former New York City police commissioner, pointed out, it was often very hard, if not impossible, to distinguish between private and public interests.[33] Surely a department should not close down a detail at a railway station or movie theater, where it was badly needed to keep order and stop crime, simply because the railway company or theater owner also benefited from its activities. Nor should a department expect a single precinct, no matter how capable its patrolmen and experienced its officers, to oversee boxing matches, baseball games, and other spectacles that brought out large and potentially explosive crowds.

Another reason was that some public officials did not see how they could carry out their day-to-day functions without police details; and given their powerful position in the city administration, the reformers could not force them to try. These officials made a plausible case. Ordinary public employees could not preserve quiet in the courts or maintain security in the jails, they claimed; nor could they force landlords and grocers to remove violations of building and health codes. Only with the aid of the police, Walter Bensel, a sanitary superintendent in the New York City Health Department, told the Curran Committee, could other municipal agencies persuade intransigent citizens to abide by unpopular regulations.[34] This situation, which was as much an indictment of the public as a compliment to the police, probably reflected the low esteem in which most Americans held public employees, a phenomenon which had impressed European visitors as early as the mid-nineteenth century. As the only municipal bureaucracy expected to work around the clock and empowered to use force, the police were therefore hard pressed to relinquish responsibility to provide temporary details to private companies and municipal agencies. As the years passed most departments transformed these details into special squads and, notwithstanding the reform critique, endowed them with a permanence in theory which they had previously enjoyed only in practice.

The big-city police also took on a wide range of other functions in the first third of the twentieth century. Some were plainly an outgrowth of the reform assumption that crime prevention was the principal task of the American police. Shortly after the turn of the century the Portland, New York City, and Washington,

D.C., police departments appointed policewomen to look after runaway, truant, and delinquent children, check on amusement parks, dance halls, and disorderly houses, and otherwise discourage youngsters from pursuing criminal careers. By 1924 more than ninety of the hundred largest cities had followed suit. To curtail juvenile delinquency and, the reformers believed, reduce adult crime, the New York City police assigned welfare officers to residential precincts; the Chicago police created an employment bureau for young men; and the Los Angeles police detached officers to the juvenile courts, another major innovation of the Progressive years. By 1930 most departments carried on at least one of these activities. Through the early 1920s the departments delegated these functions to special squads and made little or no effort to coordinate them. But Chief Vollmer of Los Angeles consolidated these squads into a special crime prevention unit in the mid-1920s. Subsequently Bruce Smith of the National Institute of Public Administration and Leonard V. Harrison of the Harvard Law School Crime Survey recommended this policy to the Chicago and Boston police forces.[35]

Other functions were probably an offshoot of the reformers' emphasis on crime prevention. Commissioner Woods of New York City organized a relief program in the winter of 1915-16, a time of widespread unemployment, on the grounds that by alleviating destitution, the department was preventing crime. He also set up a public works program in a few precincts. Applying the same reasoning, Chief Joseph A. Gerk of St. Louis established a temporary employment bureau on the eve of the Great Depression. Woods even decorated the station houses with trees at Christmas, invited the neighborhood children to stop by, and loaded them down with modest gifts on the assumption that by winning their affection the department was deterring juvenile delinquency. Following similar logic, Chiefs Peterson of Oakland and Vollmer of nearby Berkeley delivered speeches to local schoolchildren and attended meetings of the Boy Scouts, Campfire Girls, and other youth groups.[36] Along with most of their associates, these police chiefs emphatically denied charges that, by assuming these additional responsibilities, their officers were behaving more like social workers than policemen. From their perspective these activities were essential for effective crime prevention and therefore integral to proper police work.

To the dismay of many reformers, however, still other functions bore no discernible relationship to crime prevention. In the face of a strenuous campaign by a few upper-middle- and upper-class Americans to ban the use of opium and its derivatives, several police departments launched an unprecedented crusade against the use of drugs shortly before the outbreak of World War I. New York City formed its first narcotics squad in 1918; many other cities followed its lead soon after. In response to the widespread hysteria generated by the Bolshevik Revolution, several departments also activated or reactivated special units to watch over, harass, and intimidate left-wing radicals and union organizers in the 1920s. Perhaps the most notorious of these units, the Los Angeles Red squad, remained active well into the 1930s. The police forces also engaged in illegal wiretapping in New York, movie censorship in Chicago, and other activities which could not by any stretch of the imagination have much of an impact on the incidence of crime in urban America.[37] Their willingness to take on these extra functions probably reflected not only the increasing conservatism of most police officers in the postwar years but also the profound influence of the catchall tradition of American policing.

The reform movement did not derive its distinctive character from the consistency and profundity of its ideology, the originality and audacity of its strategy, or the efficacy of its activities. The reformers' diagnosis was full of serious contradictions; their prescription occasionally ran counter to their diagnosis; and the military analogy demonstrated little understanding of the military and even less of the police. Although the reformers shrewdly and often effectively exploited their influence in the state legislatures, grand juries, courts, newspapers, and other institutions beyond the machine's orbit, they drew virtually all their tactics from the standard political repertoire of late nineteenth- and early twentieth-century America. Moreover, the reformers' record was uneven. To give a few examples, they made a good deal of progress in Berkeley and very little in Kansas City; they prevailed on Chicago to establish a morals squad in 1913, only to see it disbanded in 1918; and they persuaded Los Angeles to abolish the residency requirement in the mid-1920s, only to see it reimposed in the early 1930s.[38] The reform effort derived its distinctive character rather from two closely related, extremely important, and ordinarily implicit assumptions about policing, politics, and the public interest.

The first assumption was that the tradition of American policing which had emerged out of the nineteenth century and emphasized local control, a civilian orientation, and catchall and responsive activity was inapplicable in the early twentieth century. The reformers had objections to local control. But tied by Progressive doctrine to the principle of home rule, they showed little of the enthusiasm for metropolitan policing that other reformers felt for metropolitan parks, parkways, and water districts. Mindful of the prior experiments with state control, the reformers had reservations about the wisdom of extending the state constabulary's jurisdiction from the rural communities to the metropolitan centers. And like most of their fellow Americans, the reformers refused even to consider the issue of a national police system.[39] But if, as a last resort, the reformers went along with local control, they demanded that it be lodged in the municipalities rather than the wards and with the mayors and police chiefs rather than the ward leaders and precinct captains. In light of the high probability that the political machines would continue to influence departmental policy, the reformers also insisted that the state legislatures accept the responsibility to oversee the local police and, if this proved inadequate, to supersede the municipal authorities.

The reformers had even stronger objections to a civilian orientation. They identified it with the existing political system, which in their view served the interests of the machine rather than the public. With a few notable exceptions they eventually concluded that under the circumstances the civilian orientation should be modified by a military analogy. Apart from General Butler and one or two other military officers, few reformers followed this analogy to its logical conclusion. Some were inhibited by the ideological implications of imposing a military model on a policed, as opposed to a police, society, and an exceptionally complex, mobile, and pluralistic society to boot. Others were restrained by the practical difficulties of applying it to an extremely decentralized police system which relied on individual patrolmen spread all over the city. But even though they had no intention of converting the police forces into military units, most reformers regarded the military analogy with unequivocal enthusiasm. For it not only provided a model for policing and an inspiration for police reform; it also served as the basis for a reform prescription which, if properly followed, would supposedly bring about a permanent separation of policing and politics.

The reformers had equally strong objections to catchall and responsive activity. They believed that so long as the police forces retained responsibility for health, welfare, and other nonpolice chores, they could not prevent crime, capture criminals, and otherwise carry out their principal functions with much success. Hence the reformers exerted constant pressure on the municipal authorities and police officials to narrow the department's jurisdiction, transfer its nonpolice functions, eliminate its superfluous details, and concentrate its energies on the war on crime. The reformers also thought that, so long as the police forces only responded to civilian complaints, they could not stamp out gambling, prostitution, and other victimless crimes or keep tabs on trade unions, radical parties, and other left-wing groups. Hence they supported departments that tempted bartenders to sell liquor after hours, enticed women to engage in prostitution, tapped public telephones, infiltrated labor organizations, employed agent provocateurs, and otherwise ignored long-standing restraints on police power. These practices marked a momentous departure from American tradition and left an indelible impression on American society.

The second assumption was that the mode of policing which had evolved during the nineteenth century and which stressed social mobility, political decentralization, and cultural pluralism was unacceptable in the early twentieth century. The reformers insisted that the primary purpose of the police departments, schools, courts, sanitation departments, and other municipal bureaus was not to create attractive jobs for the lower- and lower-middle-class immigrants. It was rather to provide essential public services as efficiently as possible. The reformers' view reflected the upper-middle- and upper-class Americans' assumptions about the process of mobility in urban America, which emphasized the importance of individual, economic, and private action. This view also dovetailed with the upper middle and upper classes' interest in good public services and low property taxes and rationalized their preference for a universalistic and meritocratic civil service that would perpetuate their privileged position.

Perhaps even more important, the reformers' view of the public sector led to the conclusion that all applicants to the police departments and other municipal bureaucracies should be required to meet stiff educational qualifications, pass tough competitive exams, and undergo rigorous character checks.

The reformers also claimed that local control was not a source of political legitimacy. In other words, no matter how large their majorities, the ward leaders had no authority over the police departments or other municipal agencies. Only the mayors or their appointees and other officials who held office by virtue of city-wide elections had such authority. The reformers' notion of legitimacy reflected the upper-middle- and upper-class Americans' assumptions about the social order of urban America, especially their confidence in the harmony of its social classes and ethnic groups and their faith in the existence of an overriding and easily identifiable public interest. This notion also increased the influence of the native Americans not only because they were scattered all over the city rather than concentrated in a few wards but also because they dominated the chambers of commerce, daily newspapers, bar associations, and other city- or metropolitan-wide commercial and civic associations. From the reformers' notion of political legitimacy it was only a short step to the conclusion that the locus of decision-making in the police departments should be shifted from the precincts to headquarters, which was more accessible to the upper middle and upper classes than to the lower and lower middle classes.

The reformers contended too that immigrant life-styles and the values, attitudes, and customs underlying them were not a proper expression of American culture. Only the native-American life-style and its underlying values, attitudes, and customs were worthy. The reformers' position reflected the upper-middle-class assumptions about the moral order of urban America, which favored abstinence and respectability, rejected self-indulgence and deviance, and relied on the criminal sanction to distinguish the one from the other. This position also led to the conclusion that the police, courts, schools, and other urban institutions should attempt to impose the conventional morality on ethnic minorities with little or no regard for the long-standing tradition of cultural pluralism. To the degree that these institutions were willing to put this policy into practice, they were bound to raise the status of the upper-middle- and upper-class Americans at the expense of the lower- and lower-middle-class immigrants. By rejecting the nineteenth century mode of urban policing, the reformers revealed that their campaign was an attempt not only to improve the quality of the police but also to retard the mobility, reduce the power, and lower the prestige of the newcomers.

4. Changes in Policing, 1890-1930

Writing in the *Journal of Criminal Law and Criminology* in the early 1930s, August Vollmer argued that the American police had made more progress over the past two or three decades than any other branch of municipal government. Gone were the old departments which based appointment on political grounds, provided little or no training, kept few if any records, deployed the force on a hit-or-miss basis, lacked adequate communications, and followed obsolete investigative methods. In their place were new organizations which imposed stiff entrance requirements, offered proper training, compiled detailed records, distributed the force according to scientific formulas, boasted modern communications, and applied the latest investigative techniques. The article was noteworthy not only because its author was a professor of police administration at the University of California, a former chief of police in Berkeley, a past president of the IACP, and a well-known author and consultant. The article was also noteworthy because it lent support to the position that the reform campaign had transformed the big-city police in the thirty-five years or so since the Lexow Committee investigation.[1]

At a glance this position is plausible. Between 1890 and 1930 the reformers prevailed on many states, cities, and police departments to disavow or disregard the traditions of policing that had emerged out of the nineteenth century. The states exercised a degree of authority that was inconsistent with the historic pattern of local control. Following an example set by Pennsylvania and to a lesser extent Massachusetts and Texas, some states established constabularies which bore more than a faint resemblance to the Royal Irish Constabulary and other paramilitary police agencies.[2] Many states passed laws dealing with the civil service systems, the tenure of police commissioners, the police pension systems, and the deployment of patrol units. More annoying and more threatening to the local politicians, some states empowered grand juries, attorney generals, legislative committees, and other official outfits to conduct investigations of police departments and other municipal bureaus. Indeed, the states probably exerted more influence over police policies and practices in 1930 than at any other time except the brief period in the nineteenth century when they took over most big-city forces.

Caught up in the enthusiasm for the military analogy, the cities employed their authority in many ways that were at odds with the deep-seated attachment to a civilian orientation. Some transformed the patrolmen into privates, the roundsmen into sergeants, and the superior officers into lieutenants, captains, majors, and colonels—though not, so far as I am aware, into generals. Other cities authorized the departments to hire drillmasters, build rifle ranges, and take other steps to improve their precision marching, sharpshooting, and other martial arts. One or two cities even reorganized their disciplinary procedures along the lines of a court-martial. Still others chose retired or in a few instances active military officers to lead the police forces. Among the best known of these officers were General Francis V. Greene of New York, General Smedley D. Butler of Philadelphia, Colonel James W. Everington of Los Angeles, and Major Metellus L. C. Funkhouser of Chicago. Many municipal officials also adopted a martial rhetoric. They not only identified the patrolmen as soldiers, the superior officers as military commanders, and the criminals as the enemy, but also equated police training with basic training, fighting crime with waging war, and city streets with front lines.

For their part the police departments put into practice a wide range of policies that ran counter to the long-term commitment to catchall and responsive activity. They turned over responsibil-

ity for cleaning streets, providing lodgings, distributing food, inspecting tenements, boilers, and markets, and carrying out a wide
range of other functions that were allegedly unrelated to crime
prevention to other municipal departments. They set up vice,
traffic, intelligence, and other special squads which worked
primarily in a preventive, as opposed to a responsive, style. Unlike the patrol units and detective divisions, these squads enforced
some laws that in the opinion of many Americans were aimed at
activities which were not crimes and which as a result provoked
few complaints. In the absence of complaints, these squads had
no choice but to seek out infractions and, if they found them,
bring complaints of their own. To this end they entrapped bartenders, gamblers, and prostitutes, infiltrated labor unions and
radical parties, and in the process often tempted others to break
the law and sometimes broke it themselves.[3] The special squads
thereby engaged in practices that their fellow Americans had
hitherto associated exclusively with European despotism.

At a closer look, however, the notion that the reform campaign
had transformed the big-city police is not so plausible. The campaign did not deeply erode the historic pattern of local control.
The state constabularies operated mainly in the farming regions
and mining centers, where they supplemented rather than supplanted the urban police. Despite recommendations from General Butler and other reformers, none of the states extended the
constabulary's jurisdiction to the big cities. When the state legislatures intervened in departmental affairs, it was usually at the
request of the municipal authorities, who wanted one or another
kind of enabling act, or at the insistence of the local groups,
which could not work out an agreement on their own. Although
the state investigators often compelled the police chiefs to order
shake-ups and forced the rank-and-file to restrain their cupidity,
they rarely brought about fundamental changes in departmental
policies and practices. Moreover, the federal authorities were unwilling to follow the lead of the British Parliament, which was
then consolidating its police forces, enlarging the authority of the
Home Office, and otherwise centralizing its police system. Most
federal officials were reluctant even to talk about the formation
of a national police.[4]

Nor did the reform campaign sorely weaken the deep-seated

attachment to a civilian orientation. No matter what their rank, few policemen regarded themselves as soldiers, and even fewer behaved with martial élan. Contrary to the expectations of the Greenes, Butlers, Everingtons, Funkhousers, and other military officers who went into police work, the big-city departments could not be administered in the same way as a military organization. By the 1920s, moreover, many citizens insisted that a professional model rather than a military analogy was the appropriate basis on which to restructure the big-city police. If all this were not enough, the authorities reinforced the civilian orientation in two critical ways. First, they put the police under civil service rules, a step that blocked lateral entry to every position except the chief's and thereby prevented the departments from recruiting superior officers from the military, which was a standard procedure in Germany and other countries. Second, they abolished the reserve system, an arrangement by which the rank-and-file were required to spend as many as seven hours a day on call in the station houses over and above the nine hours or more they spent on the streets. The change enabled many officers to move from the station houses into ordinary accommodations and thereby blurred the distinction between policemen and citizens.[5]

The reform campaign did not seriously undermine the long-term commitment to catchall and responsive activity either. Most police departments still accepted responsibility to regulate traffic, watch over radicals, censor motion pictures, license taxi cabs, look for missing persons, and carry on other tasks that were only remotely related to crime prevention. Moreover, the patrol units, which in spite of the great proliferation of special squads contained a large majority of the force, still labored in an essentially responsive fashion. And so, for that matter, did the detective divisions.[6] Apart from serving the political machines and filling their own pockets, most patrolmen passed their time resolving domestic disputes, giving street directions, rendering emergency assistance, dampening incendiary situations, and otherwise responding to calls from citizens. More often than not, these calls had little to do with crime prevention, no matter how broadly defined. Aside from keeping in touch with petty crooks and other disreputable types who were well informed about the workings of the underworld, most detectives usually waited for a complaint from a citizen or a report from a uniformed officer before starting to work on a case.

But the impact of the reform campaign cannot be gauged just by looking at the changes in the tradition of policing that had emerged out of the late nineteenth century. For what troubled the reformers was not so much that the police departments were strongly committed to local control, a civilian orientation, and catchall and responsive activity as that they were closely connected with the political machines. It was this connection, more than anything else, that offended the reformers and inspired their efforts to centralize the big-city police, upgrade the officers, and narrow their responsibilities. Hence the impact of the reform movement must also be gauged by the changes in the structure, personnel, and function of the big-city police in the first third of the twentieth century.

From 1890 on the reformers brought pressure on the authorities to increase the power of the police chiefs, weaken the position of the precinct captains and ward leaders, reduce the strength of the rank-and-file, and thereby centralize the police departments. The response was on the whole favorable. The authorities broadened the responsibility of the police chiefs at the expense of the police boards, enhanced their influence over assignment and discipline, though not recruitment and promotion, lengthened their term of office in some cities, and placed them under civil service in others. The authorities transferred vice control, traffic regulation, and other vital functions from ordinary patrolmen attached to the precincts to special squads assigned to headquarters. Though they refused to consolidate the precincts in Chicago and Philadelphia, they abolished the wards in Los Angeles and Cincinnati.[7] The authorities also extended civil service to patrolmen and in some cities to sergeants and captains, imposed military titles, if not martial discipline, on the superior officers, and destroyed the fledgling rank-and-file unions that had emerged in Boston, Washington, and other cities soon after World War I. Taken together, these changes gave the impression that by virtue of the reform effort the big-city police were pretty much centralized by 1930.

But as a rash of scandals that occurred in Philadelphia, Chicago, New York, and several other cities in the late 1920s and early 1930s showed, formal authority still corresponded very little with actual power.[8] With some notable exceptions most chiefs had only nominal authority over the captains, who for all practical purposes controlled the precincts, and the other superior officers, who to the reformers' dismay dominated the special squads. From the captains down to the patrolmen, most officers derived at least as much of their influence and prestige from their political connections as from their official positions. Formal organization still corresponded but slightly with actual operation. Again with a few notable exceptions, most chiefs found it hard, if not impossible, to implement departmental policies that aroused the opposition of either the precinct captains, the squad commanders, or the district leaders. Few patrolmen, detectives, and plainclothes officers were inclined to carry out orders from headquarters if this meant defying the local politicians or the superior officers on whom they depended for survival and advancement. All things considered, most big-city departments were only slightly more centralized in 1930 than in 1890.

Nothing undermined the position of the police chiefs and reinforced the pattern of decentralization more than the power of the precinct captains. From their authority to make character checks on applicants, assign tours to recruits, investigate complaints against patrolmen, and write efficiency reports about subordinates they derived enormous leverage over the rank-and-file. From time to time the captains used their power to subvert or even nullify departmental policies dealing with law enforcement, peace-keeping, and other vital functions that were still under the jurisdiction of the precinct houses. The chiefs sometimes attempted to assert their authority over the captains. But the effort usually failed, as Chief Charles C. Fitzmorris discovered. A favorite of the Chicago Crime Commission, Fitzmorris suspended Captain Donald M. Malloy on charges of incompetence and persuaded the Civil Service Commission to fire him. But under pressure from the Democratic machine the courts reinstated Malloy. As Chief Everington of Los Angeles found out, the attempt to discipline the captains sometimes backfired too. A former Marine Corps colonel, Everington dismissed Captain W. L. Spellman for failing to suppress vice and threatened to resign unless the police commission sustained his decision. The commission overruled him, however, and shortly thereafter Mayor George E. Cryer dismissed him.[9] Provided that the precinct captains retained the support of the ward leaders and other powerful politicians, they could usually disregard and even disobey headquarters with virtual impunity.

Many squad commanders were in a similar position. These officers were appointed by the chiefs and served at their pleasure. Yet as long-term veterans, ordinarily sergeants or captains, who had many friends in the departments, the machines, and the underworld, the commanders usually developed independent sources of power which effectively insulated them from head-quarters. Under most commanders the special squads went about their business in ways that not only weakened the chief's authority but also subverted his power and sometimes destroyed his reputation. The San Francisco detectives who recruited a ring of swindlers in the early 1910s were typical, and so were the New York City vice officers who framed respectable women on charges of prostitution in the late 1920s. Asked to account for these scandals, the chiefs, anxious to salvage what remained of their reputations, usually replied that they did not know what the special squads were up to and could not have done much about it anyway. A few commanders, including the heads of the confiden-tial squads organized in New York, Chicago, and other cities to keep tabs on the rank-and-file, lived up to the reformers' expectations, but they were generally transferred to much less powerful positions as soon as the machine politicians regained control of city hall.[10]

The rank-and-file could also ignore headquarters with virtual impunity, provided that they kept on good terms with the supe-rior officers and ward bosses. If the precinct captains and squad commanders withheld evidence of corruption and incompetence, the police chiefs had no way of knowing which of their men were not following orders. The chiefs could and did employ plain-clothesmen to spy on the patrolmen. But the rank-and-file loathed these officers, whom they labeled "shoe-flies," "gum-shoes," or the "Gestapo," and devised warning systems to reduce their effectiveness. If the plainclothesmen did turn up instances of flagrant wrongdoing, most chiefs lacked the authority to do more than transfer the offenders or suspend them for a few days. To demote or dismiss an officer, the chiefs were required by the civil service rules to bring formal charges and present conclusive evi-dence, which in view of the reluctance of police officers to testify against one another was hard to come by. If the chiefs did acquire the evidence, they rarely won a conviction. For most officers had what were called "rabbis" in New York City, influential politicians who looked out for their interests.[11] These politicians carried a great deal of weight not only with the police boards and civil service commissions that tried the policemen but also with the local courts that heard the appeals.

The police chiefs' position was further eroded by the influence of the rank-and-file organizations, the scores of loosely affiliated benevolent associations and fraternal orders that survived the destruction of the fledgling patrolmen's unions shortly after World War I. Besides calling for higher salaries, better pensions, and improved working conditions, which was more or less consistent with the reform campaign to upgrade the rank-and-file, these organizations lobbied against proposals to enhance the authority of headquarters. Nowhere were they more active than in New York City. In 1907 the rank-and-file organizations persuaded the state legislature to turn down a proposal endorsed by Commissioner Bingham and other reformers to increase the police commissioner's power to appoint and reduce inspectors and detectives. In 1911, after a decade of strenuous opposition by successive commissioners, these outfits prevailed on the legislature to impose an eight-hour day. In 1914 they convinced the legislators to vote down a proposal sponsored by Mayor Mitchel and other reformers to speed up the promotional process and wipe out judicial review of departmental discipline.[12] The rank-and-file organizations took part in similar struggles in Chicago, Philadelphia, and other cities, though these struggles were not always resolved to their satisfaction.

Most police chiefs were in a bind. No matter how hard they tried, they could not control their forces as long as the ward politicians dominated the mayor's offices, city councils, civil service commissions, police boards, local courts, and other official agencies—or even as long as the precinct captains, squad commanders, and rank-and-file thought that they did. Chief Fitzmorris, Chief Everington, and Commissioner Arthur Woods found this out the hard way. So did Chief Vollmer, who resigned shortly after the Los Angeles City Council refused to appropriate the funds to finish his reorganization of the police department. A few chiefs managed to carry out major reforms, but these were often short-lived. General Butler consolidated Philadelphia's precincts over the vigorous protests of many ward leaders; but a year or so after Butler resigned, Mayor Harry A. Mackey in-

structed his public safety director to restore the previous boundaries. Commissioner Woods established a confidential squad in
New York City, but Mayor John F. Hylan, a Tammany candidate, abolished it; and Deputy Commissioner Funkhouser
created a morals squad in Chicago, but Mayor William H.
Thompson disbanded it.[13] Indeed the connection between policing and politics was so close in the Windy City that through the
1920s the police chiefs maintained their office in city hall rather
than in police headquarters.

Given enough time, some chiefs might have galvanized the reform groups, cultivated the local newspapers, mobilized their
political resources, and thereby gotten themselves out of this
bind. But they seldom had enough time. Greene lasted one year
as head of the New York police, McAdoo two years, Bingham
two and a half years, and Woods three and a half years. Vollmer
survived one year in Los Angeles, Butler two years in Philadelphia, Fitzmorris two and a half years in Chicago, and Frank S.
Croul three and a half years in Detroit. This pattern was much
the same elsewhere. During the 1920s the chiefs held office an
average of only two and a half years in the ten largest cities and
barely a year longer in the nine next largest cities. The turnover
reached a peak in Detroit in 1930. Under Mayor Charles Bowles
and, after the voters recalled him, under his successor Frank
Murphy, the municipality changed police commissioners four
times in twelve months.[14] There were a few chiefs who enjoyed
fairly long terms. But ironically they were often political stalwarts
like Richard E. Enright, police commissioner of New York City
from 1918 to 1926, who had little sympathy for the campaign to
transform the big-city police.

From 1890 on the reformers also exerted pressure on the
authorities to upgrade the police personnel by weeding out unqualified applicants, attracting capable recruits, providing
proper training, protecting the policemen from the politicians,
and treating them like soldiers. The response was in general encouraging. The authorities raised the physical, mental, and
moral standards, increased salaries and improved working conditions, set up small-scale training programs and in a few departments full-fledged police academies, and enhanced the short-run
benefits, if not necessarily the long-term solvency, of the pension
systems. The authorities also applied the merit system to appoint-

ment, promotion, and dismissal, curtailed the patrolmen's right to take rewards and outside jobs, imposed martial ranks, if not military discipline, and emasculated the incipient police unions. Only in Berkeley and a couple of other cities, however, were the residency requirements abolished, and nowhere were the rank-and-file benevolent and fraternal associations wiped out. If the reformers were right, these changes should have brought about a marked improvement in the caliber of the big-city police by 1930.

But according to surveys undertaken in Kansas City, Cleveland, Los Angeles, and several other cities in the middle and late 1920s, many policemen had less than impeccable credentials.[15] Only two out of three finished grade school, only one out of ten graduated from high school, and by the reformers' own criteria, only one out of five scored high enough on intelligence tests to handle the duties. How many were physically and morally unfit is hard to tell. But some were in their sixties, seventies, and eighties; others were too infirm to patrol anywhere but in parks and cemeteries; a few had been arrested many times; and some had served time for bootlegging and homicide. Many officers still did less than exemplary work. They protected bartenders, prostitutes, gamblers, and bootleggers, intimidated reputable businessmen and ordinary citizens, and otherwise displayed about the same degree of cupidity as the New York City policemen investigated by Senator Lexow in the mid-1890s. They horsed around at roll calls, ate, drank, and slept on their beats, played cards with cronies, paid visits to women friends, and otherwise exhibited about the same level of ineptness as the Chicago policemen exposed by Captain Piper in the early 1900s. All things considered, the reform crusade had not brought about much of an improvement in the caliber of the big-city police by 1930.

There were several reasons. To begin with, most police forces had trouble weeding out unqualified applicants. According to a report issued in the late 1920s, the official standards were quite low. Most cities required that candidates know how to read and write, but only a few insisted on a grade school education and only one a high school degree. Some barred applicants over twenty-eight; others took them up to fifty; and still others fixed no age limits. Although most cities demanded that candidates be healthy and virtuous, they only rejected them for flagrant physical and moral defects. Many applicants could usually get around even these requirements. Under pressure from the ward leaders the civil service commissioners sometimes gave out advance copies of the tests and the precinct captains often ran cursory character checks. The civil service commissioners overlooked serious transgressions if they meant disqualifying a candidate with strong endorsements from influential politicians. Many officials were so lax that by the 1920s Bruce Smith, George F. Chandler, and many other reformers had lost much of their early enthusiasm for the civil service. Testifying before a national commission on public service employees in the mid-1930s, Vollmer declared that unqualified applicants slipped through the civil service about as often as through the political machine.[16]

Most police forces also had difficulty attracting capable recruits. They were severely handicapped by at least two things other than the unwillingness of the authorities to eliminate the residency requirements for police officers and thereby to enlarge the available supply of qualified candidates. First, most upper-middle-class Americans were not impressed by the salaries of patrolmen who earned more than most unskilled laborers and about as much as many skilled workers. Nor were these Americans overwhelmed by the prestige of police officers who, as one public opinion poll indicated, ranked above janitors, chauffeurs, and clerks but below accountants, draftsmen, machinists, and stenographers.[17] Second, many lower- and lower-middle-class immigrants, who were much more concerned about security than prestige, considered places on the police force and most other municipal agencies highly desirable. The newcomers could usually count on the local politicians, who regarded police jobs as a vital source of patronage, to fight every proposal to upgrade the rank-and-file that would also remove the department from political influence and reduce their constituents' access to public employment.

To make matters worse, most police forces were hard pressed to turn capable recruits into competent officers. According to the Bureau of Municipal Research, which made a survey of New York City's School for Recruits in the early 1910s, the training academies were in deplorable condition. The instructors were indifferent and the classes insipid; the students paid little attention and took few notes; worst of all, the administrators gave no tests and kept no records. Only in target practice and precision marching, which filled a large part of the schedule, did the instructors and students show much interest and the administrators measure performance. Needless to say, nobody failed this four-week course. The training academies improved in the next two decades; but according to a citizens' committee that did a study of the Chicago police, they were still in pretty bad shape in the late 1920s. The instructors, ordinary officers who knew little about criminology and less about pedagogy, did no more than pound unrelated facts into the student's head by constant repetition. Held in low esteem by the rest of the force, which regarded the classes as a waste of time, they were not even able to maintain strict discipline and high morale. No one failed this four-week course either.[18] Nowhere, except perhaps in Berkeley and Louisville, did the training academies meet the standards set by Vollmer and his fellow reformers.

Not that it mattered much. As some recruits already knew and as others eventually found out, the training academies could not have taught them the ground rules which applied in the force and on the street anyway. The instructors could not have disclosed that the patrolmen were expected not to enforce the law, keep the peace, and serve the public but to decide which laws to enforce, whose peace to keep, and which public to serve. Nor could they have revealed that the officers were rewarded not for their alacrity to obey instructions from headquarters but for their capacity to stay on the good side of the precinct captains and ward leaders. Most rookies learned these ground rules sooner or later. They discovered that a patrolman got assigned to a choice precinct or transferred to the detective division or a special squad by exploiting his political connections and not by going by the book. They found out that a patrolman won promotion to sergeant or captain by keeping out of trouble, scoring high on civil service tests, and doing well by other indicators which, as Woods acknowledged, measured political influence more than professional competence.[19] Unless the patrolmen understood the differences between their academic exercises and workaday experiences, or in other words between the rhetoric and reality of police work, their prospects for advancement were poor.

As if all this were not enough, most police forces had a rough time getting rid of incompetent and corrupt personnel. Accord ing to a study published in the late 1920s, the disciplinary procedure was extremely cumbersome. Under the civil service system most chiefs could reprimand, fine, or as the wholesale shake-ups which followed most major scandals showed, transfer their subordinates more or less at will. But they could not suspend or dismiss them without drawing up formal charges, which were difficult to substantiate. Mindful that their prestige dropped each time the authorities reinstated another policeman, most chiefs were reluctant to invoke this procedure except in cases of gross malfeasance, and not always then. By the 1920s Raymond B. Fosdick and other reformers were much concerned about the drawbacks of the civil service. They could not stand for an arrangement that not only weakened executive authority but also served, in Fosdick's words, as "a bulwark for neglect and incompetence." But neither could they tolerate a spoils system that permitted the Kansas City police board to remove 350 officers for strictly partisan reasons in 1921. They therefore concluded that the municipal authorities should give the police chiefs, as opposed to the civil service commissioners and local judges, final say on disciplinary matters.[20]

The reformers were much less concerned about the pitfalls of the pension systems. These systems, which were designed not only to help the police departments attract capable recruits but also to enable them to retain experienced policemen and retire superannuated officers, were nonvested and nonportable. In other words, policemen could not collect their benefits or any part thereof until they put in twenty or twenty-five years of service and in some cities reached the age of fifty or fifty-five; nor could they carry their rights from one force to another. These constraints may have dissuaded some competent officers from leaving the force after ten or fifteen years, but they probably encouraged as many incompetent policemen to stay in the department for an extra five or ten years. If the chiefs brought incompetent officers up on charges, neither the civil service commissions nor the local courts were likely to sustain them if, as influential politicians were certain to point out, it meant taking away not only the defendants' jobs but their pensions too. The full implications of these pitfalls were not apparent by 1930. But it was already evident that the service pensions, the civil service, and other reform measures had unanticipated consequences which might well subvert the ongoing crusade to upgrade the personnel of the big-city police.[21]

From 1890 on the reformers also put pressure on the authorities to cut down on the departments' duties, wipe out temporary details, give priority to crime prevention, and otherwise narrow the police function. The response was on the whole favorable. The authorities turned over the responsibility to clean streets, inspect tenements, supervise elections, house vagrants, operate ambulances, and carry out other so-called nonpolice chores to the other municipal departments that were allegedly better equipped to handle them. Under counter-pressure from many policemen, politicians, businessmen, and public officials, who had a great stake in the status quo, the authorities did not compel the police to abolish many temporary details; nor did they prevent them from creating new details and transforming still others into permanent units. But in the absence of stiff opposition the authorities permitted the departments to appoint policewomen, assign officers to the juvenile courts, organize employment bureaus, and in Los Angeles and a few other cities, consolidate these activities in a separate crime prevention division. Taken together, these changes made it appear that as a result of the reform campaign the big-city police had far fewer functions in 1930 than in 1890.

But according to studies conducted in Chicago, Boston, and other cities in the late 1920s and early 1930s, this conclusion was untenable.[22] Most police departments not only retained the long-standing responsibility to restrain unruly crowds, resolve domestic squabbles, render emergency assistance, suppress vice, and regulate traffic, but also assumed the additional responsibility to control narcotics, censor motion pictures, curb juvenile delinquency, and infiltrate trade unions and left-wing groups. Some of these activities were an outgrowth of the reform conviction that crime prevention was the principal purpose of the urban police, but others bore no relation whatever to crime prevention, unless criminal activity was construed to include all deviant behavior. As municipal agencies with a good many jobs at their disposal and a great deal of influence over the daily life of many citizens, the police departments also had a marked impact on the process of mobility, the distribution of power, and the struggle for status in urban America. All things considered, most big-city police had nearly as many functions in 1930 as in 1890.

The reform effort ran into stiff resistance from several sources. As expected, steamship lines, sports arenas, and other private companies did not see why they should employ their own policemen, and district attorneys, health departments, and other public bureaus did not see how they could carry out their tasks without police details. To the reformers' surprise, many other groups which supported their position in principle opposed it whenever the projected cutbacks threatened their own economic, political, and moral interests. The banks, hotels, and department stores might endorse a scheme to concentrate on organized crime, but not if it meant that the police would no longer regulate traffic and reduce congestion in the central business district. The religious organizations might back a policy to focus on dangerous criminals, but not if it meant that the police would have to stop harassing small-time gamblers, prostitutes, and bootleggers. The commercial and industrial associations might applaud a scheme to crack down on racketeers and gangsters, but not if it meant that the police could no longer keep tabs on union organizers and left-wing radicals.[23]

These groups might have gone along with the reform effort if the big-city police could have turned over the responsibility for these chores to a state or a national police force. But this was not possible. The state police, which operated in Massachusetts, Texas, Pennsylvania, New Mexico, and about half a dozen other places, did not have the manpower to do more than patrol the highways, enforce the game laws, and keep the peace in agricultural districts and mining regions. The federal police, which consisted of roughly a dozen agencies spread out among the treasury, labor, justice, and post office departments, did not have the authority to do much besides investigate counterfeiting, smuggling, bootlegging, and other infractions of federal laws.[24] From time to time the state police or the national guard helped the municipal authorities to quell a riot or break a strike. But this was a makeshift arrangement, which did not adequately compensate the local police for the time and energy spent enforcing the blue laws and other state and federal statutes. Opposed to transferring traffic regulation, vice control, and many other activities to nonpolice bureaus, the business, religious, and commercial groups had no option save to speak out against the schemes to narrow the function of the big-city police.

In the face of stiff and probably insuperable resistance the municipal authorities found the temptation to fall back on the catchall tradition nearly irresistible. A legacy of the nineteenth century, this tradition still had much to recommend it a generation or so thereafter. With the exception of the fire departments, the police departments were the only public agencies that remained on duty twenty-four hours a day and could be fully mobilized on short notice. Chosen, at least in theory, for general ability as opposed to specific skills, their personnel could adjust more quickly to unfamiliar duties than a clerk in a comptroller's office or an engineer in the waterworks plant. Since no one on the force, not even the police chief, knew the precise boundaries of its official responsibility, most police departments seldom turned down an additional assignment. Although some policemen complained about housing vagrants, rounding up drunks, and doing other messy chores, most of them, superior officers and rank-and-file alike, took pride in their readiness to deal with unanticipated problems.[25] Small wonder that the municipal authorities preferred to fall back on the catchall tradition and treat the police department as an all-purpose residual force rather than to move forward on the reform agenda.

In the meantime the reform effort ran into an even more serious problem. Contrary to the reform prescription, the conviction that crime prevention was the cardinal function of the municipal police was not a useful criterion by which to decide whether or not something was a proper police task. The problem was twofold. First, during the late nineteenth and early twentieth centuries the upper-middle- and upper-class Americans had mounted a far-reaching campaign to impose their own moral standards on the lower- and lower-middle-class immigrants. At their behest the authorities passed laws making it a crime to engage in gambling and fornication, to sell bread or show movies on Sundays, and even in some jurisdictions to wear short skirts and carry long hatpins. Despite the protests of Justice Gaynor of New York, Mayor Whitlock of Toledo, and other prominent Americans, this campaign was so successful that by 1910 fully 16,000 such federal, state, and municipal laws were on the books. By 1920 Fosdick pointed out, "Nowhere in the world is there so great an anxiety to place the moral regulation of social affairs in the hands of the police [as in the United States]."[26]

The second part of the problem was that the upper-middle-

and upper-class Americans disagreed about what caused crime and what should be done about it—though they agreed that the first- and second-generation newcomers were largely responsible for it. Some, who stressed the personal guilt of individual criminals, blamed crime on a desire for easy living, a contempt for lawful authority, the breakdown of parental discipline, and the coddling of convicted felons. They called on the authorities to fingerprint everyone, censor newspapers, magazines, and movies, deny marriage licenses to unfit applicants, revive the cat-o'-nine-tails, and build an American "Devils Island." Others, who emphasized the appalling conditions of ghetto life, traced crime to unemployment and poverty, congested tenements and teeming streets, widespread alcoholism and drug addiction. They urged the authorities to provide jobs for the newcomers, organize settlement houses for their families, construct parks and playgrounds for their children, and otherwise expose them to the benefits of American society. Still others, who adopted a narrow law enforcement perspective, attributed crime to the incompetence of the police, prosecutors, courts, and correctional institutions. They pressed the authorities to overhaul the criminal justice system and above all to insulate it from machine politics.[27]

From the reformers' viewpoint the consequences were demoralizing. If everything from murdering a relative to kidnaping a child, robbing a bank, spitting on the sidewalk, playing cards on a train, selling ice cream on Sundays, and kissing in public were a crime, what purpose would it serve to insist that the police focus exclusively on preventing crime? Such an argument made sense only if the authorities drew a precise distinction between criminal activity and deviant behavior. And if everything from promoting specialization among detectives to improving identification techniques, organizing employment bureaus, censoring motion pictures, rounding up prostitutes, and speaking to Boy Scouts might reduce crime, what good would it do to demand that the police restrict themselves to tasks related to crime prevention? Such a position made sense only if the authorities agreed about what caused crime and what should be done about it. By insisting that the authorities apply the criminal sanction to reinforce the conventional morality and by failing to come up with a coherent explanation of criminal activity, the upper middle and upper classes severely undermined the usefulness of crime prevention as a criterion of proper police chores. By so doing, they also seriously if unwittingly weakened the reform campaign to narrow the function of the big-city police.

Hence the first wave of reform fell short of its main objectives. Although the reformers weakened the connection between politics and policing, the ward leaders still had more to say than anybody else about departmental policies and practices. Other than the divisions within the reform coalition, there were several reasons that the reformers were not more successful. Among them was the opposition of the machine politicians. From their point of view the efforts to centralize the police departments, upgrade their personnel, and narrow their function posed a serious threat to the organization's hegemony. As they saw it, the issue was not whether the municipal authorities could separate politics and policing but whether the machines or the reformers would control the police departments. The machine politicians were justifiably cynical. After all, the reform campaign was part of the ongoing struggle to reduce the influence of the old-line organizations. Many of its principal proposals, including the formation of special squads, consolidation of precincts, and creation of civil service systems, were designed with precisely this goal in mind.[28] The machine politicians proved to be formidable opponents. When they dominated city hall, which was most of the time, they could usually prevail on the authorities to sidetrack, postpone, or vote down the reform schemes. Even when the reformers took over, the politicians could generally count on their cronies in the police forces, prosecutor's offices, local courts, and other agencies to undo any inopportune changes.

Another reason that the reformers were not more successful was the antagonism of the police officers. From their perspective the campaign for police reform was an impractical, uncalled for, and demoralizing attack on a system of law enforcement that had met its responsibilities pretty well over the years. To put it bluntly, they saw the reformers as misguided idealists who knew little about the police and less about their problems and who blamed the departments for all sorts of conditions over which they had no control.[29] The rank-and-file were understandably annoyed. Well insulated by their class and ethnicity from the seamy side of urban life, most reformers were out of touch with the policemen, unaware of their problems, and antipathetic to their aspirations.

By virtue of their strategy to discredit the municipal police, the reformers were driven to highlight the incompetence, corruption, and malfeasance of the ordinary patrolman. The rank-and-file proved to be formidable antagonists. They could occasionally persuade the mayor's offices, city councils, state legislatures, and other bodies to quash the reform schemes that jeopardized their vital interests. And when the authorities overrode their objections, they could usually undermine the efficacy of these schemes by ignoring orders from headquarters or by implementing them in a halfhearted way.

Many of the reform proposals were so ill conceived that they would have fared poorly even without the opposition of the machine politicians and the antagonism of the rank-and-file. How could the reformers divorce politics and policing by lengthening the police chiefs' terms, enlarging their staffs, and otherwise increasing their influence as long as the elected officials remained responsible for the conduct of the police departments? What good would it do to shift vice control from ordinary patrolmen attached to the precincts to special squads assigned to headquarters as long as so many Americans regarded the vice laws as indefensible and unenforceable? What was the point of transferring authority over appointments from the city council to a civil service commission as long as the newcomers saw the police force as a vital avenue of mobility and the politicians treated it as a prime store of patronage? What purpose would it serve to insist that the police departments concentrate exclusively on crime prevention if, in the absence of agreement among America's social classes and ethnic groups, the politicians had to draw the distinction between criminal activity and deviant behavior?

In other words, the attempt to divorce politics and policing was doomed from the outset because, contrary to Progressive ideology, they were tied to one another not only by the nature of the political machine but also by the character of the big-city police. Far from being mere administrative bodies that enforced the law, kept the peace, and served the public, the police departments were policy-making agencies that helped to decide which laws were enforced, whose peace was kept, and which public was served. Much like the courts, schools, and other vital institutions, the police thereby exercised a great deal of influence over the process of mobility, the distribution of power, and the struggle for status in urban America. To put it bluntly, no institution which had so great an impact on the lives and livelihoods of so many citizens could have been separated from the political process. Nor, so long as the nation was committed to democracy and pluralism, should it have been. None of the reform proposals —neither the schemes to centralize the police forces, upgrade their personnel, and narrow their function nor the appeals to transform them along the lines of a military organization—could have changed this situation. To contend otherwise, as the reformers did, was either naive, disingenuous, or both.

The big-city police had changed in one important, if quite unexpected, way in the thirty-five years or so since the Lexow Committee investigation. Many officers now exhibited a strong sense of alienation, a sharp feeling of persecution, and other severe anxieties which for want of a better term might be called occupational paranoia. One symptom was the chiefs' shrill complaints about other Americans. If their indictments of inept prosecutors, shyster lawyers, corrupt judges, soft-headed prison officials, idealistic parole boards, unscrupulous politicians, and apathetic citizens were to be believed, no one but the patrolman was doing his bit in the war on crime. Another symptom was the chiefs' frenzied reaction to criticism from outside. If their charges that newspapers printed only the worst abuses of the police departments and that radio stations and film studios glorified the criminals and ridiculed the officers were to be credited, everyone was out to embarrass the local police. Still another symptom was the chiefs' reckless position on vital issues. If their support for universal fingerprinting and motion picture censorship or their defense of corporal punishment and the third degree were to be taken seriously, only draconian and, if necessary, unconstitutional steps could restore law and order in urban America.[30]

Some officers were already a little anxious by the start of the century. Chief A. H. Leslie of Pittsburgh, Superintendent Richard Sylvester of Washington, D.C., Chief Fred D. Kohler of Cleveland, and many other high-ranking officials accused their countrymen of refusing to cooperate with the police and treat them with due respect. They denounced the prosecutors, judges, politicians, and newspaper publishers for failing to sustain their efforts. They even prevailed on the IACP to approve a tough resolution calling on the motion picture producers to stop depicting police officers in the ludicrous style then in vogue at the Keystone and other Hollywood studios. But most policemen grew far more anxious after World War I. Chief J. G. Laubenheimer of Milwaukee, Chief Jacob Graul of Cleveland, and many other well-known police officials not only delivered more strident protests and suggested more drastic measures but also blamed the problem on a different and far larger group. Assuming that the police forces were military units, operating in a hostile setting, they adopted the martial logic that anyone who was not for them was against them. By following this logic, they traced the problem not to a small, ill-educated, poorly informed, or highly vicious minority, as Chiefs Leslie, Sylvester, and Kohler had, but to the great and otherwise quite ordinary majority.[31]

These anxieties were not entirely groundless. Many prosecutors were inept, many judges corrupt, many politicians unscrupulous, and many citizens apathetic; few criminals were convicted, fewer incarcerated, and even fewer rehabilitated. Before World War I the motion picture studios portrayed police officers as incompetent bunglers, though not particularly frightening ones, and during the late 1920s they showed the gangland leaders as romantic figures. The policeman's lot was also extremely dangerous in the postwar decades: at no time before — or for that matter since — were so many officers killed in action. But these conditions did not explain the depth of the group's anxieties. The politicians exercised at least as much influence over the district attorneys, courts, correctional facilities, and other parts of the criminal justice process in the 1890s and 1900s as in the 1910s and 1920s. The police officers were depicted as far more capable and less comical in *Underworld, Public Enemy,* and *Little Caesar,* the most popular of the gangster films, than in the Keystone Cops pictures.[32] Although it is hard to understand, many police officials were more troubled by these trivial slights to their occupational pride than by the growing number of policemen slain on duty.

Other persons suffered from similar anxieties. Many prosecutors and judges as well as other public figures who were not directly involved in the criminal justice system believed that respect for law enforcement had dropped to an all-time low since the war. President Herbert C. Hoover shared these fears, a Buffalo police chief told his colleagues in 1933.[33] And so in all likelihood did many of the Americans who voted for the Eighteenth Amend-

ment, joined the Ku Klux Klan, or endorsed other last-ditch efforts to preserve the so-called traditional American values. But
few groups suffered from these anxieties as much as the police
officers. Few were so concerned about the breakdown of time-
honored morality and old-fashioned discipline, so perplexed by
the absence of widespread public outcry, and so pessimistic about
the long-term consequences of this inexplicable malaise. Nor
were many other groups so defensive about their inability to do
much about it. And if the speeches and resolutions at the peace
officers' conventions were indicative, few groups were so intent
upon finding an explanation that would absolve them of responsibility for this situation.

Occupational paranoia was a direct, though altogether unanticipated, outgrowth of the reform crusade. The reformers expected the big-city police to carry out a wide variety of difficult if
not impossible chores. Unlike the machines, the reformers insisted that the police do more than just regulate crime, license
vice, and exclude them from fashionable residential communities, which most officers who maintained close working relations
with the underworld did quite well in the late nineteenth century.
The reformers demanded that the police eliminate crime, even
though, as a few observers remarked, they had little control over
the outbreak of crime, less over its causes, and scarcely any over
the prosecution, adjudication, and rehabilitation of criminals.
The reformers also demanded that the police suppress vice, even
though, as a few critics observed, a sizable segment of the populace, probably a majority in the large Eastern and Midwestern
cities, did not view gambling, drinking, doing business on Sundays, and other such activities as criminal offenses.[34] By insisting
that the police concentrate on preventing crime and by defining
crime to include vice, the reformers unintentionally condemned
the officers to chronic frustration.

The reformers also expected the big-city police to meet a number of inconsistent, if not contradictory, demands, While many
reformers called on the police to behave like a military outfit,
wage war on crime, and treat criminals as enemies, a few warned
them to respect the constitutional rights of the suspects and
otherwise abide by the letter of the law. Hence the controversy
over the application of the third degree. While some reformers
pressed the police to launch an all-out attack on drinking, gam-

bling, Sunday business, and other so-called victimless crimes, other reformers asked them to adopt a broad-minded approach to these infractions. Hence the conflict over the enforcement of the sumptuary laws. While many reformers contended that the police should watch over trade unions, left-wing parties, and other disaffected groups, a few responded that the police should protect the civil liberties of all groups, no matter how unpopular or disagreeable. Hence the debate over the activities of the Los Angeles Red squad.[35] By pushing the police in two or more directions at the same time, which meant that they would antagonize some people regardless of which course they pursued, the reformers inadvertently exposed the officers to incessant criticism.

The reformers even expected the big-city police to take on several tasks that forced them into an adversary relationship with ordinarily law-abiding citizens. They compelled the police to enforce the vice laws against millions of Americans who saw nothing wrong in buying a drink after midnight, joining a friendly game of cards, or playing baseball on Sunday. Charging that these policies infringed on their private lives and squandered scarce departmental resources, many of these Americans developed a sharp antipathy toward the officers who implemented them.[36] Over the objections of Chief Vollmer and a few others, the reformers also obliged the police to enforce the traffic regulations against millions of Americans who did not view these infractions as criminal offenses. As an irate Los Angeles lawyer who had a run-in with two traffic officers wrote to the Board of Police Commissioners, "I am getting sick and tired of being treated as public enemy No. 1 every time I am stopped because my tail light is not burning."[37] By requiring the police to act against ordinarily law-abiding citizens, the reformers unwittingly deprived the officers of an invaluable source of public support that might have alleviated their deep-seated feeling of alienation and persecution.

By 1930 the reform campaign had a profound impact on the character, if not the structure, personnel, and function, of the American police. Not that it was solely responsible for occupational paranoia. In view of the remarkable heterogeneity of urban America, the police forces would probably have been subjected to intense and often conflicting pressures anyway. And if the police are by their very nature a "tainted occupation," as Egon Bittner has suggested, they might well have reacted in a defensive fashion.[38] Nor did the campaign affect all officers to the same degree. Although occupational paranoia penetrated deeply into the upper echelons, it had not yet spread widely among the rank-and-file except perhaps in an incipent way. Operating on a different set of assumptions about their obligations, the rank-and-file were spared many of the anxieties that troubled their superiors. But these qualifications did not conceal the salient point. Not until the early years of the century did the big-city police develop an occupational identity; not until then did they perceive themselves as policemen, as opposed to laborers, clerks, and railway conductors temporarily employed as policemen. And by virtue of the reform crusade a paranoid style emerged from the very start as an essential component of this occupational identity, a development that had profound consequences in the years ahead.

5.   The Impact of Reform on Urban Society

Early in 1930 Frederick Rex, head of Chicago's Municipal Reference Library, reported that the Windy City had a lower crime rate than all but thirteen of the eighty-one American cities with at least 100,000 people. Based on the FBI's *Uniform Crime Reports,* which covered murder, manslaughter, rape, robbery, assault, burglary, larceny, and auto theft, the Rex report reassured many residents, especially the backers of Mayor William H. Thompson, who was running for reelection. But many other residents, who regarded their city as the crime capital of the country, were skeptical. How, they asked, could other cities have more crime than Chicago, the home of Al Capone, the site of the St. Valentine's Day Massacre, and a place where almost 3,000 people, or nearly one a day, had been murdered in the last ten years?[1] According to John Landesco, a sociologist who studied organized crime in Chicago, conditions were indeed bad in the Windy City. But if the Rex report was accurate, they were even worse in Boston, Baltimore, Cleveland, and Los Angeles. If this was so, the reformers had made little progress in their crusade to save urban America in the thirty-five years or so since the Lexow Committee investigation.

Under constant pressure from the reformers, who held that crime prevention was the preeminent function of the big-city police, most departments took several steps to curtail criminal activity. They appointed policewomen and juvenile officers, set up employment bureaus, and created other units to deter youngsters from pursuing criminal careers. They divided the detective divisions into homicide, safe-and-lock, arson, bomb, and other squads which dealt exclusively with serious crimes and dangerous criminals. They compiled fingerprint files, which were consolidated in the mid-1920s when the Department of Justice organized a bureau of criminal identification. They established criminal laboratories, where officers conducted ballistics tests, analyzed blood samples, and for the first time in American history otherwise applied scientific techniques to criminal investigations. They devised more sophisticated signal systems, acquired swifter and sturdier patrol cars, purchased more accurate and lethal weapons, and to an unprecedented degree adapted technological innovations to day-to-day operations.[2]

Despite these changes most departments had only a slightly greater capacity to curtail criminal activity in 1930 than in 1890. For one reason, many policemen were not inclined to deal with crime. As the sensational scandals that erupted in Chicago, Philadelphia, and New York in the late 1920s and early 1930s indicated, some officers preferred to work with the gangsters. A few grew well-to-do from their share of the proceeds. Others preferred to pass their time eating, sleeping, and drinking, talking with buddies or visiting friends, and doing everything possible to stay away from trouble. These officers went after criminals only when a rash of particularly reprehensible crimes generated more complaints than the police chiefs and municipal officials could safely ignore. For another reason, some policemen did not have the ability to deal with crime. As the intelligence tests that were given to the Los Angeles, Detroit, and Kansas City police departments in the mid-1920s revealed, these officers lacked the rudimentary skills necessary to investigate crimes.[3] Poorly educated and inadequately trained, they could scarcely read and write, much less make accurate observations, conduct proper interviews, and prepare coherent reports.

The few officers who had the inclination and ability to curb criminal activity operated under severe constraints. They could not eliminate the underlying causes of crime, whether these were, as some argued, a function of poverty, discrimination, and the other conditions of ghetto life or, as others insisted, a symptom of the breakdown of parental discipline, the proclivity for easy living, and the erosion of traditional values. Nor could the officers alleviate the deep-seated flaws in a criminal justice system which, many reformers charged, was staffed by district attorneys who were loath to prosecute powerful gangsters, judges who were afraid to antagonize important politicians, and correctional officials who, in the guise of rehabilitation, turned first offenders into hardened criminals and placed dangerous criminals on probation and parole. Neither could the officers persuade the many Americans who regarded Al Capone as one of the outstanding men in the world that it was in their interest to report crime to the police departments, give evidence to the district attorneys, and otherwise cooperate with the municipal authorities.[4]

Although crime was rampant in urban America in the 1920s, it is probably impossible to figure out whether it was on the increase. The statistics are not good enough to measure the level of crime in any one year, let alone compare it from one year to another. The defects are twofold. First, the statistics included only crimes known to the police. But there is reason to believe that the citizens reported only a small proportion of crimes, probably as few as one of every four or five, to the precincts. According to a study conducted in Chicago in the mid-1920s, the precincts reported only about 10 to 20 percent of these crimes to headquarters and, to make matters worse, often misclassified them, listing burglary as larceny and bombing as malicious mischief.[5] The second defect of the statistics was that they fluctuated according to changes in public policy and police practice. The federal, state, and municipal authorities often imposed the criminal sanction on formerly legal activities, and vice versa. The police departments usually enforced the law in ways that varied not only from one city to another but also from one administration to the next. Hence an increase in the crime rate, if it had any significance at all, might have reflected a broader definition of deviant behavior and a tougher pattern of law enforcement as much as a genuine upsurge in criminal enterprise.

But these matters were academic to the great majority of upper-middle- and upper-class Americans who were virtually obsessed by crime in the postwar years. For them the daily newspapers could not print too many articles about the proliferation of fashionable speakeasies, the increase in underworld violence, the rise in insurance premiums, and other manifestations of the crime waves. Nor could the popular magazines. Even the motion picture studios could not produce enough films about the beer wars and warehouse massacres of the Mortons, Colosimos, O'Banions, and other notorious gangsters. From these sources the citizens drew the plausible conclusion that their countrymen were caught up in an orgy of bootlegging, hijacking, racketeering, kidnaping, and homicide. None of the skeptics — neither Clarence Darrow, who denied that crime was on the increase, nor Walter Lippmann, who blamed the alleged increase on the peculiar American "passion for legislative purity" — could convince the public otherwise. As a public opinion poll conducted by the National Economic League on the eve of the Great Depression indicated, most Americans agreed with President Herbert C. Hoover that crime, closely followed by disrespect for law, was the country's most serious problem.[6]

This anxiety was manifested in all sorts of ways other than by the proliferation of state and local crime commissions and the formation in 1929 of the National Commission on Law Observance and Enforcement, commonly known after its chairman, Attorney General George W. Wickersham, as the Wickersham Commission. Witness the growing demand for private detectives, whose ranks swelled from only 20,000 in 1920 to fully 100,000 in 1930, according to unofficial estimates, and whose fees ran as high as twenty-five dollars a day plus expenses. Witness also the mounting passion on the part of bankers, merchants, landlords, and even ordinary homeowners for wired doors, burglar alarms, heavy-duty locks, bullet-proof windows, armored cars, and many other ingenious but only partially effective crime prevention gadgets. Witness too the increasing support from otherwise sensible people for schemes to censor newspapers, magazines, radio programs, and motion pictures, to restore the whipping post, to sanction the third degree, to restrict the right to marry, to require universal fingerprinting, and otherwise to abridge the civil liberties of the American people in the name of crime prevention.[7]

But to draw from the Rex report and other evidence that the police had not greatly reduced crime the conclusion that the reformers had not made much progress in their crusade to save urban America would be misleading and premature. It would be misleading because the police had little control over the underlying causes of criminal activity and the alleged defects of the criminal justice system. It would be premature because the war on crime was part of a broader movement by the upper-middle- and upper-class Americans to strengthen their position vis-à-vis the lower- and lower-middle-class newcomers. To gauge the progress of the reform campaign, it is therefore necessary to look at the outcome of this movement and in particular at the results of the efforts to redeem the public service, destroy the political machine, and wipe out deviant behavior.

Many Americans viewed police reform as an essential feature of a long-standing effort to redeem the public service. As they saw it, the police forces, courts, schools, and other urban institutions were neglecting their primary responsibility. Instead of supplying the commercial, industrial, and financial establishments which were the lifeblood of the city with the best possible services at the lowest possible cost, the police were providing soft jobs for uneducated, unskilled, and unreliable immigrants whose sole qualification was loyalty to the political machine. From this perspective a change in the ethnic makeup of the big-city police was essential. Many other Americans objected that, if successful, the reform effort would deprive lots of faithful municipal employees of their hard-earned livelihood. To this the reformers replied that in a nation where social mobility was a private, economic, and individual as opposed to a public, political, and collective process, many other sources of employment and means of advancement were available. Their argument blurred but did not conceal the point that the reform movement was designed to promote the prosperity of the upper middle and upper classes at the expense of the lower and lower middle classes.

Most reformers were well aware that the Irish and other ethnic minorities who were solidly entrenched in the police forces had no intention of sacrificing their jobs on the altar of administrative efficiency. But they were unable to do much about it. They could not fire every police officer who was unsympathetic to their cause without violating the principles that politics and policing should be strictly divorced and that officers should be removed only for cause. So they resorted to less drastic and, it turned out, less effective measures. They brought charges against a few corrupt and incompetent officers, only to learn that the disciplinary process was so cumbersome and time-consuming, the crucial witnesses so hard to find, and the appellate process so susceptible to political influence that this tactic was effective only in the case of gross malfeasance.[8] They also raised the service pensions to levels that led a few unqualified officers to retire, only to find out that these benefits also tempted a few qualified officers to leave and had little impact on the great majority of officers who were far from retirement age. Short of adopting the ruthless methods of political machines, which would have alienated many of their supporters, the reformers could drive out only a fraction of the most avaricious and least dedicated police officers.

Nor could the reformers prevent many other immigrants, no matter how self-serving their motives, from getting into the police forces. Not that the reformers failed to try. Year after year they urged the state and local authorities to tighten the physical, mental, and moral requirements in ways that would have discriminated against, or perhaps even disqualified, the overwhelming majority of first- and second-generation newcomers. But under cross-pressure from the political machines and rank-and-file organizations the authorities refused to do more than order minor revisions in the entrance requirements and subject all applicants to civil service tests. Unlike the entrance requirements, which were anything but stringent and could be easily circumvented, the civil service tests, which were conducted in English, probably kept out many first-generation Italian-, Polish-, Slavic-, and Russian-Americans. But as the tests were otherwise fairly easy, they did not bar many second-generation German- or Scandinavian-Americans.[9] Nor did they exclude many first- and second-generation Irish-Americans, who were the largest ethnic minority in most police departments, the staunchest supporters of the political machine, the chief beneficiaries of the spoils system, and so far as the reformers were concerned, the symbol of all that was wrong with the big-city police.

Moreover, the reformers could not prevail on many native Americans, qualified or otherwise, to consider seriously a career as a police officer. There were several reasons. First, the number of potential applicants was fairly small. The native Americans were a minority in all but a handful of big cities; and except in Berkeley and a few other places where the reformers had persuaded the authorities to abolish the residency requirements, the police forces were not allowed to recruit outside the city. Second, few of these Americans were interested in public service. Although they wanted to redeem the public sector, they shared the conventional wisdom that private enterprise was the proper path for ambitious and worthy youths and that public service was the sorry refuge of nitwits, loafers, and scoundrels.[10] Third, even fewer of these Americans were attracted to police work. The low prestige, irregular hours, and often disagreeable tasks put them off; and despite sizable increases in the postwar years, the salaries, service pensions, and fringe benefits left them unimpressed. These obstacles were so formidable that the reformers should not have been surprised that few native Americans applied to the police departments, only skeptical of the claim that they did so for more altruistic reasons than the first- and second-generation immigrants.

The attempt to change the ethnic makeup of the big-city police was therefore less than a smashing success. Under the administration of Theodore Roosevelt, who was named head of the New York City police board in the aftermath of the Lexow Committee investigation, the reformers, as Roosevelt put it, "greatly raised the proportion of native-born [recruits], until, of the last hundred appointed, ninety-four per cent were Americans by birth." But the reformers did less well under subsequent administrations. Between 1890 and 1920, the last year for which the census bureau classified occupational groups by nativity and parentage, the proportion of native Americans in the New York police force, which by then included many third-generation Irish-Americans, went up only from about 18 to 25 percent. The turnover was much the same in most other cities. The proportion of native Americans rose a little more in Pittsburgh, Cleveland, St. Paul, and Milwaukee, a bit less in Newark and Philadelphia, and stayed about the same or fell a little in Boston, Chicago, Minneapolis, and San Francisco. As a result, the first- and second-generation immigrants retained roughly two out of three police jobs in Boston, Newark, Cleveland, and Buffalo, three out of four in Minneapolis, St. Louis, San Francisco, and New York, four out of five in Chicago and Providence, and five out of six in Milwaukee.[11] Hence the newcomers had a fair share of the jobs in some cities and a lot more in others in 1920 — and there is no reason to think that it was otherwise in 1930.

On the basis of the census bureau reports, which ceased classifying police officers by country of origin in 1910, it is impossible to figure out with much precision the ethnic makeup of the big-city police in 1930. But it is possible to calculate that the blacks filled roughly 4 percent of the slots in Philadelphia, 3 percent in Omaha, 2 percent in Pittsburgh, Chicago, and Los Angeles, and 1 percent or less in Cleveland, Detroit, Oakland, and New York. It is also possible to work out a rough gauge of the relative standing of the other ethnic groups. After 1890 the second-generation immigrants, whose parents migrated mainly from northern and western Europe, steadily increased their share of the jobs at the expense of the first-generation immigrants, who came largely from southern and eastern Europe. By 1920 the second generation held around one out of every three jobs in Philadelphia, one out of two in Boston, Chicago, Buffalo, Newark, St. Paul, New York, Detroit, and San Francisco, and two out of three in Milwaukee.[12] If this trend persisted through 1930, and again there is no reason to think otherwise, it follows that notwithstanding the great influx of Italians, Poles, Slavs, and Russians in the late nineteenth and early twentieth centuries, the Irish-Americans, the German-Americans, and in one or two cities the Scandinavian-Americans retained the lion's share of the slots. The Irish cop, celebrated in gangster films and political cartoons, was indeed a fitting symbol of the big-city police.

In the meantime the number of policemen rose sharply. It more than doubled in Baltimore and Minneapolis, tripled in Boston, Philadelphia, St. Louis, and Washington, quadrupled in Buffalo, Chicago, Denver, and New Orleans, and quintupled in Cleveland and Milwaukee. On a per capita basis the number also went up, but less sharply. During the postwar decade police salaries also regained so much of the ground lost in the prewar years that they were about as good in 1930 as in 1890. Service pensions and fringe benefits were far better too. By then some big cities even paid for the policemen's uniforms, weapons, and ammunition. If the estimates of General Smedley D. Butler were accurate, many patrolmen pocketed $150 to $200 a month in payoffs in Philadelphia, less whatever assessments the local politicians levied on them. If the revelations of the Seabury Committee were indicative, a few officers, usually captains, sergeants, and plainclothesmen, collected hundreds of thousands of dollars in graft in New York City. For most policemen, who were recruited mainly from the ranks of laborers, clerks, truck drivers, and railwaymen, according to surveys conducted in Cleveland, Los Angeles, and Boston, this was no mean living.[13] Despite the reform effort, the police forces not only served many first- and second-generation newcomers as a vital avenue of social mobility in 1930 but also served more of them and served them better than ever before.

In light of the size of the forces — which in 1930 came to roughly 17,700 in New York, 6,700 in Chicago, 5,500 in Philadelphia, 4,000 in Detroit, 2,700 in Los Angeles, 2,600 in Boston, 2,300 in St. Louis, 1,900 in Baltimore, 1,600 in Cleveland, 1,400 in Washington, 1,300 in Buffalo, and 1,100 in Milwaukee — only a small fraction of the newcomers could be employed as policemen.[14] And though most policemen moved from the lower class into the middle class, only a handful of unscrupulous officers who accumulated enough graft to build sizable bank accounts, buy single-family homes, and drive expensive motor cars made it into the upper middle class. But most police departments were a crucial part of a far larger political system that included the fire and sanitation departments, schools and courts, and other municipal bureaucracies and had at its disposal tens and even hundreds of thousands of remunerative and secure jobs. For most lower- and lower-middle-class newcomers who wanted to climb into the middle class but lacked the skills, funds, and connections to do so by way of the private sector, these jobs were well worth fighting for.

Many Americans also viewed police reform as an integral component of a long-term campaign to destroy the political machine. The police, fire, sanitation, and other municipal departments were, in their opinion, disregarding their official mandate. Far from operating as a branch of the municipal government, responsible to the city-wide officials and devoted to the public interest, they were serving as adjuncts of the political machines, accountable to the ward leaders and dedicated to their organization's hegemony. From this point of view a reduction in the day-to-day influence of the local politicians was imperative. Many other Americans complained that, if successful, the reform movement would deprive the ward bosses of a principal source of their hard-earned leverage in municipal politics. The reformers countered that local control was not a source of political legitimacy in the United States and that, no matter how large their majorities in the wards, the district leaders had no authority over the policies or practices of the municipal police. This argument obscured but did not hide the crucial point that the reform movement was designed to increase the influence of the upper middle and upper classes at the expense of the lower and lower middle classes.

Most reformers were well aware that the ward bosses derived much of their influence from their close relationship with the precinct captains. But they were hard put to do much about it. The reformers tried to destroy this relationship by pressing the authorities to consolidate or close down the precincts and thereby to separate them from the wards. But this tactic foundered in the face of opposition from the local politicians. The reformers also attempted to undermine the captains by urging the authorities to appoint inspectors, deputy chiefs, and other high-level police officials to keep tabs on them and, if need be, to bring charges against them. But this strategy failed because these officials, most of whom had come up through the ranks, had little inclination to harass, much less prosecute, the captains except in cases of flagrant misconduct. The reformers sought to downgrade the precincts as well by asking the authorities to transfer traffic regulation, vice control, and many other functions from ordinary patrolmen attached to the precincts to special squads assigned to headquarters. But even this proposal, which was implemented to one degree or another in most cities, did not greatly diminish the power of the precinct captains or sharply decrease the influence of the ward leaders.

The reformers also pressed the authorities to weaken and, if possible, to break the ward bosses' hold over the rank-and-file by shifting authority over appointments, promotions, and discipline from the police boards and city councils to the civil service commissions. In time most authorities went along with them. But the commissions, which were largely staffed by members of the machines who were personally and professionally committed to the spoils system, were eager to accommodate the ward bosses and afraid not to.[15] They were quite prepared to violate the civil service rules if they would otherwise have been forced to reject an applicant or remove an officer who had the organization's endorsement. To curb these abuses, the reformers demanded that the authorities spell out the civil service rules as precisely as possible and insulate the civil service examiners from political influence. But in the face of counterpressure from the old-line machines, which were intent on preserving what remained of the spoils system, the authorities responded halfheartedly in some cities and not at all in others. Consequently the ward leaders retained their say on most personnel decisions. In view of the weakness of the rank-and-file associations, many of which had been crushed or coopted in the aftermath of World War I, most patrolmen had no alternative but to follow their orders.

The reformers also called on the authorities to enhance the police chiefs' tenure, increase their power, and otherwise strengthen their position vis-à-vis the ward bosses. The response varied from city to city, but nowhere did the situation change very much. By virtue of the bosses' strong ties to the mayors, councilmen, prosecutors, and judges, they could still prevent most chiefs from introducing any but minor reforms in departmental policies and practices. If by chance the chiefs slipped through a major reform, the bosses could still exert enough pressure on the superior officers and rank-and-file to ensure that it would be loosely if at all enforced. Most chiefs worked out an accommodation with the local politicians. But if they did not — and if, like Butler of Philadelphia and Everington of Los Angeles, they considered compromise worse than defeat — the politicians could usually prevail on the authorities to dismiss them. If a reform administration held office, the ward bosses might have to wait until the political machine returned to power. But to the annoyance of Commissioner Woods, who was removed as soon as Tammany regained the mayor's office in 1917, the bosses generally got their way sooner or later. If the chiefs needed a reminder of their vulnerability, they had only to look to Los Angeles, where the local politicians drove Chief James E. Davis out of office against his wishes and in violation of the spirit if not the letter of the civil service rules.[16]

The campaign to reduce the day-to-day influence of the ward politicians was therefore less than an unqualified success. With a few exceptions, these politicians could no longer close a criminal investigation, protect a line of pickets, or break up a rally of socialists or anarchists simply by issuing instructions to the precinct captains. By virtue of the proliferation of special squads, which as a result of reform pressures was well underway by the 1920s, these decisions were now made not by the captains but by the squad commanders, many of whom took a hard line vis-à-vis union organizers and left-wing radicals in the postwar period.[17] Most ward politicians were not troubled by this crackdown. Not only did they feel little sympathy for trade unions and even less for radical groups, but they saw little connection between the treatment of these groups, which spoke for few voters and commanded meager resources, and the prospects of their ward organizations. To put it bluntly, the politicians did not worry much about the proliferation of special squads largely because they did not believe that these squads threatened their vital interests.

So far as most ward leaders were concerned, their vital interests were twofold. In the first place, it was incumbent on them to oversee the appointment and, to a lesser degree, the assignment, promotion, and discipline of the policemen, as well as the firemen, garbagemen, schoolteachers, building inspectors, judges, and other municipal employees. If they could not provide jobs for the first- and second-generation immigrants, they could not expect them to vote for their candidates, contribute to their treasury, bring out more voters, and assist in other ways to keep the local organization in power. The ward leaders probably had less, but not much less, of a say in personnel decisions in 1930 than in 1890. In Chicago, New York, and San Francisco they mobilized so much opposition to the effort to tighten the entrance requirements and insulate the civil service from political influence that their constituents stood a fair chance of getting appointed regardless of their qualifications. In Kansas City, where as a result of a successful lawsuit the Pendergast machine regained control of the police department in the early 1930s, the ward bosses summarily dismissed 200 Republican policemen, or about one-third of the force, and replaced them with Democratic officers, most of whom were Irish-Americans.[18]

In the second place, it was imperative for the ward leaders to shape the polices and practices of the police departments, courts, schools, building departments, and other municipal agencies which directly impinged on the lives and livelihoods of their constituents. If they could not provide protection for the gamblers, prostitutes, and saloon keepers, not to speak of the peddlers, storekeepers, contractors, and other reputable businessmen who occasionally violated municipal ordinances, they could not count on them to lend the organization political, economic, and moral support on election day. The ward leaders probably had less, but not much less, of a voice in policy matters in 1930 than in 1890. In Philadelphia, Detroit, and New York they usually brought enough pressure on the precinct captains or squad commanders to ensure that so long as their constituents ran an orderly enterprise, kept up their payments, and otherwise abided by the prevailing ground rules, they would not be bothered by the police department. In Chicago, where the Democratic organization controlled the police force, the ward leaders, as the Citizens' Police Committee protested in the late 1920s, forced the officers to distribute partisan handbills on election day, though they no longer compelled them to round up influential Republicans on the eve of the municipal elections.[19]

Viewed in the context of the fire and sanitation departments, courts and schools, public utilities and private contractors, and other sources of jobs, retainers, premiums, and kickbacks, the police departments were only one of the ward bosses' bases of power. Moreover, the police departments traced missing persons, gave traffic directions, resolved domestic disputes, operated emergency ambulances, and rendered many other everyday services that could not be manipulated in ways which would redound to the benefit of the political machines. But along with the fire and sanitation departments, the courts, the schools, and the prosecutorial and correctional agencies, the police departments were one of the urban institutions that were critical, and in the long run probably indispensable, to the ward bosses. For these politicians, who sought leverage over the profitable but vulnerable business enterprises that operated on or beyond the borders of illegality and were prepared to pay well for the privilege, the police were well worth fighting over.

Many Americans also viewed police reform as an essential feature of an ongoing crusade to wipe out deviant behavior. The police and other parts of the criminal justice system were, in their opinion, shirking their sworn duty. Rather than enforcing the ordinances against gambling, drinking, prostitution, and other illicit activities, the police were ignoring them on the grounds that most officers, politicians, and citizens considered these laws unenforceable and perhaps even indefensible. From this viewpoint a revision in the prevailing patterns of law enforcement was vital. Many other Americans protested that, if successful, the reform movement would deprive many respectable newcomers of some of their cherished cultural traditions. The reformers replied that the ethnic life-styles, as well as the attitudes and mores underlying them, were incompatible with the country's values and that wherever necessary the authorities should employ the criminal sanction to bring them into line with the conventional morality. This argument confused but did not refute the critical point that the reform movement was designed to reinforce the values of the upper-middle- and upper-class native Americans at the expense of the lower- and lower-middle-class first- and second-generation immigrants.

Most reformers were well aware that many Americans had strong doubts about the feasibility of the vice laws, but they were hard pressed to dispel them. As William J. Gaynor, Brand Whitlock, Raymond B. Fosdick, and other skeptics charged, many of the vice laws were unenforceable. The police could not possibly prevent the citizens from kissing in public, wearing short skirts, playing blackjack at home, or selling groceries on Sunday. To begin with, they lacked the manpower. For every 1,000 residents most departments had only 1.5 to 3.3 officers; and as a result of shifts, vacations, and sick leaves, only one-fifth to one-quarter of the officers were on duty at any one time.[20] What is more, the police lacked the authority. They could not hire an army of spies and informants, break into houses without search warrants, and employ the other chilling measures that are often the only way to deal with criminal offenses when complainants are unavailable and witnesses uncooperative. In the absence of widespread public support, these obstacles were insuperable. To put it another way, the police could not enforce many of the vice laws unless urban America was transformed from a policed into a police society, a course of action that even the most dedicated reformers shied from.

But not all the vice laws were unenforceable, the reformers insisted. Provided that the municipal authorities shifted responsibility from ordinary patrolmen attached to the precincts to special squads assigned to headquarters, the reformers claimed, the police could crack down on the gamblers, prostitutes, and liquor dealers. Under vigorous pressure from the reformers, most cities made this change. But as one scandal after another erupted in these cities, revealing that in return for regular payments most gamblers, prostitutes, and liquor dealers were allowed to go about their business, the reformers realized that the vice squads were as susceptible to financial inducements and political influence as the uniformed officers. The situation was so bad in Detroit during the mid-1910s that Commissioner John Gillespie resigned under fire and his successor, Commissioner James Couzens, abolished the vice squad, which remained defunct until Mayor Charles Bowles reestablished it a decade and a half later. The situation was no better in Philadelphia where Public Safety Director Butler, who took office in the mid-1920s, denounced the vice squad as a "barnacle" on the police department and disbanded it as part of his campaign against vice.[21] Nowhere in urban America, except perhaps in Chicago under Deputy Commissioner Funkhouser, did the vice squads justify the reformers' confidence in them.

But as the reformers learned, neither the vice squads nor the uniformed officers had much inducement to enforce the vice laws. As Director Butler, Superintendent Henry G. Pratt, and other high-ranking police officials lamented, the prosecutors and courts more or less hamstrung their operations. During his term in office, Butler remarked, the Philadelphia police raided more than 3,000 speakeasies and arrested more than 10,000 liquor dealers, but fewer than 2,000 were indicted and barely 300 were convicted. During his administration, Pratt told a congressional committee, the Washington police were unable to drive gamblers out of the District of Columbia largely because no sooner were they arrested than they were released.[22] No doubt the police sometimes handled things so sloppily that the prosecutor had no option but to drop the charges and, if he pressed ahead anyway, the judge had no choice but to dismiss the case or levy a nominal fine. But according to the Chicago Crime Commission, the Cleveland Foundation, the Missouri Association for Criminal Justice, and the Seabury Committee, few prosecutors and judges were inclined to deal harshly with the offenders, especially if they were on good terms with the ward bosses.

The campaign to revise the prevailing patterns of law enforcement was therefore less than a resounding success. From 1890 on the reformers brought mounting pressure on the state and municipal authorities and, through them, the police, prosecutors, and courts to close down the red-light districts, which were the most conspicuous symbols of the official attitude toward vice that had emerged in urban America during the late nineteenth century. By 1930 the authorities had cracked down on many of the illicit activities and dangerous hangouts which had given nationwide and even worldwide notoriety to Chicago's Levee, New Orleans' French Quarter, New York's Tenderloin, and San Francisco's Barbary Coast. But the destruction of the red-light districts did not, it turned out, mean the elimination of deviant behavior. As the Minneapolis Vice Commission and other reform organizations that led a crusade against segregated districts in the prewar decades pointed out, neither prostitution nor drinking, gambling, and other vices was strictly confined to the red-light districts.[23] For the millions of Americans who were often tempted to bet on the horses, join a friendly game of cards, buy a bottle of beer, hire a prostitute, and violate one or another of the hundreds of less serious sumptuary laws, there were plenty of opportunities available elsewhere in urban America.

The range of these opportunities in the late 1920s was wide. The public printer told a congressional committee that Washington, D.C., bookmakers did a land-office business with Government Printing Office employees, who spent most of their time figuring out the odds, looking for tips, placing bets, and waiting for the results, which came over an official wire. Justice Samuel Seabury reported to the New York State Supreme Court that Billy Warren, Johnny Baker, and other big-time gamblers ran their card games out of the city's Democratic clubhouses and turned a share of the take over to the district leaders, who protected the players from the police. A former bootlegger declared that for years he had brought booze into Los Angeles, paid a dozen or so police officers about $100,000 a year for protection, and would still have been in business were it not that the officers got too greedy and demanded more than he could afford. According to Landesco's report to the Illinois Association for Criminal Justice, several hundred Chicago prostitutes worked out of houses in the Loop that enjoyed the protection of the Democratic aldermen and the tacit approval of the Thompson administration.[24] Similar opportunities abounded in Philadelphia, Detroit, Denver, and San Francisco.

Millions of Americans took full advantage of these opportunities. To meet the tremendous demand for illicit activity, gambling dens, bookie joints, speakeasies, and brothels proliferated, gamblers, bookmakers, bartenders, and prostitutes multiplied, and news bureaus, policy bankers, bootleggers, and madams enlarged their operations. Whether vice was more prevalent in 1930 than in 1890 is impossible to tell. None of the available sources, neither the arrest statistics, the police reports, nor the official surveys, is reliable enough. But most citizens were afraid that vice was on the increase. Their concern gave rise to innumerable articles, books, radio programs, and motion pictures about immorality and lawlessness and even prompted President Hoover to appoint the Wickersham Commission not long after his inauguration in 1929. Most gangsters were also convinced that vice was on the rise. This conviction was manifested in the extraordinary lengths to which the Capones, Buchalters, Schultzes, O'Banions, Diamonds, Lanskys, and their underlings were willing to go to gain and retain control over gambling, policy, bootlegging, prostitution, off-track betting, and other illicit activities in their cities.[25]

Viewed from a broad perspective, alongside the prosecutors, courts, and correctional institutions, on the one hand, and the schools and welfare bureaus, on the other, the police departments were but one of the municipal bureaucracies that were responsible for discouraging and deterring deviant behavior. If the families, churches, and voluntary organizations had failed to instill the conventional morality in the ethnic ghettos, as many reformers contended, it was highly unlikely that the police force or any other public agency, no matter how committed and competent their personnel, would be more successful. But for the millions of upper-middle- and upper-class Americans who were severely troubled by the inability of the families, churches, and voluntary associations to transmit their values and attitudes to their fellow citizens, the policies of the municipal authorities took on a symbolic significance out of all proportion to their actual effectiveness. As far as these Americans were concerned, the practices of the police departments served as a better guide than the activities of the schools, courts, and other public agencies to whether the authorities were trying hard to stamp out vice.

Hence the first wave of reform fell short of its principal objectives. Despite many changes, the big-city police still served as a vital avenue of mobility for the newcomers, reinforced the pervasive decentralization of municipal government, and sanctioned the prevailing pluralism of urban life. Other than the opposition of the machine politicians and police officers, there were several reasons that the reformers did not do better. High among them was the antagonism of the lower- and lower-middle-class newcomers. From their perspective, which was shaped by a natural desire to hold on to what little they had acquired in their adoptive country, the attempt to redeem the public service, destroy the political machine, and wipe out deviant behavior was ominous. It was also gratuitous. Crime might well be on the increase, they admitted, but most sensible people knew which streets to avoid; and if they wanted to place a bet, pick a horse, or buy a drink, it was no one else's concern. Least of all was it the concern of the upper-middle- and upper-class Americans whose communities were relatively free of crime. The reformers tried hard to persuade the newcomers that it was in the public interest to tighten the entrance requirements for policemen, overthrow the ward leaders and their henchmen, and support the crusade against immorality. But most newcomers remained skeptical and, under the circumstances, justifiably so.

Another major reason that the reformers did not do better was the diffusion of municipal authority. The ethnic composition of the big-city police, the day-to-day influence of the ward politicians, and the prevailing patterns of law enforcement were shaped by many official agencies other than the police departments. The civil service commissions not only certified the candidates but also conducted the promotional exams in several cities and presided over the disciplinary proceedings in a few others. The city councils and mayor's offices fixed the terms and powers of the police chiefs and their aides, set the salaries and fringe benefits of the rank-and-file, and defined the chores of the police forces. The prosecutors and courts decided not only whether to press or drop charges, admit or exclude evidence, and discharge or incarcerate criminals but also whether to bring charges against corrupt officers or allow them to resign. From the mid-1890s on the reformers attempted to prevail on these institutions to support their campaign while mounting a separate campaign to divorce them from municipal politics. But the scandals which rocked many cities in the late 1920s and early

1930s indicated that these institutions remained tied to the political machines and unresponsive to the reform proposals.[26]

Many reform proposals were so ill conceived that they would have fared badly even without the antipathy of the ethnic minorities and the diffusion of municipal authority. To put it bluntly, what was the point of raising the salaries, service pensions, and fringe benefits if most upper-middle-class Americans regarded the police departments and other branches of the public service as the last refuge of halfwits, misfits, and knaves? Why bother to extend the police chiefs' term and enlarge their authority if under the civil service rules that applied in most cities they had no voice in appointments, little say about promotions, and scarcely more power over discipline? Why shift responsibility for vice control from ordinary patrolmen attached to the precinct to special squads assigned to headquarters if most first- and second-generation newcomers regarded the vice laws as indefensible? And why establish flying squads, juvenile divisions, criminal laboratories, fingerprint files, rogues' galleries, and other crime-fighting facilities if the police forces had little control over the everyday incidence of criminal activity and even less over its underlying causes?

In other words, the attempt to redeem the public service, destroy the political machine, and wipe out deviant behavior was hamstrung from the outset by flaws in the reform ideology. So was the effort to suppress criminal activity. The misplaced confidence in the efficacy of the big-city police was probably the most serious of the flaws. But the ambivalence toward the public service, the conflict between a strong executive and an autonomous civil service, and the excessive reliance on the criminal sanction were far from trivial flaws.[27] These flaws might not have mattered much if the reformers' assumption was tenable that waste, graft, vice, and crime were functions of the shortcomings of the big-city police. But it was not. Much of what the reformers saw as waste, graft, vice, and crime was rather a manifestation of the efforts of the newcomers to enhance their mobility, increase their power, and enjoy their style of life. To thwart these efforts, it was not enough just to change the big-city police. It was also necessary to transform the mayor's offices, city councils, courts, schools, and other urban institutions, a task that was well underway but by no means finished by the late 1920s.

Although the reformers had not made much progress in their crusade to save urban America since the Lexow Committee investigation, they had profoundly influenced the development of the big-city police in at least one important though easily over-looked way. By the late 1920s and early 1930s they had trans-formed the quintessential principles of the Progressive movement into the conventional wisdom of the American people. By this I do not mean that the reformers had entirely persuaded their fellow countrymen, including the many who were otherwise un-interested in municipal affairs, that as a result of a defective structure, unqualified officers, extraneous functions, and the insidious influence of machine politics the big-city police were in deplorable condition. Nor do I mean that the reformers had eroded the tradition of American policing which emphasized local control, a civilian orientation, and catchall and responsive activity. I mean rather that the reformers had established a con-sensus of their own about the big-city police which denied that public service was a means of social mobility, that local control was a source of political legitimacy, and that immigrant life-styles were an expression of American culture.

This consensus was based on three assumptions. The first assumption was that the primary purpose of the police forces, as well as of the schools, courts, and other municipal bureaucracies, was to provide the best possible service at the lowest possible cost and not to reward the lower- and lower-middle-class newcomers for voting the right way in local elections. An explicit critique of the spoils system, this assumption gained such widespread support after the turn of the century that by the 1920s even the politicians and bureaucrats who were prone to violate it in private were obliged to honor it in public. They no longer followed the lead of James J. Martin, a Tammany Hall district leader and New York City police commissioner who, when asked by the Lexow Committee to account for the partisan cast of his personnel poli-cies, testified, "All things being equal, I accept the recommenda-tion of political friends." Instead, most officials now employed reform rhetoric to deflect reform criticism. When Chief Robert Phelan, a loyal Democrat, was called upon to explain why the police department, which by virtue of a court decision had just been returned to the Pendergast machine, had replaced several hundred native-American Republicans with Irish-American

Democrats, he replied, "The Irish make the best cops in the world."[28]

The second assumption underlying the new consensus was that all authority over the police forces, fire departments, and other municipal agencies was vested in the mayors or their appointees and other city-wide officials and not in the ward leaders. A sharp refutation of political decentralization, this assumption not only expressed the reformers' conviction that municipal administration should be completely insulated from local politics. It also reflected their contention that when the ward bosses and their allies exerted pressure on the police officers, it was political interference, but that when the chambers of commerce, municipal leagues, and crime commissions did so, it was civic responsibility. The reform assumption did not deter the ward bosses from playing an active and in some instances a decisive role in most police departments down through the late 1920s, but it discouraged them from defending these activities as a prerogative of their electoral majorities. Acknowledging the tremendous power of the reform ideology, the bosses now downplayed their own influence.

The third assumption behind the new consensus was that the ethnic life-styles, as well as the values, attitudes, and customs underlying them, were incompatible with the conventional morality and the values, attitudes, and customs underlying it and that the police, prosecutors, courts, and other municipal bureaus should take whatever steps were necessary to bring the one into line with the other. An out-and-out repudiation of cultural pluralism, this assumption won such wide acceptance in the early twentieth century that by the 1920s many police chiefs and public officials adopted it, and many others who were skeptical felt compelled to pay lip service to it. No longer did most chiefs and officials insist, as Justice Gaynor of New York had in 1903, that the police lacked authority to impose the conventional morality on the ethnic minorities or argue, as Chief O'Neill of Chicago had in 1904, that even if the police had the authority, they lacked the capacity. On the contrary, most public officials now went along with Public Safety Director Butler, who declared not only that the police departments should enforce the sumptuary laws but also that, if adequately staffed, supervised, and supported, they could wipe out vice in urban America.[29]

The emergence of this consensus about policing can be attributed to several things other than its superficial plausibility. The reform ideology was supported by most of the institutions that molded public opinion. The newspapers, magazines, churches, commercial organizations, and civic associations promoted scores of investigations and conferences which focused attention on the incompetence and corruption of the big-city police. The universities created a few professorships in police science, organized several schools of public administration, and in one case even published a journal of criminology that transmitted the Progressive·viewpoint to the upcoming generation. The research institutes turned out dozens of surveys and reports, full of elaborate charts, tables, and figures, which under the guise of objective scholarship carried the gospel of reform from one city to the next. The ward leaders did not appreciate the import of this ideological barrage; and even if they had, they would have been unable to do much about it. Fully occupied with helping their constituents, getting out the vote, and making a living, they did not have the time.[30] Nor, as a result of a deep-seated reluctance to speak in public and put anything in writing, did they have the knack.

The reform ideology was also reinforced by several momentous changes that were underway in urban America. The critique of the spoils system struck a responsive chord in a society which, as Samuel Haber has observed, had fallen under the spell of Frederick W. Taylor, the apostle of scientific management, and had come to equate technical efficiency with moral uplift. The refutation of political decentralization made a profound impression at a time when many Americans were calling for city, metropolitan, and regional planning commissions and public works agencies whose jurisdictions crossed not only ward but even city and state boundaries. The repudiation of cultural pluralism sparked a good deal of enthusiasm in a nation whose anxieties about social change had recently culminated in the Red scare, the Eighteenth Amendment, the restriction of immigration, and the resurgence of the Ku Klux Klan.[31] The ward bosses were well aware of these changes. But they failed to perceive that the changes seriously threatened the old consensus and the assumptions underlying it on which their control of the police forces and other municipal agencies rested. Unwilling or perhaps unable to join the debates on the social costs of managerial efficiency, the political implications of centralized authority, and the civil liberties of unpopular minorities, the ward leaders gave way without much of a struggle.

The reform ideology was also strengthened by the recurrent scandals that rocked the political machines and police departments. As the scandals revealed, the politicians not only treated public service as a means of social mobility. They also appointed recruits who were alcoholic, incapacitated, or virtually illiterate, promoted officers who had been convicted of major crimes, and retained policemen who were in their seventies and eighties. The politicians not only regarded local control as a source of political legitimacy. They also turned their clubhouses over to professional gamblers and, in return for a share of the take, protected the gamblers from precinct officers, special squads, and even prosecutors and judges. The politicians not only considered immigrant life-styles an expression of American culture. They also worked with the Torrio, O'Banion, Capone, and other gangs which, in addition to selling beer and running numbers, intimidated businessmen, exploited prostitutes, and infiltrated labor unions. Some politicians realized that these practices placed the machines in a vulnerable position. But operating on the assumption that so long as the ward leader brought out the vote, the organization had no grounds to meddle in his affairs, other politicians could not as a rule do much about it.[32]

The new consensus about policing did not greatly change the structure, personnel, and function of the big-city police by the late 1920s and early 1930s; nor did it completely sever the connection between policing and politics. Most ward bosses had more than enough power to thwart the reform efforts; so did some of the mayors.[33] But the consensus did generate a set of norms to evaluate the policies and practices of the big-city police and, by implication, to judge the integrity and competence of the policemen and politicians responsible for them. It also undermined the traditional assumptions about policing, discredited the policies and practices that derived from them, and in the process placed the ward leaders and their friends in the police departments on the defensive. In other words, this consensus laid the groundwork on which a later generation of reformers would attempt to transform the big-city police. More than the patrol cars, call boxes, and signal systems, and even more than the civil service, special squads, and service pensions, this consensus was the enduring legacy of the first wave of police reform.

6. The Professional Model

On October 19, 1933, Dr. William Jay Schieffelin, Judge Samuel Seabury, and several hundred other notable New Yorkers assembled in Town Hall to pay tribute to the Reverend Charles H. Parkhurst, who had died several weeks before at the age of ninety-one. The meeting was a memorable occasion. It started out as a service for Dr. Parkhurst, the fiery pastor who had led the campaign against the New York City Police Department in the 1890s. But it turned into a rally for Fiorello H. La Guardia, the colorful ex-congressman who had been picked by the reformers to run for mayor on the fusion or anti-Tammany ticket in the first municipal election after the Seabury Committee investigation.[1] The meeting thus marked the passing of the first generation of reformers—which included, in addition to Dr. Parkhurst, Clarence Lexow, Gustav Schwab, John Goff, Theodore Roosevelt, and William Strong—and the arrival of the second generation. It was the second generation that carried on the reform campaign from the early 1930s through the late 1960s.

The second generation of reformers was in some ways more heterogeneous than the first. Bruce Smith, an associate and later director of the Institute of Public Administration and perhaps the nation's preeminent police consultant, was the son of a wealthy New York banker whose Scottish forefathers had settled on Long Island in the seventeenth century. Lewis J. Valentine, who joined the New York police in the early 1900s, rose slowly through the ranks, and on the basis of a well-deserved reputation for integrity was named commissioner in the mid-1930s, was a second-generation Irish-American whose father had owned and lost a small fruit business in the late 1890s. Orlando W. Wilson, who headed the Wichita police in the 1930s and the Chicago force in the 1960s and spent the time between as professor of police administration and dean of the School of Criminology at Berkeley, was the son of a well-to-do Norwegian-American lawyer who had moved his family from South Dakota to California early in the twentieth century. And Herbert T. Jenkins, who joined the Atlanta police in the early 1930s and was named chief in the late 1940s, a post he filled with distinction until his retirement twenty-five years later, was the third genera-tion of his family to go into law enforcement.[2]

Neither Valentine nor Jenkins went to college; nor did James P. Allman, commissioner of the Chicago police in the 1930s and 1940s, Jeremiah O'Connell, chief of police in St. Louis in the 1940s and 1950s, Thomas J. Gibbons, commissioner of the Philadelphia police in the 1950s, or Charles R. Gain, chief of the Oakland police in the 1960s. But Wilson had a bachelor's degree, as did Eliot Ness, an FBI agent who was appointed public safety director of Cleveland in the 1930s, Virgil W. Peterson, another FBI agent who was named operating director of the Chicago Crime Commission in the 1940s, and Quinn Tamm, still another FBI agent who became executive director of the IACP in the 1960s. Smith graduated from law school; so did J. Edgar Hoover, director of the FBI from 1924 to 1972, Franklin M. Kreml, director of the Northwestern University Traffic Institute from 1932 to 1955, William H. Parker, chief of the Los Angeles police in the 1950s and 1960s, and Clarence M. Kelley, an FBI agent who retired to head the Kansas City police but returned in 1973 to succeed Hoover.[3] Patrick V. Murphy, who led the Syracuse, Detroit, and New York City departments, had a master's degree; and A. C. Germann, a Los Angeles police officer who organized a police science department at Long Beach State College, had a doctorate. Hoover, Wilson, Peterson, and a handful of others were awarded honorary degrees too.

But the second generation of reformers was in at least one way

more homogeneous than the first. With a few noteworthy exceptions, among them George Edwards, a prominent lawyer, politician, and judge who left the Michigan Supreme Court to head
the Detroit police force in the early 1960s, its members were
drawn in large part from the law enforcement community. They
had come to that community by diverse paths. Jenkins, Murphy,
and to a lesser degree Parker followed a family tradition that
went back one or more generations; but Valentine joined the
police force because there were no openings in the fire department.[4] Stanley R. Schrotel, chief of police in Cincinnati during
the 1950s and 1960s, got his appointment in the depths of the
Depression; but Jerry V. Wilson, chief of the Washington police
in the 1960s and 1970s, signed up in the aftermath of World War
II. Once in law enforcement, these reformers proceeded along
one of two tracks. A majority, which included Parker, Murphy,
Valentine, Gain, Gibbons, Schrotel, Stephen P. Kennedy,
commissioner of the New York police in the 1950s, and Curtis
Brostron, chief of the St. Louis police a decade later, started as
ordinary patrolmen. But a large minority, which included Ness,
Peterson, Tamm, Kelley, Lear B. Reed, chief of police in Kansas
City during the 1930s and 1940s, and W. Cleon Skousen, chief of
the Salt Lake City police in the 1950s, began as FBI agents.

Most of the reformers worked their way up through the ranks.
Valentine, who was appointed in 1903, was promoted to sergeant
in 1913, lieutenant in 1917, captain in 1926, and deputy chief
inspector in 1928; he was then demoted to captain in 1928,
promoted to chief inspector in 1934, and later that year named
commissioner, a job he held for eleven years.[5] Jenkins, Gibbons,
Parker, Schrotel, and Gain followed similar, though less tortuous,
routes. So did Jerry Wilson, who was appointed in 1949, promoted to sergeant in 1958, lieutenant in 1960, captain in 1961,
inspector in 1964, and deputy chief in 1966, and in 1969 chosen
chief, a post he filled for roughly six years. But a few reformers
moved up by moving around. Before taking charge of the Chicago police, O. W. Wilson pounded the beat in Berkeley, ran the
Fullerton and Wichita police departments, taught at Berkeley
and Harvard, and served as a consultant to more than half a
dozen police forces. Ness and Kelley changed places two or three
times. So did Murphy, a veteran New York policeman who later
served as head of the Syracuse, Detroit, and New York City po-

lice departments, public safety director of Washington, D.C., head of the Law Enforcement Assistance Administration (LEAA), director of research on public order at the Urban Institute, and president of the Police Foundation. But whether the reformers stayed put or moved around, and whether they worked in a police force, the FBI, a research institute, a university, or a foundation, they usually remained within the law enforcement community.

Hence most reformers shared a wide range of organizational affiliations. They belonged not only to the state peace officers associations but also to the IACP, which admitted many members who were not police chiefs or even police officers. Some spoke at its annual conventions, others sat on its standing committees, and a few, including Brostron, Jenkins, Schrotel, and Thomas J. Cahill, chief of the San Francisco police in the 1960s, were elected president of the association. A few attended the meetings of the University of Louisville's Southern Police Institute, Florida State University's Southern Institute for Law Enforcement, and Southern Methodist University's Southwestern Police Institute. Several went to the FBI's National Training Academy, which was set up in the mid-1930s to provide specialized instruction to promising officers, and later joined the National Academy Associates. Others participated in seminars at the Harvard Business School, Operations Research Center of the Massachusetts Institute of Technology, and American Society for the Advancement of Criminology, which O. W. Wilson presided over in the 1940s. Some served as consultants to the President's Commission on Law Enforcement and Administration of Justice, otherwise known as the President's Crime Commission, and the National Advisory Commission on Civil Disorders, commonly known as the President's Riot Commission. One or two even sat on these commissions.

Most reformers also held a common set of underlying assumptions, which were an outgrowth of the Progressive movement. They not only believed that the primary purpose of the police was to provide the best possible service at the lowest possible cost rather than to reward impoverished immigrants whose sole qualification was political loyalty. They also insisted that the police officials were in a better position than the municipal authorities to figure out how to deliver this service. They not only thought that the ward leaders, no matter how large their majorities at the polls, had no authority over the big-city police. They also argued that the mayors and other city-wide officials, aside from choosing chiefs, passing laws, and appropriating funds, had no business interfering in departmental policies and practices. Whether or not they held that the state and municipal authorities should use the criminal sanction to impose the conventional morality on the lower- and lower-middle-class immigrants, they assumed that the police had no choice but to apply it. A single standard of law enforcement was in the reformers' view an essential feature of proper policing. Provided the public and its elected officials honored these assumptions, the reformers were confident that the big-city police could handle their responsibilities.

Hence Dr. Parkhurst's death marked not only the departure of one generation of reformers and the arrival of another but also the end of the first wave of police reform, which was inspired by the Progressive movement, and the beginning of the second, which was dominated by the law enforcement community. This is a vital, if not a rigid, distinction. August Vollmer of Berkeley, Richard Sylvester of Washington, James L. Beavers of Atlanta, William P. Rutledge of Detroit, and other high-level police officials had supported the reform effort before 1930. But the chambers of commerce, ministerial alliances, municipal leagues, and other nonpartisan organizations had led the first wave of reform. Far from abandoning the reform campaign, these groups rendered invaluable and in some cases indispensable financial, political, and moral assistance after 1930. But outside of Chicago and a few other cities where most policemen and politicians felt little or no sympathy for the reform effort, the voluntary associations had a deep-seated reluctance to take a commanding role in the second wave of reform. This transition, in which the leadership of the reform crusade shifted from the Progressive elites to the law enforcement groups, was far from over by the 1930s; but it was well underway and, with hindsight, just about irreversible.

The second generation of reformers was troubled by much the same things as the first, though not necessarily to the same degree or for the same reasons. Although its members were broad-minded about some infractions of the blue laws, they were offended by gambling, prostitution, pornography, and other forms of commercial vice and were appalled by the use and sale of marijuana, heroin, and other so-called dangerous drugs. They were disturbed by the insidious influence of partisan politics, which in their opinion undermined the integrity of the police forces and other parts of the criminal justice system.[6] They were irritated by the incompetence of the welfare bureaus, school boards, and other institutions, which in their judgment increased the responsibility of the police departments and decreased the legitimacy of the public authorities. They were dismayed by the sharp rise of serious crime, particularly of racketeering and extortion in the 1930s and 1940s, of organized crime and juvenile delinquency in the 1940s and 1950s, and of muggings, attacks, and drug abuse in the 1950s and 1960s. Unlike their predecessors, however, these reformers were driven not so much by their distaste for deviant behavior, machine politics, administrative inefficiency, and criminal activity as by their concern about the low status of the big-city police.

An outgrowth of the occupational paranoia of the American police, which was an unanticipated consequence of the first wave of police reform, this concern spread from a handful of police chiefs to the great majority of law enforcement officials after World War I. According to these officials, who aired their opinions in speeches to the IACP conventions, statements in the FBI *Bulletin,* articles in the *Journal of Criminal Law and Criminology,* and remarks to congressional committees, the problem was a result of two unfortunate practices. First, out of a misguided sympathy for criminals and an unwarranted hostility toward policemen, many Americans refused to cooperate with the police, to lend them moral support, to provide them the necessary wherewithal, and otherwise to help them carry out their vital chores. Second, out of a perverted sense of the public interest, the media constantly criticized the police and frequently portrayed the officers as incompetent, corrupt, and lawless buffoons with strong bodies and weak minds.[7] These practices might have been understandable in the late nineteenth and early twentieth centuries, a few law enforcement officials conceded, but in view of the great progress in policing since then, they were no longer defensible.

Most law enforcement officials fell into two major camps. One camp, which included Hoover, Parker, and Peter J. Pitchess, sheriff of Los Angeles County in the 1960s, regarded the antipathy to the police as part of an all-out attack on constituted authority that was inspired by Communists and other left-wing radicals in the 1950s and by militant blacks and dissident students in the 1960s. By subverting the so-called "thin blue line," which as Parker declared time and again stood between civilization and barbarism, these agitators hoped to plunge the country into anarchy. The other camp, which included Jenkins, O. W. Wilson, and Howard R. Leary, commissioner of the Philadelphia police in the 1960s, perceived the antipathy to the police as a sign of a pervasive breakdown of civic consciousness and a symbol of the apathy, as opposed to the animosity, that gripped millions of otherwise ordinary Americans.[8] By ridiculing the police officers, implying that they were so inept it was hardly worthwhile cooperating with them, these citizens tried to excuse their own irresponsibility. But whether the law enforcement officials fell into the first or second camp, most of them agreed that the widespread criticism of the big-city police lowered their status and thereby reduced their effectiveness.

According to most of these officials, the low status of the big-city police was partly a public relations problem. Extremely busy, unduly modest, and perhaps overly reticent, the police had neglected to explain their position to the public, present their viewpoint to the media, and without concealing their blunders, publicize their achievements. They had failed to counter the widespread criticism which downplayed the impressive advances in municipal policing in recent decades and thus cost the officers the understanding, respect, and support of their fellow citizens. As Carl Hansson, chief of the Dallas police in the 1950s, put it, the police had not sold themselves to the community—a singularly inappropriate metaphor under the circumstances. Many chiefs tried to overcome this problem. They persuaded the IACP to set up a public relations committee in the late 1930s, which cultivated the goodwill of newspaper and magazine publishers as well as radio, television, and motion picture producers. They prevailed on many police departments to follow suit after World War II. These departments formed public relations units that gave handouts to reporters and editors, supplied brochures and pamphlets to citizens' groups, sent speakers to public meetings, and otherwise conveyed the organization's point of view to the community.[9]

But as most officials realized, the low status of the big-city police was only partly a public relations problem. Many policemen were incompetent. During the mid-1930s Atlanta patrolmen not only horsed around at roll calls, goosing one another and ignoring their superiors, but also hosted poker games at headquarters for out-of-town officers. Reminiscing about his career on the Los Angeles police force, particularly his assignment to the Central Booking Office in the 1930s, Chief Parker told a reporter that "there were mornings when I was the only sober man in the office." If a few memos written for the Chicago Crime Commission in the 1940s were reliable, many officers left their posts after dark, going home to sleep or out to gamble, and paid the switchboard operators a dollar or two a month to call them if anything unusual took place on their beats. According to the Senate Committee to Investigate Organized Crime in Interstate Commerce, popularly known after its chairman, Estes Kefauver of Tennessee, as the Kefauver Committee, gangsters violated vice laws with impunity in Philadelphia, Miami, New Orleans, and Detroit in the 1950s. According to New York State's Commission on Investigation, which was set up to keep tabs on organized crime, the situation was just as bad in Buffalo in the 1960s.[10]

Many policemen were also corrupt. Late in the 1930s a special investigator reported to the San Francisco district attorney that several officers belonged to a ring that was involved in gambling, prostitution, and other illegal activities. A few years later similar scandals erupted in Philadelphia, where a grand jury indicted dozens of politicians and policemen, and in Detroit, where another grand jury amassed the evidence that sent a former mayor, police chief, and scores of other officials to prison. Things quieted down during World War II. But in the wake of the Kefauver Committee report a citizens commission revealed that in return for regular payoffs many New Orleans policemen were staging fake raids, giving advance warnings, and otherwise protecting local racketeers. Similar scandals broke out in Pittsburgh, Philadelphia, Cleveland, and Washington, D.C., where Major Robert J. Barrett, unable to explain the sources of his income to a Senate committee, stepped down as superintendent of the Metropolitan Police in 1951. The chief investigator of the Emergency Crime Committee found that corruption was commonplace in Chicago in the mid-1950s. The State Commission on Investigation disclosed that corruption was pervasive in Syracuse in the 1960s. The Commission to Investigate Allegations of Police Corruption, commonly known, after its chairman Whitman Knapp, a prominent Wall Street lawyer, as the Knapp Commission, charged that corruption was widespread in New York City in the early 1970s.[11]

Many policemen were lawless too. Early in the 1930s a veteran reporter wrote that many New York City policemen employed the wide range of illegal methods popularly known as the third degree to pry confessions out of uncooperative suspects. Shortly thereafter the Wickersham Commission revealed that the third degree was commonly practiced in most other cities. Late in the 1930s Captain Earle E. Kynette and Lieutenant Roy J. Allen of the Los Angeles Police Department's Special Intelligence Unit were convicted of attempting to murder Harry Raymond, a private investigator for a civic group that had recently mounted an all-out attack on police corruption. The intelligence unit committed a variety of other criminal offenses as well. Early in the 1950s, in the wake of a Senate probe of the District of Columbia police, a grand jury indicted Lieutenant Hialmar H. Carper, chief of the narcotics squad, and his assistant, Sergeant William L. Taylor, for organizing and operating a small drug ring of their own. Although acquitted after a long drawn-out trial, both officers resigned from the department. Early in the 1960s about thirty Denver policemen, the major part of a loosely organized gang of officers assigned to the night shift, were convicted of breaking into stores and restaurants and carrying away the loot in squad cars. Similar crimes rocked the Atlanta and Chicago forces at the same time.[12]

The law enforcement officials reacted to these revelations in different ways. Some defended the officers, insisting that they were the innocent victims of irresponsible publishers trying to boost sales or unscrupulous politicians attempting to impress voters. Others contended that though a few policemen might have given in to temptation, the rest of the department was fundamentally sound, the so-called "rotten apple" theory. Still others conceded that some policemen were venal, but no more so and perhaps even less than many businessmen, labor leaders, politicians, and other citizens. One or two officials even admitted that the recurrent investigations exposed only a small fraction of the skullduggery and malfeasance of the big-city police. But no matter how the law enforcement officials reacted to these revelations, most of them drew the conclusion that so long as even a few policemen were incompetent, corrupt, and lawless, the status of the big-city police would remain low and that so long as their status remained low, they would be hard pressed to do their job. From this conclusion it was only a short step to the position that in order to raise the status of the big-city police and increase their effectiveness, a campaign had to be mounted to change the structure, personnel, and function· of the police forces in ways that would put an end to these abuses.

To lay the groundwork for the campaign, the reformers had to explain why, after four or more decades of investigations, reorganizations, and other changes, so many policemen were still incompetent, corrupt, and lawless. To this end they spoke at state and national peace officers' conventions, worked with city and state crime commissions, testified before grand juries and legislative committees, and lectured at schools of criminology and departments of police science. Out of these efforts came a host of studies, surveys, reports, essays, articles, speeches, pamphlets, and textbooks which presented a fairly coherent diagnosis of the nation's police problems. According to the reformers the incompetence, corruption, and lawlessness of the big-city police were only partly a function of political interference in departmental policies. It was also a function of the long-standing tradition of American policing and, though most reformers were hesitant to say so explicitly, the unanticipated consequences of the first wave of police reform. This diagnosis was worked out by Vollmer in the 1920s and 1930s. But not until O. W. Wilson and Vollmer's other disciples refined and popularized it after World War II did it emerge as the conventional wisdom of the reform movement.[13]

According to the reform diagnosis, most police departments violated the fundamental rules of sound organization.[14] Notwithstanding the growing consensus that the police were an administrative body and should be strictly divorced from partisan politics, the ward bosses still interfered in departmental policies and practices. They still exerted pressure not only on the chiefs but also on the precinct captains and squad commanders and, through them, on the patrolmen, detectives, and other specialists. But as the reformers admitted, the ward leaders could not be blamed for all the structural defects of the big-city police. It was not their fault that few chiefs showed much interest in planning and research and that the proliferation of special squads blurred the division of responsibility among the precincts, squads, and other units. Nor was it their fault that the superior officers, highly protective of their own bailiwicks, provided chiefs with extraneous and often unreliable information and that the multiplication of high-level officers who reported directly to the chiefs tangled the chain of command. Although most departments had made some progress in the 1920s, they still had a long way to go.

Not much could be expected of the departments, the reformers pointed out. By virtue of the civil service, the rank-and-file were better protected after 1930 than before, but they were not so well protected that they were ready to follow orders if it meant antagonizing the ward leaders and precinct captains. The commanding officers were also less vulnerable than in the past, but they were vulnerable enough to be reluctant to press charges against well-connected policemen save in cases of gross misconduct. In the absence of systematic planning and research, most chiefs were hard put to spell out the goals of the force; and in light of the hazy division of responsibility among the precincts, squads, and other units, they were hard pressed to say which of them were supposed to do what. In the absence of reliable sources of information, most chiefs had no way of finding out whether their men were on the job; and in view of the tangled chain of command, they were in a poor position to figure out who, if anyone, to hold accountable. Small wonder that when asked about the charges of incompetence, corruption, and lawlessness, most chiefs replied either that they did not know anything about it or, if they did, that they could not have done much about it.

To make matters worse, the reformers charged, many police officers lacked the necessary physical, mental, and moral qualifications. Notwithstanding the growing awareness that the police were supposed to supply the best possible service at the lowest possible cost, most ward leaders still regarded the force as a prime source of soft jobs for their constituents. They still brought pressure on the mayors, city councilmen, civil service commissioners, police administrators, and other municipal officials who had a say over the appointment, promotion, and discipline of the rank-and-file. But as the reformers acknowledged, the personnel problems of the big-city police could not be traced exclusively to the ward bosses. Political interference was only one of many reasons that the municipal authorities had not yet raised the salaries and prestige of policing to levels that would have attracted what the reformers regarded as qualified candidates. Nor was political interference the only reason that the police departments had not yet set up decent training facilities, designed promotional standards related to on-the-job performance, and devised swift and just disciplinary proceedings. Many qualified recruits had joined the police during the 1930s, but not enough to compensate for several decades of political favoritism.

Not much could be expected of the rank-and-file, the reformers insisted. Though better qualified than their predecessors, many officers were overage and overweight; some had little education and less intelligence; and a few had criminal records of one sort or another. Most officers owed their primary allegiance not to the departments but to the machines which had gotten them their jobs and, providing they carried out the organization's orders, would sponsor them for promotions and defend them against their superiors. With few exceptions most officers considered policing not so much a vocation as a livelihood and, when compared with the opportunities available in the urban economy to men of their means, skills, and connections, an attractive livelihood at that. From the job they received a fair salary and, if promoted to sergeant, lieutenant, or captain, a good salary and, providing they stayed out of trouble for twenty or twenty-five years, a nice pension. Little wonder that in the absence of strict supervision, rigorous discipline, and other hallmarks of centralized authority so many recruits turned into incompetent, corrupt, and lawless officers.

As if all this were not enough, the reformers contended, most police forces neglected their principal responsibility. Notwithstanding the growing realization that the police were first and foremost a crime prevention bureau, the local politicians still pressed the departments to operate ambulances, manage jails, and assign special details to private companies and public agencies. They also encouraged the departments to employ police officers in all sorts of clerical, secretarial, technical, and other semi-skilled and unskilled positions which could have been filled just as effectively and far less expensively by nonpolice personnel. But as the reformers conceded, the local politicians could not be blamed for all the functional difficulties of the big-city police. It was not their fault that the criminologists had not yet come up with a theory of crime prevention that rested on anything more substantial than dubious assumptions and antiquated prejudices. Nor was it their fault that most departments compiled criminal statistics in so careless and capricious a manner that criminal activity could not be compared from one precinct to another, one city to the next, and one year to another. Although many big-city departments had made some headway in the 1920s, they still left a good deal to be desired.

Not much could be expected of the departments, the reformers argued. With so many officers operating ambulances, managing jails, watching over courthouses, railway depots, theaters, and amusement parks, and working as typists, clerks, telephone operators, and lab technicians, the remaining policemen were overwhelmed by the crime problem. True, most departments expanded a great deal after World War I, but this expansion barely compensated for the manpower lost as a result of the eight-hour day, six-day week, two-week vacation, and other improvements in working conditions. Following the conventional wisdom of orthodox criminology, most police departments set up juvenile squads, formed boys clubs, organized employment bureaus, sponsored police athletic leagues, and engaged in other ventures whose connection to crime prevention was tenuous. Lacking accurate criminal statistics that could be compared from precinct to precinct, city to city, and year to year, most departments had no way of telling whether or to what degree these ventures reduced criminal activity. No wonder that in the face of intense pressure to do something about the rising crime rates many policemen contended that they had no alternative but to resort to the third degree.

The reformers' diagnosis was a noteworthy political achievement. It presented an explanation for the incompetence, corruption, and lawlessness of the big-city police that not only satisfied the law enforcement community but also affirmed the broad assumptions, if not necessarily the narrow conclusions, of the first generation of reformers. This diagnosis was consistent with the notions that public service was not a means of social mobility, local control was not a source of political legitimacy, and immigrant life-styles were not an expression of American culture. It was also consistent with the belief that the disparities between the principles and practices of big-city policing were a manifestation of political interference in departmental policies. Hence the reform diagnosis profoundly impressed the many upper-middle- and upper-class Americans who adhered to the Progressive ideology long after the Progressive movement was over. To complete the ideological groundwork for the upcoming campaign, however, the reformers were obliged to come up not only with a diagnosis of the problem but also with a model of policing that would inspire the efforts to transform the departments in the years ahead.

The second generation of reformers was very much drawn to the military analogy, which had guided the first wave of police reform. To William P. Capes, executive secretary of the New York State Conference of Mayors, the officers were "front line troops"; to Schrotel, chief of the Cincinnati police, each patrolman was a "field soldier"; and to Edmund L. McNamara, commissioner of the Boston police, the patrol force was the "infantry." Hoover and Parker believed that criminals were enemies of society; so did Earl Warren, district attorney of Alameda County, Donald S. Leonard, captain of the Michigan State Police, and Paul L. Kirk, professor of criminalistics at the University of California.[15] The military analogy made so strong an impression that when the fear of crime spread thoughout the nation and turned into an explosive political issue in the mid-1960s, President Lyndon B. Johnson pledged his administration to an all-out "war on crime," a war that his successor promised to carry on with even more vigor. Yet under the influence of Vollmer, Rutledge, and several other prominent figures who were less than enthusiastic about the military analogy, the reformers were also very much attracted by a professional model.

Conceived in a rudimentary way by Sylvester, superintendent of the Washington, D.C., police and president of the IACP in the early years of the twentieth century, the professional model generated little enthusiasm before 1920. But as developed by Vollmer, Rutledge, and their colleagues it struck so responsive a chord that the IACP set up a Committee on Professionalization of Police Service in the late 1930s. This committee, chaired by Chief J. A. Greening, Vollmer's successor in Berkeley, issued a report that more or less established the professional model as the conventional wisdom of the association.[16] O. W. Wilson and Vollmer's other protégés later spread the gospel of professionalism throughout the law enforcement community. They wrote about it in articles for the FBI *Bulletin,* IACP *Yearbook, Journal of Criminal Law and Criminology,* and other semischolarly periodicals. They talked about it at meetings of the Southern Police Institute, Southern Institute for Law Enforcement, Southwestern Police Institute, and other quasi-academic outfits. They made such an impression that even the National (later International) Conference of Police Associations (ICPA), which was founded by a dozen rank-and-file organizations in the early 1950s, formed a Committee on Professionalization.[17] As a result of these efforts the professional model largely, though not completely, superseded the military analogy after World War II.

According to this model, policemen were professionals and policing was a profession. Like doctors, lawyers, teachers, and engineers, policemen were expected to meet high admission standards, undergo extensive training, serve their clients, devote themselves to the public interest, subscribe to a code of ethics, and possess a wide range of extraordinary skills. As Joseph J. Casper, assistant director of the FBI told the IACP in 1964, the country was rapidly approaching a point where each police officer would need "the mind of a law professor, the agility of a professional athlete, the patience and restraint of a Sunday School superintendent, and the technical ability of a graduate engineer."[18] Like the other professions, policing had a specialized body of knowledge, known as criminology, a nationwide professional organization, the IACP, and a number of institutions of higher learning, known as departments of police science and schools of criminology. These institutions were vital, E. Wilson Purdy, superintendent of the Pennsylvania State Police, said to the Southern Institute for Law Enforcement in 1963, because policing is "as complicated, exacting, and technical as almost any profession today." All things considered, Tamm declared in the mid-1960's, "professionalization has indeed come to law enforcement."[19]

Not all the reformers were so sure. Harry Caldwell, assistant director of training and personnel of the Houston Police Department, insisted that despite recent progress toward professionalism the big-city police still had "a long way to go." Chief W. D. Booth of Clearwater, Florida, agreed with him. So did Paul H. Ashenhust, a Dallas police. inspector and an associate editor of the *Texas Police Journal,* and Gene S. Muehleisen, a Los Angeles police officer and later an associate director of the President's Crime Commission. Peterson, operating director of the Chicago Crime Commission, blamed this lag on partisan interference in departmental affairs. Don S. Kooken, a former treasury agent and later an assistant professor of police administration at Indiana University, attributed it to the power of the rank-and-file unions. Ed Davis, head of the Los Angeles Fire and Police Protective League and later chief of the Los Angeles police, traced the lag to the absence of statewide standards. But virtually all the reformers were certain that professionalism was the appropriate model on which to base the ongoing campaign and that the big-city departments were on the way to reaching it. As Chief Booth told an audience of the Southern Institute for Law Enforcement in the mid-1960s, anyone who does not already recognize the need for professionalization "might as well leave now."[20]

In view of the early history of police reform, it is hard to tell why the second generation of reformers chose a professional model instead of the military analogy. True, the military analogy left much to be desired. As Murphy testified to the National Commission on the Causes and Prevention of Violence, unofficially called the Violence Commission, policemen were not soldiers, policing was not warfare, and urban America was not a battleground.[21] But as William J. Gaynor, Raymond B. Fosdick, and one or two other skeptics had already pointed out, the military analogy left as much to be desired before 1930, and the first generation of reformers had adopted it just the same. What is more, the professional model was not much of an improvement over the military analogy. According to social scientists, policemen did not qualify as professionals. And according to the nationwide surveys of occupational prestige conducted after World War II, most laymen did not regard policing as a profession either.[22] The reformers might have had reason to compare police officers with librarians, nurses, journalists, social workers, and other paraprofessionals but not with doctors, lawyers, architects, and engineers.

The second generation of reformers probably chose a professional model on the grounds that it would somehow raise the status of the big-city police. These grounds were by no means unrealistic. Not only were the professions more prestigious and, with the exceptions of teaching and the clergy, more remunerative than most vocations; but they also were otherwise ordinary occupations whose practitioners had prevailed on the public to accord them special recognition. Doctors, lawyers, and engineers had done so in the middle and late nineteenth century; professors had followed suit not long after. The lesson was not lost on other groups. By the early twentieth century librarians, nurses, planners, journalists, and social workers asserted their claims to professional status. A few decades later firemen, salesmen, realtors, and beauticians insisted that they too were professionals. Indeed by the mid-1960s sociologists were calling attention to the trend toward "the professionalization of everyone."[23] If these groups could claim to be professionals and thereby acquire the prestige that comes with it, the reformers reasoned, so could the police. The obstacles were formidable, but no more so for the police than for many other groups demanding professional recognition.

Apart from providing a plausible concept of the big-city police and completing the ideological groundwork for the upcoming campaign, the professional model served the reformers well in other ways. The model was so vague, its meaning susceptible to so many different interpretations, that it united many law enforcement figures who were divided on just about everything else. Hoover was a staunch advocate of professionalism; so was Ramsey Clark, attorney general during the Johnson administration, who sharply disagreed with Hoover on many other issues. Parker was committed to professionalism; so was Jenkins, chief of the Atlanta police and later president of the IACP, who strongly objected to Parker's ideas about the function of the police in a democratic society. The leaders of the IACP supported the proposals to professionalize the police; so did the leaders of the ICPA, who headed the rank-and-file associations that many chiefs viewed as the main obstacle to professionalization. Hence the professional model drew together a generation of reformers who were otherwise so split along ideological and organizational lines that they would probably have found it hard to work as a group for long.

What is more, the model ensured this generation of reformers the backing of many upper-middle- and upper-class Americans outside the law enforcement community who were unalterably opposed to political interference in departmental matters. If policemen were professionals, they should be as insulated from political pressure as doctors, lawyers, professors, and engineers. They should be guided exclusively by professional, as opposed to political, considerations in setting standards, evaluating personnel, disciplining misfits, and otherwise managing their departments. If policing was a profession, the officers should not be accountable to elected officials, not even to the degree that the soldiers, to whom the previous generation of reformers had compared them, were answerable to civilian authorities. Like doctors, lawyers, teachers, and engineers, the officers should be accountable solely to their colleagues. In other words, the professional model not only tied the second generation of reformers together but also linked it to the first generation. Not without reason were the reformers optimistic that they could stamp out the incompetence, corruption, and lawlessness of the big-city police and thereby raise their status if they could persuade their fellow citizens to grant them professional recognition.

The reformers realized that they could not carry the professional model too far without calling for changes in policing that were inconceivable at the time. They could not argue that the police should operate in a collegial fashion without pressing the departments to dismantle the elaborate hierarchy created in the late nineteenth century and, in line with the military analogy, reinforced by the first wave of police reform. They could not demand that the recruits should have a college or graduate degree without urging the authorities to raise the salaries and benefits of police officers to levels their fellow citizens would have viewed as altogether unwarranted. And they could not insist that the police should reserve the right to choose their "clients" without asking the departments to abdicate many responsibilities taken on in the late nineteenth century and fully accepted by the early twentieth. Provided the professional model was not carried too far, however, most reformers believed that it could serve as a source of the criteria by which to formulate and evaluate proposals for changing the structure, personnel, and functions of the big-city police.

Or to put it more succinctly, the model could serve as the basis of their prescription for police reform.

Applying the professional model to the big-city police, the reformers arrived at three distinct yet closely related recommendations, which incorporated and extended the Progressive prescription for police reform.[24] The first recommendation was that the departments had to overcome the obstacles that had stymied their attempts to gain the same degree of autonomy as medicine, law, and the other professions. Hence the reformers called on the authorities to increase the chiefs' power, enhance their tenure, insulate them from partisan pressures, and otherwise strengthen their position vis-à-vis ward and even city-wide politicians. Close down as many additional precincts as possible, they proposed, and transfer as many additional activities as possible from ordinary patrolmen attached to the precincts to special squads assigned to headquarters. In line with contemporary organizational theory, the reformers urged the departments to set up planning and research units, reorganize the force along functional instead of territorial lines, and clarify the division of responsibility among the precincts, squads, and other units. Form special inspectional units to keep a close watch over day-to-day operations, they suggested, and untangle the chain of command by reducing the number of officials who reported directly to the chiefs.

These changes would enhance the autonomy of the big-city police, the reformers reasoned. Protected against arbitrary dismissal and insulated from partisan pressures, the chiefs would make departmental decisions on professional rather than political grounds. Once the precincts were closed down and the long-term connection between the precincts and wards was severed, the captains would be insulated from the ward bosses. So would the commanders, whose power would increase as one function after another was shifted from ordinary patrolmen to special squads. As a result the ward bosses would lose their power over the rank-and-file. Once the departments were restructured according to contemporary organizational theory, the chiefs would be able to spell out the goals of the force, specify which outfits were responsible for what chores, find out which of their officers were off the job, and figure out who, if anyone, to hold accountable. No longer could the chiefs defend themselves against revelations of incompetence, corruption, and lawlessness on the grounds that they did not know anything about it or, if they did, that they could not have done much about it. The big-city police would hereafter have a good deal of autonomy; but by the same token they would have no one else to blame for their shortcomings.

The second recommendation was that the departments had to surmount the hurdles which had thwarted their plans to bring the rank-and-file up to the same level as architects, professors, and other professionals. Thus the reformers pressed the authorities not only to accept only high school or college graduates, subject them to a thorough psychiatric screening, and otherwise tighten the physical, mental, and moral requirements, but also to raise salaries, increase pensions, improve working conditions, abolish residency requirements, and permit lateral entry. The reformers further encouraged the departments to expand existing training programs for recruits and develop in-service training facilities for veterans; to forbid the rank-and-file to solicit rewards, take part-time jobs, join labor unions, and engage in other activities that were inconsistent with professional status; and to devise promotional procedures that inhibited political interference, emphasized on-the-job performance, increased the chief's discretion, and reduced the number of years an officer had to serve at one rank to be eligible for advancement to another. Lastly, the reformers implored the authorities to shift the disciplinary proceedings from the city councils, police commissions, and civil service boards to the police chiefs, departmental trial boards, or other internal bodies.

These policies would raise the caliber of the big-city police, the reformers claimed. By tightening the entrance requirements and increasing the material inducements, the departments would discourage unqualified applicants and attract capable recruits. The recruits would owe their loyalty to the forces as opposed to the machines. By augmenting the recruit and in-service training programs, the departments would also convert the recruits into competent officers and keep them abreast of technological and other changes in law enforcement. The officers would soon come to regard policing as a vocation as well as a livelihood. Fully aware that the commanders expected them to perform as professionals and would judge them on the basis of their performance, the policemen would enthusiastically carry out departmental orders. After a while they would develop a deep commitment not only to the force but also to the profession. Their enthusiasm would be

reinforced by the knowledge that the chiefs would summarily remove any and all incompetent, corrupt, and lawless officers. No
longer could they count on influential politicians to intervene on
their behalf. From now on the police officers would be less inclined to break the rules; but when they did, they would be more
likely to be dismissed from the force.

The third recommendation was that the departments had to
deal with the constraints which had handicapped their efforts to
develop the same degree of proficiency as engineering, accounting, and the other professions. Hence the reformers suggested
that the authorities should relieve the police of the responsibility
to run ambulances, operate lockups, take censuses, provide special details for private concerns and public agencies, and carry out
other tasks remotely if at all related to crime prevention. The departments should not only employ civilians in all sorts of clerical,
secretarial, technical, and other positions currently filled by policemen but also curtail foot patrols, replace two-man with one-
man squad cars, and deploy the uniformed force according to
scientific formulas. Possibly in conjunction with sociologists,
psychologists, criminologists, and other experts on deviance and
delinquency, the profession should work out a theory of crime
prevention that rested on something more substantial than dubious assumptions and antiquated prejudices. The departments
should also compile and report criminal statistics in a more careful and less capricious style so that police administrators and
ordinary citizens could compare criminal activity from one precinct to another, one city to the next, and one year to another.

These changes would increase the proficiency of the big-city
police, the reformers argued. Once the so-called nonpolice functions were shifted from the police forces to other municipal agencies and enough civilians were employed to replace patrolmen in
unskilled and semiskilled positions, the departments could
strengthen the uniformed and plainclothes divisions. By abolishing or curtailing foot patrols, two-man squad cars, and unscien-
tific deployment strategies, they could raise the productivity of
the rank-and-file. Once the profession came up with a sound theory of crime prevention, the departments would have a criterion
by which to judge whether their juvenile units, employment bureaus, boys clubs, and other special squads were a worthwhile investment of resources. By reporting accurate criminal statistics

and deriving from them reliable performance measures, they would give police administrators and interested citizens a means of figuring out whether and, if so, to what degree police practices reduced criminal activity. The big-city police would henceforth have no excuse to resort to the third degree and other unprofessional tactics to curb crime.

The reformers' prescription was an impressive political accomplishment. It offered a set of recommendations to put an end to the incompetence, corruption, and lawlessness of the big-city police that was not only satisfactory to the law enforcement community but also consistent with the general proposals, if not necessarily the specific details, of the first generation of reformers. This prescription incorporated the Progressive proposals to centralize the structure, upgrade the personnel, and narrow the function of the big-city police. By following the professional model, it also reinforced the Progressive conviction that political influence was out of place in a well-organized police system. Hence this prescription greatly impressed the many upper-middle- and upper-class Americans who subscribed to the Progressive ideology long after the Progressive movement was over. But the projected changes in the structure, personnel, and function of the big-city police were bound to have an uneven impact on the well-being of urban America's social classes and ethnic groups. For this reason, if for no other, a full-scale struggle over police reform was virtually inevitable in the second third of the twentieth century.

The second generation of reformers was well prepared for this struggle. Although they had little money of their own, they had access to a host of extremely affluent institutions which had backed the first wave of police reform and now supported the second. Chief among these institutions were the philanthropic foundations. The Laura Spelman Rockefeller Memorial financed the IACP committee that devised the system of uniform crime reports in the late 1920s. Several years later another offshoot of the Rockefeller fortune, the Spelman Fund, gave the International City Managers' Association the funds to prepare and publish *Municipal Police Administration,* one of the two or three most influential texts of the reform movement. The Carnegie Corporation and the Rockefeller Foundation put up the money to launch the Southern Police Institute in the early 1950s. The Ford

Foundation not only made large grants to the IACP to devise professional standards and create a National Registry and Testing Service in the mid-1960s but also set up an independent Police Foundation in 1970 and gave it $30 million to encourage innovations in policing. Seventy-five years after the New York Chamber of Commerce had financed the Lexow Committee probe, the Field Foundation, Stern Fund, New World Foundation, J. M. Kaplan Fund, and half a dozen other philanthropic outfits underwrote the Knapp Commission investigation.[25]

With some exceptions — among them Bruce Smith, who came from a prominent family, and J. Edgar Hoover, who grew into an authentic folk hero — most reformers had little personal influence. But as leaders of the law enforcement community, they had a good deal of political influence. Congressional committees invited them to testify on crime control, drug addiction, and public safety; so did state legislatures, city councils, and presidential commissions. Civic groups, commercial organizations, and bar associations asked them to speak at dinners and conventions; prestigious universities called on them to join seminars and help on research projects. President Johnson appointed Chiefs Cahill and Jenkins to his crime and riot commissions, respectively. Hoover, Parker, Murphy, and Kelley took advantage of these opportunities to proclaim the virtues of professionalism. So did Tamm, executive director of the IACP, whose membership rose from several hundred to several thousand and whose budget grew from a few thousand to several hundred thousand dollars after World War II.[26] So did Roy C. McLaren, Nelson A. Watson, and William H. Franey, who served under Tamm as chiefs of the association's field operations, professional standards, and highway safety divisions, respectively.

In addition to the philanthropic foundations, the reformers could count on the support of the newspapers, universities, and research institutes. The Brooklyn *Eagle* exposed the ties between local bookies and police officers, which drove the Kings County district attorney to conduct a full-scale investigation in the early 1950s. Subsequently the New Orleans *Item,* the Baltimore *Sun,* and the New York *Times* uncovered evidence of official malfeasance, which forced the municipal and state authorities to launch a rash of other inquiries.[27] The universities were so impressed by the reform campaign that between 1930 and 1970 they set up roughly two hundred associates, bachelors, masters, and doctoral programs in police science, criminology, and law enforcement. Combined with numerous research projects, these degree programs strengthened the reformers' case for professional recognition. In the meantime the Institute of Public Administration, Public Service Administration, National Municipal League, and local and state bureaus of governmental research turned out a barrage of studies and reports on the big-city police. Filled with organizational charts, statistical tables, and scientific jargon, these documents covered the reform ideology with a veneer of pseudoscholarly objectivity.[28]

The reformers could even count on the backing of many state and federal bureaus which objected to the current practices of the big-city police on political, ideological, and professional grounds. The State Commission of Investigation carried out a far-reaching inquiry in Buffalo in the late 1950s; the state's attorney uncovered a front-page scandal in Chicago in the early 1960s; and grand juries found widespread incompetence and corruption in Philadelphia in the late 1930s, in Detroit in the early 1940s, and in New York City in the early 1950s. The state legislatures also imposed uniform standards for recruitment and training in some cities, abolished the residency requirements in others, and otherwise implemented the reform proposals in still others. The Kefauver Committee exposed the close connections between local racketeers and crooked officers. The United States Postal Service, Federal Bureau of Narcotics and Dangerous Drugs, Internal Revenue Service, Department of Justice, and Law Enforcement Assistance Administration helped out the Knapp Commission. And the President's Crime Commission placed the prestige of the presidency behind the campaign for police reform.[29]

The reformers could not expect much support from the patrolmen because most of them opposed the reform effort. But they could count on the backing of a small but rapidly growing, fairly articulate, and as the years passed, extremely influential segment of the rank-and-file. Little is known about these officers. As Arthur Niederhoffer, a one-time New York City policeman and later professor at the John Jay College of Criminal Justice, has argued, a few may have been drawn from the ranks of the college graduates who had hoped to enter law, accounting, or business but in the wake of the Depression had joined the police instead.[30]

Of the rest it is possible to say only that they were much more likely than their fellow officers to have come from middle-class backgrounds and to work in Cincinnati, Los Angeles, and other cities where Progressivism had made a good deal of headway in the first third of the twentieth century. These officers were also set apart from their fellow policemen by their organizational affiliations. Some belonged to the Peace Officers Research Association of California and the Association for Professional Law Enforcement, both of which were rank-and-file groups committed to police reform.[31] A few also served on the professionalization committee of the ICPA.

The segment of the rank-and-file which backed the reform campaign did so for two major reasons other than their expectations that it would raise salaries, improve working conditions, increase pensions, and otherwise enhance the policeman's lot. For one thing, some officers were troubled by the low status of the big-city police. They were outraged that, with the exception of Sergeant Joe Friday and his partner Detective Frank Smith, the incorruptible and unflappable heroes of the television series *Dragnet,* most policemen were still depicted by the media as strong-bodied and weak-minded clods. They were tired of defending their buddies against charges of incompetence, corruption, and lawlessness and then apologizing to friends and neighbors when another round of investigations or another slew of indictments substantiated these charges. Convinced that the police rendered a more valuable service than many more prestigious occupations, they were infuriated that so many Americans, above all so many ordinary law-abiding Americans, treated them with little respect and even less deference.[32] These officers responded favorably to the reform movement because it not only attempted to enhance the status of the big-city police and the self-esteem of the rank-and-file but also aspired to transform policing into a profession and policemen into professionals.

For another thing, some officers were annoyed by the persistent meddling of the ward politicians. Viewing policing as a vocation rather than a sinecure, they could not accept a system that drove the rank-and-file to neglect their duties and violate their oaths or which forced them to man special details, oversee local elections, and carry out all sorts of other functions which might please the district leaders but would not reduce the level of criminal activity.

Dedicated to the force instead of the machine, these officers could not tolerate a system wherein the rank-and-file were rewarded for anything but their performance and punished by anyone save their peers or were compelled to find themselves a "rabbi," a "hook," or another influential outsider to intercede on their behalf whenever they were put up for a promotion or brought up on charges. To put it bluntly, these officers could not go along with a system that demeaned their partners and demoralized their departments.[33] They responded favorably to the reform movement because it not only proposed to separate policing and politics but also planned to transform the big-city police into autonomous bureaucracies.

The backing of even a small segment of the rank-and-file was vital to the reformers. To begin with, it protected the reform campaign against charges of elitism. This protection was critical because the reformers were for the most part drawn from the upper echelons of the law enforcement community, and though they were unwilling to admit it, their prescription was elitist. If the reform proposals were carried out—if, in other words, the police force were forbidden to take outside jobs, accept rewards from citizens, and reside in the suburbs—the burdens would fall mainly on the patrolmen and not their superiors. Moreover, the support of even a few officers weakened the opposition of many other officers. This support was crucial because many policemen were prepared to fight the reform recommendations in the state legislatures, city councils, and local courts. If these recommendations were adopted over the objections of the rank-and-file, some officers were even ready to implement them in a way that would undermine and in the end probably destroy the reform movement. By persuading a segment of the rank-and-file to back the general aspirations of their campaign, if not all their specific proposals, the reformers rounded out the formidable coalition that would carry on the struggle for control of the big-city police in the years ahead.

7. The Second Wave of Reform

Tammany Hall mounted a counterattack shortly after the Seabury Committee started its probe in 1930. The local politicians denounced Seabury and intimidated his assistants; the city's corporation counsel refused to pay the salaries of the committee's lawyers; and in an attempt to find out where the investigation was heading, a resourceful underling infiltrated the staff in the guise of a process server. Branding the inquiry a "criminal waste of public funds," the Democrats opposed a bill to extend the committee's mandate and, when the Republican-dominated state legislature passed the bill, pressed Governor Franklin D. Roosevelt, who needed Tammany's support to win the presidential nomination in 1932, to veto it. In the meantime Commissioner Edward P. Mulrooney complained that the probe was demoralizing the force; several policemen refused to answer the committee's questions; and an important witness was strangled to death on the eve of an appointment with the committee's lawyers.[1] The political machines or the remnants thereof employed similar tactics to head off official investigations in Philadelphia, San Francisco, and Los Angeles. Apparently they would go to almost any lengths to retain control of the big-city police.

But there was little reason to believe that they would succeed. Some machines were well on the wane by 1930. The Minneapolis organization fell apart early in the century after a grand jury in-

dicted Albert A. Ames; and the San Francisco machine broke
down a few years later after Abraham Ruef pleaded guilty to a
charge of extortion. The Los Angeles machine never recovered
from the Progressive takeover in the early 1910s; and the Cincinnati organization, which had once thrived under the leadership
of George B. Cox, collapsed after the Progressives revised the city
charter in the mid-1920s. Other machines started to crumble
after 1930. The Pendergast machine lost much of its power in
Kansas City after Tom Pendergast pleaded guilty to two counts of
income tax evasion in the late 1930s. Despite efforts by Carmine
DeSapio and his cronies, Tammany Hall never rebounded from
the La Guardia administration, which governed New York from
the early 1930s to the mid-1940s. The Republican organization,
which had ruled Philadelphia since the late nineteenth century,
was routed by the Democratic party in the early 1950s.[2] By the
1960s the machines were able to deliver the electoral majorities
that had heretofore protected them from the reformers only in
Chicago, where Mayor Richard J. Daley was in charge, and a
handful of other cities.

Nor were the machines able to generate the political pressure
that had hitherto forced the district attorneys, municipal judges,
and other public officials to sidetrack and otherwise stymie the
reform movement. The Philadelphia organization could not prevent Judge Curtis Bok from authorizing a grand jury to investigate the connections between politics, policing, and racketeering
in the late 1930s. Nor could Tammany Hall dissuade District
Attorney Miles McDonald from convening a grand jury to inquire
into accusations that the police were protecting bookies in the
early 1950s. The Chicago organization could not stop State's
Attorney Benjamin S. Adamowski from ordering raids on the
homes of eight officers who belonged to a burglary ring in the
early 1960s.[3] The machines ran into similar trouble wherever the
Progressives or their successors had prevailed on the authorities to
transfer control over the district attorneys, municipal judges, and
other public officials from ward clubs to city and state agencies,
which were ordinarily outside the natural orbit of the local politicians.

The machines were also unable to count on the lower- and
lower-middle-class newcomers whose loyalty had helped them
withstand the reform crusade in the past. After World War II

many second-generation newcomers moved up into the middle and upper middle classes and, as the emergence of reform clubs in New York and other cities revealed, adopted their notions of good government. Some of these newcomers even left the cities for the suburbs, where they battled over property taxes, school budgets, and zoning appeals or dropped out of politics entirely. In their place came millions of blacks and, in a few cities, Mexicans and Puerto Ricans who were not part of the political machines and did not trust the Irish, Italians, and other ethnic groups that ran them. The machines were hard pressed to win the support of the new minorities because the civil service and other Progressive reforms had reduced the number of jobs, contracts, and other favors at their disposal.[4] To make things worse for the machines, many blacks, Mexicans, and Puerto Ricans grew extremely concerned about the increase in violent crime in the 1960s. Although these groups did not share the reformers' worries about the status of the big-city police or their anxieties about the integrity of municipal government, they responded favorably to the reformers' pledges to stamp out street crime.

The machines could expect some support from the many officers who were related to the party leaders, tied to the ward organizations, and otherwise committed to the status quo. But they could not count on much sympathy from the rest of the officers. To be sure, the rank-and-file were not enthusiastic about the reform movement. They were annoyed by the frequent investigations which in their view maligned the police departments and subjected the police officers to all sorts of violations of their civil liberties. They were skeptical of the reform aspirations which in their eyes were designed not so much to increase the autonomy of the policemen vis-à-vis the politicians as to strengthen the position of the chiefs vis-à-vis the patrolmen. And they were dismayed by the reform proposals to undermine the civil service, downgrade the importance of seniority, destroy the rank-and-file associations, and change the departments in other ways that seriously threatened their vital interests.[5] In other words, most officers objected to the reform campaign not because they were content with the low status of the big-city police but because they were reluctant to pay so high a price to raise it.

But neither were the rank-and-file enthusiastic about the political machine. They were pretty much fed up with their subservience to the ward bosses, though not for the same reasons as the small group of policemen who supported the reform movement. Most policemen were prepared to go along with the incompetence, corruption, and lawlessness that were an outgrowth of political interference in departmental affairs. But they were unwilling to put up with the deep-seated insecurity that was another outgrowth of political interference. This insecurity, which was exacerbated by the purges that hit the Kansas City police in the 1930s and the Los Angeles police a decade later, was offensive to the long-term veterans.[6] To the younger officers, who had grown up during the Depression, fought in World War II, and went into policing because it promised a steady job, a modest salary, and a decent pension, this insecurity was outrageous. So far as these officers were concerned, the postwar machines were a menace. They were strong enough to influence the department's deliberations, but not to dictate its decisions, and powerful enough to intimidate the rank-and-file, but not to protect them from the reformers.

By the 1940s and the 1950s most police officers realized that the reformers and the machines were ready to sacrifice the rank-and-file's interests for their own purposes and that, to defend these interests, they would have to play the one against the other. Hence in Boston the rank-and-file joined forces with several politicians to block a proposal to cut the number of precincts from seventeen to twelve, a proposal that had been put forth in a survey of the force by Bruce Smith in the late 1940s. In Chicago the rank-and-file worked with the Democratic organization to cripple the Emergency Crime Committee, which was set up by the city council in the mid-1950s to inquire into allegations that policemen and politicians were protecting racketeering in the Windy City. But the rank-and-file lined up with the reformers in Chicago to prevent the Democratic machine from bypassing the civil service rules in the 1950s, even though most policemen had opposed the effort to put the force under these rules sixty years earlier. The rank-and-file also labored with the reformers in New York to persuade the state legislators to waive the residency requirements for police officers in the 1960s, even though most policemen had fought to maintain these requirements a few decades before.[7]

During the 1930s and 1940s, and in some cities even later, the machines did not need the support of the rank-and-file, which was not worth much anyway, to deflect the reform attack. But the situation changed shortly after. Many ward organizations, which had held their own in the first third of the twentieth century, fell apart in the second third, and by the 1960s they were a force to be reckoned with in only a handful of big cities. A few influential politicians, who were aware of the many administrations that had been brought down by police scandals, were even beginning to wonder whether it was worth their while to fight for control of the police. What is more, the rank-and-file, who had been rather subdued during the Depression, came into their own after World War II when their fraternal and benevolent associations developed into de facto labor unions. By the mid-1960s these unions emerged as one of the highly organized and extremely militant municipal employee groups that Theodore J. Lowi and other scholars have described as the successors to the old-line machines.[8] By then, however, the machines, or what remained of them, could rarely count on the rank-and-file to support their attempts to hold back the second wave of police reform.

By the start of World War II it was fairly clear that the reformers enjoyed a sharp edge over the machines in the upcoming struggle. As the years passed, this edge became even sharper. Outside of Chicago, where by a process that remains somewhat of a mystery Mayor Daley centralized the Democratic organization, the machines grew more and more decentralized or fell apart entirely. Hard pressed to win the loyalty of the newcomers and get out the vote on election day, the machines were in no position to put pressure on the few ward leaders who were able to do so or on the police officers who were connected with them. If it had been hard to prevail on the bosses to pursue their short-run goals in ways that were consistent with the organization's long-run interests before the 1930s, it was virtually impossible afterward. Thus many politicians and policemen continued to engage in all sorts of improper and illegal practices which enraged their enemies, embarrassed their friends, and appalled the public. When the grand juries, legislative committees, muckraking journalists, and other advocates of reform exposed these practices, the ensuing scandals not only demoralized the big-city police but also discredited the old-line machines.

These scandals rocked one city after another. Not long after the Seabury Committee investigation a federal grand jury disclosed that on orders from the Pendergast machine the Kansas City Police Department had connived with party hacks to intimidate, assault, and thereby disfranchise the organization's opponents. A year or two later Edwin N. Atherton, a former FBI agent working as a special investigator for the San Francisco district attorney, reported that local gamblers, bookies, numbers runners, and liquor dealers were paying police officers upward of one million dollars a year for protection. Late in the 1940s a Los Angeles grand jury revealed that the city's vice squad was taking care of dozens of prostitutes and call girls, for roughly $100 a week per woman, and doing other favors for underworld figures. A year or so later the Brooklyn *Eagle* reported that Harry Gross, the kingpin of the borough's bookmaking business, kept scores of New York City police officers on his payroll, which came to several million dollars a year. Shortly afterward a Philadelphia grand jury, set up as a result of the Kefauver Committee's revelations, turned up evidence that the police were overlooking prostitution, gambling, and other forms of vice in return for about $3,000 to $4,000 a month per precinct.[9]

Matters were much the same in other cities. Early in the 1960s State's Attorney Adamowski announced that over the last couple of years several Chicago officers had planned the jobs and served as lookouts for a small-time burglar who divided the proceeds with them, the so-called Summerdale scandal. A year or so later the Columbia Broadcasting System presented a nationwide television program entitled "Biography of a Bookie Joint" which showed nearly a dozen Boston policemen going into a Back Bay shop where they were presumably placing bets and collecting payoffs. Shortly thereafter the Baltimore *Sun* published a long series of articles charging that the Baltimore police were refusing to answer calls, failing to report crimes, hanging out in bars, protecting vice, and mismanaging funds. Other front-page scandals broke out in Philadelphia in the 1930s, Detroit in the 1940s, Pittsburgh and New Orleans in the 1950s, Denver and Syracuse in the 1960s, and New York City and Philadelphia in the early 1970s.[10] These scandals showed that in the absence of effective sanctions the machines could not force the local politicians or police officers to exercise a reasonable degree of restraint, prudence, and common sense.

Nor could the machines prevent the reformers from capitalizing on these scandals. In the wake of the Atherton report, which rocked San Francisco in the late 1930s, the Chamber of Commerce and other civic groups prevailed on Mayor Angelo J. Rossi to ask Bruce Smith to work on a survey of the San Francisco Police Department. A year or so later Governor Lloyd Stark, a Democrat who had broken with the Pendergast machine largely because of the election frauds, persuaded the Missouri legislature to place the Kansas City police force under state control and appointed a four-man board to run it, which named Lear B. Reed, a former FBI agent, as chief of police. In the aftermath of the grand jury's exposé of the Los Angeles vice squad in the late 1940s, Mayor Fletcher Bowron accepted the resignation of Chief C. B. Horrall and chose William A. Worton, a former Marine Corps general, to succeed him. Following the Brooklyn *Eagle*'s series on police corruption in the early 1950s, the newspapers and reform groups prevailed on Mayor Vincent R. Impellitteri to authorize the Mayor's Committee on Management Survey to invite Smith to do a survey of the New York City Police Department. Shortly afterward Mayor-elect Joseph S. Clark, who had won a smashing victory in the wake of the recent grand jury exposé of the Philadelphia police force, picked Inspector Thomas J. Gibbons, one of the few veteran officers untainted by the investigation, to head the department.[11]

Events took a similar turn in other cities. The reformers raised such a furor over the Summerdale scandal that Mayor Richard Daley was forced to dismiss Commissioner Timothy J. O'Connor and appoint a five-man board, which was dominated by O. W. Wilson, Virgil W. Peterson, and Franklin M. Kreml, to select a new commissioner and make recommendations for a full-scale reorganization. The outcry that followed "Biography of a Bookie Joint" drove Governor John Volpe of Massachusetts to request the resignation of Commissioner Leo J. Sullivan, to call in the IACP to do a survey of the Boston Police Department, and to ask the state legislature to give the municipal officials the authority over the force taken from them eighty years before. The response to the Baltimore *Sun*'s exposé of the Baltimore Police Department prompted Governor J. Millard Tawes of Maryland to set up a blue-ribbon committee that sponsored a survey by the IACP which not only confirmed the *Sun*'s charges but also forced Commissioner Bernard J. Schmidt and Chief Inspector George J. Murphy to resign.[12] The reformers skillfully exploited the recurrent scandals to gain control of the police departments and to bring in outside experts to help reorganize them virtually everywhere except in Albany and a handful of other cities where the old-line machines still carried a good deal of weight.

Besides Chiefs Reed, Worton, and Gibbons, Lewis B. Valentine, who commanded the New York City police under Mayor La Guardia, came to power in 1934 in the wake of a serious scandal. So did William H. Parker, who followed General Worton as chief of the Los Angeles police in 1950. Robert V. Murray was named superintendent of the Washington, D.C., police when Robert J. Barrett resigned under fire from a Senate committee in 1951. Francis W. Adams was appointed commissioner of the New York police in 1954 in the aftermath of the Gross scandal; and Stephen P. Kennedy succeeded him in 1956. Wyman W. Vernon took over as chief of the Oakland police in 1956 after a state investigating committee forced the incumbent to step down. O.W. Wilson was nominated for superintendent of the Chicago police in 1961 by the four other members of Mayor Daley's advisory board. James Slavin was picked to head the Denver force in 1962 after the authorities uncovered a burglary ring in the department. Patrick V. Murphy was asked to rebuild the Syracuse police force in 1963 after the State Commission of Investigation tore it apart. And Edmund L. McNamara, a former FBI agent, was chosen commissioner of the Boston police when the city regained control over the force in the early 1960s.[13] A few reformers, among them Herbert T. Jenkins of Atlanta and Stanley R. Schrotel of Cincinnati, came to power by other routes; but they were the exceptions.

In addition to San Francisco, New York, Baltimore, and Boston, several other cities called in outside experts in the wake of a serious scandal. Following the exposure of the police burglary ring in Denver, the city council employed an IACP team, which included Quinn Tamm, Schrotel, and other eminent reformers, to find a new chief and make recommendations for an overhaul of the department. As a result of newspaper reports of police incompetence in Indianapolis, the municipal authorities invited the Police Services Group of Indiana University, which was headed by a one-time high-level IACP official, to look into the day-to-day operations of the force. After taking over as superintendent of the Chicago police, Wilson brought in a group of consultants from the IACP and the Public Service Administration, at a cost of roughly a quarter of a million dollars, to help plan the reorganization of the force. In the aftermath of an exposé by the Seattle *Post-Intelligencer,* which led to the indictment of dozens of police officers and public officials, Mayor J. D. Braman hired the IACP to do a survey of the force and come up with proposals for change.[14] The IACP, Public Service Administration, Institute of Public Administration, and other consulting firms took advantage of these opportunities to spread the conventional wisdom of police reform.

Now that the reform chiefs were taking over one department after another and the outside consultants were drawing up plans for their reorganization, the reformers had several reasons to be optimistic. For one, the same scandals that had brought the reform chiefs to power had mobilized the civic leaders, newspaper publishers, and other influential citizens and thereby generated a ground swell of support for the reform administrations. For another reason, the scandals had discredited the machine politicians, weakened their hold over the reform chiefs, and to a degree inconceivable a generation or two before, undermined their capacity to obstruct the reform proposals. For still another reason, the scandals had documented the incompetence and corruption of the current system in such mind-boggling detail that for the time being almost anything the reform administrations did would be received with approbation. Whether the second generation of reformers could raise the status of the big-city police by changing their structure, personnel, and function remained to be seen. But it would have plenty of opportunities, and compared with the first generation, it would have fairly good conditions under which to make the most of these opportunities.

In line with their prescription, the reformers first attempted to enhance the autonomy of the big-city police. Accordingly they sought to strengthen the chief's hand. At their insistence the San Francisco voters approved a charter amendment in the late 1930s that increased the chief's power at the expense of the police board. A few years later the Atlanta City Council shifted authority over promotions from the police committee to the chief's office. With the strong support of the reform groups Chief Parker turned the Los Angeles police commission into a rubber stamp in the 1950s. The reformers raised such a furor over the Gross scandal that Mayor Robert F. Wagner was loath to overrule Commissioners Adams and Kennedy. They made such an uproar about the Summerdale scandal that Mayor Daley was reluctant to override Superintendent Wilson.[15] The chiefs did not, of course, operate in a political vacuum. By the very nature of their position they were subjected to tremendous pressure from all sorts of groups other than the old-line machines. But as a result of the reform movement they were fairly well insulated, and as the years passed, increasingly so, from the day-to-day meddling in departmental affairs that had been commonplace a generation before.

The reformers sought to reinforce the chief's tenure as well. But alarmed, as Bruce Smith put it, that the incumbents might be frozen in regardless of competence, they rejected August Vollmer's advice that the chiefs "should be surrounded with every protective civil service device imaginable."[16] They suggested instead that the chiefs hold office on good behavior and that the voters give notice that they would deal harshly with any politician who dismissed a chief for partisan purposes. Apparently the politicians were impressed. Chief Parker, who was a civil servant, outlasted several administrations; so did Chief Jenkins, who served at the pleasure of the mayor. Chiefs Schrotel, Clarence M. Kelley, and Curtis Brostron stepped down at their own convenience. Commissioner McNamara, who was appointed to a five-year term by Mayor John F. Collins, held on long after Mayor Kevin H. White had made it known he wanted to replace him.[17] Not all the incumbents fared so well. Commissioner Vincent L. Broderick, a holdover from the Wagner administration, was not reappointed by Mayor John V. Lindsay, and Commissioner Donald F. Cawley was forced to step down by Lindsay's successor, Mayor Abraham D. Beame. But unless overtaken by a scandal or, in the case of Commissioner Ray Girardin of Detroit, a riot, most chiefs enjoyed a degree of security virtually unheard of a generation ago.

The reformers also tried to close down as many precincts as possible. In line with Smith's survey of the San Francisco police force, Chief William J. Quinn abolished six of the city's fourteen precincts in the late 1930s. Over the protests of Cleveland's ward bosses, Public Safety Director Eliot Ness eliminated all but six of the city's sixteen precincts at the same time. The reformers made similar reductions in Pittsburgh, Rochester, Cincinnati, Providence, Syracuse, and New Orleans. They got rid of more precincts in the postwar years. With the Republican organization in shambles, Commissioner Thomas J. Gibbons closed down twelve of Philadelphia's thirty-six precincts in the mid-1950s. Despite the objections of the aldermen, Superintendent Wilson wiped out seventeen of Chicago's thirty-eight precincts several years later. On the advice of the IACP and the President's Commission on Crime in the District of Columbia, the Washington police followed suit.[18] The reformers did less well in Boston, where Commissioner McNamara's shutdown of three of the Hub's sixteen precincts in the mid-1960s aroused so much opposition that he was forced to shelve plans to get rid of several others. The reformers made little headway in New York and even less in Buffalo. Despite these setbacks, the reformers managed to sever the close connection between the ward leaders and precinct captains in all but a handful of cities.

The reformers also tried to transfer as many functions as possible from ordinary patrolmen to special squads. Backed by the rank-and-file, the superior officers, and the civic and commercial groups, they proceeded along more or less the same lines as the first generation of reformers. Only they went much further. The reformers subdivided many of the old squads into even more specialized units. They also formed new squads, among them special intelligence squads, which kept tabs on organized crime, internal investigation squads, which looked into police malfeasance, and community relations squads, which dealt with racial problems. The reformers even devised tactical patrol squads, highly mobile units designed to control riots and other disturbances, which encroached on the precinct's historic function to maintain order and preserve the peace.[19] By the 1960s the proliferation of special squads had reached its peak. Some reformers, who realized that many chiefs were having difficulty staying in touch with all these squads and coming up with the manpower to patrol the streets, started to wonder whether this process had gone too far. But with one or two exceptions even they were not ready to recommend that these functions be transferred back to the precincts.

In the meantime the reformers endeavored to restructure the

departments according to the basic principles of organizational theory. At the suggestion of Wilson, then dean of the School of Criminology at Berkeley, Chief Vernon formed a planning and research unit in the Oakland Police Department in the early 1950s and hired Wilson's students to work in it. Chief Parker followed suit not long after. So did Wilson, when he took charge of the Chicago police in the early 1960s, and Slavin, when he assumed command of the Denver police a year or so later. Commissioner Robert J. diGrazia of Boston appointed Mark H. Furstenberg, an associate director of the Police Foundation, to revitalize his planning and research division in the early 1970s. At the suggestion of the Indiana University Police Services Group the Indianapolis police jumped on the bandwagon. So did the Houston force, which was under pressure from the Houston Crime Commission, and the Washington force, which was under pressure from the President's Commission on Crime in the District of Columbia.[20] By the 1960s virtually every big-city department boasted a planning and research bureau of one sort or another. Although some did nothing but apply to the LEAA for funds, others made an attempt to help the chiefs analyze the department's problems, review its options, and spell out its goals.

The reformers also reorganized the departments along functional, as opposed to territorial, lines, a measure that was supposed to clarify the division of responsibility among the precincts, squads, and other units. Conceived by Vollmer in the prewar years and incorporated into his plans for the Los Angeles police in the mid-1920s, this scheme was subsequently put into practice in Chicago in the early 1930s. Following the recommendations of Smith, who had just made a survey for the Citizens' Police Committee, Commissioner James P. Allman combined dozens of precincts, squads, and other units into eight major bureaus. In addition to the patrol force, around which the department had hitherto been organized, these bureaus were personnel, traffic, morals, detective, crime prevention, information and statistics, and records and property. The reformers reorganized the departments in much the same way in New Orleans and San Francisco later in the 1930s and in St. Louis, Boston, and many other big cities after World War II.[21] By the 1960's some officers, who believed that a modest amount of overlapping responsibility was inevitable in police work, wondered whether the reformers had gone too far. But not even they challenged the underlying assumption that the chiefs would be in a better position to say which units should carry out what chores once the departments were organized along functional lines.

The reformers also set up special units, which usually reported directly to the chiefs, to keep close watch over the rank-and-file. In the wake of a major scandal in the late 1940s Chief Worton of Los Angeles created a Bureau of Internal Affairs and appointed Inspector Parker, who had a well-deserved reputation for honesty, to head it. On the advice of the IACP, Commissioner McNamara of Boston followed suit a decade or so later; so did Commissioner Wilson of Chicago and Chief Jenkins of Atlanta. Shortly afterward Commissioner Howard R. Leary formed an Inspection Service Bureau that brought together the eight or nine separate outfits which monitored the integrity and efficiency of the New York City police.[22] The rank-and-file loathed these units, especially in Washington, Chicago, New York, and other cities where their members attempted to entrap their fellow officers. But the rank-and-file could not stop them from spreading from one city to the next or from gaining a degree of permanence that sharply distinguished them from the shoe-fly, confidential, and other undercover squads which had emerged early in the century. By the 1960s the internal affairs units were so well established that, if they worked as well as the reformers expected, the chiefs should have had little trouble finding out which of their men were not on the job.

The reformers also reduced the number of high-level officials who reported directly to the chiefs, a measure that was supposed to untangle the chain of command. Devised by Vollmer, refined by Smith, and later on popularized by Wilson, this scheme was put into practice in Chicago during the early 1930s. On the basis of Smith's conclusion that the commissioner's so-called "span of control" was too broad, Commissioner Allman cut the number of officials who reported to him from nineteen to eight. In line with Smith's other findings, he tightened the command of the patrol force, which was placed under a chief inspector, and the other seven units. The reformers reorganized the departments in roughly the same way in San Francisco and St. Paul later in the decade and in St. Louis, Los Angeles, and many other cities after World War II.[23] These changes, which placed a far greater emphasis on the hierarchical than the collegial character of big-city policing, were plainly inconsistent with the reformers' notion that policemen were professionals. But this inconsistency did not alter their conviction that the chiefs would be in a much better position to figure out whom to hold accountable once the lines of authority were untangled.

The reformers also attempted to raise the caliber of the big-city police. To this end they urged the authorities to tighten the entrance requirements, many of which were an outgrowth of the first wave of police reform. Their efforts were fairly successful. Charging that the departments were full of overage officers who had come to policing after failing in some other line, the reformers convinced one city after another to lower the maximum age limits for applicants. By 1968 only Boston, Dallas, and a handful of other cities accepted recruits over thirty-five years old; Chicago, Detroit, and St. Louis turned them away at thirty-one; and Memphis, Minneapolis, and Oakland drew the line at twenty-nine, the age recommended by the IACP though considered too low by the President's Crime Commission. Contending that the departments were full of officers who lacked the intelligence befitting their professional stature, the reformers persuaded one city after the next to raise the educational credentials too. By 1968 none of the big cities and very few of the medium-sized ones accepted applicants without a high school degree. In the face of vigorous opposition from the rank-and-file, however, the authorities shelved the reform proposals to require two or more years of college everywhere except in Flint, Michigan, Ogden, Utah, and a few small California cities.[24]

Claiming that too many immoral, unstable, and otherwise undesirable types were going into policing, the reformers prevailed on one department after another to toughen its character checks as well. Besides asking the FBI to search its files, most departments examined the applicants' school records, interviewed their past and present employers, and spoke with their friends and neighbors. In New York City, Commissioner Michael Murphy boasted, each dossier normally ran from sixty to seventy-five pages. Many departments subjected the applicants to Rorschach and Minnesota Multiphasic tests; and a few supplemented these tests with psychiatric examinations of one sort or another. Operating on the principle that all doubts should be resolved in favor of the force, the departments turned away some who had been convicted of a felony and others who had been arrested for a misdemeanor. They also turned down some who were chronic alcoholics and confirmed gamblers and others who had played hooky, changed jobs too often, or followed something other than a conventional life-style. Applying these requirements, plus the written tests and fitness standards, most departments winnowed out a staggering proportion of the applicants. During the late 1950s and early 1960s they rejected roughly five out of six in New York City, nine out of ten in Washington, D.C., fourteen out of fifteen in Tucson and Portland, and nineteen out of twenty in Dallas and Los Angeles.[25]

But it was not enough to set stringent standards, the reformers insisted; it was also necessary to attract capable recruits. At their insistence the authorities steadily increased starting salaries, which rose in the 1940s and 1950s from $2,400 to $6,200 in San Francisco, $2,100 to $4,900 in Chicago, $2,000 to $4,800 in New York, and $1,800 to $4,400 in Baltimore. But other groups fared as well, if not better, after the war. By 1960, therefore, big-city policemen earned more than musicians, social workers, medical technicians, carpenters, and auto mechanics, but less than reporters, draftsmen, electricians, teachers, and plumbers.[26] The rank-and-file got much larger raises in the 1960s and 1970s, but for these they had to thank the unions not the reformers. In the meantime most departments went on a five-day week and eight-hour day, extended sick leaves and annual vacations, supplied uniforms, paid for overtime, and provided life and health insurance. The departments also built new police headquarters, demolished old station houses, equipped the officers with late-model cars and up-to-date walkie-talkies, and otherwise improved working conditions. The authorities even increased the pension benefits, which were already the envy of the civil service; but here too the impetus came from the unions rather than the reformers.

As a result of strong opposition from the rank-and-file, who insisted that the superior officers should be drawn exclusively from the ranks, the authorities withstood reform pressures to allow lateral entry. But at the insistence of the rank-and-file, who claimed that they should be permitted to live in single-family homes in outlying suburbs, the authorities gave in to reform demands to get rid of the residency requirement. The Dallas police dropped the residency requirement during World War II, a time of severe manpower shortage; the Los Angeles police abolished it in the 1950s, roughly a decade after the city attorney had declared it illegal. The Seattle Civil Service Commission waived it for patrolmen in the late 1950s; and by approving a charter amendment, the Portland electorate eliminated it for all municipal employees in the early 1960s.[27] The state legislatures repealed it in New York and Boston shortly afterward. By the late 1960s only Philadelphia, Buffalo, Milwaukee, and a few other big cities retained the residency requirement; and not all of them enforced it. Few police departments systematically recruited outside the cities, let alone the states and the regions. But by virtue of the increased salaries and improved working conditions, plus the job security and generous service pensions, most departments attracted a large and growing number of capable recruits in the postwar years.

Capable recruits were one thing and competent officers quite another; and to turn the one into the other, the reformers pressed the departments to expand and improve their training facilities. Most departments did. Shortly after Ness took over as public safety director, the Cleveland police reopened its training academy; on Smith's recommendation the San Francisco police set up a school for recruits. Not long after Jenkins assumed command, the Atlanta police organized a training school modeled along the lines of the FBI training academy. By the late 1940s virtually every department boasted a training facility of one sort or another. During the next two decades most departments extended the training periods to anywhere from one to four months in the big cities and a bit less in the medium-sized ones. They enriched the programs by adding courses on criminal justice and racial prejudice to a curriculum that had hitherto stressed precision marching, target practice, and other martial arts. They often appointed as instructors veteran officers who had studied at the FBI National Academy, Southern Police Institute, and Northwestern University Traffic Institute.[28] But to the reformers' dismay, few departments, no matter how sympathetic to the reform campaign, gave much in the way of in-service training.

Besides providing better training, the reformers urged the departments to prevent the rank-and-file from engaging in activities that were inconsistent with their professional stature. Quite a few departments went along with this recommendation. On instructions from Chief Worton the Los Angeles police forbade the rank-and-file to accept rewards, a long-standing tradition that had survived the first wave of reform in a good many cities. Many other reform chiefs issued similar instructions after World War II. On orders from Superintendent Wilson the Chicago police barred the rank-and-file from holding outside jobs which required them to wear police uniforms, release departmental records, or work more than twenty-four hours a week, or which might in any way discredit the force. Many other reformers gave similar orders or prohibited moonlighting altogether. To make sure that these and other regulations were observed, many departments demanded that the rank-and-file submit to income probes, take polygraph tests, testify without immunity, and otherwise relinquish some of their civil liberties. Not until the 1960s did the officers effectively challenge the constitutionality of these practices. At the urging of the reformers, who claimed that unionism was incompatible with professionalism, most departments forbade the rank-and-file to join labor unions; but these restrictions were ineffective.[29]

The reformers also sought to revamp the promotional procedures, but this was an uphill struggle. Superintendent Wilson revised the Chicago rating system in a way that increased his discretion, but he was unable to reduce the influence of written tests in the promotional process. Commissioner Murphy proposed to restrict promotion to officers with a college education, but he was forced to back down by the Detroit Police Officers' Association. Deputy Chief Jerry V. Wilson urged the Washington police to cut down the number of years before a patrolman was eligible for the sergeant's exam, but he was overruled by Chief John B. Layton.[30] The reformers made some headway. By virtue of an arrangement worked out by the Atlanta City Council, Chief Jenkins enjoyed full authority over promotions; and over the objections of the rank-and-file other chiefs created high-ranking positions that were exempt from the civil service rules. But in general the chiefs failed to weaken the influence of seniority, written tests, and other reform measures which had been designed to curb the meddling of ward politicians but now allegedly served to block the advancement of capable leaders.

The attempts to revise the disciplinary procedures ran into much less resistance. Late in the 1930s the Los Angeles voters approved a charter amendment, which was drafted by the Los Angeles Fire and Police Protective League and backed by several reform groups, stipulating that police officers could be removed only by departmental trial boards and imposing a one-year statute of limitations on all infractions. This amendment, which withstood periodic attacks, emerged as a hallmark of the heralded autonomy of the Los Angeles Police Department. Early in the 1960s the Illinois legislature passed a law, which was sponsored by Superintendent Wilson and supported by the Chicago Crime Commission and, with modifications, by the Chicago Patrolmen's Association, shifting authority over discipline from the Civil Service Commission to a five-man police board.[31] This shift weakened the long tradition of political interference in disciplinary proceedings. Similar changes took place in most other big cities. In conjunction with previous reforms that had increased the chief's authority over short-term suspensions and high-level demotions, these changes pretty much transferred discipline from external or allegedly political to internal or allegedly professional bodies. As a result self-policing became the norm virtually everywhere in urban America — a development that helps explain why the big-city police reacted so vehemently against proposals for civilian or civilian-controlled review boards in the 1960s.

The reformers attempted to increase the proficiency of the big-city police too. Accordingly they called on the departments to cast off all sorts of functions that were remotely, if at all, related to crime prevention. The results were mixed. Under Chief Worton the Los Angeles police turned the management of the municipal jail over to the newly formed department of corrections. Under Commissioner Adams the New York police gave the responsibility for guarding school crossings to housewives and other part-time city employees. Under Superintendent Wilson the Chicago police abolished special details that served the hospitals, schools, and Chicago Transit Authority. Under Commissioner diGrazia the Boston police closed down the city prison and wiped out the harbor patrol.[32] Other departments took similar steps. And still others stopped running emergency ambulances, a chore assumed by public hospitals and private companies, or writing parking tickets, a task taken over by municipal "meter maids." Despite vigorous pressure from the reformers, however, many departments still operated lockups, regulated traffic, censored motion pictures, and carried out several other functions that were not closely related to crime prevention.

Of all these functions traffic regulation was by far the most time-consuming. Upon learning that at a time of rising crime rates the Washington, D.C., police allocated 20 percent of their manpower to traffic regulation, Congressman Jerome H. Waldie asked Chief Wilson whether the police should be relieved of this chore. Wilson replied no. Following the conventional wisdom, he pointed out not only that motorists kill more people than murderers but also that in the course of making routine traffic stops the officers often find evidence of criminal activity. This may well have been true, but there were probably other more compelling reasons that the police were reluctant to give up the task. One was that traffic regulation helped the departments develop close ties with engineers, academics, and other prestigious groups which strengthened the law enforcement community's case for the professional recognition. Another reason was that traffic squads provided an important avenue of mobility for many run-of-the-mill officers who had little chance of being promoted to sergeant or transferred to a detective division or other plainclothes unit. Yet another reason was that the IACP over the years had accepted tens of thousands of dollars from the Association of Casualty and Surety Companies, the Automotive Safety Foundation, and other outfits with a great stake in highway safety.[33] Having solicited these funds to set up a Highway Safety Division and to underwrite its wide-ranging projects, the association had no alternative but to oppose the notion that traffic regulation was not a proper police function.

The reformers also favored employing civilians to fill many of the clerical, secretarial, and other semiskilled slots that had traditionally been filled by policemen. On taking office, many reformers put this proposal into practice. During Parker's fifteen years as chief the Los Angeles police increased their civilian personnel three times as fast as their sworn officers. During Wilson's first two years as superintendent the Chicago police relieved nearly 900 officers of desk jobs and replaced most of them with civilians. During Jerry V. Wilson's first two years as chief the Washington, D.C., police hired 300 additional civilians in order, Wilson said, to get more officers "out on the street." Shortly after diGrazia took over as commissioner the Boston police adopted a similar policy over the objections of the patrolmen's association. As a result of these changes, the number of civilian employees, most of whom worked in the personnel, budget, data-processing, and equipment maintenance units, rose steadily in the postwar years. The proportion of civilian employees increased too. Between 1950 and 1970 it went up a little in Boston and Detroit, roughly doubled in Los Angeles, Philadelphia, St. Louis, Washington, D.C., Chicago, and New York City, and more than tripled in San Francisco. By 1970 civilians made up about 10 percent of the force in Boston, Baltimore, New York, Philadelphia, Chicago, and Washington, 15 percent in San Francisco, 25 percent in Los Angeles, and a whopping 30 percent in St. Louis.[34]

The reformers favored replacing two-man with one-man squad cars too. But this proposal generated a good deal of controversy—more than the proposal to employ civilians in place of sworn officers and much more than the proposal to shift from foot to motorized patrols. Supporting the proposal were the reform chiefs, who claimed that one-man cars would not only save money but also ensure wider coverage, quicker response, and more effective use of available manpower. Opposing it were the rank-and-file groups, which charged that, by requiring the officers to drive and patrol at the same time, one-man cars would reduce the efficiency and increase the hazards of policing. The rank-and-file groups forced the chiefs to shelve plans to change over to one-man cars in Boston and New York, but the chiefs got their way in most other cities. Parker of Los Angeles introduced one-man cars in the early 1950s, and Bernard C. Brannon of Kansas City, Jenkins of Atlanta, and Wilson of Chicago followed suit not long after. Indeed so many chiefs put this proposal into practice that between 1947 and 1964 the number of departments which used two-man cars dropped from eight out of thirteen to four out of twenty in the large cities and fell even more sharply in the medium-sized cities.[35] The number of departments that relied exclusively on one-man cars also rose, though not quite as much.

In the meantime Parker, O.W. Wilson, and a few other prominent reformers came up with an alternative to the theory of
crime prevention that had been worked out by Woods and Vollmer a generation before. The police, they insisted, could not alleviate poverty, stamp out prejudice, cure mental illness, care for
neglected youngsters, and otherwise solve the social problems
that gave rise to criminal activity. These were jobs for the families, churches, schools, hospitals, and other institutions. Dealing,
as Parker put it, with "effects" not "causes," the police could only
apply "emergency treatment" to "surface wounds"; they could
contain but not convert criminals, repress but not prevent crime.
As the so-called "thin blue line" that separated the lawless from
the law-abiding, the police could deter criminal activity by
increasing the likelihood of intervention, apprehension, and punishment. Or as Wilson explained, the police could reduce the
opportunities but not the motives for crime. Jenkins and a few
other well-known reformers rejected this alternative on the
grounds that it presented too dismal a view of crime prevention
and implied too narrow an approach to the police function. But
the theory gained momentum and, as the 1961 report of the
IACP's Committee on Crime Prevention indicated, eventually
emerged as the conventional wisdom of the second wave of police
reform.[36]

From this theory Parker, Wilson, and other reformers drew
three obvious conclusions. First, the police departments should
close down the boys' clubs, employment bureaus, athletic
leagues, and other welfare and recreational programs that had
proliferated in the first third of the century. Second, they should
teach the citizens to lock their cars, beware of con men, report
suspicious strangers, and take whatever other safeguards were
necessary to protect themselves. Third, they should seek out the
criminals rather than wait for complaints from their victims, or
in other words, follow a policy of preventive instead of responsive
patrol. This policy, which was commonly known as stop-and-
search, field interrogation, or stop-and-frisk, was epitomized by
the San Francisco Police Department's Operation S, which was
launched in the late 1950s. On orders from Chief Cahill a special
S (or saturation) squad flooded high-crime neighborhoods and
attempted to round up potential offenders by stopping, quizzing,
and frisking suspicious characters. During its first year of opera-

tion the S squad stopped 20,000 people, filed 11,000 reports, and arrested 1,000 persons, most of whom were blacks and youths.[37] An outgrowth of the emergent theory of crime prevention, preventive patrol was a momentous departure from the American tradition of policing.

Led by Commissioner Rutledge of Detroit and several other police chiefs who were dismayed by the slipshod quality of criminal statistics, the reformers also urged the IACP to do something about reporting procedures. After much discussion the association created a Committee on Uniform Crime Records in the late 1920s. It consisted of two subcommittees, one headed by Rutledge and including Vollmer and ten other police administrators, the other chaired by Lent D. Upson of the Detroit Bureau of Governmental Research and including J. Edgar Hoover and nine other powerful figures. With a gift from the Laura Spelman Rockefeller Memorial the committee hired Bruce Smith and a small staff to analyze the reporting problems. On the basis of their work the committee issued a lengthy report in 1929 that set forth a uniform classification of criminal offenses, laid out an administrative procedure for recording them, and recommended that the police departments report their statistics to the FBI, which would then collect and publish them. In other words, it devised a uniform system of criminal reporting for the entire country.[38] The IACP accepted the report; the FBI agreed to operate the system; and though the document was not legally or otherwise binding, so many departments went along with its recommendations that by World War II this system, known officially as the *Uniform Crime Reports*, was one of the monuments of the second wave of police reform.

But the *Uniform Crime Reports* were only as accurate as the department figures, which left much to be desired, and so the reformers pressed each force to centralize and rationalize its reporting procedures as well. On Bruce Smith's advice the Chicago police, whose statistics were notoriously unreliable, set up a central complaint bureau in the early 1930s. Following Smith's recommendations, the San Francisco and St. Louis police overhauled their records systems not long afterward. Under sharp criticism from the press for concealing hundreds of criminal offenses the Washington police invited the FBI to make a study of their records system in the late 1940s. Again on Smith's advice the New

York City police, whose figures were so inaccurate that the FBI refused to publish them, shifted record-keeping from the precincts to headquarters a few years later. Thus outside of Buffalo, where as many as three out of four crime reports were somehow buried, misplaced, or lost in the precincts, most departments provided reliable statistics of reported crime by the 1960s.[39] But as the President's Crime Commission and the LEAA revealed, the American people did not report most crimes to the police.

The second wave of police reform differed from the first in several ways. Its leaders were drawn not so much from the ministerial associations, municipal leagues, chambers of commerce, and other voluntary organizations as from the law enforcement community. They were driven not so much by a desire to wipe out deviant behavior, destroy the political machine, and stamp out administrative inefficiency as by a determination to raise the status of the big-city police. Although they traced many of the problems of policing to political interference in departmental affairs, they believed that the force should be reorganized on the basis of a professional model rather than a military analogy. Despite these differences, the second generation of reformers came up with pretty much the same recommendations as the first generation for changing the structure, personnel, and function of the big-city police. The second generation also shared with the first a common set of assumptions about policing, politics, and other matters which were an integral part of the conventional wisdom of the upper middle and upper classes.

To begin with, the second generation of reformers had strong reservations about local control. From their point of view, which was influenced by a keen appreciation of the highly centralized police systems of Western Europe, this tradition hamstrung the police in their efforts to deal with criminals who were free to plan their operations in one city, carry them out in another, and hide away in a third. This tradition also stymied the reformers, whose proposals needed the approval of hundreds of municipalities, each of which had its own social structure and political culture, rather than a handful of high-level officials in the state or national capital. But the reformers had deep suspicions of the state and federal authorities too. Anxious to protect their own bailiwicks, the reformers therefore opposed the introduction of metropolitan policing, the extension of state policing, and the consolidation of existing forces along the lines of the British system. They demanded assurances and reassurances from Patrick V. Murphy, then head of the LEAA, that the federal government would not interfere in the management of the local police. They praised Hoover, who declared time and again that the creation of a national police force would not only violate the traditions of American society but also subvert the foundations of democratic government.[40]

The reformers had strong reservations about a civilian orientation as well. From their perspective, which was shaped by the painful recollection of the Lexow, Seabury, and other investigative committees, this tradition increased the likelihood that the departments would be run in the interests of the political machine rather than of the general public. To the degree that the civilian orientation left the departments unprepared to deal with the frequent rioting and intermittent terrorism that broke out in the middle and late 1960s, it also posed a serious threat to the well-being of the police officers and ordinary citizens. But the reformers had grave doubts about the military analogy too. If pressed, they conceded that the policemen were not soldiers, criminals were not their enemies, policing was not warfare, and urban America was not a battleground, though it might sometimes appear to be. Citing the experience of doctors, lawyers, and other groups, the reformers insisted that so long as the civilian orientation was based on a professional model, it was compatible with a strict separation of politics and policing. They also pointed out that, unlike the national guard and federal troops, the big-city police had many tasks other than riot control which were better approached from a civilian than a military point of view.

The reformers had even stronger reservations about catchall and responsive activity. From their standpoint, which was molded by the conviction that the overriding responsibility of the big-city police was not to give traffic directions, resolve domestic squabbles, censor motion pictures, or find lost children but to prevent crime, this tradition undermined the efficiency of the police. It also weakened the case for professional recognition, which rested to a great degree on the contention that effective police work required scientific expertise and technical know-how as well as stamina, courage, and common sense. The reform position had far-reaching implications. If crime prevention, as defined by Parker and Wilson, was the essence of policing, it was incumbent on the departments not only to get rid of their other chores but also to adopt a preventive instead of a responsive posture. If implemented, this strategy would force the precincts to follow the lead of the special squads, which in their efforts to wipe out vice, regulate traffic, and keep tabs on radicals had long ago abandoned the responsive tradition.

What is more, the reformers were highly critical of the view that the big-city police should expedite social mobility. They agreed with the Progressive conviction that the primary purpose of the police departments, schools, courts, and other municipal agencies was to supply the best possible service at the lowest possible cost and not to create soft jobs for impoverished immigrants. Following the logic of the professional model, some reformers even went so far as to insist that under no conditions should the departments lower their entrance requirements. As a result several departments operated at levels well below their authorized strength in the 1950s and 1960s, a situation that would have been inconceivable during the heyday of the political machines in the late nineteenth century. The reform position well served the upper-middle- and upper-class elites. It had only a slight impact on the second- and third-generation Irish-Americans and other ethnic groups, who were ordinarily able to meet the entrance requirements or, if need be, to find other opportunities outside the police forces. But the reform position ill served the first- and second-generation blacks, Mexicans, and Puerto Ricans, who lacked the credentials to get into the public service as well as the capital and connections to get ahead in the private sector.

The reformers were just as critical of the notion that the big-city police should promote political decentralization. They went along with the Progressive theory that no matter how large their majorities, the ward bosses should exercise no authority over the police departments, schools, courts, and other municipal bureaus. Carrying the professional model to its logical conclusion, some reformers went so far as to contend that not even the mayors, councilmen, comptrollers, and other city-wide officials had a right to interfere in departmental affairs. As a result many chiefs ran their forces with a degree of independence that would have been unheard-of under the system of machine politics a generation or two earlier. The reform position did not inhibit the upper middle and upper classes, who exerted strong pressure on the force through the daily newspapers, chambers of commerce, and civic organizations. Nor did it frustrate the Irish-Americans and other ethnic groups, who were well entrenched in the big-city departments and well represented by the rank-and-file outfits. But the reform position stymied the blacks, Mexicans, and Puerto Ricans, who had no way of shaping official policies and practices other than by bringing pressure on the local politicians.

The reformers were also critical of the idea that the big-city police should foster cultural pluralism. True, they did not fully share the Progressive sentiment that immigrant life-styles were largely inconsistent with American morality. Adopting a position spelled out by Vollmer in the 1920s, a few reformers even argued that the public should not call on the police to enforce sumptuary legislation. But applying the logic of the professional model, most reformers concluded that the police should uphold a single standard of law enforcement. If this meant imposing the conventional morality, so be it. The reform position pleased many upper-middle- and upper-class Protestants, whose values, attitudes, and customs were embodied in the state and municipal ordinances. It also satisfied many middle-class Catholics, who emerged after the war as the staunchest supporters of the sumptuary legislation originally aimed at them by the Protestants. But the reform position frustrated many lower- and lower-middle class blacks, Mexicans, and Puerto Ricans, who were often reluctant to conform to the conventional morality. And the reformers would eventually pay a high price for their long-standing indifference to these newcomers and their problems.

8. Unionism Comes to Policing

Shortly before the end of World War II the IACP issued a pamphlet entitled *Police Unions and Other Police Organizations* which spelled out the reform position on recent efforts to organize the American police. The pamphlet, which was based largely on a questionnaire submitted to two hundred cities, a survey of union activity in five of them, and a report of the National Institute of Municipal Law Officers, made three main points. First, unionism was incompatible with policing, which as a semimilitary pursuit required the undivided allegiance of its personnel, and inimical to the profession and the public. Second, the rank-and-file would gain little by affiliating with trade unions because the municipal authorities had no power to enter into collective bargaining agreements, set up a dues check-off, or establish a closed shop, which were the cardinal benefits of unionism. Third, according to a large body of legal opinion, the authorities had the right, indeed the duty, to prohibit police officers from joining a union and to fire them if they persisted in so doing.[1] The association's pamphlet left no doubt that the reformers would not tolerate the unionization of the municipal police.

The first campaign to organize the police started shortly after World War I, when the AFL reversed a long-standing policy and issued charters to police unions in Boston, Washington, D.C., and about thirty other cities. August Vollmer, Martin O'Brien, and many other police chiefs promptly condemned this move. Following the logic of the military analogy, they insisted that policemen had no more right to join a union than soldiers and sailors and no more right to affiliate with the AFL than with the National Association of Manufacturers. The officers could not give their allegiance to any group other than an independent fraternal or benevolent association without abandoning the traditional neutrality that was the hallmark of proper policing. This argument was lost on the thousands of policemen who were caught up in a nationwide inflation that had just about doubled the cost of living since the outbreak of World War I. Forced to cut back on necessities and go into debt but still, as several officers told a congressional committee, unable to make ends meet, the rank-and-file were fed up with the indifference of the authorities. If the chiefs, who admitted that salaries had lagged way behind prices, could not get the police long-overdue raises, perhaps the unions could. Capitalizing on this resentment, the fledgling unions signed up about six out of seven policemen in Washington, three out of four in Boston, and a smaller proportion in a dozen or so other cities.[2]

Their success was short-lived. Commissioner E. U. Curtis refused to recognize the Boston police union, forbade the rank-and-file to join it, and filed charges against several union officials, and Commissioner Louis Brownlow ordered the Washington police to quit the union or face dismissal. The Washington union secured a temporary injunction that stayed Brownlow's order. But when Commissioner Curtis — ignoring a settlement worked out by a citizen's committee and, though it called on the union to give up its charter, endorsed by the union officials — suspended more than a dozen policemen, roughly three-quarters of the force went out on strike. The strike — or to be more accurate, the newspaper accounts of it, which exaggerated the accompanying surge of crime and violence — generated a furor not only in Massachusetts but throughout the nation. On orders from Governor Calvin Coolidge the Commonwealth dismissed the strikers and destroyed the union, an action hailed by President Woodrow Wilson, who claimed that policemen had the same obligation as soldiers and branded the walkout "a crime against civilization."[3] Shortly thereafter the Congress, which had opposed the Washington union from its inception, upheld Brownlow's ultimatum. The AFL, which was under heavy criticism, revoked the outstanding charters; and by 1920 the organizing effort was defunct.

It remained so until World War II, when the American Federation of State, County, and Municipal Employees (AFSCME), an affiliate of the AFL with jurisdiction over all public employees except teachers, and the State, County and Municipal Workers of America (SCMWA), an affiliate of the Congress of Industrial Organizations (CIO) and a rival of AFSCME, mounted a second campaign to unionize the police. With the approval of the AFL and CIO leaders, who were fresh from the victories of the 1930s and anxious to extend their influence into the public sector, these unions issued charters to a few dozen locals all over the nation and sent in organizers to help them present their case to the rank-and-file. Most police chiefs, citing the devastating consequences of the Boston police strike, spoke out against these efforts. But their appeal did not move the thousands of police officers who found that by virtue of the wartime inflation their economic position was deteriorating and concluded that it would not improve until the rank-and-file had an organization to press for higher salaries and better fringe benefits. By promising to do just that, AFSCME and, in one or two cities, SCMWA organizers prevailed on anywhere from one-third to two-thirds of the rank-and-file to join locals in Los Angeles, St. Louis, Detroit, Portland, Miami, Chicago, and many other cities.[4]

The authorities reacted swiftly and harshly. With the strong support of Mayor Fletcher Bowron and Chief C. B. Horrall, the Los Angeles Police Commission banned the union, gave the members thirty days to resign from it, and dismissed the few who refused to do so. Under strong pressure from Governor Phil Donnelly of Missouri and other state officials, the St. Louis Police Board ordered the rank-and-file to sever their connection with the union in two weeks and later fired a few officers who held out. The authorities took similar steps in Detroit, Chicago, and Jackson, Mississippi, where Mayor Walter A. Scott and the City Commission delivered a forty-eight hour ultimatum to the force and then got rid of the thirty-six policemen who defied it. Arguing that their constitutional rights had been violated, the officers appealed to the courts for redress. But in a series of rulings, which included *Perez* v. *Board of Police Commissioners, King* v.

Priest, and *City of Jackson* v. *McLeod,* the courts, using the military analogy to distinguish police officers from other public employees, upheld the right of the authorities to ban police unions.[5] Reluctant to call for a strike, which would probably have been futile, the unions had no option save to disband; and by the end of the war, just one year after the IACP published its bulletin, most of them had done so.

The unions were survived by scores of benevolent and fraternal organizations. Some were patrolmen's benevolent associations (PBAs), which had been formed in New York, Chicago, Washington, Rochester, Milwaukee, and other cities in the late nineteenth and early twentieth centuries. These associations, which were usually restricted to patrolmen, were completely autonomous, and remained so even after a few of them set up the National (later International) Conference of Police Associations (ICPA) in the early 1950s. Others were fraternal orders of police (FOPs), which had emerged in Philadelphia, Cincinnati, Cleveland, Detroit, and other mid-Atlantic and Midwestern cities in the 1910s and 1920s. Unlike the PBAs, the FOPs were open to officers of all ranks and, though largely autonomous, were affiliated with state and national lodges, an arrangement that prompted the authorities to ban them in Detroit and a handful of other cities in the 1940s. Still others were superior officers' or, in New York, Chicago, and several other very large cities, sergeants', lieutenants', detectives', and even captains' benevolent associations, which had been founded early in the twentieth century. These groups, which were fairly small, normally followed the lead of the PBAs and FOPs on most policy issues that did not vitally affect their own special interests.[6]

Besides providing insurance against sickness and death, sponsoring picnics and parties, and otherwise looking out for the health and well-being of the members, most benevolent and fraternal organizations also carried the rank-and-file's demands to the authorities and, if need be, to the voters. The New York PBA pressed the state legislators for an eight-hour day in the 1900s, and the Chicago Patrolmen's Social and Athletic Association petitioned the city aldermen for a six-day week in the 1920s. The Philadelphia PBA brought pressure on the municipal officials in the 1910s to give the rank-and-file a full accounting of the pension fund and to guarantee a secret ballot when they chose the delegates who picked a majority of the fund's directors. The Los Angeles Fire and Police Protective League urged the voters to amend the city charter in the 1930s so that policemen could be dismissed only after a departmental trial held within one year of the alleged infraction. The Cleveland FOP lobbied in the 1930s to limit the policemen's contribution to the pension system to only two percent of their salary rather than the four percent that was paid by all other municipal employees except firemen.[7] And the rank-and-file groups in these and other cities regularly implored the authorities to raise salaries, improve fringe benefits, and increase service and disability pensions.

With some exceptions — notably the Cleveland Bureau of Governmental Research, which was so offended by the soliciting and lobbying of the Cleveland FOP that it called on the authorities to ban the lodge — the reformers did not worry much about these groups.[8] Indeed, in the same bulletin that denounced the police unions the IACP praised the benevolent and fraternal organizations for helping out police officers, raising departmental morale, and contributing to charitable causes. Two things accounted for the reformers' attitude. For one, the rank-and-file groups spent most of their time fighting over salaries, pensions, and working conditions. Only rarely did they oppose reform schemes, as when the New York PBA lobbied against Mayor John P. Mitchel's reform proposals to abolish judicial review of disciplinary decisions and to downgrade seniority in promotional procedures. For another, these groups did not have much clout. Despite vigorous protests, they were not able to dissuade the authorities from reducing salaries by roughly 10 percent in New York, 25 percent in Chicago, and similar amounts in other cities during the early years of the Depression.[9] The future was uncertain. But if the past was any guide, the reformers had little reason to fear that these outfits would be more troublesome after World War II than before, much less that they would be transformed from pressure groups into de facto labor unions in the next two decades.

Prior to World War II most police were fairly well off. For men who had little education and few skills — who, as a Washington patrolman told a congressional committee, were not "fit for anything except police duty or some kind of laboring work" — they received a decent salary, which could be supplemented by regular payoffs and, if they put in their twenty or twenty-five years, a modest pension.[10] Although they worked six days a week for eight or ten hours a day, under disagreeable and sometimes dangerous conditions and subject to stringent and often pointless regulations, so did factory laborers, truck drivers, and other unskilled and semiskilled workers, who did not enjoy as high a degree of job security as police officers. Most officers also had a number of ways of improving their lot. If they wanted a transfer, a promotion, or a raise or if they needed protection from their superiors, they could appeal to the political machines to intercede on their behalf. If they felt that salaries should be raised, pensions increased, work loads reduced, or work rules changed, they could urge the benevolent and fraternal associations to lobby for them in city halls and state capitols. If neither the machines nor the associations gave them satisfaction, they could as a last resort join, or threaten to join, one or another of the labor unions.

All this changed in the war and postwar years. Between 1939 and 1950 the salaries of policemen and other public employees went up slightly less than the cost of living and much less than the earnings of factory workers. Thus many officers found it hard to support their families—even harder, to their dismay, than many less skilled workers in the private sector. By the early 1950s, the Chicago *American* reported, many of them lived in crowded and run-down quarters, with little money for food or clothes and none for cigarettes or movies, dependent on the earnings of their wives or children and, in some cases, indebted to credit unions and loan sharks. These conditions, which were very likely at their worst in the early and mid-1940s when AFSCME and SCMWA launched the second campaign to organize the police, improved somewhat in the mid-1950s when police salaries rose faster than the cost of living. But according to a survey of the Washington, D.C., police force in the late 1950s, many officers were leaving for better-paying spots in private firms and federal agencies, others were holding second jobs as laborers, painters, paper hangers, and salesmen, and still others were encouraging their wives to look for employment.[11]

So far as the rank-and-file were concerned, things were going from bad to worse. Forced not only to put in five or six days a week, as often as not on Saturdays and Sundays, but also, as a result of the rising cost of living, to moonlight in their off hours, most officers had little time for their wives and, as the wife of a Chicago patrolman complained, even less for their children.[12]

After a decade of numbing depression that left most cities unable to carry out ordinary maintenance, many police stations, some of which had been erected in the late nineteenth and early twentieth centuries, were drafty, dark, and filthy. The pipes leaked, the paint was peeling, and the walls were crumbling. By virtue of the changes brought about by the first wave of reform, most departments had greatly increased the number of regulations, the amount of paperwork, and the emphasis on martial demeanor, which was particularly offensive to the World War II veterans on the force. These conditions prompted a good deal of grumbling in the late 1940s and early 1950s. This grumbling grew into a deep-seated sense of outrage in the late 1950s and early 1960s, when the American Civil Liberties Union (ACLU) called for the creation of civilian review boards to handle complaints against the police and the Supreme Court handed down a series of landmark rulings upholding the constitutional rights of suspected criminals.

The rank-and-file's grievances were severely, if inadvertently, exacerbated by the reformers' rhetoric. If the police were professionals, as the reformers insisted, why, the rank-and-file wondered, did they earn less than draftsmen, designers, electricians, plumbers, and carpenters, not to speak of doctors, lawyers, engineers, and teachers? If policemen were not paid like professionals, why were they forbidden to moonlight in Chicago, Detroit, Milwaukee, San Francisco, and other cities, a prohibition that was no less infuriating because it was commonly violated? Again, if the police were professionals, why were they bound by so many nitpicking rules, subjected to so many arbitrary decisions, and obliged to submit to income probes, polygraph tests, and other violations of their civil liberties? And if policemen were not treated like professionals, why were they forbidden to belong to labor unions? Unable to answer these questions, or in other words to reconcile the differences between the reformers' rhetoric and their own workaday experience, the rank-and-file were driven to do something to improve their position.

Their options were sharply limited, however. They could ask the political machines to intercede on their behalf, a strategy that was employed frequently before World War I. But the machines were defunct in some cities, on the wane in others, and stymied by civil service rules and other offshoots of the first wave of police reform in still others. Even if the machines were inclined to help the rank-and-file—which as a result of the dwindling influence of the police over municipal elections and other matters vital to the ward bosses, not many were—they could not do much. The situation was only slightly different in Chicago and the handful of other cities where the local politicians carried a good deal of weight and the police departments were full of the politicians' friends, relatives, and associates. The politicians were willing to support individual officers who wanted to be assigned to another post, transferred to a plainclothes unit, or protected from their superiors. But as the Chicago Patrolmen's Association complained, the politicians were reluctant to back the rank-and-file's demands for across-the-board increases in salaries, benefits, and pensions or for changes in work rules that affected them as a group.[13]

The rank-and-file could also urge the fraternal and benevolent associations to lobby for them in state capitols and city halls, another strategy that was followed quite often after World War I. But the associations carried little weight. In some cities they were hamstrung by the legacy of the Boston police strike; in others they were immobilized by the shock of the Great Depression; and in still others they were under the thumb of the political machine. It was precisely because they were so weak, so hard put to prevent salary cutbacks during the Depression and to win sizable raises during World War II, that many officers joined the AFSCME and SCMWA locals in the early and mid-1940s. Nor was there much evidence to suggest that the fraternal and benevolent groups would do much better in the postwar years. Most of them attracted so few members, many of whom refused to pay their dues, that they were ordinarily on the verge of destitution. They were also challenged so often by militant labor unions and vigorous insurgent groups that their claim to speak for the rank-and-file was open to question. Lacking official recognition, they were compelled to engage in what Carl Parsell, head of the Detroit Police Officers Association (POA) during the 1960s, referred to as "collective begging."[14]

As a last resort the rank-and-file could affiliate with one or another of the labor unions, a strategy that was adopted in several cities during and soon after both world wars. But outside of Denver, Portland, Seattle, and a few dozen small and medium-sized cities in Connecticut, Illinois, Michigan, and Washington where police unions were tolerated by the authorities, this was not feasible. According to a survey conducted by the District of Columbia police in the late 1940s, most departments had issued orders forbidding the rank-and-file to belong to a labor union; and most chiefs were determined to enforce these orders. The Baltimore police organized an AFSCME local in the early 1950s but, under pressure from Commissioner Beverly Ober and the superior officers, dissolved it a year or two later. AFSCME launched a drive to unionize the Oakland police in the mid-1950s but, in the face of opposition from Chief Wyman W. Vernon and the city council, called it off shortly afterward. Commissioners George Monaghan and Stephen P. Kennedy responded in much the same way when the Transport Workers' Union and the Teamsters' Local 237 attempted to organize the New York City police in the 1950s.[15] A decade after World War II the unions still represented only a small fraction of the rank-and-file and, inasmuch as many of the unions were not recognized by the authorities, did not represent them very well.

By the mid-1950s, if not earlier, three things were clear to the rank-and-file. First, they could not prevail on the authorities to raise their salaries, benefits, and pensions or improve their working conditions unless they were well organized. In view of the countless claims and conflicting pressures on the elected officials, it was futile to rely solely on the intrinsic merit of the requests. Second, only a labor union could mobilize the political, economic, and other resources to make an impression on the city councilmen and state legislators. Contrary to the reformers' rhetoric, the police were not professionals; for them the American Medical Association and American Bar Association were not appropriate models. Third, in view of the outcome of the previous attempts to organize the police, the rank-and-file could not follow the lead of the firemen and other municipal employees and join forces with a nationwide union. The shock of the Boston police strike, the tenacity of the military analogy, and the opposition of the second generation of reformers were for the time being insuperable. Hence the rank-and-file were in a bind. Whether their leaders could find a way out and, if so, whether the authorities would go along with it remained to be seen.

The prospects were not bright. Veteran officers who had entered policing in the 1920s and 1930s, the rank-and-file leaders had developed a style that was based largely on their close personal relations with prominent politicians and high-level police officials. Like John Carton, head of the New York PBA from 1944 to 1958 and, in Commissioner Monaghan's words, a sound, decent fellow who knew his place, the leaders were unwilling to take any steps that might jeopardize these relations.[16] They were ill informed about labor unions. As a result of the long history of violent confrontations between police officers and striking workers, they were not well disposed toward the unions either. The rank-and-file leaders were also reluctant to go outside normal channels. They were content to work for candidates, lobby in legislatures, bring cases to court, and sponsor referenda—or in other words, to stick pretty much to the standard repertoire of American pressure groups. This policy was well advised because the leadership could count on no more than a small minority of the rank-and-file to support a walkout or slowdown, let alone a full-fledged strike.

During the late 1950s and early and mid-1960s, however, a new group of rank-and-file leaders came to power. John Cassese, a New York City patrolman who was elected a delegate to the PBA in the mid-1940s and named a vice-president a decade later, ousted Carton as the association's president in 1958. Carl Parsell, a twenty-year veteran of the Detroit force who had long been active in rank-and-file affairs, gained control of the Detroit POA in 1965. In the same year Richard MacEachern, a little-known Boston patrolman, and a dozen or so fellow officers founded the Boston Police Patrolmen's Association (PPA), which soon superseded the other rank-and-file groups.[17] Each leader came to power in a different way, but all faced the same problem. To win leadership, they had been obliged not only to articulate the rank-and-file's grievances and promise to alleviate them but also to call on their fellow officers to put aside personal sentiments and hold their leaders accountable. Henceforth the new leaders of the fraternal and benevolent associations could not expect to retain their positions, as well as the perquisites and prestige that went with them, unless they could fulfill their campaign promises.

But could they? Veteran officers who had entered policing during or shortly after World War II and were products of the civil service rather than protégés of the political machines, the new leaders lacked the close ties to prominent politicians and ranking police officials on which their predecessors had relied so heavily. They could probably have developed these ties, but it would have taken far more time than they could afford. It would also have opened them to charges that they were company men, to cite Harold Melnick, a New York patrolman who helped Cassese engineer Carton's downfall and later went on to head the Sergeants' Benevolent Association.[18] As events in Chicago indicated, these ties were not worth much anyway. Despite their connections, the patrolmen's, sergeants', and other benevolent associations, which were banded together in the Joint Council of Chicago Police Organizations, could not prevail on the municipal authorities in the early 1950s to provide cash allowances for uniforms, impose an eight-hour day and forty-hour week, or give them more than a token raise. Nor could these groups prevent Superintendent O. W. Wilson a decade later from going ahead with his plans to shift from two-man to one-man squad cars, fill so-called nonpolice jobs with civilian employees, set up an internal investigative unit, and reduce political involvement in disciplinary proceedings.[19]

Forced for these reasons to review their options, the rank-and-file leaders were struck by two things. The first was that during the postwar years the labor unions not only consolidated their position in the private sector but also increased their influence in the public sector. Early in the 1950s the Philadelphia Civil Service Commission, following the provisions of a recently approved city charter, authorized the personnel director to enter into collective bargaining agreements with AFSCME. Shortly afterward Mayor Robert F. Wagner of New York issued executive orders recognizing the right of city employees to join unions and instructing all mayoral departments except the police to bargain with them. Early in the 1960s the Wisconsin legislature passed a statute that authorized Milwaukee and other cities to bargain collectively with all municipal employees except policemen and firemen. Not long afterward President John F. Kennedy signed an executive order that gave these rights to federal employees. By the late 1960s, only ten years or so after George Meany, head of the AFL-CIO, had argued, "It is impossible to bargain collectively with the government," a large majority of the states and big cities had taken similar steps. Public employee unionism had apparently come of age everywhere but in the police departments.[20]

The second thing that struck the rank-and-file leaders was that

despite the previous failures of AFSCME and SCMWA, a few
other labor unions were preparing to mount yet another campaign to organize the police, a campaign that if successful would
destroy the fraternal and benevolent groups. Nothing tempted
the unions more than the New York City Police Department with
its roughly twenty thousand officers. Early in the 1950s Michael
Quill, head of the Transport Workers' Union, announced his
intention to unionize the city's police. Asked why a transit union
was going after police officers, he answered, "They ride in subways, don't they?" Quill's efforts attracted the rank-and-file, two-
thirds of whom allegedly signed pledge cards, but dismayed
Commissioner Monaghan, who forbade the men to join the
transit union and thereby stopped the organizing drive. A few
years later Henry Feinstein, head of the Teamsters' Local 237,
mounted another campaign, which prompted Cassese, then
president of the PBA, to state, "We do not need, nor want, the
help of any outside union to achieve our aims." Several thousand
policemen who thought otherwise welcomed the Teamsters. But
under strong pressure from Commissioner Kennedy and Mayor
Wagner, who threatened to strip Feinstein of a city job, the union
backed down.[21] Viewed along with similar efforts in Baltimore,
Seattle, Oakland, and other cities, these campaigns revealed that
the rank-and-file were well aware of the advantages of unionism
and saw no reason why they alone should be denied them.

Moreover, the rank-and-file leaders realized that they could
not count on the municipal authorities to hold off the labor
unions forever and that, if the authorities gave in, the fraternal
and benevolent associations were doomed. From this point it was
only a short step to the conclusion that, in order to retain their
power, the leaders would have to win for the rank-and-file the
same rights as other public employees. But in view of the vigorous
opposition to unionization, especially from the second generation
of reformers, the rank-and-file leaders were aware that they
might well have to engage in more militant tactics than electioneering, lobbying, and litigation. To put it bluntly, they might
have to call for slowdowns, speed-ups, sick-ins, strikes, and other
unprofessional and possibly illegal job actions unthinkable to
their predecessors. The leaders were ready to do so. Their confidence in direct action was rising, which was understandable
among Americans who had come of age at a time when the

United Automobile Workers and other unions were resorting to sit-ins and other militant tactics to gain recognition. For reasons that are unclear, their commitment to orderly social change, or in other words, to the assumption that in a democracy necessary reform can always be achieved through normal political channels, was waning too.

The new leaders could count on the support of a large majority of the rank-and-file for several reasons other than that they shared their faith in direct action and their doubt about orderly social change. For one thing, these leaders worked hard to gain the allegiance of the rank-and-file. Besides pressing the authorities to raise salaries, benefits, and pensions, they prevailed on the fraternal and benevolent associations to offer their members free legal aid, low-cost life insurance, and other valuable services. They also voiced the rank-and-file's protests against the civilian review boards, Supreme Court decisions, official investigative bodies, and income probes, polygraph tests, and other violations of their civil liberties.[22] For another thing, the rank-and-file had elected the new leaders largely on the basis of their promises to provide more forceful leadership than the incumbents. If the rank-and-file turned against the new leaders, it would probably not be because they were too militant but rather because they were not militant enough.

Thus from the mid-1950s on, the leaders of the fraternal and benevolent associations pressed the municipal and state authorities for a formal grievance procedure, in which the associations would represent the rank-and-file vis-à-vis their superiors; for a dues check-off, whereby the departments would deduct the rank-and-file's dues from their salaries and turn the money over to the associations; and for collective bargaining rights, by which the associations would negotiate salaries, benefits, and work rules for the rank-and-file. In other words, they demanded that the authorities recognize these groups as the representatives of the rank-and-file and treat them accordingly. To bring the authorities into line, the leaders worked in local elections, lobbied in city halls and state legislatures, and with the help of such prestigious law firms as Philips, Nizer, Benjamin, Krim, and Ballon, appealed to the courts. From time to time they also called upon or at least encouraged the rank-and-file to engage in slowdowns, sick-ins, and other job actions.[23] These activities generated so much pressure that the authorities were forced seriously to consider reversing their long-standing policies and giving in to the rank-and-file's demands.

The IACP and other reform groups appealed to the authorities to stand firm. Citing the conventional wisdom of organizational theory and a large body of legal opinion, which drew a sharp distinction not only between public employees and private employees but also between police officers and public employees, they charged that the rank-and-file's demands were misguided and illegal. A formal grievance procedure would destroy the authority of the police chief and the integrity of the civil service; a dues check-off would violate the judicial rulings that state and local agencies cannot be used to collect private debts; and collective bargaining agreements would be an unconstitutional delegation of authority. A firm stance was not only proper, the reformers insisted, it was also politic. A firm stance had not hurt Governor Coolidge of Massachusetts, whose suppression of the Boston police strike earned him the enviable reputation for decisiveness that served as a springboard for the vice-presidency and the presidency. Nor had it hurt Mayor Fletcher Bowron of Los Angeles, who won reelection in the late 1940s not long after he vetoed an ordinance that would have mandated a dues check-off for the Los Angeles Police Employees Union, an affiliate of the AFL.[24]

But these arguments lost a good deal of their force in the postwar years. During the 1950s and 1960s the authorities gave the firemen, teachers, garbagemen, and other public employees a formal grievance procedure, a dues check-off, and collective bargaining rights in Philadelphia, New York, Milwaukee, Boston, and many other big cities.[25] By so doing, they severely undercut the reform position. The reformers could still argue that a formal grievance procedure would handicap the police chief to a much greater degree than the fire chief or superintendent of schools. But under the circumstances they could not contend that it would undermine the integrity of the civil service. They could not claim that it was illegal for the authorities to make deductions from the rank-and-file's salaries and turn them over to their associations, and they could not insist that it was unconstitutional for the authorities to bargain with the rank-and-file's representatives. Hence the reformers were obliged to base their case against unionization on other grounds.

They were, by and large, unsuccessful. Falling back on the military analogy, they argued that policemen were not entitled to the same rights as firemen, sanitationmen, teachers, and other civil servants. But most Americans were not convinced by this agrument. They had long been urged by the second generation of reformers to think of policemen not as soldiers but as professionals. Though many Americans had reservations about the professional model, they no longer took it for granted that the police force was, in the words of Senator Sherman of Illinois, "the standing army against lawlessness" and should therefore be treated differently from other public agencies. The reformers also insisted that the rank-and-file's demands would lead inevitably to unionization, which would be "a death knell of *profession-alization,*" as the IACP put it.[26] But most Americans were not impressed by this argument either. The authorities had already given collective bargaining to teachers and other public employees who had fairly strong claims to professional status. To extend collective bargaining to the police might be misguided; but in the absence of the military analogy, which implied that unionization was seditious and strikes were treasonous, it would hardly be catastrophic.

The rank-and-file groups further weakened the reform position by claiming that all they wanted was to be recognized, not unionized, and by arguing that police officers should be represented by independent associations rather than by labor unions. Commissioner Kennedy, who strongly opposed the New York PBA's demands for recognition in the late 1950s, charged that this distinction was meaningless. Insisting that the nature of a group was determined by its function not its title, he declared, "When an organization acts like a union, talks like a union, makes demands like a union and conducts itself like a union, it cannot be heard to say that it is not a union."[27] Kennedy's logic was impeccable but not compelling. Along with the reformers, who objected to unionization on the grounds that it would subvert the neutrality of the police, the authorities were worried mainly about the organizing campaigns of the labor unions. They did not fully realize that if the PBAs and FOPs won a formal grievance procedure, a dues check-off, and collective bargaining, it would be hard, if not impossible, to distinguish them from the Transport Workers, Teamsters, and AFSCME locals.

Even if the authorities had foreseen the consequences, it would not have made much difference. During the 1950s and 1960s many elected officials — especially though not exclusively the reform mayors, who could not count on the support of the old-line machines — began to wonder whether it really was politic to resist the rank-and-file's demands and proceeded to calculate the costs of continuing to do so. Two trends in particular impressed them. First, the rank-and-file were starting to play a much more active role in electoral politics. Along with the firemen, teachers, garbagemen, and other municipal employees, they were developing into one of the most powerful groups in urban America and, as Lowi has argued, were emerging as the successors to the political machines. They were also beginning to flex the political muscle that later helped elect Charles Stenvig, former head of the Patrolmen's Association, as mayor of Minneapolis; Frank Rizzo, the controversial police commissioner, as mayor of Philadelphia; and Wayne Larkin, one-time head of the Police Officer's Guild, as Seattle city councilman.[28] The local politicians could win election and, as Kevin H. White of Boston and John V. Lindsay of New York demonstrated, reelection in the face of the rank-and-file's opposition; but their opposition did not make the job any easier.

Second, the rank-and-file were starting to take a much more militant stance in municipal affairs. With the tacit support, if not active encouragement, of the fraternal and benevolent associations, they engaged in a slowdown in New York in the early 1960s, a sick-in in Detroit a few years later, and similar job actions in Pittsburgh, Boston, and Atlanta not long afterward. They even went on strike in New York, Milwaukee, and Baltimore, though not until the early 1970s.[29] These job actions placed the local officials in an awkward spot. If they took no action, they would infuriate many citizens who were sorely troubled by the increase of criminal activity, the surge of violent protests, and the alleged breakdown of law and order. Inasmuch as law enforcement and peace-keeping were two of the few vital functions that were still handled at the local level, these officials were in no position to disclaim responsibility for the situation. But if they cracked down, they would alienate many policemen who were crucial to their schemes to raise productivity, enhance accountability, and otherwise improve the quality of public services. Unless the authorities punished the entire force, which would probably violate the civil service rules, they would also have to figure out which of the many officers who phoned in sick were malingering, a difficult and demeaning task.

Hence the elected officials concluded that it would be hazardous to resist the rank-and-file's demands. Even if they could survive the onslaught, they wondered what good would it do them. If they refused to give the PBAs and FOPs a formal grievance procedure, a dues check-off, and collective bargaining rights, the rank-and-file would probably turn to the Teamsters or AFSCME. These unions would welcome another opportunity to organize the police; and in view of their growing political influence and financial resources, they might well succeed this time. So far as the politicians were concerned, it would be hard to deal with Cassese and Parsell; but it would be much harder to deal with Jimmy Hoffa, the head of the Teamsters, and Jerry Wurf, the head of AFSCME. Their constituents were particularly apprehensive about the Teamsters. Late in the 1950s the New York City press appealed to the Wagner administration to go along with the PBA's demands for recognition on the grounds that it would undermine the Teamsters' organizing efforts. The fraternal and benevolent outfits often exploited the public's anxieties. During the mid-1960s the Detroit POA attempted to compel Mayor Jerome Cavanagh's administration to negotiate by threatening to affiliate with the Teamsters.[30] Although the union officials were bluffing, the mayor and his staff were reluctant to call them.

Hard pressed to defend the invidious distinction between police officers and other public employees on either ideological or political grounds, many elected officials realized that it was pointless to resist the rank-and-file's demands any longer. A few officials perceived that it might even be possible to get some sort of quid pro quo. In return for a formal grievance procedure, a dues check-off, and collective bargaining rights, the leaders of the rank-and-file might support organizational and other changes that would enhance the efficiency of the force. The response to the so-called Little Wagner Act, which extended collective bargaining to all of New York City's mayoral departments save the police, indicated that they might even settle for nominal increases in salaries and fringe benefits for the time being. By making these concessions, the authorities would transform the fraternal and benevolent associations from pressure groups into labor unions. And in the long run these unions might block reform proposals and demand exorbitant raises. But so far as most elected officials were concerned, the long run was someone else's problem; in the short run, which was all that mattered, a policy of accommodation was just about irresistible.

The rank-and-file groups made the most of the situation. Not long after taking over the New York PBA in 1958, Cassese asked for a dues check-off and, to strengthen his case, obtained authorizations from roughly 90 percent of the force. Commissioner Kennedy refused to consider it. Cassese appealed to the courts, which in the wake of Mayor Wagner's endorsement of the PBA's position ruled that the check-off would not undermine the commissioner's authority and ordered Kennedy to set it up. Cassese demanded a formal grievance procedure too. Kennedy, who regarded it as the harbinger of unionization, turned the request down and threatened to resign if overruled. Though under strong pressure from Cassese, Wagner backed the commissioner. When Kennedy quit a couple of years later, Wagner, who was coming up for reelection, appointed Chief Inspector Michael Murphy to succeed him; and with Wagner's approval, Murphy established a grievance procedure. Cassese next pressed the administration to give the police force the same collective bargaining rights that had been given the other mayoral departments by the Little Wagner Act. The mayor procrastinated. But when Cassese and Murphy reached an agreement whereby the PBA was forbidden to affiliate with a union and required to renounce the right to strike, he issued an executive order recognizing the association as the bargaining agent for the rank-and-file.[31]

Events took a somewhat different course in Detroit where, as a result of a long campaign by AFSCME and several other rank-and-file groups, the Michigan legislature passed a law in 1965 that authorized collective bargaining for all city and county employees. Several months later the Detroit POA, headed by Parsell, was recognized as the bargaining agent for the rank-and-file. The POA had won a dues check-off a decade before when the municipal authorities, in an attempt to head off an outcry from the taxpayers and yet maintain a working relationship with the association, offered the check-off in lieu of an across-the-board raise. But the association still lacked a formal grievance procedure. When the authorities declined to bargain over it and several other issues, the POA filed charges of unfair labor practices against the city and then encouraged the rank-and-file to join a sick-in, the so-called "blue-flu" epidemic of 1967. The job action brought the authorities to the bargaining table. Not long afterward the union and the city worked out an agreement whereby the POA's representatives would be permitted to look into grievances during working hours, sit in on disciplinary proceedings, and appeal any disputed trial board decision to arbitration.[32]

Events also took a slightly different turn in Boston, where AFSCME and a few other rank-and-file unions prevailed on the Massachusetts legislature to pass a bill in 1965 that authorized collective bargaining for all municipal employees except police officers. But this distinction was no longer defensible, not even at the site of the great police strike. Under pressure from the Boston Police Patrolmen's Association (PPA), which had just been set up by MacEachern and a few other officers, the legislature approved an amendment less than a year later that extended the privilege to the police. Shortly thereafter the Collective Bargaining Federation, an amalgamation of four state and city police employee organizations other than the PPA, petitioned the Massachusetts Labor Relations Commission to hold an election to determine which group should represent the rank-and-file. But the PPA, which attacked the federation for siding with management and otherwise conveyed a more militant impression, won the election by a two to one majority and was certified as the bargaining agent for the patrolmen. The association and the city made little progress in the first round of negotiations. But after the state labor relations commission sent in a mediator, an agreement was reached that gave the PPA a dues check-off and a formal grievance procedure, which was later expanded into a full-fledged "bill of rights."[33]

By the early 1970s the outcome was no longer in doubt. The rank-and-file organizations had in one way or another obtained a dues check-off, a formal grievance procedure, and collective bargaining rights not only in New York, Detroit, and Boston but also in Philadelphia, Buffalo, Milwaukee, Omaha, Oakland, Seattle, and Los Angeles. It was only a matter of time before they gained these privileges in Atlanta, where in spite of the adamant opposition of Chief Herbert T. Jenkins and the city council, the rank-and-file formed an FOP lodge in the late 1960s and persuaded the Georgia Supreme Court to overturn a state.law forbidding them to join a labor union.[34] The consequences were momentous. For years the rank-and-file organizations had lived a hand-to-mouth existence; now, without even dunning their members, they received a steady and sizable income that could be spent on lobbying, litigation, and electioneering. For years they had drawn only a small fraction of the force; now they attracted an overwhelming majority, which needed their financial, moral, and political support at disciplinary proceedings. For years they had pleaded with the municipal authorities to pay attention to their requests; now for the first time they held the legal right to insist that the authorities sit down at the bargaining table.

Once the rank-and-file got collective bargaining, three distinct though closely related issues surfaced. First, which of the many outfits that claimed to speak for the rank-and-file would be certified to bargain with the authorities? This issue was resolved without much fuss in New York, where the PBA was certified by the mayor's executive order, and Detroit, where the POA was recognized by the authorities. The outcome was much the same in Philadelphia, where the FOP had informally represented the rank-and-file for decades, and Seattle, where the Police Officers' Guild, the successor to the Police Union, was just as well entrenched. But the issue was settled only after hard-fought elections in Boston, where the PPA upset the Collective Bargaining Federation; in Hartford, where the International Brotherhood of Police Officers, an affiliate of the National Association of Government Employees, defeated AFSCME Local 234; and in Omaha, where the National Union of Police Officers, an outfit that later affiliated with the Service Employees International Union, beat AFSCME Local 531.[35] No matter how the issue was resolved, however, one and only one group emerged as the representative of the rank-and-file everywhere except in the handful of cities which had not yet adopted collective bargaining.

Second, where would the line be drawn between work rules, which were negotiable, and managerial prerogatives, which were not? This issue was settled in different ways in different cities, but in most of them the unions prevailed on the authorities to accept an extremely broad interpretation of the scope of bargaining. Soon after the Washington legislature authorized collective bargaining for public employees, the Seattle Police Officers' Guild persuaded the city council to sign a contract that covered virtually every working condition and created machinery through which the union could challenge almost any change in policy. The Boston PPA worked out a similar agreement with Mayor White. In the aftermath of the "blue-flu" epidemic the Detroit POA forced Commissioner Ray Girardin to back down from his previous position that the department would not negotiate over one-man squad cars, overtime rates, or any other rule included in the police manual.[36] The unions were less successful in Cincinnati and a few other cities. But even there they prevailed on the authorities to bargain not only over salaries and benefits but also over deployment, work load, discipline, and many other things that were heretofore the exclusive province of the chiefs.

Third, how far could the unions go to force the authorities to give in to their demands? Or to put it another way, had the police the right to strike or otherwise withhold their services? To resolve this issue, many states outlawed strikes by all public employees; many others—including Pennsylvania and Hawaii, the only ones that allowed strikes by public employees—banned walkouts by policemen and firemen. Some cities passed similar laws. Despite these restrictions, the rank-and-file engaged in numerous job actions, up to and including full-fledged strikes, in Detroit, Milwaukee, Pittsburgh, Rochester, New York, Baltimore, and other cities in the late 1960s and early 1970s.[37] So did the teachers, garbagemen, transit workers, and other municipal employees. The authorities sharply denounced these job actions; but they were so anxious to get the officers back on the streets and so reluctant to tangle with the unions that, instead of invoking the legal sanctions, they usually gave in to the demands and granted amnesty to the strikers. So long as the laws were on the books, it was risky for the police to withhold their services; but as their recent experiences indicated, it was not too risky, and it probably was not much more risky for them than for other municipal employees.

By the early 1970s, less than thirty years after the IACP published its pamphlet opposing unionization, the fraternal and benevolent organizations had been transformed from pressure groups into de facto labor unions. As unions, they were unique in one way. With the exception of a few unions that belonged to the National Association of Government Employees, the Service Employees International Union, or AFSCME, most of them were independent, affiliated, if at all, with the FOP or the ICPA and not with a national union. Their autonomy was potentially a grave disadvantage. But most unions more than compensated for it by developing a knack for getting from the city councils, state legislatures, courts, and voters what they could not win at the bargaining table. These outfits were so successful that they showed little interest in the efforts by Cassese and others to set up a nationwide police union in the early 1970s. The attitude of the Los Angeles Fire and Police Protective League was typical. Invited by Cassese to join the new union, the board of directors replied with "a definite *no*" and, pointing out that the rank-and-file were well represented by the league, went on to say, "We cannot foresee the need for a union."[38]

Down through the early 1960s the reformers spoke out strongly against the unionization of the big-city police. In a rash of speeches, articles, and official statements, which drew heavily on the military analogy and the professional model, they stressed time and again that this movement would nullify the achievements of the campaign for police reform. It would undermine the police officers' claims to professional status, infringe on the police chiefs' managerial prerogatives, inject partisan politics into departmental affairs, and by encouraging the rank-and-file to strike or otherwise withhold their services, weaken public confidence in the police. The reformers also fought hard against the attempts to unionize their departments. Chief Vernon of Oakland issued an ultimatum forbidding the rank-and-file to join a union shortly after AFSCME started a drive to organize the Oakland Police Department. And Commissioner Kennedy of New York threatened to resign if Mayor Wagner gave in to the PBA's demands for a formal grievance procedure and collective bargaining rights.[39]

Some reformers carried on the struggle into the late 1960s and early 1970s. Perhaps the most formidable was Chief Jenkins, who assumed command of the Atlanta police in the late 1940s and over the next twenty years turned it into one of the few so-called professional forces in the region. A liberal who desegregated the

Atlanta police at the beginning of his term and served on the President's Riot Commission near the end, Jenkins was opposed to any and all rank-and-file groups. Supported by Mayor William B. Hartsfield and other civic leaders who shared his views that these outfits were an impediment to police reform, Jenkins had crushed an FOP lodge in the late 1940s. When the rank-and-file, who were fed up with their low salaries and the chief's arbitrary power, founded another lodge in the late 1960s, Jenkins tried hard to cripple it too. Besides assigning its president and secretary-treasurer to beats so far apart they could seldom get together for meetings, he attacked their scheme to challenge the city attorney's ruling that the FOP was a labor union and as such violated state law. The FOP won the case. But in the face of continued opposition from Jenkins and Mayor Ivan Allen, Jr., the rank-and-file could not prevail on the city council to authorize a dues check-off, a formal grievance procedure, or collective bargaining rights.[40]

For most reformers, who lacked Jenkins' long tenure, political know-how, and professional standing, it was foolhardy to continue the struggle. The rank-and-file outfits, whose support was vital to the efforts to improve the quality of service and the image of policing, were far too powerful. They could urge the officers to ignore the chief's orders, carry them out in a halfhearted way, and thereby sabotage his law enforcement policies. They could speak out against his reforms in city halls and state capitols and, if they were adopted, challenge them in the courts. They could sponsor slowdowns, sick-ins, and other job actions that were hardly likely to enhance the chief's reputation. If greatly aroused, the rank-and-file groups could even raise doubts about the chief's integrity. Shortly after Donald D. Pomerleau, a staunch opponent of unionization, took over as head of the Baltimore force the police union, an AFSCME affiliate, let it be known that he had hired a contractor who employed off-duty officers to paint his house.[41] For this action Pomerleau was censured by the governor. With only a few exceptions, which included Jenkins, Stanley R. Schrotel of Cincinnati, and Clarence M. Kelley of Kansas City, most reformers were no longer willing to run these risks by the late 1960s and early 1970s.

Even if they had been, it would not have made much difference. By the time Howard R. Leary took over the New York City police in the mid-1960s the PBA had already been transformed from a pressure group into a labor union. Patrick V. Murphy, who headed the Detroit police in the late 1960s and then succeeded Leary in New York, found himself in much the same spot. So did Robert J. diGrazia, who assumed command of the Boston police in the early 1970s, and Charles R. Gain, the head of the Oakland police who was appointed acting chief of the Seattle force in the early 1970s. The reformers could try to pre-serve their managerial prerogatives, to insist that the unions stick to monetary issues and leave the administration of the department to the chiefs, as Chief Schrotel, then president of the IACP, put it.[42] They could also attempt to block legislation to legalize police strikes and other job actions. But in view of the tre-mendous influence of the rank-and-file groups the reformers could not hope to prevail on the authorities to rescind the dues check-off, formal grievance procedure, or collective bargaining rights and thereby turn these groups back into fraternal and benevolent associations.

As the reformers feared, the unions often opposed their attempts to improve policing. The Detroit POA fought Commis-sioner Murphy's proposal to restrict promotional exams to patrol-men who had completed a year or two of college. The Providence FOP blocked the chief's plan to introduce lateral entry. The New York PBA prevented several commissioners from shifting from two-man to one-man squad cars. The Boston PPA lobbied against Mayor White's plan to hire fifty civilian clerks and fifty civilian traffic directors. The Seattle Police Officers' Guild went to court to stop the chief from using polygraph tests to investigate allegations of corruption. The unions also resorted to militant tactics that were incompatible with reform aspirations. The Boston PPA set up pickets at headquarters to prevent tailors from sewing name tags on their uniforms. The Trenton PBA handed out a rash of speeding tickets to force the city fathers to come to terms on a new contract. The Pittsburgh FOP came down with the so-called "blue-flu" to protest the chief's decision to transfer white officers out of a black community. The Milwaukee Police-men's Protective Association (PPA) went on strike when the municipality refused to give in to their demands after nearly a year of negotiations.[43]

But as the reformers found out, the unions often went along

with their efforts to upgrade policing. The Boston PPA and the Detroit POA appealed to the legislatures and courts to abolish residency requirements for police officers. The Cincinnati FOP and the Milwaukee PPA supported schemes that encouraged the rank-and-file to attend classes at nearby colleges and universities. The San Francisco POA and the New Haven AFSCME Local 530 backed proposals to reduce political interference in the promotional process. The New York PBA and the Philadelphia FOP led the campaign to destroy the civilian or civilian-controlled review boards set up in the early and mid-1960s. As the years passed, many unions also developed close working relationships with the chiefs. Under Ed Kiernan, who succeeded Cassese in the late 1960s, the New York PBA, which had bitterly fought a proposed fourth platoon, sat down with Commissioner Murphy to devise a more flexible deployment schedule. Under Thomas Rappanotti, who served as its business agent in the late 1960s, the Baltimore union, AFSCME Local 1195, engaged in an ongoing dialogue with Commissioner Pomerleau. Realizing that they and the chiefs shared common problems, if not similar objectives, some of the unions even worked out a style that Margaret A. Levi has aptly referred to as "collusive bargaining."[44]

As the reformers also found out, the unions sometimes acted as a brake on the rank-and-file. Probably the outstanding example took place in New York after the city and the PBA reached an agreement in the late 1960s that fixed the ratio between patrolmen's and sergeants' salaries at 3.0 to 3.5. The city subsequently reneged on the agreement, and the association filed suit shortly after. The courts ruled in favor of the PBA and held that the city, which had given the sergeants a raise in 1968, owed the patrolmen about $2,700 each. The city appealed, and early in 1971 the courts ordered a new trial. The verdict, which was completely unexpected, infuriated the rank-and-file, three-quarters of whom joined in the first wildcat strike in the department's history. The city obtained a back-to-work order, which the patrolmen ignored, and as the strike dragged on, the city called on the PBA to use its influence to end the walkout. Kiernan, who had opposed the strike, was willing to try. He issued an appeal to the strikers, hundreds of whom were picketing the association's headquarters to express their dissatisfaction with his leadership. When the appeal failed, Kiernan began to work on the PBA delegates, the rank-and-file's representatives to the association. Shortly afterward the delegates called for an end to the walkout, a move which, in conjunction with a pledge from the courts to expedite the pending trial, prompted the rank-and-file to return to work.[45]

For these reasons the reformers abandoned the struggle against unionization in the late 1960s and early 1970s. Addressing the annual convention of the IACP, Commissioner Pomerleau conceded that police unions were inevitable and possibly even desirable: "They are here to stay, and we must work with them." His fellow chiefs apparently agreed. Late in the 1960s the IACP, which had hitherto ignored the existence of the ICPA, appointed several members to sit on a joint committee that served as a liaison between the two associations. At about the same time the IACP printed a report from a Special Committee on Police Employee Organizations, chaired by Chief Curtis Brostron of St. Louis, which advised the chiefs to adopt a conciliatory attitude toward the unions. The IACP went even further in the early 1970s. Along with the Police Foundation and the Labor Management Relations Service, it drafted a set of guidelines that acknowledged the right of the rank-and-file to join labor unions.[46] It also started publishing the *Public Safety Labor Reporter*, a monthly journal that keeps track of collective bargaining and other activities which were virtually inconceivable two decades ago. A unique compilation, the *Reporter* reflects the transformation of the rank-and-file groups and documents their impact on the campaign for police reform.

9. Changes in Policing, 1930-1970

Late in the 1960s a panel of journalists asked O. W. Wilson, who was about to retire as superintendent of the Chicago police, whether he had done what he set out to do seven and a half years before. At the risk of sounding smug, Wilson replied, he thought that he had. Was he apprehensive that the department might abandon his reforms after his departure, the panel went on. Not at all, Wilson responded. Its leadership was able and its structure sound; although a few pockets of resistance remained, they would be wiped out before long. During the next ten or twenty years, Wilson assured the panel, the Chicago police would "continue to increase its effectiveness, quality, and level of service."[1] Wilson confined his remarks to the Chicago force, but other reformers were impressed by the striking changes in the Cincinnati, Los Angeles, Atlanta, St. Louis, and Kansas City police. They were convinced that by virtue of their efforts most departments had been pretty much transformed in the thirty-five years or so since the Wickersham Commission report of 1931.

The reform efforts had some impact on the tradition of policing that had emerged out of the nineteenth century and survived the first wave of police reform. One result of these efforts was that the state and federal authorities took numerous steps that were inconsistent with the pattern of local control. Besides supporting paramilitary constabularies and authorizing official investigations, which were common practices by the 1920s, many state legislatures imposed minimal training standards and built regional training facilities. A few, including New York, Illinois, and California, set up bureaus of identification, intelligence, and investigation, which served as statewide clearinghouses for criminal records and other sources of information. Besides managing the National Division of Identification and Information, which was formed in the 1920s, the FBI assumed responsibility first for the *Uniform Crime Reports* and later for the National Crime Information Center, a nationwide clearinghouse for criminal histories.[2] In response to the fear of crime, which spread throughout the nation in the early and middle 1960s, the Congress created the Law Enforcement Assistance Administration (LEAA), a division of the Justice Department which made grants to police forces and other parts of the criminal justice system.

Another result of the reform efforts was that most police departments adopted various policies which were at odds with the attachment to a civilian orientation. In addition to employing the rhetoric of the "war on crime" and stressing the martial arts in the training academies, these departments ordered grenade launchers, infrared screening devices, and other weapons that were more appropriate for a military or paramilitary outfit than for a civilian police force. Chief Ed Davis even asked the Los Angeles City Council to appropriate funds for two jet helicopters, presumably to cut off the narcotics traffic that flowed north from Mexico, and added that he would request a submarine in the near future. "Why don't you go to the Navy for that?" Councilman Thomas Bradley retorted. In the aftermath of the 1960s riots, which overwhelmed the police forces in Los Angeles, Newark, Detroit, and several other cities, many departments attempted to turn groups of ordinary officers who were accustomed to working on their own into highly centralized and tightly disciplined riot control units. Following recommendations proposed by the FBI and the army, the departments taught these units how to form lines, circles, diamonds, wedges, and other formations that were designed to disperse unruly crowds.[3]

Still another result of the reform effort was that most police forces implemented many changes that ran counter to the commitment to catchall and responsive activity. Following a trend that was well underway by the 1920s, they turned the responsibility for operating local lockups, guarding school crossings, running emergency ambulances, writing parking tickets, and carrying out other tasks that were allegedly unrelated to crime prevention over to other public agencies. Most departments also increased the number of special squads that functioned in a preventive style. Like the vice and traffic squads on which they were modeled, these special units were compelled to seek out infractions because they enforced laws which in the eyes of many citizens dealt with activities that were not crimes and which therefore generated few complaints. Applying the principles of O.W. Wilson and other reformers, most departments even extended a preventive style of policing, which had hitherto been restricted to the plainclothes units, to the uniformed force. They instructed the patrolmen to stop, quiz, and search a citizen not only if they saw him commit a crime or received a complaint about him but also if they felt that he was behaving in a suspicious way, a practice that sometimes verged on out-and-out harassment.

But these changes did not have much impact on the pattern of local control. The state training standards and regional training facilities did not infringe on the autonomy of the big-city forces because most of them had more stringent standards and more elaborate facilities of their own. The state bureaus of identification, intelligence, and investigation, which were set up to facilitate the flow of information, did not intervene in the day-to-day operations of the police departments. Outside of Florida, Tennessee, and to a lesser degree California, the state legislatures did not encourage the municipal police forces to consolidate along metropolitan or regional lines. The situation was much the same at the federal level. Despite its great prestige the FBI did not wield much power over the big-city police, though by virtue of its publication of the *Uniform Crime Reports* it had something to say about their reporting procedures. According to the House Committee on Government Operations, the LEAA, far from interfering in the everyday working of the departments, did not even attempt to monitor how they spent federal funds.[4] Few officials recommended that the LEAA issue guidelines for the local police, and in the face of the vigorous opposition of J. Edgar Hoover and other reformers, none suggested that the Congress set up a national police force.

Nor did the changes have much impact on the attachment to a civilian orientation. The military weapons, which were more often than not acquired as a result of the largesse of the LEAA, were incidental to the day-to-day operations of the big-city police; so were the riot control squads and their martial formations. If anything, the military style lost a lot of its force in the second third of the century. Not only did the second generation of reformers adopt a professional model instead of a military analogy but the rank-and-file associations also prevailed on the authorities to institute grievance procedures, collective bargaining, and other practices that were out of place in a military or paramilitary outfit. The results were striking. No longer did the municipal authorities look for former military officers to head their police forces. No longer did the police chiefs insist that the rank-and-file stand at attention at roll calls, salute their superiors, and otherwise maintain a martial bearing. No longer did the police forces engage in the annual displays of precision marching that were so brilliantly satirized by Buster Keaton in *Cops*.

These changes did not have much impact on the commitment to catchall and responsive activity either. Many police departments still managed local jails, censored motion pictures, regulated traffic, looked for missing persons, and carried out a wide range of other tasks that were not closely related to crime prevention. Moreover, the uniformed force, which contained a large if, as a result of the proliferation of special squads, dwindling proportion of the sworn personnel, operated largely in a responsive fashion. According to Albert J. Reiss, a sociologist who conducted a survey of police-citizen encounters in a few high-crime neighborhoods in Boston, Chicago, and Washington, D.C., in the late 1960s, nearly nine of every ten encounters were initiated by the public.[5] Nor did all of the special squads, or even most of them if the vice and traffic squads are excluded, operate in a preventive manner. The community relations, missing persons, and juvenile squads ordinarily waited for a complaint before taking action; so did the detective squads and the homicide, safe-and-lock, pickpocket, rape, and other subdivisions thereof. The planning and research, internal affairs, and intelligence units did not as a rule deal directly with citizens; neither did the special units which were responsible for the training academies, crime labs, records systems, and communications networks.

But the campaign for police reform was not primarily an attempt to undermine the tradition of policing that had emerged

out of the nineteenth century. Wilson, Herbert T. Jenkins, and
their associates were more willing than the first generation of reformers to work within the context of local control, a civilian
orientation, and catchall and responsive activity. They were less
prepared, however, to put up with the low status of the American
police and to go along with the widespread incompetence, corruption, and lawlessness which in their opinion were largely responsible for it. From their viewpoint the campaign for police reform was above all a struggle to put an end to these abuses and
thereby to raise the status of the police. These objectives inspired
the efforts to enhance the autonomy, raise the caliber, and increase the proficiency of the big-city police. And these efforts had
a profound impact on the structure, personnel, and function of
policing in the second third of the century.

The drive to enhance the autonomy of the big-city police was a
qualified success. For one reason, the reformers reduced the ward
politicians' influence over the chiefs, which had long been a
principal source of leverage over the departments. By exploiting
the scandals that racked one city after another in the postwar
years to discredit the machines, the reformers made it harder for
the politicians to browbeat the chiefs. By persuading their fellow
Americans, the lower and lower middle classes as well as the
upper middle and upper classes, that politics should be strictly
divorced from policing, the reformers also made it much riskier
for the politicians to get rid of the chiefs. Thus most chiefs now
enjoyed a degree of independence in New York, Chicago, and
Kansas City that would have been virtually inconceivable a generation or two earlier. This phenomenon was most striking in Los
Angeles, where Chief William H. Parker paid so little attention
to the city councilmen that they were hard pressed to get an appointment to talk with him in the late 1950s and early 1960s. But
it was so commonplace by the mid-1960s that the President's
Crime Commission, by no means a radical outfit, warned that in
many cities the elected officials no longer accepted responsibility
for the conduct of the police force.[6]

Another reason for the increased autonomy of the big-city
police was that the reformers had weakened the ward politicians'
hold over the captains, which had been another principal source
of leverage over the departments. By pressing the authorities to
close down many station houses, the reformers severed the nexus

that had tied the precincts to the wards, bound the captains to the bosses, and in conjunction with the spoils system, subordinated the departments to the machines. By encouraging the proliferation of special squads, the reformers also undermined the captain's position. This process had gone so far that not long after taking over as commissioner of the New York City police, Patrick V. Murphy made it clear that he intended to restore to the captains some of their former authority.[7] Hence the politicians lost much of their clout after World War II just about everywhere save in Albany, Buffalo, and a few other cities where the old-line machines still carried a great deal of weight. Even the Knapp Commission and the Pennsylvania Crime Commission, which published stinging indictments of the New York and Philadelphia police in the early 1970s, found little evidence that the ward leaders played much of a role in departmental affairs.[8] The police did not treat the politicians as ordinary citizens, as Wilson boasted; but neither did the politicians treat the departments as adjuncts of the machines whose primary purpose was to strengthen their hold over urban America.

At the insistence of the reformers most departments set up planning and research units, which were supposed to cut down the opportunities for outside interference by spelling out, or at any rate helping to spell out, the goals of the force in an unambiguous way. But here things went awry. While most Americans agreed that the police should enforce the law, keep the peace, and serve the public, they disagreed whether they should arrest citizens for getting drunk, issue permits for potentially violent demonstrations, and maintain special details at railway stations. While most Americans agreed that the police should use their resources as efficiently as possible, they disagreed whether they should operate out of the precincts or headquarters, work in three or four platoons, and patrol on foot or in cars, or in one-man or two-man cars.[9] No matter how ably staffed and well funded, which few of them were, the planning and research units could not do much to prevent these controversies from surfacing in the city councils, state legislatures, and other public arenas, where the local politicians and pressure groups often exerted a degree of influence over departmental policies and practices that was inconsistent with the aspirations of the reformers, if not necessarily incompatible with the wishes of the voters.

Most departments also reorganized their forces along functional lines, a step that was supposed to reduce the opportunities for outside interference by clarifying the division of responsibility between the precincts and the squads. Here too things did not work out quite right. The reorganizations did little good because the opportunities were a result not so much of the hazy division of responsibility as of the dubious legitimacy of vice control, traffic regulation, and other police chores. These changes even did some harm because the members of the special squads and other functional units often developed a sense of loyalty to their outfits instead of their departments and to their commanders rather than their chiefs. Far from reducing the opportunities for outside interference, the reorganizations simply shifted them from the precincts to the squads, a trend that was well underway by the late 1920s, and from the ward politicians to the policy bankers, narcotics dealers, and other disreputable types. Thus it was hardly surprising that the squads replaced the precincts as the primary source of police corruption in New Orleans, New York, and most other big cities after World War II.[10]

On the advice of the reformers most departments formed special inspectional units, which were supposed to reduce the amount of outside interference by keeping close watch over the rank-and-file and letting the chiefs know which of their men were not on the job. The results were disappointing. Manned by a small cadre of officers, some of whom were inhibited by a concern for the reputation of their departments, these units found it hard to expose their incompetent, corrupt, and lawless peers, who often went to great lengths to conceal their malfeasance. They found it even harder to substantiate their suspicions because most citizens were unwilling to file complaints against policemen and most officers were reluctant to testify against one another. Not until the Justice Department made a report in 1964 did Superintendent Wilson find out that a score of Chicago officers, including a confidential investigator who served as his administrative assistant, were operating a protection and shakedown racket. And not until the New York *Times* broke the story in 1968 did Commissioner Howard R. Leary learn that dozens of New York patrolmen were spending part of the night shift sleeping in parking lots, school yards, and other quiet spots, a practice popularly known as "cooping."[11]

Most departments also cut down the number of high-ranking officials who reported directly to the chiefs, a step that was supposed to reduce the amount of outside interference by helping the chiefs figure out which of the superior officers to hold accountable when things went wrong. Here too the results were less than satisfactory. Most high-ranking officials were prone to praise the efforts of their units and, in the face of clear evidence to the contrary, to shift the responsibility to other parts of the force or other branches of government. If this tactic failed, they were ready to deny responsibility on the grounds that apart from preparing unfavorable efficiency reports, which might or might not be taken into account when promotions were handed out, they had few effective sanctions over their subordinates. Hence most chiefs were hard put to figure out which of the superior officers to hold accountable; and with a few exceptions, they were even harder put to do anything about it. As Wilson showed, the chiefs could pass over candidates for promotion, demote inspectors to captains, and restructure the high command.[12] But they could not dismiss superior officers without a trial; nor could they handpick their successors, who worked their way up mainly via seniority and test scores.

Hence the reformers had a profound impact on the structure of the big-city police. In all but a handful of cities they weakened the position of the ward leaders, undermined the influence of the precinct captains, severed the connections between them, and thereby destroyed the territorial basis of decentralization that had heretofore been an integral feature of the American police. But by the same token the reformers also encouraged the proliferation of the special squads, stimulated the transformation of the rank-and-file associations, and brought about other changes that reinforced the functional basis of decentralization that is now one of the hallmarks of most police forces. As a result the big-city police were more autonomous in the mid-1960s than in the late 1920s, and far more so than in the early 1890s; but nowhere, not even in Los Angeles and Cincinnati, which boasted highly apolitical departments, were they as autonomous as doctors and other professionals. There was one striking and ironic difference. By the early and middle 1960s the municipal and state officials intervened in departmental policies and practices not so much at the request of the ward politicians as at the insistence of the rank-and-file leaders.

The campaign to raise the caliber of the big-city police was a partial success. To the reformers' delight, most departments did a pretty good job of weeding out unqualified applicants. They turned away everyone who was over thirty-five years old, or in some cities thirty, and had not graduated from high school; and they subjected everyone else to thorough physical exams, exhaustive character checks, stiff civil service tests, and some sort of psychiatric or psychological screening. Nowhere in urban America — not even in Chicago, Virgil W. Peterson conceded — could the politicians force the medical examiners to overlook chronic ailments, compel the civil service officials to circulate copies of the tests in advance, or otherwise help the candidates circumvent the requirements.[13] By the 1960s most recruits were in their twenties or at most their early thirties and had at least a high school degree or its equivalent; they did not suffer from alcoholism and other debilitating diseases, nor had they been arrested, let alone convicted and incarcerated. Since they did not owe their jobs to the local politicians and could not count on them to defend their interests, most recruits were not inclined to give their primary loyalty to the old-line machines, much less to follow their orders when they ran counter to instructions from headquarters.

But to the reformers' dismay, most departments had a hard time attracting the most qualified candidates. Apart from the rules against lateral entry, which allegedly discouraged many first-rate young men from embarking on a career as a police officer, the reasons were twofold. Despite the efforts to increase the salaries of the big-city police, which were fairly successful, policing was not especially remunerative. Nor, despite the attempts to raise the status of the big-city police, which were fairly successful too, was it particularly prestigious. As a result policing was in a poor position to compete with business, medicine, law, and engineering for upper-middle-class college graduates. During the 1950s and early 1960s the New York City police drew the great majority of their recruits from the lower middle class; so did the Portland police. Only a small fraction of the recruits were college graduates — roughly two percent in Portland and six percent in

Los Angeles, where nineteen out of every twenty applicants were rejected. According to surveys conducted in New York and a few other cities, most of the recruits went into policing not so much out of a commitment to public service as out of a concern for personal security.[14]

Most departments also had trouble turning capable recruits into competent officers. They bowed to pressures from the reformers to set up training academies and, after they were set up, to lengthen their programs, enrich their curricula, and upgrade their instructors. But though these academies put an end to the practice of sending the recruits out with only a badge, a gun, a billy, and perhaps a few pointers on a pistol range and a few classes in self-defense, they left a lot to be desired. For one reason, the training academies did not teach much about the theory of police work, a subject that would probably have been well above the heads of most of the students and many of the teachers. The schools of criminology and departments of police science offered courses on this subject, but the recruits were not required to take them.[15] For another reason, the training academies did not deal much with the everyday problems of police work, a policy that presumably reflected the reluctance of most reformers to acknowledge how much of their time the patrolmen spent on things other than crime prevention. But in all fairness the police academies probably trained their recruits to patrol the streets about as well as the graduate schools prepared their students to teach classes.

Most departments also gave in to demands from the reformers to forbid the rank-and-file to accept rewards, hold outside jobs, and engage in other activities that were allegedly inconsistent with their professional stature. But though these changes served as a curb on some officers who felt no compunction about supplementing their salary by exploiting their position, they had a couple of unintended consequences which more or less defeated the reformers' purposes. The restrictions on moonlighting infuriated the rank-and-file, who badly needed the extra income and, now that they were forbidden to take rewards, knew of no other legitimate way of earning it. The rank-and-file were also incensed by the income probes, polygraph tests, and other degrading and perhaps unconstitutional measures which were widely employed to find out whether the officers were violating these restrictions.[16] If policemen were supposed to behave like professionals, the rank-and-file wanted to know why they were paid little better than skilled laborers and treated little better than common criminals. In the absence of satisfactory answers, many of them drew the conclusion that they were not professionals but workers and that, as workers, they should unionize to defend their vital interests.

Most departments also had a hard time moving up their best officers and getting rid of their worst. The authorities went along with the reformers' proposals to insulate the promotional process from the local politicians in all except a handful of cities. But in the face of strong opposition from the rank-and-file they turned down most of the reformers' proposals to increase the chief's discretion, stress on-the-job performance, allow lateral entry, and otherwise downgrade the importance of seniority and written tests. So far as the reformers were concerned, the results were less than satisfactory. As the President's Crime Commission pointed out, the promotional process slowed down the advancement of many capable policemen and perhaps drove some to move on to other jobs where their abilities would be recognized sooner.[17] It also gave the patrolmen who had a knack for taking exams and biding their time the edge over their fellow officers who, on the basis of past performance, educational achievement, and personal experience, had greater leadership potential. Although some of these officers managed to work their way up through the ranks, the promotional process increased the likelihood that by the time they reached a position of authority, most of them would be strongly committed to the status quo.

The authorities also followed the reformers' recommendations to insulate the disciplinary process from the local politicians in all except a handful of cities. But at the same time they overrode the reformers' objections to the rank-and-file's requests for a grievance procedure, legal representation, and a host of other devices that improved their prospects before the departmental trial boards. So far as the reformers were concerned, the results were far from gratifying. As the Pennsylvania Crime Commission pointed out, the disciplinary process was full of loopholes. If brought up on charges — which in view of the difficulty of finding witnesses who would appear at the trial and getting policemen to testify against one another was quite unlikely — the accused could file for retirement and, if he had served long enough, collect his pension. If he chose to fight the charges, he or his lawyer had the right to cross-examine the witnesses; and if he was convicted, he could appeal to the courts, which were fairly lenient when an officer stood to lose his pension as well as his job.[18] Some unscrupulous officers were removed by this process. But enough escaped through one or another of the loopholes to reveal that policemen were no more inclined to police themselves than doctors, lawyers, academics, and other groups which enjoyed this privilege.

Hence the reformers had a pronounced impact on the personnel of the big-city police. By virtue of their efforts, the departments were able to turn away many overage, ill-educated, illiterate, incapacitated, and unsavory applicants who regarded policing as a livelihood and planned to draw their salary, stay out of trouble, put in their twenty or twenty-five years, and then live on their pension. But the departments were not able to attract many upper-middle-class college graduates who, the reformers believed, were inclined to view policing as a calling and to dedicate themselves to the public service; nor were they able to promote them over the heads of their less competent fellow officers. According to the reformers' criteria, the big-city police were therefore better qualified in the mid-1960s than in the late 1920s, and far more so than in the early 1890s; but nowhere, not even in Portland and Tucson, which had fairly stringent standards, were they as well qualified as lawyers and other professionals. Whether the reformers' criteria were sound was another matter. But this issue did not surface until the late 1960s and early 1970s when several blacks and Puerto Ricans filed suits in Boston, Oakland, Philadelphia, and other cities charging that the entrance requirements bore little or no relation to on-the-job performance.

The drive to increase the proficiency of the big-city police was marginally successful. Most departments sloughed off a few of their so-called nonpolice functions, employed civilians in positions previously filled by sworn officers, and shifted from foot to motorized patrols and from two-man to one-man squad cars. By virtue of these changes many officers who had been running jails, typing reports, and doing other tasks that were unrelated to crime prevention were shifted to the uniformed force. Yet despite these reforms, relatively fewer officers were out on the street in the mid-1960s than in the late 1920s. The reasons were twofold.

First, under pressure from the reformers, who wanted to raise the caliber of the big-city police, most departments went on a five-day week and an eight-hour day, gave longer vacations and sick leaves, and made so many other improvements in working conditions that only about one-fifth of the force was on duty at any one time.[19] Second, again under pressure from the reformers, who hoped to enhance the autonomy of the big-city police, most departments created so many special squads and set up so many high-level positions that only about one-half of the officers on duty were out on patrol or assigned to a unit that was directly involved in crime prevention.

Moreover, the patrolmen spent most of their time — perhaps as much as 80 percent, according to Reiss, who did research in several high-crime neighborhoods in Boston, Chicago, and Washington, D.C. — dealing with what they considered noncriminal matters.[20] They resolved domestic disputes, helped out at accidents, broke up noisy parties, headed off potential rumbles, looked for stray children, handed out traffic directions, and responded to all sorts of calls that were generated by something other than a violation of the criminal law. By responding to these calls, which were a sign of the remarkable tenacity of the catchall tradition of American policing, the patrolmen rendered a valuable service to the urban community. But according to the reformers, the proficiency of the big-city police was essentially a function of their capacity to prevent criminal activity, a notion that had been adopted in the postwar years not only by the rank-and-file but also by a large majority of the American people. By this criterion most departments left much to be desired. In other words, the reform schemes had only a slight effect on the proficiency of the big-city police because they could not offset the relative decrease in the size of the patrol force or weaken the tenacity of the catchall tradition of American policing.

Most departments also adopted the theory of crime prevention advanced by Parker and Wilson in the 1950s. According to this theory, the police could do more to prevent crime by reducing the opportunities for criminal activity than by trying to solve the social problems underlying it. This theory, which was embodied in the tactic of preventive patrol, was plausible. But whether it was sound was another matter, especially because neither Parker nor Wilson provided any evidence to substantiate the claim that preventive patrol was the most effective way to curb crime. According to the Police Foundation, which conducted a systematic, though by no means flawless, experiment in Kansas City in the early 1970s, the reformers may well have exaggerated the efficacy of this strategy.[21] The Kansas City experiment raised doubts that preventive patrol—or at least a form of preventive patrol that stressed random and nonaggressive patrolling by uniformed officers—had much of an impact on the level of crime. As the foundation admitted, its experiment did not resolve the issue. But it did highlight the fact that there was no evidence to prove that preventive patrol—and by implication the theory of crime prevention underlying it—increased the proficiency of the big-city police.

There are even some grounds to think that preventive patrol reduced their proficiency. For one thing, it sometimes turned into outright harassment, from which it was separated by a narrow line, and thereby generated a good deal of hostility, especially though not exclusively in the black ghettos. Out of this hostility emerged a reluctance to report criminal activity, supply essential information, and otherwise volunteer the unselfish cooperation that is indispensable for a successful crime prevention campaign in a policed society. For another thing, preventive patrol sometimes resulted in unwarranted arrests, a practice that was commonplace in the ghettos but was not unheard-of in other neighborhoods as well.[22] Although the charges were usually dropped, the arrestees were stuck with a criminal record which handicapped their efforts to find legitimate employment and often left them with no option but to resort to criminal activity. In other words, this theory of crime prevention so overestimated the benefits and underestimated the costs of preventive patrol that it was only a slight improvement over the notions of August Vollmer and Arthur Woods.

Most departments also compiled, classified, and published their criminal statistics according to guidelines that were drawn up by the IACP, approved by the FBI, and incorporated into the *Uniform Crime Reports*. The guidelines greatly enhanced the accuracy of these statistics which, as the Chicago Crime Commission and other reform groups pointed out, were extremely unreliable down through the first third of the century. Nonetheless, it was still hard to generalize about the level of crime in one place at one time, much less to compare it from one precinct to the next, one city to another, or one year to the next. For the *Uniform Crime Reports* were based entirely on crimes that were reported to the police; and according to one study of criminal victimization, which was published by the President's Crime Commission in the late 1960s, roughly one-half of all crimes were not reported. Indeed, according to another victimization study, which was sponsored by the LEAA a few years later, unreported crime exceeded reported crime by a multiple of 1.5 in St. Louis, 2.1 in New York, 2.6 in Dallas, 2.9 in Los Angeles, and 5.1 in Philadelphia.[23]

What is more, the *Uniform Crime Reports* were open to diverse and often conflicting interpretations. If they registered a sharp rise in criminal activity, did this mean that the police were getting worse and therefore more crimes were being committed, or that the police were getting better and as a result more crimes were being reported? The rise may even have had nothing to do with the police. If so, did it reflect flaws in the prosecutor's offices, courts, and correctional institutions or changes in demographic patterns, economic conditions, and other matters that were not related to the criminal justice system? If the *Uniform Crime Reports* could not answer these questions, they could not reveal much about the relative efficiency of alternative crime prevention practices. The police could not use them to figure out whether to focus on the causes of crime, as Vollmer and Woods proposed, or to concentrate on the opportunities for crime, as Wilson and Parker insisted. Nor could the police use them to find out whether to assign detectives to the precincts or to headquarters, to upgrade or downgrade vice control, and to rely on ordinary patrolmen or special squads. In other words, the *Uniform Crime Reports* had only a slight effect on the proficiency of the big-city police not only because they were extremely inaccurate but also because, in the absence of a coherent theory of criminal behavior, they were virtually unfathomable.

Hence the reformers had a noteworthy impact on the function of the big-city police. Applying the logic of the professional model and, to a slight degree, the military analogy, they prevailed on most departments to place a higher priority on crime prevention than on peace-keeping, crowd control, and the other chores that had been their raison d'être in the late nineteenth century. But despite their efforts, most departments could not assign more than a small fraction of the force to this task; nor, in the absence of a sound theory of criminal behavior and a reliable set of criminal statistics, could the departments figure out the most effective ways in which to deploy the few officers available. As a result, the big-city police were more proficient in the mid-1960s than in the late 1920s, and far more so than in the early 1890s; but nowhere, not even in New York City and Chicago, which boasted highly sophisticated criminal laboratories, were they as proficient as engineers and other professionals. The fault was not with reformers, except perhaps for exaggerating the potential efficacy of the police. For the big-city police, no matter how well organized and ably staffed, probably cannot do very much about the incidence of crime in urban America.

Whether the reform campaign raised the status of the big-city police, which was the overriding objective of the second generation of reformers, is hard to figure out. Occupational prestige is a highly elusive concept. Not until the mid-1920s did scholars start to study it; not until the late 1940s did they analyze it in a systematic way; and not until the early 1960s did they attempt to replicate any of the previous surveys.[24] As a result, the studies have little to say about occupational prestige in the postwar years, even less about it in the prewar years, and not much more about the changes that took place. Many of the studies tried to measure the occupational prestige of the police. But they did not take into account rank and function, even though there was plenty of evidence to suggest that superior officers stood higher than patrolmen and that plainclothesmen stood higher than uniformed officers. Nor did the studies make allowance for the reputation of the different departments, even though, if the reformers were correct, policemen should have ranked higher in Los Angeles and Cincinnati than in Chicago and Buffalo. Notwithstanding these limitations, the data suggest that the status of the big-city police rose a good deal after World War II.

According to the National Opinion Research Center (NORC), which interviewed about three thousand Americans in 1947, policemen ranked fifty-fifth out of ninety occupations, standing just above railroad conductors, mail carriers, carpenters, auto mechanics, and plumbers and just below bookkeepers, insurance agents, tenant farmers, traveling salesmen, and playground directors. This was approximately where they had stood in 1925, according to George S. Counts, a sociologist whose pioneering research, which relied heavily on the opinions of teenagers, probably overestimated the prestige of the police. Between 1947 and 1963, when three sociologists replicated the NORC survey, policemen not only held their own against most other groups but also moved ahead of reporters, radio announcers, tenant farmers, insurance agents, managers of small stores, traveling salesmen, and bookkeepers.[25] Policemen now ranked forty-seventh out of ninety, standing just below newspaper columnists, welfare workers, undertakers, farmers, and trained machinists and not far below self-employed printers, county agricultural agents, electricians, engineers, and national labor leaders. They were firmly established on the higher echelons of skilled labor and even had a toehold on the lower echelons of the paraprofessionals.

The surveys were corroborated by other evidence from popular novels, motion pictures, and television programs, which are valuable, if imperfect, indicators of social standing. This evidence too revealed a sharp rise in the status of the big-city police. The rise was reflected in at least two notable trends other than the increasing emphasis on the competence and commitment of the rank-and-file, an emphasis that was epitomized by the shift from the Keystone Cops to *Dragnet*. Down through the 1930s most policemen were shown as lower- and lower-middle-class ethnics, often hefty Irish-Americans, who lived in immigrant neighborhoods and spoke, after the introduction of sound, with a heavy brogue. After World War II they were portrayed as ordinary middle-class Americans, who had no discernible accent, lived in residential suburbs, and like the heroes of Donald Westlake's *Cops and Robbers,* relaxed in backyard swimming pools. Down through the 1930s most of the officers were romantically involved with cooks, domestics, waitresses, governesses, and other lower-class first- and second-generation newcomers.[26] After World War II most of these officers went out with and married women who, if Joseph Wambaugh's *The New Centurions* is indicative, came from well-to-do families, attended college, worked as paraprofessionals, and plainly belonged to the middle class.

The rise in the status of the police should not be exaggerated. Three decades after the second generation of reformers launched its campaign, the rank-and-file still stood on the lower half of the

NORC occupational ladder. Notwithstanding the rhetoric of professionalism, they ranked well below doctors, lawyers, and architects, all of whom were in the top fifteen occupations, and even below engineers, accountants, and teachers, all of whom were in the top thirty. So far as the reformers were concerned, the American people did not accord the big-city police the recognition to which the recent changes in structure, personnel, and function entitled them. But neither should the rise in the status of the police be underestimated. After all, policemen moved up eight rungs between 1947 and 1963, a gain that was equaled only by chemists and lawyers and exceeded only by nuclear physicists and local labor leaders. The gain was impressive not only because it occurred at a time when occupational prestige was, to quote the second NORC survey, "remarkably stable."[27] This gain was also impressive because it took only sixteen years, a short span of time considering how long lawyers, dentists, and other groups had struggled to achieve a prominent position in American society.

But it is one thing to measure occupational prestige and another to explain it, one thing to work out the progress of the big-city police and another to find out whether it was a result of the reform campaign. The literature does not help much. The theory, which holds that occupational prestige is closely correlated with income and formal education, is irrelevant and perhaps fallacious. It is irrelevant because it does not preclude the possibility that income and education are reflections of occupational prestige rather than the other way around. And it is fallacious because the occupational prestige of the big-city police probably rose faster than their income and education in the postwar years. The surveys are only slightly more helpful. They show that the status of the police was not just a function of the prestige of public employees. While schoolteachers went up on the occupational ladder, welfare workers and garbage collectors stayed put, and big-city mayors and state governors went down.[28] But the surveys do not suggest any more satisfactory explanations. Despite the inadequacies of the theory and the data, there is evidence that the reformers may have helped raise the status of the police in at least two ways in the postwar years.

One way was that the reformers worked hard to change the image of the police. Following a tradition that went back to the early years of the century, when the IACP first condemned the movies for ridiculing policemen, the reformers continued to press the studios to portray the police in a more favorable light in the postwar years. They also started to exert pressure on the radio and television networks. Early in the 1950s the IACP commended the National Broadcasting Company for *Dragnet,* then a popular radio program; and in 1956 it invited Ben Alexander, who played alongside Jack Webb in the television version, to address its annual conference. In the mid-1950s the association formed a Radio and Television Committee, which monitored programs, reviewed scripts, cultivated producers, and otherwise attempted to influence the depiction of the police. In 1965 the ICPA, which spoke for many of the rank-and-file associations, filed a vigorous protest against NBC's *Car 54, Where Are You?,* a short-lived television series that drew what little inspiration it had from the Keystone Cops. A year later the IACP produced a film of its own. Entitled *Every Hour . . . Every Day* and narrated by Danny Thomas, the television celebrity, it was sold at $200 a print to hundreds of civic groups and other organizations.[29]

Another way was that the reformers tried hard to change the milieu of the police. The reformers sought to associate policing with a host of prestigious activities, institutions, and individuals, a strategy which rested on the assumption that some of their prestige would rub off on the police. During the second third of the century, for example, the reformers stressed crime labs, ballistics tests, fingerprint files, computers, and other scientific and technical devices to a degree that was out of all proportion to their value in police work. They called for close ties between law enforcement and higher education and particularly for the creation of schools of criminology and departments of police science, which spread throughout the United States after World War II. They invited mayors, governors, judges, and other prominent figures to speak to the IACP, and year after year the association adopted a resolution extolling J. Edgar Hoover for his magnificent contributions to law enforcement.[30] The reformers' opposition to parity, a common arrangement by which the salaries of policemen and firemen are set at the same level, suggested that they wanted to dissociate the police from less prestigious groups as well.

So far as the reformers were concerned, the status of the big-city police was a function not so much of their image and milieu as of their performance, which improved somewhat in the second third of the century. But the relationship between performance and prestige is ambiguous. The efforts to change the image of the police probably would have been doomed if the rank-and-file had continued to behave like the Chicago patrolmen whose incompetence was exposed by Captain Alexander Piper around the turn of the century. The attempts to change the milieu of the big-city police would also probably have been stymied if the departments had not set up the labs and rented the computers or the universities had not sanctioned the programs in criminal justice and police science. But if prestige is essentially a function of performance, it is hard to explain why college professors and congressmen stood so high and bartenders and garbage collectors so low. Surely not because the students were so well educated and the nation so well governed, nor because the saloons were so poorly run and the streets so poorly cleaned. It is also hard to figure out why lawyers and barbers rose so much and bankers and artists fell so much in the postwar years. Whether further research will reveal a closer relationship between performance and prestige remains to be seen.

In view of the survey data and other evidence it is paradoxical that most policemen believed that their status had fallen in the postwar years. Of 200 Boston, Chicago, and Washington, D.C., officers who were interviewed by Reiss in the mid-1960s 59 percent said the prestige of the police was lower than twenty years ago, 26 percent said it was higher, and 9 percent said it was about the same. Of 170 New York policemen who were interviewed by John H. McNamara a few years earlier three-quarters disagreed with the statement that respect for patrolmen had been "steadily increasing over the years." These findings were confirmed by several less systematic surveys conducted in New York, Washington, D.C., and other cities in the mid-1960s. In one interview after another the officers complained that the relations between the public and the police had gotten worse in recent years, that with few exceptions the citizens had little regard for the policemen's position and little sympathy for their problems.[31] Running through these complaints was a deep strain of nostalgia, a vision of a time, somewhere in the not-too-distant past, when the officers enjoyed the respect of the citizens and commanded the authority necessary to do their job.

This paradox was only one of many symptoms of the occupational paranoia of the big-city police. Among other symptoms were a strong sense of alienation, a deep feeling of persecution, and an extreme sensitivity to criticism. These symptoms were quite common in the 1960s. To give a few examples, Parker told the Governor's Commission on the Los Angeles Riots, popularly known after its chairman, John A. McCone, former director of the Central Intelligence Agency, as the McCone Commission, that the police were "the most downtrodden, oppressed, dislocated minority in America." This opinion was shared by John Harrington, president of the FOP, and his supporters. Hoover warned the IACP that law enforcement was the prime target of "the communists, the hatemongers, the pseudoliberals and others who would destroy the very foundations of this great Republic." For Hoover's defense of the profession the association pledged him its "undying gratitude" and "unwavering support." Parker, Hoover, and many other well-known figures also attacked the Supreme Court for the Mallory, Escobedo, Miranda, and other landmark decisions which put restrictions on the standard investigatory practices of the American police.[32] Their attacks were supported by John Cassese and many other rank-and-file leaders.

Occupational paranoia, an outgrowth of the first wave of police reform, changed in at least two striking ways during the second third of the twentieth century. First, it struck the rank-and-file as well as the chiefs. It was the ICPA and not the IACP that formed a special committee to keep its members informed of the activities of the Communist party, ACLU, Black Muslims, and other allegedly subversive groups. It was the PBAs and FOPs which led the nationwide struggle against the proposed police review boards. It was the ICPA and not the IACP that condemned the report of the President's Riot Commission for reprimanding the local police and national guard, exonerating the rioters, and encouraging further lawlessness. It was the Law Enforcement Group (LEG), a cadre of New York policemen, which attacked the prosecutors, judges, and probation officers for coddling criminals. And it was the Fire and Police Research Association (FiPo), a group of Los Angeles firemen and policemen, that distributed *Human Events,* an ultraright tabloid, in the station houses and sponsored a talk by Fred Schwarz of the Christian Anti-Communism Crusade. Representing the right wing of the rank-and-file, LEG and Fi-Po reflected the anxieties of a great many otherwise ordinary police officers.[33]

The second change was that occupational paranoia got a lot worse. The big-city police now saw themselves not only as an object of scorn, a subject for caricature, and in the words of Chief Fred Kohler of Cleveland, "a target for the poisoned arrow of abuse and ridicule," but also as a scapegoat for all sorts of social problems that were not their responsibility. They felt that they were under siege, attacked on the one side by well-to-do whites who expected them to compensate for the breakdown of the churches, families, and other sources of social control and on the other side by impoverished blacks who viewed them as the symbol of oppression, a veritable army of occupation. The big-city police now talked less about soldiers, armies, wars, and battlefields and more about the downfall of American society and the collapse of Western civilization; their metaphors were drawn not so much from the military analogy as from an apocalyptic vision. They were, in the words of Chief Parker, the "thin blue line" that stood between civilization and barbarism, served as the bastion against crime and subversion, and remained the only hope for the preservation of the rule of law and the American way of life.[34] A profound misreading of the role of the big-city police and the character of the American people, this vision struck a responsive chord in many otherwise levelheaded police officers.

The changes in occupational paranoia were partly an outcome of the turbulent conditions of the postwar years. During the late 1950s and early 1960s the National Association for the Advancement of Colored People (NAACP), ACLU, and other liberal groups charged that the American police were systematically depriving the blacks, radicals, and other minorities of their civil liberties. Coming in the wake of a decade or so of anti-Communist frenzy, the charges drove many officers into the arms of the John Birch Society and other conservative outfits which were wooing them with the slogan "Support Your Local Police." To make matters worse, a rash of riots erupted in Harlem, south-central Los Angeles, and most of the nation's other black ghettos in the middle and late 1960s, the worst racial disorders in nearly half a century. Most policemen were stunned by the riots, and they had barely recovered when some of the blue-ribbon commissions appointed to look into the disorders issued reports that placed much of the blame on the local police. As if all this were not enough, the number of officers killed on duty, which had dropped sharply in the 1940s and leveled off in the 1950s, began to rise in the mid-1960s and continued to go up in the late 1960s and early 1970s. Although fewer officers were slain then than in the late 1920s and early 1930s, when most departments had only one-half to two-thirds as many men, the killings shocked even hardened veterans.[35]

The changes in occupational paranoia were also partly an outcome of the second wave of police reform. The reformers had worked hard to impress on the rank-and-file the view that policemen were professionals akin to doctors, lawyers, teachers, and engineers. According to McNamara, they were quite successful. Of the 170 New York City officers with whom he spoke in the early 1960s three-quarters believed that policing should be ranked alongside medicine and law.[36] If McNamara had done his research in Cincinnati, Los Angeles, and other cities where the reform movement had made more headway, the proportion would probably have been even higher. If policemen were professionals, the rank-and-file asked, why were they obliged to put up with so much pressure from local politicians and community groups? Why were they forced to submit to income probes, testify without immunity, refrain from political activity, and relinquish many of their other civil liberties? And why were they subjected to so many nitpicking regulations, arbitrary decisions, and official investigations, most of which were often nothing but fishing expeditions? In the absence of satisfactory answers the rank-and-file drew the conclusion that for some reason or other the police were being singled out for the sort of treatment that no other profession would have tolerated for long.

The reformers had also worked hard to prevail on the police to shift from a responsive to a preventive strategy, or in Reiss's terms from a reactive to a proactive one. Here too they were fairly successful. Most departments transferred vice control, traffic regulation, crime prevention, and many other chores from ordinary patrolmen to special squads. They also authorized uniformed officers to stop, question, and if they deemed it necessary, frisk anyone who aroused their suspicion. As a result of these changes, the big-city police now intervened in all sorts of situations which in the absence of a strong complaint they would have ignored a generation or two before. By so doing — by arresting a taxpayer for gambling, citing a motorist for speeding, and ordering a few teenagers to keep moving — they generated a great deal of resentment.[37] Challenged by the suspects, who denied that they had done anything wrong and claimed that they were being harassed, many policemen felt obliged to reassert their authority. All too often the encounters turned into confrontations in which the policemen were verbally and physically abused and the suspects were booked for resisting arrest. From the viewpoint of the rank-and-file, who believed that they were doing their duty, the confrontations were one of many signs of the declining respect for police officers and the growing contempt for lawful authority in urban America.

Occupational paranoia was a severe affliction. Estranged from the community, which was in their view indifferent if not downright antagonistic to their efforts, the big-city police, or at any rate a large majority thereof, were sorely frustrated in their work and highly uncertain about their role. After confessing his rage at a group of radical college students to a sympathetic priest, a Boston sergeant blurted out, "Father, if you know what we're trying to do, I wish you'd let me know, and that would be two of us that know."[38] It was hard enough for the big-city police to keep the peace and enforce the law under ordinary circumstances. It was much harder now that they saw themselves as the scapegoat for a host of social problems which in their opinion were a function of the profligacy, depravity, and misguided idealism of the very people whom they were supposed to protect. And it was even harder now that they regarded themselves as the so-called "thin blue line," on whose shoulders rested not only the safety of the citizenry but also the fate of American society and the future of Western civilization. A direct, if unintended, consequence of the reform movement, occupational paranoia was a high price to pay for the transformation of the structure, personnel, and function of the big-city police.

10.   The Price of Progress

On July 16, 1966, Chief William H. Parker, who
had turned the Los Angeles Police Department into what many
reformers regarded as the nation's preeminent police force, died
of a heart attack at the age of sixty-four. The response was mind-
boggling. Governor Edmund G. Brown praised him; so did
Mayor Samuel W. Yorty, Attorney General Thomas Lynch, and
former Mayor Fletcher Bowron, who called Parker "the outstanding police chief of the United States." After paying tribute to the
chief, the city council voted to adjourn; and the board of education, the county grand jury, and the executive committee of the
California Peace Officers' Association followed suit. Thousands of
people filed through the city hall rotunda where Parker lay in
state for two hours surrounded by an honor guard of uniformed
officers. After Cardinal McIntyre presided over a solemn pontif-
ical requiem mass, a funeral procession led by 300 motorcycles
and 280 police cars slowly wound its way from downtown Los
Angeles to a San Fernando Valley cemetery. Six rookies carried
the casket to the graveside where the chaplain of the police post
of the American Legion conducted the service, which included a
twenty-one gun salute, and the police band played "My Buddy"
and "Hail to the Chief."[1] By the time that the final notes of
"Taps" died out, it was clear that the crowd was not only mourn-
ing the chief but also celebrating his lifework, the transformation
of the Los Angeles Police Department.

There was much to celebrate, and not only in Los Angeles. By virtue of the efforts of Parker, Thomas J. Gibbons, O.W. Wilson, Herbert T. Jenkins, and the other reformers the big-city police had made a good deal of headway in the second third of the twentieth century. To begin with, they were less incompetent. A few officers still spent a fair amount of time hanging around bars, wandering in and out of bookie joints, and taking naps in school yards, parking lots, and other quiet spots. But according to Jerome Skolnick, L.H. Whittemore, and Jonathan Rubenstein, who have reported on the everyday activities of the big-city police, these officers were the exceptions. Whether they were afraid of their superiors, anxious to meet their quotas, or as the reformers hoped, committed to serving their fellow citizens, the rank-and-file worked hard in the mid-1960s. They worked harder than in the late 1940s, when the Chicago Crime Commission pointed out that many officers left their posts after dark, went home to sleep or out to play cards, and paid the switchboard operators to call them if anything unusual took place on their beats. The rank-and-file also worked much harder than in the mid-1900s, when Captain Alexander Piper reported that most officers passed the day eating, drinking, talking, sleeping, visiting friends, and doing all sorts of things other than policing.[2]

The police made plenty of blunders. The New York City police wrung a confession out of an innocent youth for the Wylie-Hoffert murders in the mid-1960s; and as Deputy District Attorney Vincent Bugliosi has shown, the Los Angeles police mislaid vital evidence and otherwise bungled the Tate-LaBianca slayings a few years later. But such blunders were fairly common a generation before too. Late in the 1920s the Los Angeles police mistook one youth for another who had been missing for five months, ignored his mother's claim that the youth was not her son, forced her to take him home with her, and when she brought him back, committed her to a psychiatric ward. Shortly afterward the Washington, D.C., police concluded on the basis of a cursory investigation that a young woman who was found dead in her apartment had committed suicide and then suspended a veteran officer who insisted — quite rightly, it turned out — that she had been murdered. Early in the 1930s, several days after a gang known as the Tape Bandits had abducted a man in broad daylight on a busy thoroughfare, the Kansas City police force acknowledged that it had not been able to identify the victim, much less to apprehend the kidnappers.[3] Although by no means conclusive, the evidence seems to suggest that the big-city police probably made fewer blunders in the mid-1960s than in the late 1920s and early 1930s.

The big-city police were also less corrupt. Some officers still solicited payoffs from bartenders, gamblers, prostitutes, numbers runners, narcotics peddlers, and even shopkeepers and contractors who were hard pressed to comply with municipal ordinances. But according to Albert J. Reiss, Jr., who estimated that of a few hundred Boston, Chicago, and Washington, D.C., policemen whom he studied in the mid-1960s only one-sixth to one-quarter were "on the take," these officers were in the minority. Whether from a fear of exposure, a lack of opportunity, or as the reformers hoped, a preference for integrity, most policemen were fairly honest in the mid-1960s. Or at worst they were, in the Knapp Commission's words, "grass-eaters," who accepted small gratuities and seasonal gifts from shopkeepers, rather than "meat-eaters," who shook down policy bankers and drug dealers for substantial sums. Fewer officers were on the take in the mid-1960s than in the mid-1920s when a reporter told Colonel Henry B. Chamberlin, operating director of the Chicago Crime Commission, that only one percent of the Chicago police force was honest. And far fewer were on the take than in the mid-1890s when the Lexow and other investigative committees discovered that virtually all officers regarded payoffs as a perquisite of police work.[4]

The police were sometimes extremely rapacious. A few New York City officers demanded such high payoffs from the policy shops in the early 1960s that they drove many small-time operators out of business and cleared the way for the big-time syndicates to take over the numbers racket. But such venality was quite common a generation before as well. Late in the 1920s District Attorney John Monaghan reported that a bunch of high-level Philadelphia police officers had organized a system of payoffs which covered nearly the entire city and, after the patrolmen and sergeants took their share, netted each of them around $500 a week. A year or so later Harry "Bathhouse" McDonald, a well-known bootlegger who had been paying several members of the Los Angeles Police Department roughly $100,000 a year for protection, protested that the officers had raised their demands to a point which forced him out of business. Early in the 1930s the Seabury Committee discovered that several members of the New York City vice squad had framed respectable women for prostitution, arrested them, and booked them at the station house, for which the officers got a cut from avaricious bondsmen and unscrupulous lawyers.[5] These incidents suggest that the big-city police were probably less rapacious in the mid-1960s than in the late 1920s and early 1930s.

The big-city police were less lawless too. Some officers still broke into homes and terrorized the residents, attacked prisoners without provocation, shot fleeing juveniles suspected of minor crimes, and employed the third degree in the station houses. But according to the President's Crime Commission, which sent out observers to accompany policemen in high-crime neighborhoods and watch for cases of unnecessary and excessive force, these officers were the exceptions. Whether the officers were moved by the protests of the bar associations, the opinions of the courts, or as the reformers hoped, the logic of the professional model, police brutality was on the wane in the mid-1960s. And so was police harassment, a term that refers to investigatory arrests, extended detention, and other improper and illegal tactics which were justified in the name of vigorous law enforcement. These practices were less pervasive in the mid-1960s than in the early 1930s when Ernest J. Hopkins, Emanuel H. Lavine, and other journalists revealed that most police departments regularly employed the third degree. And they were much less widespread than in the early 1900s when Chief John W. Ball reported that the Atlanta police force had come across a few well-known criminals and, lacking "evidence sufficient to prosecute," drove them out of town instead.[6]

The police were at times quite repressive. The Cleveland police severely manhandled a group of civil rights activists in the mid-1960s, and the Los Angeles police savagely attacked a crowd of antiwar demonstrators a few years later. But such tactics were fairly common a generation earlier too. Early in the 1930s the Los Angeles Intelligence Bureau, commonly known as the Red squad, joined forces with the American Legion to prevent the ACLU, John Reed Club, Communist party, and other left-wing groups from holding meetings in and around Los Angeles. Not long afterward a few New York City detectives tossed several tear-gas canisters into a large but orderly crowd that had gathered in Harlem to demonstrate against the trial of the Scottsboro Boys. Late in the 1930s a bunch of Chicago officers, armed with revolvers, clubs, and tear gas, killed ten and wounded nearly a hundred members of a vast but peaceful crowd that was trying to organize a picket line around a Republic Steel factory.[7] Although far from conclusive, the evidence seems to indicate that the big-city police were probably less repressive in the mid-1960s than in the late 1920s and early 1930s.

For these improvements the reformers and their allies deserved much of the credit. Aside from exhorting the rank-and-file to do their job, the police chiefs pleaded with the municipal authorities to give the rank-and-file the facilities and equipment to do it well. Apart from exposing corrupt officers and urging elected officials to get rid of them, the local newspapers and crime commissions attempted to destroy the political machines that encouraged and protected these officers. In addition to attacking the third degree and other lawless forms of law enforcement, the bar associations, civil liberties unions, and civil rights groups appealed to the courts to toss out confessions and other evidence obtained through these tactics. And though the IACP had formed a special committee in the mid-1930s to refute the Wickersham Commission's report on the third degree, most chiefs sharply criticized this practice on professional grounds after World War II.[8] But if the reformers and their allies deserved much of the credit for reducing the incompetence, corruption, and lawlessness of the big-city police, they also deserved much of the blame for changing the police in other less salutary ways.

Starting before World War I, continuing up to the Depression, and resuming during and after World War II, several million blacks moved from the farms and towns of the rural south to the large cities of the Northeast, Midwest, and Far West. Along with them came a few hundred thousand Mexicans, who went to Los Angeles, San Antonio, and other Southwestern cities, and several hundred thousand Puerto Ricans, who settled in and around greater New York. These newcomers, who were the latest, though not the last, in a long line of impoverished immigrants who sought to improve their lot in urban America, soon changed the ethnic makeup of their adoptive cities. By 1965 New York City had more Puerto Ricans than San Juan, Los Angeles had more

Mexicans than Vera Cruz, and Detroit had more blacks than
Atlanta. More than a million of these newcomers lived in New
York City, more than half a million lived in Chicago and Philadelphia, and more than a quarter of a million lived in Detroit,
Cleveland, Los Angeles, Baltimore, and Washington, D.C. A
small minority in 1930, they now made up over 25 percent of the
population in New York, Chicago, Los Angeles, and Cincinnati,
over 30 percent in Philadelphia, Detroit, Cleveland, and St.
Louis, over 40 percent in Newark, and over 60 percent in Washington, D.C.[9]

Despite the great influx of blacks, the big-city police remained
overwhelmingly white. According to the President's Riot Commission, which drew on a study made in 1967, the blacks made
up only 11 percent of the force in St. Louis, 10 percent in Newark, 7 percent in Cleveland and Pittsburgh, 6 percent in San
Francisco, 5 percent in Detroit and New York, and 4 percent or
less in Oakland, Boston, and Buffalo. According to the President's Crime Commission, which relied on a survey done in 1966,
they made up only 9 percent of the force in Atlanta, 5 percent in
Winston-Salem, 4 percent in New Orleans, 3 percent in Tampa,
and less than one percent in Birmingham.[10] Nowhere, not even in
Chicago, Philadelphia, and Washington, D.C., where by dint of
vigorous recruiting in the 1950s and 1960s the proportion of
black policemen climbed to 17, 20, and 21 percent respectively,
did the blacks get a fair share, much less the lion's share, of the
jobs. According to the United States Commission on Civil Rights,
which did a study of its own in 1967, the Mexicans and Puerto
Ricans fared no better than the blacks and perhaps a bit worse.
Things had improved somewhat since 1930, when most police
forces had few blacks and some none at all, but not enough to
obscure the point that by the mid-1960s the American police no
longer served to enhance the mobility of the lower- and lower-
middle-class first- and second-generation newcomers.

The reformers were not solely responsible for this situation. It
was not their fault that down through World War II, fully eighty
years after emancipation, blacks were prohibited from serving on
the police forces in most Southern cities and for that matter some
Northern ones. On the contrary, it was Chief Jenkins, a prominent reformer, who in the face of strenuous opposition from
many citizens opened the Atlanta police to blacks in the late

1940s. Nor was it the reformers' fault that in Boston and several other cities the Irish-Americans enjoyed a virtual stranglehold on the police force and exploited their political influence and bureaucratic know-how to exclude blacks and other newcomers. On the contrary, it was Commissioner Gibbons, another prominent reformer, under whose leadership the Philadelphia Police Department raised the proportion of black officers from 3.6 percent to 13.6 percent in the 1950s.[11] Neither was it the reformers' fault that as a result of their prior experience with the police many blacks were reluctant to go into policing or that by virtue of inferior schooling and inadequate health care many others were unable to meet the entrance requirements.

But the reformers were partly responsible for this situation. In their efforts to attract qualified recruits they not only urged the authorities to raise salaries, increase benefits, and improve working conditions. They also pressed the departments to do their recruiting outside their own communities. At a time when tens of thousands of blacks and Mexicans were pouring into south-central and southeastern Los Angeles, the Los Angeles police sent recruiters, loaded down with posters and pamphlets, to county fairs, Boy Scout jamborees, military bases, and college campuses all over the country. At a time when more than a quarter of the population of Oakland was black, the Oakland police dispatched recruits to the campuses of Michigan State, Florida State, Washington State, and other universities with schools of criminology. At a time when more than half the population of the District of Columbia was black, the Washington police sent recruiters all over the Eastern United States, in particular to Appalachia and other regions that were then plagued by higher than average rates of unemployment. And at a time when tens of thousands of blacks were pouring into the south and west sides of Chicago, the Chicago Police Department requested permission from the city council to extend its recruiting efforts into the predominantly white suburbs of Cook County.[12]

Supported by the rank-and-file associations, the reformers also prevailed on the authorities to abolish the residency requirements in all save a handful of cities. This change, which was justified on professional grounds, handicapped the blacks, Mexicans, and Puerto Ricans in two principal ways. First, it slowed down the ethnic turnover of the big-city police. It allowed thousands of white officers, often third- and fourth-generation Irish-Americans, who were troubled by the quality of life and cost of living in the big cities, to move to the suburbs and still hold on to their jobs. Had the residency requirements been retained, these officers would have been forced to return to the city or leave the force, and many of them would probably have quit.[13] Second, this change cut down the competitive edge of the recent immigrants. It made millions of whites who lived outside the cities eligible for the thousands of jobs that opened up when police officers retired, resigned, or were dismissed and when elected officials voted to increase the size of the force. Had the residency requirements been retained, the blacks, Mexicans, and Puerto Ricans would have had to compete for these jobs not with the many whites who lived in the suburbs but with the few who resided in the cities.

In their efforts to exclude unqualified applicants the reformers not only pleaded with the authorities to insulate the civil service from partisan politics, but also appealed to them to impose stiff entrance requirements, which severely, if inadvertently, discriminated against blacks, Mexicans, and Puerto Ricans. Chief among them were the written exams. Multiple choice tests, which according to critics revealed less about the intelligence of the applicants than about the biases of the examiners and the shortcomings of the schools, these exams winnowed out a far higher proportion of blacks than whites. The examiners flunked 75 percent of the blacks as opposed to 35 percent of the whites in Boston in 1970, 72 percent of the blacks as opposed to 24 percent of the whites in Atlanta in 1970, and 65 percent of the blacks as opposed to 31 percent of the whites in New York City in 1968. The Mexicans and Puerto Ricans fared even worse, perhaps because the tests were given in English. Whether the written exams were, as critics charged, a violation of the Fourteenth Amendment is a moot point. But as Peter Smith Ring, special assistant to the commanding officer of the New York City Police Department's Personnel Bureau, admitted, they were a major roadblock to the blacks, Mexicans, and Puerto Ricans who wanted to go into police work.[14]

Another major roadblock were the character checks, which were thorough investigations run by the departments on every applicant who passed the written exams. These checks also winnowed out a far higher proportion of blacks and, though the evidence is scanty, of Mexicans and Puerto Ricans than of whites. The investigators rejected 41 percent of the blacks as opposed to 29 percent of the whites in St. Louis in 1966, 68 percent of the blacks as opposed to 56 percent of the whites in Cleveland in 1966, and 58 percent of the blacks as opposed to 32 percent of the whites in Philadelphia in 1968.[15] The disparities were a function of two things other than racial prejudice. First, many departments were loath to accept anyone who had been arrested or at any rate convicted for any criminal offense, no matter how trivial, other than a traffic violation. And according to a study published by the President's Crime Commission, blacks were far more likely to have criminal records than whites.[16] Second, most departments were reluctant to appoint anyone who had played hooky, changed jobs too often, hung around with known criminals, or broken military regulations. These practices were much more prevalent in black, Mexican, and Puerto Rican communities than in white neighborhoods.

Hence the blacks and other newcomers paid a high price for police reform. Regardless of their intentions, the reformers made it much harder for the newcomers to get a fair share of the available jobs, which in 1967 came to roughly 27,600 in New York City, 11,100 in Chicago, 6,900 in Philadelphia, 5,200 in Los Angeles, 4,300 in Detroit, 3,000 in Baltimore, 2,700 in Washington, D.C., and more than 2,000 in Boston, Cleveland, and St. Louis. These jobs paid a pretty good salary. Excluding overtime and other extras, the patrolmen in 1967 earned from $8,200 to $8,800 in San Francisco, $7,700 to $9,100 in Los Angeles, $7,400 to $8,300 in Detroit, $7,000 to $8,500 in New York, $6,800 to $8,300 in Chicago, $6,300 to $7,100 in New Orleans, and $4,800 to $6,000 in Atlanta.[17] Their superiors received a good deal more. These jobs also provided a high degree of security, liberal sick leaves, inexpensive health insurance, generous annual vacations, the best pensions outside the military, and other material benefits that made them more remunerative than other positions which paid higher wages. There were of course more rewarding positions elsewhere. But for the many blacks, Mexicans, and Puerto Ricans who were immobilized by unemployment or underemployment and lacked the capital, connections, and credentials to move up via the private sector, these jobs would have done nicely for a start.

The newcomers arrived at a time when most cities were more

or less segregated along class and ethnic lines. In the face of a deep-seated commitment to racial homogeneity, which was promoted by real estate interests, supported by banks and insurance companies, and sanctioned by local and federal officials, the newcomers had no choice but to settle in ghettos of their own. By the hundreds and then the thousands they moved into New York's Harlem and East Harlem, Chicago's south and west sides, Boston's Roxbury, Cleveland's Hough, and south-central and southeastern Los Angeles. As the years went by, these places grew into the largest black, Mexican, and Puerto Rican communities in the country. The ghettos did not offer much in the way of adequate housing, job opportunities, and public services; but they did establish a political base for aspiring newcomers. They provided the constituencies that enabled the blacks to name a ward committeeman in Chicago in the early 1920s, choose a district leader in New York City in the mid-1930s, and elect city councilmen in St. Louis, Cleveland, and Los Angeles after World War II.[18] In other words, they provided the votes with which William L. Dawson, Adam Clayton Powell, Herman Badillo, Augustus Hawkins, and other newcomers gradually eased out the Irish-Americans and other second- and third-generation immigrants who had hitherto dominated local politics.

But these politicians did not wield much power over the big-city police. Unlike Jim Pendergast, "Big-Tim" Sullivan, "Duke" Edwin H. Vare, Michael "Hinky-Dink" Kenna, and other late nineteenth and early twentieth century ward bosses, the black, Mexican, and Puerto Rican politicians had little to say about which laws would be enforced, whose peace would be kept, and which public would be served. They could not offer protection to gamblers and saloon owners, or for that matter to peddlers, contractors, storekeepers, and other businessmen who were hard put to abide by local ordinances. As a result they could not count on their support come election day. Their influence was on the wane not only because Parker, Jenkins, Wilson, and the other reform chiefs enjoyed a considerable degree of autonomy. It was also on the wane because most departmental policies were now made at headquarters, in the mayor's office, at the bargaining table, or in other places that were outside the orbit of the local politicians. During the late 1960s and early 1970s several blacks and one or two Puerto Ricans won city-wide offices. But these victories did not alter the fact that by the mid-1960s the big-city police no longer served to increase the power of the lower- and lower-middle-class immigrants.

The decline of the ward politicians was partly a function of the movement for municipal reform. This movement, which started in the late nineteenth and early twentieth centuries, drew its support from the upper-middle- and upper-class Americans, and derived its recommendations from a corporate model, had a profound impact on local government in urban America. In one city after another the reformers prevailed on the authorities to adopt the initiative, referendum, and recall, establish nonpartisan elections, set up at-large councils, organize a civil service system, and increase the clout of the mayor's office. They persuaded the authorities to shift the locus of power over the schools, courts, and other urban institutions from ward organizations to city-wide, metropolitan, or state outfits and in a few instances to independent authorities or other quasi-public bodies.[19] In conjunction with other political and social changes, these reforms destroyed most of the old-line machines and compelled most of the others to centralize their operations. By putting an end to the tradition of urban politics that had laid the foundation for the old-line machines in the middle and late nineteenth century, the reform movement severely undermined the influence of the ward politicians.

The decline of the ward politicians was partly a function of the campaign for police reform too. Outside of Albany, Buffalo, and a few other cities, the reformers not only reduced the politicians' influence over the chiefs and the captains but also weakened their hold over the rank-and-file. In the first place, the politicians were stripped of much of their power over appointments. Gone were the days when the Chicago City Council gave each ward committeeman a share of the new slots and allowed him to fill them with the party faithful. Gone were the days when the New York City Police Board permitted the Tammany Hall district leaders to choose recruits whose sole qualification was dedication to the ward organization.[20] It was still possible for the local politicians to bring pressure on the municipal authorities to increase the size of the force, prohibit lateral entry, raise the age limits, and retain the residency requirements — though in Boston and several other cities these issues were normally resolved by the state legislature.

But by the mid-1960s, if not earlier, it was no longer possible for a well-connected but unqualified candidate to get a job as a patrolman and no longer necessary for a well-qualified candidate to get an endorsement from a ward boss.

In the second place, the politicians were stripped of much of their power over promotions. Not for some time had the Philadelphia ward leaders handpicked the sergeants and captains, a procedure that, as a grand jury pointed out in the late 1930s, made a mockery of the merit system. Not for some time had the Tammany district leaders sold positions to the rank-and-file, who were willing to pay roughly $300 to be a roundsman, $1,600 to be a sergeant, and a whopping $12,000-$15,000 to be a captain. Not for some time had the ward bosses been able to order the police chiefs to shift an uncooperative officer from one precinct to another or transfer a compliant officer from the uniformed force to a plainclothes unit.[21] It was still possible for the local politicians to exert pressure on the municipal authorities to increase the number of superior officers and change the relative importance of seniority, test scores, efficiency ratings, and other promotional criteria. In other words, they still had some say over the ground rules of the promotional process. But it was no longer possible for a well-connected patrolman who could barely read or write to move up through the ranks and no longer necessary for a competent officer with a knack for taking tests to be certified by a ward leader.

In the third place, the politicians lost much of their influence over salaries. By virtue of the reform efforts, which standardized police salaries according to rank and years of service, the politicians could not put much pressure on the authorities to pay their protégés more than their fellow officers. Nor could they exert much pressure on the authorities to make across-the-board changes, for as a result of initiatives by the rank-and-file associations, most municipalities had much less discretion over salaries in the mid-1960s than ever before. By virtue of a municipal ordinance that was approved by the city council in the mid-1950s, Los Angeles was required to adjust salaries each year according to the so-called Jacobs formula, which was based on changes in prevailing wages in greater Los Angeles. By virtue of a charter amendment that was adopted by the voters in the late 1950s, Oakland was obliged to adjust salaries each year according to a formula that was based on average salaries of industrial workers in the San Francisco Bay area. And by virtue of an executive order that was issued by Mayor Robert F. Wagner, Jr., in the early 1960s, New York City was required to bargain in good faith with the rank-and-file's representatives over salaries and other forms of remuneration.[22]

In the fourth place, the politicians lost much of their influence over discipline. As a result of the reform efforts, which placed disciplinary authority in the hands of trial boards and other departmental bodies, the politicians could not shield the rank-and-file from the superior officers. Nor, as a rule, did the rank-and-file need their protection. By the mid-1960s they were fairly well insulated against unfounded accusations, and even against well-founded ones, as several critics charged. The civil service rules forbade the chiefs to demote or dismiss an officer, though not to transfer him from one precinct to another or from a plainclothes unit to the uniformed force, without drawing up charges and convening a trial board. The rank-and-file associations prevailed on the municipal authorities to set up formal grievance procedures that guaranteed the officer the right to be represented by counsel and to cross-examine witnesses. And the Supreme Court ruled in *Gardner* v. *Broderick* that a police officer could not be removed for refusing to waive his privilege against self-incrimination before a grand jury or other official outfit.[23] Nor was there much reason to think that the local politicians would regain much if any of their influence over appointments, promotions, salaries, and discipline in the foreseeable future.

Again the blacks and other newcomers paid a high price for police reform. By insulating the big-city police from the ward politicians, the reform campaign undermined the historic localism that had long been a major source of power for the lower- and lower-middle-class first- and second-generation immigrants. Few other sources of power were available to the newcomers. Unlike the upper-middle- and upper-class Americans, who dominated the commercial and civic groups and controlled the press and other media, they had little influence over the city-wide officials. Nor, unlike the Irish-Americans and other second- and third-generation immigrants, who held the great majority of jobs in the police departments and other municipal agencies, did they have much influence over the rank-and-file unions. They had virtually no influence over the metropolitan and state agencies, independent authorities, and quasi-public bodies that had assumed responsibility for transit and other functions in the second third of the century. Other sources of power would become available to the blacks, if not the Mexicans and Puerto Ricans, in the 1970s and 1980s when they would emerge as a majority in most big cities. But in the meantime they were unable to shape the policies and practices of the police forces in ways that might have increased their share of the power in urban America.

The newcomers brought with them a set of values, attitudes, and customs that were in part incompatible with the conventional morality, which had been more or less incorporated into the criminal law. Feeling little of the upper middle class's professed commitment to abstinence and abhorrence of self-indulgence, many of them saw nothing wrong with buying a drink, betting on a horse, playing the numbers, or doing business on Sundays. Nor, feeling little of its prejudice against socializing in public, did many of them see anything wrong with hanging around the block with their friends and treating the streets as extensions of their apartments.[24] The Germans, Italians, and other European immigrants had felt much the same way a generation or two before. They had worked out an arrangement with the police whereby they were allowed to behave as they saw fit provided they kept a semblance of public order and stayed out of upper-middle- and upper-class neighborhoods. Many blacks, Mexicans, and Puerto Ricans were prepared to abide by the same ground rules. According to the Knapp Commission and other investigative agencies, which found that most police departments were reluctant to crack down on the numbers racket and other so-called victimless crimes, many police officers were inclined to accommodate them.

Not all officers were so accommodating. According to other sources, many policemen enforced the law and preserved the peace in a rather heavy-handed way in the black, Mexican, and Puerto Rican neighborhoods. Late in the 1950s Judge David W. Williams charged that the Los Angeles police made about 90 percent of their gambling arrests in the black community, which was the home of only a tenth of the city's population and the host of only a fraction of its illegal games. In an effort to defend Chief Parker and his force the Los Angeles Board of Police Commissioners stressed that only 82 percent of the arrestees were blacks and insisted that things were much the same in most other cities. During the mid-1960s Carl Werthman and Irving Piliavin, two Berkeley sociologists, reported that the San Francisco police often harassed black teenagers who hung out on the streets and, if they protested, sometimes ran them in for disorderly conduct and other offenses. Shortly thereafter the President's Riot Commission, which was trying to explain why so many blacks deeply resented the police, concluded that this practice was common in many other cities.[25] In these and other ways the big-city police made it clear by the mid-1960s that they were no longer inclined to reinforce the life styles of the lower- and lower-middle-class immigrants.

The reformers were not entirely responsible for this turn of events. It was not their fault that most patrolmen—roughly three out of four, according to a study of the Boston, Chicago, and Washington, D.C., police by Donald J. Black and Albert J. Reiss, Jr.—were prejudiced against blacks. Nor was it their fault that, as Richard Simon, a member of the Los Angeles Police Department told the McCone Commission, most officers did not view blacks as individuals and therefore could not distinguish between the lawless and the law-abiding. Neither was it the reformers' fault that many policemen—far too many, according to Paul Jacobs and Paul Chevigny, who wrote exposés of the Los Angeles and New York City police—felt much the same way about Mexicans and Puerto Ricans.[26] Most reformers were not racist. Even Chief Parker, who had a well-deserved reputation for insensitivity to racial minorities, was not so much prejudiced against blacks as he was antagonistic to anyone, whatever his color, who criticized the police. Indeed, many reformers opened their departments to blacks and launched minority recruiting campaigns, encouraged the training directors to add courses on social studies and race relations to the curriculum of the training academies, and disavowing a tradition that went back to the nineteenth century, instructed the rank-and-file to employ a single standard of law enforcement throughout the city.

But the reformers were partly responsible for this turn of events. At their insistence most police departments made a genuine effort to apply the same standards of law enforcement in the black, Mexican, and Puerto Rican neighborhoods as in the white communities.[27] Applied to violent crimes, a single standard posed few problems. Few Americans, least of all the blacks and other newcomers who lived in the most dangerous parts of the cities, were prepared to argue that the police should maintain a double standard. But extended to morals offenses, a single standard posed several difficult questions. How could the police apply the same standards to well-to-do whites and impoverished blacks? How could they enforce the gambling laws in the same way against whites who played poker in private casinos and blacks who shot craps in public parks? How could the police enforce the liquor laws in the same way against whites who belonged to exclusive clubs and blacks who hung out in after-hours drinking spots commonly known as "blind pigs"? And how could they apply the same standards to white call girls who worked out of posh apartments in respectable districts and black hookers who cruised the streets of the "combat zones"? The answer was that they could not. And so a single standard of law enforcement, even if applied in an evenhanded way, tended to discriminate against blacks, Mexicans, and Puerto Ricans.

And the standard was rarely applied in an evenhanded way. Not only were many police officers prejudiced against blacks and, to a lesser degree, against Mexicans and Puerto Ricans but, as the sons and grandsons of European immigrants, they also had a good deal of empathy for the other ethnic groups. So far as they were concerned, it was one thing for a group of Irish- or Italian-Americans to sponsor a rousing bingo game at a neighborhood club and quite another for a group of black teenagers to run a friendly crap game on a side street. Although the gambling laws did not as a rule draw such a distinction, many officers were prone to overlook the one and to break up the other. Some officers preferred to go by the book; but as Deputy Chief Inspector Louis Goldberg of New York learned, this was quite risky. Under pressure from Protestant groups and reform outfits which were outraged by the bookie scandal of the early 1950s, Goldberg, commander of the Brooklyn Public Morals Squad, ordered roughly a dozen Catholic and Jewish organizations to halt their bingo games, which were then illegal in New York State. The orders aroused such a storm of protest that Commissioner Francis W. Adams, a reformer who was unsympathetic to the antibingo laws but unwilling to instruct his subordinates not to enforce them, demoted Goldberg to captain, a reduction of three grades, and thereby drove him to apply for retirement.[28]

At the reformers' insistence most police departments also adopted the tactic of preventive patrol worked out by O. W. Wilson and other reformers in the 1950s and 1960s. Employed in the white neighborhoods, preventive patrol created few problems. Outside of Boston's North End, San Francisco's North Beach, and other ethnic enclaves few whites used the streets in ways that aroused the suspicions of the patrolmen. But extended to the black ghettos, where many teenagers and young adults spent much of their time on the streets, preventive patrol presented several questions. How could the police practice preventive patrol without resorting to out-and-out harassment? How could officers, who dealt with blacks professionally as lawbreakers and personally not at all, distinguish between law-abiding blacks and black criminals? How could these officers figure out which of the many young men who hung out on the streets to stop, search, and interrogate? In other words, how could the police follow the recommendations of the reformers without challenging the life style of many ghetto residents? Thus the tactic of preventive patrol, even if employed in a dispassionate way, also tended to discriminate against the blacks, Mexicans, and Puerto Ricans.

And the tactic was seldom employed in a dispassionate way. Besides being hard pressed to distinguish between law-abiding blacks and black criminals, many police officers also suffered from a sense of alienation, a feeling of persecution, and other symptoms of occupational paranoia. Hence the officers sometimes mistook respectable blacks for black offenders. When the blacks expressed their displeasure, either refusing to submit to a field interrogation or, after submitting, asking for an explanation or complaining about racial discrimination, some policemen felt obliged to reassert their authority or, in effect, to get tough. "I'm gonna give you three minutes to get off the street!" a San Francisco officer told a group of black teenagers who had rubbed him the wrong way. "When I call you next time, come see what I want!" another San Francisco officer said as he grabbed a black youth who had slighted him.[29] Frustrated by a long history of subordination and segregation, acutely, sometimes unduly, sensitive about their status, quick to take offense and slow to hide resentment, some blacks often responded in a provocative way.

Whereupon a confrontation often developed because few groups were less willing to hear a reasonable gripe than the police, few groups were less inclined to accept an honest error than the blacks, and though each might prefer to avoid a showdown, neither was secure enough to back down.

Once again the blacks and other newcomers paid a high price for police reform. The adoption of a single standard, which was long overdue, did not curb, much less eradicate, crime in the ghettos, which remained by far the most dangerous neighborhoods in urban America. Neither did the employment of a preventive strategy. To the dismay of some blacks, Mexicans, and Puerto Ricans, moreover, these changes seriously threatened their life styles and the values, attitudes, and customs underlying them. It was as if insult had been added to injury. So far as most newcomers were concerned, the big-city police had apparently joined forces with the schools, courts, welfare agencies, and other public bureaucracies which had long tried to impose the conventional morality on them. True they were less than completely successful. At a time when the conventional morality had lost so much of its force that some states were setting up lotteries and sanctioning off-track betting, many persons wondered why the police even attempted to enforce the sumptuary laws. But to many blacks, Mexicans, and Puerto Ricans, who could not understand why the police spent so much energy on morals offenses at a time when violent crime was skyrocketing, these reforms seemed little more than an excuse for racial and ethnic discrimination.

If the reform movement was a mixed blessing—a boon for the middle- and upper-middle-class whites and a bane for the lower- and lower-middle-class blacks, Mexicans, and Puerto Ricans—it is necessary to deal with two distinct though closely related questions. First, how widespread were the above-mentioned changes? Did they take place in most big cities or only in Oakland, Cincinnati, Kansas City, and a few others where, to apply one scholar's distinction, the police departments employed a "legalistic," as opposed to a "watchman" or a "service," style?[30] To put it another way, has the impact of the second generation of reformers been exaggerated because the differences from one department to another have been downplayed? Second, how important were these changes? How much of an impact did the big-city police, which were only one of many municipal agencies, have on the mobility, power, and standing of urban America's social classes and ethnic groups? Or to put this another way, has the impact of the second generation of reformers been exaggerated because the focus has been on the police forces rather than on the whole range of urban institutions?

There were, it is true, many differences from one department to another. Some departments were more accessible than others. According to the President's Riot Commission, which made a survey in the late 1960s, the Philadelphia police employed 1,377 blacks, roughly one for every 450 black residents or about five times as many as the Detroit police, which employed 277 blacks, roughly one for every 2,420 black residents. Some departments were also less autonomous than others. The elected officials had much more to say about rank-and-file salaries in Chicago, where the patrolmen's association dealt directly with Mayor Richard J. Daley or his aides, than in Los Angeles, where the authorities had pegged salaries to prevailing wages in the private sector. Some departments were more broad-minded than others too. According to a study done in the mid-1960s, the Albany police, which put their principal emphasis on keeping the peace, were fifty times less likely to arrest a black man for gambling than the Oakland police, which placed their highest priority on enforcing the law.[31]

But these differences were overshadowed by several striking similarities. Nowhere in urban America, not even in Philadelphia and the few other cities where the police departments had made a strong effort to recruit minority applicants, did the blacks hold a fair share, much less a lion's share, of the jobs. Neither did the Mexicans and Puerto Ricans, who were even more severely underrepresented than the blacks. Nowhere in urban America, not even in Chicago and the few other cities where the old-line machines had survived the reform movement, did the ward politicians have much of a voice over the appointment, promotion, and discipline of the rank-and-file. They were superseded by citywide officials in some places, police chiefs in others, and rank-and-file outfits in still others. Nowhere, not even in Albany and the few other cities where the reform campaign had run into strong resistance, did the officers refuse to enforce the sumptuary laws on the grounds that they were incompatible with the values and attitudes of the newcomers. Neither, for that matter, did the other parts of the criminal justice system. The differences were significant, but in view of the striking heterogeneity of urban America, the similarities were more impressive.

Underlying these similarities was the consensus about policing that had been created by the first generation of reformers and preserved by the second. At the core of this consensus were three assumptions which are worth repeating. In the first place, public service was not a means of social mobility. The big-city police were supposed to provide the best possible service at the lowest possible cost and not to supply jobs for first- and second-generation newcomers whose sole qualification was party loyalty. In the second place, local control was not a source of political legitimacy. No matter how commanding their majorities at the polls, the ward leaders had no right to interfere in departmental affairs, which were the exclusive province of the chiefs, mayors, and other city-wide officials. In the third place, immigrant life-styles were not an expression of American culture. The police forces were supposed to apply the criminal sanction not only to prevent crime but also to impose the conventional morality on the newcomers and their families. This consensus, which was the great legacy of the first generation of reformers, shaped the nationwide debate over the policies and practices of the big-city police down through the second third of the twentieth century.

The police were, it is also true, only one of many public agencies which had an impact on the mobility, power, and standing of urban America's social classes and ethnic groups. They handed out enough jobs to enhance the mobility of some groups at the expense of others. But so did the fire, sanitation, and public works departments, the welfare bureaus, hospitals, and transit authorities, and the schools, which employed by far the largest segment of the municipal labor force. The police made enough decisions to increase the weight of some groups at the expense of others. But so did the highway departments, the transit authorities, the urban renewal agencies, and the public authorities, which, as Robert A. Caro has shown, often enjoyed a degree of freedom from legislative, executive, and judicial oversight that even Chief Parker might have envied. The police also enforced enough rules to raise the standing of some groups at the expense of others. But so did the schools, courts, and welfare bureaus which, whatever their ostensible purpose, had long attempted to impose the conventional morality on deviant and dependent groups.[32]

But many of these institutions, notably the schools, courts, and fire, sanitation, and public works departments, had been transformed in much the same way as the police. The process started around the turn of the century when the Progressives launched their campaign to upgrade the public service and destroy the political machine. The schools and other bureaucracies, which functioned as adjuncts of the machine and furnished the ward bosses a steady supply of jobs and favors, were among the reformers' prime targets. Following a corporate model in some cases and a quasi-military model in others, the reformers urged the authorities to sever the connection between public service and machine politics. As Samuel P. Hays and other scholars have pointed out, they were fairly successful.[33] They set up at-large councils, instituted nonpartisan elections, strengthened the mayor's office, instituted the initiative, referendum, and recall, and otherwise reorganized city government. They stripped the ward boards of their authority over the schools, deprived the ward leaders of their power to appoint judges, and put the firemen, sanitationmen, and most other municipal employees under civil service. They even shifted authority over highways and other public works from ward organizations to city, metropolitan, and state agencies, and in a few cases to independent quasi-public authorities.

By the mid-1960s the reformers had centralized, bureaucratized, and to a lesser degree professionalized the schools, courts, fire, sanitation, and public works departments, and most other municipal agencies. (For different reasons they had also made changes in institutions that were not cogs in the political machine, such as prisons, almshouses, and asylums.)[34] As a result municipal agencies no longer eased social mobility, reinforced political decentralization, fostered cultural pluralism, or otherwise promoted the interests of the lower- and lower-middle-class newcomers. Most of these institutions aroused less animosity than the police, though it is hard to see why. The fire departments were no more accessible to the newcomers. The urban renewal agencies and state highway departments were no more responsive to their demands. The schools and welfare bureaus were even less tolerant of their life styles. Although these institutions may have provided slightly better service in the mid-1960s than in the mid-1890s, the evidence is hardly conclusive, and in any event the lower- and lower-middle-class newcomers paid a stiff price for it.

Some of the newcomers were fed up. So far as they were concerned, the police, schools, courts, hospitals, welfare bureaus, and other municipal agencies were less responsive to the residents who needed them than to the civil servants who manned them. Half a century of centralization, bureaucratization, and professionalization was enough, they argued; now was the time for a move to administrative decentralization, political accountability, and .citizen participation. Hence they called for community control of schools and neighborhood health centers. They demanded the abolition of civil service tests and the reimposition of residency requirements. They filed suits against the welfare bureaus and public housing authorities. They continued to fight against urban renewal and started the struggle against inner-city highway construction. They pressed for civilian review boards for the police and ombudsmen for other public agencies. The newcomers did not have much leverage over the big-city police. But by the mid-1960s many upper-middle- and upper-class Americans, some of whom had hitherto supported the reform movement, shared their concerns; and thus for the first time since the early twentieth century the campaign for police reform was in serious trouble.

The reformers themselves evaluated the big-city police according to quite different standards. These standards emerged in the late 1920s when the reformers, who had long held that the police were supposed to provide the best possible service at the lowest possible cost, started looking for a way to measure the quality of this service. They thought about using the crime rate, an indicator which was consistent with their position that crime prevention was the principal function of the big-city police. But this indicator was severely flawed. As Donald C. Stone, director of research for the International City Managers' Association, pointed out, the crime rate reflected not only the caliber of the prosecutors, courts, and other outfits besides the police, but also the impact of social, economic, and other changes over which the police had little or no control. The reformers therefore decided to use the so-called clearance rate, an indicator that had been invented by the IACP's Committee on Uniform Crime Records. According to the committee, the clearance rate expressed the percentage of crimes solved by the police, or more accurately, the percentage of crimes known to the police that the police believe they have solved. This indicator appealed so strongly to most police officials that by World War II it was regarded as the principal measure of police performance throughout the country.[35]

But the clearance rate left much to be desired. For one thing, it was inaccurate. It underestimated the number of crimes because only a small fraction—ranging from two-thirds in St. Louis to one-half in New York, one-third in Los Angeles, and one-fifth in Philadelphia—was reported to the police. The fraction varied from city to city not only because of the attitudes of the citizens but also because of the policies of the departments. In some departments the officers recorded just about every complaint as a crime; but in others they often refused to file a report on the grounds that the victim could not be trusted or that he could not produce any evidence to support his complaint. The clearance rate also exaggerated the number of crimes solved. So far as the statisticians were concerned, the police solved a crime when they arrested a suspect, even though, as the President's Crime Commission reported, a large majority of the suspects was subsequently released or acquitted. To make matters worse, the officers employed a host of gimmicks to boost the clearance rate. To give one example, they sometimes promised to reduce the charges provided that the suspect confessed to several other offenses, which he may or may not have committed, and thereby helped them clear a good many unsolved cases.[36]

For another thing, the clearance rate was misleading. Based on the untenable assumption that the big-city police spent all their time solving crime, the clearance rate did not reveal how well they performed their other tasks. It did not measure how well they prevented crime, even though most reformers contended that crime prevention was the prime function of the big-city police. This chore was very difficult to measure. Hard as it was to figure out how many crimes were committed, it was much harder to figure out how many were prevented and even harder to figure out how many were prevented by the police. Yet it made little sense for the reformers to urge the police departments to focus on preventing crime and then evaluate them on the basis of solving crime. Nor did the clearance rate measure how well the police kept the peace and served the public, even though they spent 80 to 90 percent of their time on these tasks.[37] It revealed nothing about how well they resolved domestic disputes, handled unruly crowds, protected unpopular demonstrators, responded to emergencies, and looked for lost children. These chores too were difficult to measure. But again it made little sense for the public to call on the police to deal with so many noncriminal matters and then evaluate them according to the clearance rate.

The reformers attempted to remedy these defects in two ways. First, they devised techniques to increase the accuracy of the statistics on which the clearance rate was based. Perhaps the most promising of these techniques were the so-called victimization surveys, which measured the incidence of crime by asking a random sample of residents and businessmen whether, and how often, they had been victims of crime. Pioneered by the President's Crime Commission in the District of Columbia during the mid-1960s, these surveys were later sponsored by the LEAA in several other major cities.[38] Although the surveys were only as reliable as the respondents, they provided a far more accurate estimate than the *Uniform Crime Reports* — and inasmuch as they showed that reported crime was only a small fraction of total crime, a far more ominous estimate too. Apart from urging the departments to centralize their reporting procedures, some reformers also called on them to keep track of the disposition of the charges. But as Clarence E. Ridley, the executive director of the International City Managers' Association, and Herbert A. Simon, a graduate student at the University of Chicago, pointed out in the late 1930s, the disposition of the charges depends on all sorts of things other than the efficiency of the police.[39] Few departments have given this scheme a try. Unless they do — or unless they find another way to figure out how many crimes have been solved — the clearance rate will remain an unsatisfactory measure of police performance.

Second, the reformers looked for alternatives to the clearance rate. Following the lead of Ridley and Simon, who had recommended that the number of serious auto injuries per 100,000 people be used as a measure of how well the police regulated traffic, the reformers analyzed a good many chores other than crime prevention. With the support of the National Commission on Productivity and other organizations they developed additional indicators, most of which were based on simple input-output measures or standard survey research methods. Chief among them were the percentage of patrolmen assigned to patrol duty, the percentage of time patrolmen spent on beats, the percentage of calls responded to in a reasonable time, and the percentage of calls responded to in a satisfactory way. Other measures were the number of people served per policeman and per dollar, the number of arrests per policeman and per dollar, the percentage of arrests leading to conviction, and the percentage of the population satisfied with the service. Given the Police Foundation's interest in raising police productivity and finding ways to measure it, some of these indicators will no doubt be tested, refined, and adopted in the not-too-distant future.[40]

Even so, these indicators will probably provide a measure of police performance that is only slightly more satisfactory than the clearance rate. For they deal with only one of the many functions of the big-city police. An offshoot of the reform movement, these indicators focus on what is commonly referred to nowadays as service delivery. They measure what the police claim to do, what the reformers want them to do, and to be fair to the many people who have worked hard to develop these indicators, what most Americans think they do. To draw sociologist Robert K. Merton's distinction, they look at the manifest, as opposed to the latent, functions of the big-city police. But the police do many other things. They help to decide which laws are enforced, whose peace is kept, and which public is served. They hand out a good many jobs, which pay high salaries and come with adequate benefits and handsome pensions. They shape the structure of local politics, which regulates access to the locus of decision-making. And they legitimize or stigmatize competing life-styles. Along with the schools, courts, welfare bureaus, and other public institutions, the police influence the process of mobility, the distribution of power, and the struggle for status in urban America. About these functions the indicators are not the least bit informative.

At best the indicators tell whether the police have improved their service; but they do not tell what these improvements have cost, who has paid for them, or whether they are worth the price. Hence they beg the question. Suppose, for a moment, the indicators showed that during the twentieth century the clearance rate went up, response time went down, auto accidents fell, and citizen satisfaction rose. Suppose they revealed that corruption, incompetence, and lawlessness were on the wane. And suppose, after a careful analysis of the pertinent variables, they indicated that these changes were a direct result of the reform campaign. A favorable evaluation would presumably be in order. But suppose the big-city police at the same time became less accessible to the newcomers, less responsive to their leaders, and less tolerant of their life styles. Suppose the police no longer fostered social mobility, political decentralization, and cultural pluralism. And suppose, after another careful analysis of the pertinent variables, it turned out that these changes were also a direct outcome of the reform movement. So far as most upper-middle- and upper-class whites were concerned, a favorable evaluation would still be in order. But most lower- and lower-middle-class blacks, Mexicans, and Puerto Ricans would not have thought so.

The reformers would not have been fazed, for with few exceptions they had never paid much attention to the newcomers' views. As they put it, they listened to no group other than the great majority of hard-working, law-abiding, and upstanding Americans; they spoke for no interest other than the public interest. To pay much attention to the newcomers' views would have been to admit that their campaign might have had a different impact on the various social classes and ethnic groups. To admit this possibility, much less to develop indicators to measure the differences, would have been to renounce their moral superiority and weaken their long-range prospects. So long as the debate over policing focused on service delivery, which was by far the least controversial function of the big-city police, the reform campaign was in good shape. Once the debate turned to social mobility, political legitimacy, cultural pluralism, and other highly inflammatory issues, the campaign was in serious trouble. Down through the second third of the twentieth century few Americans thought much about these issues, which was perhaps the most revealing indicator of the long-term impact of the reform movement. But how much longer the reformers could count on this myopia remained to be seen.

11.   Reform at a Standstill

On October 24, 1968, Gordon E. Misner appeared before the National Commission on the Causes and Prevention of Violence. A prominent criminologist, Misner had impeccable reform credentials. As a product, in his words, of "California policing," he had preached the gospel according to August Vollmer, earned his Ph. D. at Berkeley's School of Criminology, and worked with Joseph D. Lohman, who had succeeded O. W. Wilson as dean of the school. Yet in his testimony Misner expressed grave reservations about the conventional wisdom of the reform movement.[1] He observed that the Philadelphia police, which "nobody ever accused of being a professional [force]," did a pretty good job without imposing stiff entrance requirements and maintaining high professional standards. He remarked that several other departments, which had carried out most of the reform recommendations, had run into all sorts of problems that Vollmer, Wilson, and other reformers had failed to anticipate. Misner's testimony, given two years after Wilson had retired and only one year after William H. Parker had died, revealed that by the late 1960s a few reformers were having second thoughts about some of the cardinal tenets of the reform movement.

A few of their second thoughts were predictable. Some reformers were worried about the growth of the special squads, a concern that had been voiced by Public Safety Director Smedley D.

Butler of Philadelphia as early as the mid-1920s. Some of these units were essential, the reformers conceded; but if allowed to proliferate, they subverted the command structure, blurred the responsibility between patrolmen and plainclothesmen, and provided the uniformed force with an excuse for inaction. The Knapp Commission revealed that, unless closely supervised, they also turned into the principal sources of graft and corruption in most departments. As Jerry V. Wilson, chief of the Washington, D.C., police, remarked, these squads posed still other problems that were less obvious but even more serious. They developed a strong esprit de corps, a conviction that they were superior to the uniformed force, which severely undermined the morale of the rest of the department. They also siphoned off from the uniformed force many of its most competent and committed members, who regarded a transfer to a plainclothes unit as the next best thing to a promotion.[2] Since the patrolmen and not the plainclothesmen dealt with ordinary citizens on a day-to-day basis, this practice did little to enhance the public image of the big-city police.

Some reformers were troubled as well by the operation of the civil service, an anxiety that had been articulated by Commissioner Arthur Woods of New York City as early as the late 1910s. Some regulations were necessary, they acknowledged, to insulate personnel practices from partisan politics. But the promotional procedures, which relied heavily on written tests, seniority, oral interviews, and field evaluations, were not reliable indicators of potential leadership, Commissioner Robert J. diGrazia of Boston charged. Instead of moving up promising commanders, the civil service rewarded run-of-the-mill patrolmen who were anxious to increase their pay and raise their status and had a knack for taking tests and avoiding trouble. In a striking departure from the conventional wisdom, a few reformers even criticized the appointments process. According to James M. Murray, personnel director of the Washington, D.C., police in the late 1960s, there was little correlation between IQ levels, test scores, or other recruitment criteria and ordinary performance measures. According to the Rand Corporation, which did a survey of minority recruitment in New York City in the early 1970s, the civil service was so slow that many qualified candidates dropped out of the running.[3]

Some reformers were also critical of the efforts to enforce the vice laws, a position that had been spelled out by Chief August Vollmer as early as the mid-1920s. Gambling, prostitution, and drunkenness were deplorable, they admitted. But in the face of the pervasive indifference, not to mention the out-and-out opposition, of many Americans, there was nothing much the police could do about these activities. As James F. Ahern, chief of the New Haven police in the late 1960s, wrote, the police also paid a high price for trying.[4] Well aware that gamblers, bookies, prostitutes, and numbers runners often operated with virtual impunity, many citizens drew the conclusion that the police were either corrupt or incompetent. And according to the Seabury, Knapp, and other official commissions that looked into the activities of the vice squads, this conclusion was not wide of the mark. To many reformers, this price seemed exorbitant in the early 1970s. They did not see how the police could justify spending so much time and money on gambling and other morals offenses at a time when murder, rape, robbery, and burglary were on the rise. Nor did these reformers see how the police could justify assigning so many officers to vice squads at a time when many departments were being forced to put a freeze on appointments and even to lay off veteran officers.

But some of the second thoughts about the cardinal tenets of the reform movement were unexpected. A few reformers were skeptical about the validity of the professional model, a notion that had been sacrosanct down through the late 1950s. This skepticism took several different forms. To Misner, professionalism had gone too far; the gap between politics and policing had grown too wide. "I don't want City Hall to be out of the police department," he told the Violence Commission. "I don't want the day-to-day interference with operating routine . . . But I do want the participation of . . . the political leadership in the long-range planning and policy development." To Ahern, however, professionalism had not gone far enough; it had reached the chiefs, but it had not been extended to the patrolmen. Most departments paid lip service to the professional model, he pointed out; in practice, they continued to treat the rank-and-file like "military operatives." And to Jerry Wilson, professionalism was simply inappropriate, a reflection of an elitist attitude toward ordinary work. Rather than following undertakers, salesmen, janitors, and other groups in the ludicrous quest for professional status, Wilson wrote, police officers should model themselves on carpenters, bricklayers, plumbers, and the other so-called "master crafts-men."[5]

A few reformers also doubted the wisdom of requiring a college degree of all recruits, a requirement that had been endorsed by the President's Crime Commission in the late 1960s. Jerry Wilson based his objections on several grounds other than the difficulty of persuading college graduates to go into policing. First, the police should be "reasonably representative" of the community, which was full of citizens who did not start, much less finish, college. Second, the police should serve as "a ladder" to the mid-dle class for blacks and other newcomers who would be hard pressed to meet this requirement. And third, the police do a good deal of tedious work which would probably bore many college graduates, a point also stressed by Misner. Wilson did not object to higher education for police officers; on the contrary, he encouraged the rank-and-file to attend college classes and sup-ported plans to give them extra pay for college credits. But he strongly objected to the proposal to make the college degree an entrance requirement, a proposal that in his view reflected the law enforcement community's drive for professional status and its infatuation with formal credentials. Attacking the conventional wisdom of the reform movement, Wilson insisted that anyone with a solid education through the tenth grade should have no-trouble assimilating police training and understanding depart-mental regulations.[6]

A few reformers were critical too of the rhetoric of the "war on crime," a rhetoric that had been employed by the Johnson Administration in the mid-1960s. As Misner pointed out, the police spend most of their time, probably as much as 90 percent, directing traffic, helping people, and doing all sorts of other things which by no stretch of the imagination are related to crime prevention. The police do not use the remaining 10 percent of their time very well, Ahern added. They still do not know what causes crime, and notwithstanding the widespread acceptance of the *Uniform Crime Reports,* they still cannot measure criminal activity with much precision. A few reformers also insisted that the public tended to expect too much of the police. Addressing a Police Foundation conference, Patrick Murphy spoke out against this tendency, which he attributed to the tradition of the frontier marshal, a susceptibility to easy solutions, and the rhetoric of law and order. "Somehow," he told his audience, "we must let the American public know that neither the police nor other elements in the criminal justice system have anything approaching a complete answer to the problems of crime."[7]

Misner, Murphy, Ahern, and Jerry Wilson did not repudiate the campaign for police reform. They had no wish to return to the days when public service was a means of social mobility, local control was a source of political legitimacy, ethnic life-styles were an expression of American culture, and the police department was an adjunct of the political machine. Nor did they speak for the majority of their fellow reformers. Most of them were more concerned about political interference than bureaucratic isolation, more troubled by undereducated officers than overeducated officers, and more inclined to stress the progress of policing than to emphasize its limitations. But Misner and the other skeptics expressed reservations about the reform campaign which cannot be lightly dismissed. These reservations not only raised questions that threatened the ideological consensus on which the reform movement was based — questions about the relationship between policing and politics, credentials and qualifications, crime and society. These reservations also reflected a growing concern about the course of police reform among millions of Americans, many of whom had supported the reform campaign down through World War II and even into the 1960s.

Many Americans were concerned about the course of police reform for traditional reasons. These Americans, who were represented by the crime commissions, chambers of commerce, taxpayers outfits, and other agents of the financial and commercial elites, placed a high priority on public order, managerial expertise, and governmental efficiency. Direct descendants of the Progressives, they had long accepted the reformers' assumptions about the nature of public service, political legitimacy, and American culture as well as their convictions about the relationship between politics and policing. They had also shared the reformers' confidence that if the local authorities changed the structure, personnel, and function of the police departments in line with the reform prescription, they would solve the police problem and in time the crime problem as well.

But lately these Americans had begun to think that their confidence was misplaced. For despite the special squads and precinct consolidations, the civil service and service pensions, and the *Uniform Crime Reports* and preventive patrol, the big-city police still left much to be desired — not so much as in the 1890s, when the Lexow Committee held its hearings, or in the 1930s, when the Wickersham Commission issued its report, but enough to raise serious doubts about the long-run efficacy of the reform movement.

Two things in particular troubled these Americans. The first was that the reformers had not put an end to the corruption, incompetence, and lawlessness of the big-city police. In 1974, a decade and a half after Commissioner Thomas J. Gibbons left the Philadelphia police, the Pennsylvania Crime Commission uncovered evidence "of systematic, widespread corruption at all levels of the Department." Similar revelations rocked New York, Seattle, Indianapolis, and several other cities in which the reformers had gained control of the police force after World War II. In 1972, a decade and a half after Commissioner Stephen P. Kennedy quit the New York City police, the New York *Times* reported that many officers were working at what one senior commander estimated at no more than 50 percent efficiency. Although the New York City Police Department had an unenviable reputation, there was no reason to believe that it was much less efficient than other big-city forces. In 1973, less than a decade after Superintendent O.W. Wilson retired from the Chicage police, a blue-ribbon panel charged that many officers employed excessive force in the black and Puerto Rican communities. Shortly thereafter the Chicago *Tribune* published an eight-part series that not only confirmed the panel's charges but also concluded that police brutality was common in the white neighborhoods as well.[8]

The second source of concern was that the big-city police had not put an end to crime in the streets. Notwithstanding the saturation squads, field interrogations, crime labs, *Uniform Crime Reports,* and other innovations, the police were hard put to do much about what *Newsweek* magazine referred to in 1965 as "a condition of epidemic criminality." Whether crime was worse in the 1960s than in the 1920s, when the second wave of police reform got underway, is impossible to say because the available statistics are not reliable enough to permit generalizations from one decade to another. But crime was probably on the rise in the 1960s, and in any case most citizens thought it was. Of five hundred persons who were asked in the mid-1960s whether violent crime had increased in the District of Columbia over the last five years, 60 percent said very much, 22 percent a little, 10 percent not much, and 3 percent not at all. Only one percent said it had decreased.[9] Conditions were much the same in most other big cities. Out of a respect for the FBI and a reverence for hard data most Americans took at face value the results of the *Uniform Crime Reports,* which as a rule revealed a steady and often sharp rise in criminal activity in urban America. And they accepted as gospel the jeremiads of Hoover, Parker, and other well-known law enforcement officials who were not averse to exploiting the fear of crime to justify their requests for additional manpower and increased resources.

The critics were no doubt too hard on the reformers. The big-city police were less corrupt, incompetent, and lawless in the late 1960s than in the early 1930s and the middle 1890s, a mark of progress for which the reformers deserved much of the credit. And if the police had not made much headway against crime, neither had the prosecutors, courts, and correctional institutions. But the reformers had only themselves to blame for the growing skepticism about the reform movement. For two decades they had claimed that the big-city police would be free of corruption, incompetence, and lawlessness once their structure, personnel, and function were revised according to the reform prescription. They had also contended that once the police were reorganized along the lines of the military analogy or the professional model, they would greatly cut down, if not completely wipe out, crime in urban America. The reformers had been persuasive. Over the years they had prevailed on most Americans not only to adopt their goals and support their efforts but also to accept their standards. Hence their fellow citizens evaluated the reform movement not from an historical viewpoint, which might have given a proper perspective, but by the reformers' own criteria. By these criteria the results were somewhat less than satisfactory.

Perhaps for lack of a viable alternative, some Americans remained loyal to the reform campaign. Along with the Knapp Commission and the Pennsylvania Crime Commission, they held that the big-city police were still prone to corruption, incompetence, and lawlessness not because the reform proposals were ill-advised but because they had not been put into practice. Despite the valiant efforts of Wilson, Murphy, and the other reformers, the police still bowed to pressure from the local politicians, still appointed too many unqualified applicants, and still spent too much energy on chores other than crime prevention. Now was the time to rally behind the reformers, these Americans concluded, not to abandon them. This viewpoint was not limited to conservatives. Testifying before the Violence Commission, Ramsey Clark, attorney general in the Johnson Administration and a Democrat with outstanding liberal credentials, insisted that the solution to the police problem was, in a word, professionalization. Two years later Clark recommended that the big-city police require college degrees of all recruits, appoint specialists with graduate degrees in medicine, law, criminology, and related disciplines, and focus their efforts exclusively on crime prevention.[10] Although characterized by Tom Wicker of the New York *Times* as "the most revolutionary public voice in America," Clark said little that ran counter to the conventional wisdom of the reform movement.

But many Americans lost faith in the reform campaign. Stunned by the revelations of the Knapp Commission and other investigative agencies, they no longer believed that the big-city police could stamp out corruption and incompetence, much less wipe out violent crime. The great popularity of *Serpico* and *Dirty Harry* was one sign of the dwindling confidence in the big-city police. *Serpico,* a movie about the New York City police, described how Officer Frank Serpico discovers that with one or two exceptions everyone is "on the take" and no one, not the commissioner and not even the mayor, does anything about it. A dedicated officer, who to the delight of the middle- and upper-middle-class audiences combines an Italian-American background with a Greenwich Village life style, Serpico is shot in the head for his attempts to expose the system. *Dirty Harry,* a film about the San Francisco police, depicted the plight of Detective Harry Calahan, another dedicated and courageous officer, who is stymied by self-serving politicians, woolly-headed judges, and nitpicking commanders. Calahan finally gets his man, but only by defying his superiors and taking the law into his own hands. In

Magnum Force, the sequel to *Dirty Harry,* Calahan has no choice but to throw away his badge.[11]

Another sign of the dwindling confidence in the big-city police was the deep-seated reluctance to report criminal activity. According to the nationwide victimization survey sponsored by the LEAA in the early 1970s, roughly one of every three crimes went unreported in Newark and St. Louis, one of every two in New York, Baltimore, and Atlanta, three of every five in Cleveland, Dallas, and Portland, two of every three in Chicago, Denver, and Los Angeles, and a whopping four of every five in Philadelphia. There were many reasons that the victims failed to call the police. According to another nationwide victimization study, published by the President's Crime Commission in the late 1960s, some Americans felt the crime was a private matter; others were afraid of reprisals; some could not spare the time; a few were worried about the offenders; and others were too confused or upset by the incident. But according to this and other surveys, the victims did not report crimes partly because they lacked confidence in the police forces. Of several hundred victims who were asked to account for their reluctance to call the police, 28 percent replied that the officers would not want to be bothered, 58 percent said that the police could not do anything about it anyway, and 31 percent answered that even if they tried, the police would not necessarily arrest the right person.[12]

Still another sign of the dwindling confidence in the big-city police was the widespread enthusiasm for community policing, self-defense, and even vigilante activity. The North Ward Citizens Committee patrolled the Italian neighborhoods of Newark and the Maccabees Safety Patrol policed the Jewish communities of Brooklyn. The Crime Prevention Institute set up an escort service in New York's Harlem; and with the support of LEAA the Sav-Mor Association organized a house-watch program in Boston's Roxbury. As the President's Crime Commission reported, many persons stayed home after dark, put iron bars on their windows, left the lights on at night, and kept a dog on the premises. Many others attended judo and karate classes, bought mace cans and tear-gas pens, carried knives or handguns, and took other drastic steps to protect themselves. Few Americans were ready to tangle with dangerous criminals. But many were quick to applaud Paul Kersey, the hero of the movie *Death Wish,* a well-to-do architect who seeks out muggers and summarily executes them after his wife and daughter are brutally assaulted. A one-man vigilante squad, Kersey reflects the growing sentiment that the lone gunman was, in the words of Penelope Gilliatt, one of the *New Yorker*'s film critics, "a big city's only hope of law and order."[13]

To make matters worse for the reformers, the price of policing and other public services was, as the Washington *Post* put it, "skyrocketing." The rise was steep in New York. Between 1963 and 1973, a decade in which the size of the force increased from 26,700 to 31,500, or roughly 18 percent, the cost of operations went up from $299 million to $587 million or roughly 96 percent. But the rise was just as steep, if not steeper, in most other big cities. By the early 1970s Chicago spent more than $200 million, on policing, Los Angeles, Detroit, and Philadelphia more than $100 million, Baltimore and Boston more that $50 million, and Cleveland and Houston more than $25 million. Assured by the reformers that the departments had to raise salaries, benefits, and pensions in order to attract and retain qualified officers, most citizens were willing to go along with the increases through the 1960s. But dismayed by the inflation of the early 1970s and the recession that followed, they now began to wonder not only whether the cities were getting their money's worth but also whether they could afford the mounting costs of the reform movement. Summing up this sentiment, Vice-President Nelson A. Rockefeller, chairman of the National Commission on Productivity and Work Quality, told a conference, "Our citizens' right to have safe streets can no longer be sought 'at any cost.' "[14]

The costs of policing were skyrocketing for two principal reasons other than the steady increase in the number of officers. One reason was that under pressure from the police unions and to a lesser degree the reform groups most big cities gave the rank-and-file substantial raises in the late 1960s and early 1970s. New York was extremely generous. Between 1966 and 1974 a patrolman's base pay after five years' experience went up from $8,500 to $15,300, an increase of close to 80 percent, and his direct earnings, which included longevity increments, paid holidays, and night-shift differentials, rose from $8,800 to $16,800, an increase of over 90 percent. By virtue of a pegging system the superior officers — who as a result of a trend that went back to the turn of the century and reached a peak in the early 1970s now made up one-third of the sworn personnel and one-fourth of the entire force in most cities — received comparable raises. But many other cities were just as generous. By 1974 a patrolman started at more than $14,000 in San Francisco, more than $11,000 in Seattle, Los Angeles, Chicago, Cleveland, and Detroit, more than $10,000 in Boston and Houston, and more than $9,000 in Pittsburgh, Denver, and Phoenix. A patrolman with five to nine years' experience earned that year at least $15,000 in San Francisco, Los Angeles, and Detroit, at least $14,000 in Chicago, Boston, and San Diego, and at least $13,000 in New Orleans, Milwaukee, and Philadelphia.[15] The superior officers received 33 to 100 percent more in most of these cities.

Another reason that the costs of policing were skyrocketing was that during the postwar years most big cities made what later turned out to be expensive improvements in fringe and pension benefits. Many cities provided a uniform allowance; some paid for health insurance; a few contributed to a welfare fund; and some improved the service pensions by increasing the benefits and reducing the age and service requirements. Many cities even raised the pension benefits after retirement. Detroit gave the beneficiaries an extra 2 percent every year; St. Louis provided an additional 3 percent a year if the Consumer Price Index rose 3 percent or more. Washington, D.C., tied retirement benefits to starting salaries; and Los Angeles pegged them, point by point, to the cost of living.[16] The results were mind-boggling. For a patrolman with five years' experience New York City spent about $400, or 60 percent, more in fringe benefits and around $2,400, or 80 percent, more in pension benefits in 1974 than in 1966. For a patrolman with five to nine years' experience Detroit paid more than $9,000 in benefits alone in 1974; Los Angeles shelled out more than $6,000, San Francisco more than $5,000, and New Orleans more than $4,000. All told, a veteran patrolman cost that year at least $25,000 in Detroit, $22,000 in New York and Los Angeles, $21,000 in San Francisco, $17,000 in New Orleans, San Diego, and Chicago, and $16,000 in Milwaukee, Phoenix, and Washington, D.C.[17] The superior officers were a good deal more expensive.

For these increases the reformers bore much of the responsibility. Besides mounting a campaign for higher salaries, they formulated the arguments that the rank-and-file leaders put forward in their negotiations with the municipal officials. In the drive to separate policing from politics the reformers also developed the formulas and other devices that deprived the municipal authorities of their influence over personnel expenditures. Small wonder that at a time when the rank-and-file groups were turning into de facto unions and the cost of living was rising at a record clip police salaries were skyrocketing. Besides launching a campaign for better pensions, the reformers called on the authorities to turn away applicants who were more than thirty or at most thirty-five years of age. Thus many officers joined in their early or middle twenties, put in twenty to twenty-five years, and retired in their late forties or early or middle fifties. Small wonder that at a time when most pensioners lived into their seventies and eighties and many retirement benefits were pegged to the cost of living police pensions were skyrocketing too. Thanks in part to the reformers, many cities were now supporting two police forces, one made up of active officers and another, which was growing rapidly, made up of retired officers. Quite a few citizens wondered whether they could afford both forces.

Some thought that they could, but only if the big-city police made an all-out effort to increase their productivity. Speaking on behalf of New York's financial, commercial, and real estate interests, which were deeply troubled by the rising costs of municipal services, the Citizens Budget Commission praised the New York City Police Department for a productivity program that it had started in the early 1970s. Following the reform prescription, the commission also called on the department to press ahead with its plans to employ civilians in clerical and other positions currently filled by sworn officers, shift from two-man to one-man squad cars, and apply computers to patrol allocation and other mundane tasks. The National Commission on Productivity and Work Quality came up with similar recommendations. Addressing a conference on productivity sponsored by the Police Foundation in the mid-1970s, Mayor Tom Bradley of Los Angeles suggested that in view of the spiraling costs of policing the departments should begin to reexamine their function. Following an argument laid out by Vollmer more than a generation earlier, he proposed that the police consider devoting a smaller share of their limited resources to victimless crimes and traffic violations.[18] The San Francisco Committee on Crime had already adopted this position, and the Washington *Post* followed suit not long afterward.

But others felt that these proposals did not go far enough. Departing from the conventional wisdom of the 'reform movement, they insisted that it was time for the authorities to put a stop to the rising costs of policing. Some of them tried to do so. Late in the 1960s Mayor Jerome Cavanagh, whose administration was facing a $10 million deficit, concluded that Detroit could no longer afford the present policemen's and firemen's pension system. Under the current provisions, which allowed the officers to retire after twenty-five years of service at 50 percent of their salary plus 50 percent of future raises, the cost of the system had gone up from $1.5 million in 1946 to $27.6 million in 1968. It already came to more than one-third of the total budget of the two departments. With 3,400 more policemen and firemen eligible to retire in the next ten years, many of them first-rate officers in the prime of life, Cavanagh feared that the system would soon be completely out of control. He therefore proposed a charter amendment that set a minimum age requirement of fifty-five, added a modest cost of living escalator of 2 percent a year, and as an incentive to the veterans to stay on the job, based the benefits on years of service. Drawing on the reform rhetoric, the Detroit POA charged that the changes would make it harder to attract qualified recruits; but despite the opposition of the association, which spent about $250,000 on the campaign, the voters adopted the amendment by a narrow margin.[19]

Early in the 1970s the city administrative officer advised the Los Angeles City Council that according to the so-called Jacobs formula, which pegged starting salaries to prevailing wages, the city's policemen and firemen were entitled to a 7.8 percent raise. But the council, which was caught in a severe fiscal squeeze, authorized only a 3.8 percent raise. As expected, Mayor Samuel Yorty vetoed it; and after failing in an attempt to override his veto, the council, stressing its past generosity to the policemen and firemen and its present obligation to the taxpayers, approved a raise of 5.5 percent. Mayor Yorty went along. But the Los Angeles Fire and Police Protective League filed suit charging that the city council had exceeded its authority by disregarding the formula and demanding back pay equal to the difference be-

tween 7.8 percent and 5.5 percent. Three years later the courts
upheld the league's position. Complaining that the city council
had "lost control over the salary setting of policemen and firemen," Councilman Ernani Bernardi promptly urged his colleagues to repeal the Jacobs formula, which was one of the monuments of the reform movement. Mayor Bradley agreed that the
system required an overhaul; but while he evaluated the alternatives, the city and the league worked out a settlement that gave
the policemen and firemen $31.3 million in back pay, the largest
settlement of its kind in the city's history.[20]

During the mid-1970s the PBA demanded that New York City
abandon "parity," the long-standing arrangement whereby the
uniformed forces received the same salary, and instead pay policemen 11 percent more than firemen. If implemented, the proposal would have brought a patrolman with three years' experience up to $19,700 in 1975 and made the New York City police
force the highest paid in the country. The PBA based its case
on the grounds that policemen were professionals, that unlike
firemen they exercised great discretion, worked under little supervision, and needed all sorts of exceptional skills in addition to
stamina, patience, and courage. The city rejected the demand,
pointing out that it could not afford the increase, that police officers were already very well paid, and that contrary to the association's claim policing was no more "demanding" than firefighting.
The negotiations eventually broke down, and the issue went to a
three-man impasse panel. After lengthy proceedings, at which
Murphy and other reformers strongly supported the union's case
for professional recognition, the panel ruled in favor of the city.
Whether or not the ruling was a "major victory" for responsible
labor relations, as Mayor Abraham Beame put it, it was a stun-
ning setback for the reform movement.[21]

Many Americans were concerned about the course of police
reform for different reasons. These Americans, who were represented by the civil liberties unions and civil rights groups, put a
high priority on personal liberty, racial equality, and bureaucratic accountability. What troubled them was not so much the
corruption and incompetence of the police or the high cost of policing as the much-heralded autonomy of the police. To put it
another way, these Americans were distressed not because the reform movement had done too little or because it had gotten too

expensive but because it had done too much. From their perspective, which was shared by Misner and a few other reformers, the movement had not only separated policing from politics, which was admirable, but also removed it from popular control, which was deplorable. In addition to denying the local politicians their sources of influence, the movement had deprived the ordinary citizens of their avenues of redress; if scrupulous officers could operate with impunity, so could the unscrupulous. The reform movement had improved the quality of policing in a number of ways, these Americans conceded; but in the process it had fostered a degree of bureaucratic irresponsibility that was out of place in a democratic society.

This concern surfaced in the late 1950s and early 1960s when the United States Commission on Civil Rights revealed that many blacks felt powerless to do anything about police malpractice. Some of the commission's advisory committees later confirmed these revelations; so did the University of California School of Criminology and the Atlanta, Boston, and New York City chapters of the ACLU. According to the President's Crime Commission, the blacks had reason to feel this way. Drawing on a nationwide survey of police-community relations by Michigan State University, the commission reported that police officers were rarely convicted and punished on the basis of a complaint by citizens. These revelations had a strong impact on many Americans, whites as well as blacks. For one thing, they came in the wake of a number of studies by the NAACP and ACLU which showed that a generation after the Wickersham Commission report on lawless law enforcement the big-city police still arrested citizens without a warrant, detained them without cause, and otherwise violated their civil liberties. For another thing, they came in the heyday of the civil rights crusade, a time when the intense emotions aroused by the Montgomery bus boycott, the Birmingham sit-ins, the March on Washington, and the other efforts to undermine the racial status quo had reached their peak.[22]

As some Americans realized, this problem was largely an outgrowth of the reform movement, which had persuaded the authorities that the responsibility for handling complaints against the police should be entrusted to the police, and to them alone. Out of a deep concern for the reputation of their departments the internal affairs units and other special squads that assumed this responsibility employed a host of reprehensible tactics to discourage citizens from filing complaints against officers. They threatened complainants with criminal libel in New York City, demanded that they take a lie detector test in Cleveland, and charged them with disorderly conduct, resisting arrest, and other offenses in Philadelphia, Washington, D.C., and Los Angeles. If the citizens filed a complaint anyway, many departments intimidated them and their witnesses. If the citizens requested a hearing, which in light of the expensive, complicated, and protracted proceedings involved was highly unlikely, many departments refused to provide them with counsel or allow them access to the files. In other words, the police behaved as if the complainants, not the officers, were on trial.[23] As a result most departments upheld so small a fraction of the complaints that many citizens concluded that self-policing, one of the principal corollaries of the professional model, was a sham.

Led by the ACLU and NAACP, these citizens called on the authorities to shift the responsibility for handling complaints from the police departments to outside review boards, or as they were commonly referred to, civilian review boards. These boards would serve several purposes, their sponsors claimed. They would restrain the many officers who in the absence of an effective disciplinary system engaged in brutality, harassment, and other improper and even illegal practices. By ensuring a thorough and impartial investigation of all complaints, they would protect the other officers against malicious, misguided, and otherwise unfounded accusations. They would provide the blacks and other ethnic minorities an avenue of redress, which would help restore their dwindling confidence in the police departments and other municipal agencies. They would explain police procedures to the citizens, review enforcement requirements with the police, and start a genuine dialogue in place of mutual recrimination. By curbing police malpractice and improving police-community relations, the review boards would greatly enhance the quality of law enforcement in urban America.[24] The boards would have "no disciplinary powers whatever," their backers assured the police; they would only make recommendations to the departments, which would deal with the officers as they saw fit.

The proposed boards incensed most police officers, who regarded them as a severe threat to their professional aspirations and especially to their determination to set their standards and discipline their colleagues without outside interference. Led by the IACP, ICPA, and FOP, the police lashed out against the proposal. The amount of malpractice is greatly exaggerated, they insisted; the cries of brutality and harassment are usually nothing but attempts to subvert law enforcement. The police departments, the courts, and the Justice Department all provide adequate avenues of redress on the rare occasions when a citizen is mistreated by an officer. The review boards would be inequitable, impractical, and undesirable — inequitable because they would draw invidious distinctions between the police departments and other municipal agencies, impractical because they would ask people with no expertise or experience to sit in judgment on police officers, and undesirable because they would inject politics into policing and set the reform movement back several decades. If put into practice, these boards would demoralize the police, weaken their authority, impair their efficiency, and thus exacerbate the crime problem. Rather than press ahead with this harebrained scheme, the police spokesmen concluded, the civil liberties and civil rights groups should lend their support to the ongoing efforts to professionalize the big-city police.[25]

The issue came to a head in one city after another. At the insistence of the Philadelphia branches of the ACLU and NAACP and the Philadelphia Fellowship Commission, a civic group devoted to promoting interracial harmony, Mayor J. Richardson Dilworth set up a Police Advisory Board in the late 1950s, a step that was strongly opposed by John Harrington, head of the Philadelphia FOP. A few years later the Genessee Valley Civil Liberties Union and the local offices of the NAACP and AFL-CIO prevailed on the Rochester City Council to establish a Police Advisory Board over the vigorous objections of the Locust Club, a fraternal association that spoke for the members of the Rochester police force. In the mid-1960s Mayor John V. Lindsay, who owed his election in large part to New York City's blacks and Puerto Ricans, added four civilians to the police department's three-man Civilian Complaint Review Board, a move that was sharply criticized by John Cassese, head of the New York PBA. About the same time the National Capital Area Civil Liberties Union joined forces with the District of Columbia Bar Association to persuade the Board of Commissioners to enlarge the existing civilian review board, which operated largely out of the police force, from three to five members, two of whom would have to be lawyers.[26] All told, about half a dozen cities had followed Philadelphia's lead by the mid-1960s.

But they were the exceptions. Supported by the Los Angeles *Times,* the Fire and Police Protective League prevailed on the Los Angeles City Council to turn down a proposal by the Southern California Civil Liberties Union to set up a civilian review board in the early 1960s. Backed by the Denver Junior Chamber of Commerce, the Police Protective Association persuaded the Denver City Council to reject an ordinance empowering the Commission on Human Relations to look into allegations of police brutality. With the support of civic groups, daily papers, and reform outfits, the rank-and-file organizations defeated similar proposals in Cincinnati, Seattle, Detroit, Newark, San Diego, Hartford, Baltimore, and San Francisco. In the meantime these organizations launched an attack on the existing review boards. The Philadelphia FOP brought so many suits against the Police Advisory Board that even though the state supreme court eventually ruled in its favor, the board was moribund by the mid-1960s. The Locust Club also appealed to the courts, which held that the Rochester City Council had exceeded its authority by establishing the Police Advisory Board. Despite the vigorous opposition of the ACLU, NAACP and most of New York's leading politicians, the PBA prevailed on the voters to approve a proposition that put the city's review board out of business.[27] By the late 1960s, when Mayor James Tate of Philadelphia formally disbanded the Police Advisory Board, all the civilian review boards were defunct.

The controversy was not particularly inspiring. The ACLU and NAACP overstated the case for the review boards almost, though not quite, as much as the ICPA and FOP exaggerated the case against them. If the experience of the Philadelphia advisory board is indicative, the review boards would not have greatly curbed police malpractice or improved police-community relations, but neither would they have severely hamstrung the police forces or exacerbated the crime problem. The controversy was illuminating, however. It not only revealed that the rank-and-file groups were now a force to be reckoned with in most cities and that they would use their formidable power to conserve many of the reform legacies of which their members were the principal beneficiaries. More than any other issue of the decade, it also showed that many citizens who had hitherto supported the reform campaign were no longer willing to go along with the notion of self-policing and the assumptions about politics, policing, and professionalism underlying it. The controversy indicated too that out of a genuine concern for the plight of the blacks and other minorities some of these citizens were prepared to tolerate a degree of political interference and to sacrifice a degree of professional autonomy in order to enhance the accountability of the big-city police.

The civil liberties and civil rights groups would probably not have pushed so hard for the civilian review boards if the big-city police had been representative of the communities they served. But as the President's Riot Commission pointed out, most departments were overwhelmingly white. Nowhere did nonwhites hold a fair share of the jobs. They were underrepresented by a factor of two in Philadelphia and San Francisco, three in New York and Kansas City, four in Atlanta and Newark, five in Boston and Cincinnati, six in Baltimore and Buffalo, and eight or more in Oakland, Detroit, and New Orleans.[28] To many citizens it seemed that in an effort to upgrade the force the big-city police had excluded not only the illiterate, incapacitated, and unsavory but also the blacks, Mexicans, and Puerto Ricans. No doubt some of the minority candidates were unqualified, but what, these citizens asked, about the rest of them? In the absence of a satisfactory answer some Americans who had previously supported the reform campaign concluded that exclusion of these racial and ethnic minorities was indefensible.

This issue emerged in the South in the late 1940s and early 1950s when the Southern Regional Council reported that with one or two exceptions none of the region's leading cities employed more than a handful of black police officers. But the issue did not surface outside the South until the early and middle 1960s when the United States Commission on Civil Rights pointed out that blacks and other minorities fared only slightly better in the rest of the nation. And it did not come to a head until the late 1960s when the President's Crime Commission and the President's Riot Commission, whose reports reached a wide audience and generated a good deal of interest, confirmed the findings. These reports had a profound impact on many Americans, whites as well as blacks. For one thing, they came out in the midst of the civil rights movement, when the campaign to prohibit discrimination in private employment which culminated in the passage of the Civil Rights Act of 1964 had left Americans extremely sensitive to charges of discrimination in the public sector. For another thing, the reports came out at the height of the 1960s riots, when Los Angeles, Newark, Detroit, and the other major cities were so racked by violent protest that for the first time in history Americans were forced to consider whether the big-city police could maintain law and order in the black ghettos.[29]

As some Americans realized, this problem was largely an outgrowth of the reform movement, which had persuaded the authorities to adopt a number of policies that severely, if inadvertently, discriminated against blacks and other groups. Under pressure from the reformers the authorities abolished the residency requirements, which slowed down the turnover of the Irish-Americans and other second- and third-generation immigrants and also reduced the competitive edge of blacks and other first- and second-generation newcomers. They underwrote vigorous recruiting efforts, which were aimed not at central city churches, YMCAs, and high schools, which were mainly black, Mexican, and Puerto Rican, but at out-of-town colleges, universities, and military bases, which were predominantly white. They put great emphasis on written tests, which winnowed out a higher percentage of blacks, Mexicans, and Puerto Ricans than of whites. They tightened the character checks, which disqualified a disproportionate number of blacks and other newcomers on the grounds that they had picked up a criminal record, changed jobs too often, or received a less than honorable discharge from the armed forces. Surely, many Americans concluded, it was time for the authorities to find other ways to raise the caliber of the big-city police.

It was also time for them to take steps to increase the number of black officers. Following this line, many Americans called on the authorities to do their recruiting in the central cities, a move, they claimed, that would encourage more blacks and other newcomers, at least some of whom would be qualified, to consider a career in policing. The authorities were responsive in Washington, D. C., where the Civil Service Commission sent mobile recruiting facilities into black neighborhoods, placed ads in local papers and on radio stations, and used black athletes and other celebrities to promote the campaign. They were also responsive in Detroit, New York, and Philadelphia, where the police departments asked blacks for the names of candidates, set up "Instant Testing Centers" to speed up the certification process, and put up posters which read "cop in, don't cop out." But according to the New York *Times,* which made a survey in the early 1970s, these efforts had little impact on the racial makeup of the big-city police except in Atlanta, Chicago, and Washington where the percentage of black officers doubled between 1967 and 1971. In some cities the authorities did not try very hard, and in others they were stymied because many potential candidates resented the police for mistreating black citizens and discriminating against black officers.[30]

Many Americans also called on the authorities to reimpose the residency requirements, a move, they argued, that would not only increase the competitive edge of the blacks and other minorities but also improve the quality of law enforcement and alleviate the fiscal crisis of the cities. But the rank-and-file outfits strongly objected to this proposal. Stressing that it would violate the civil liberties of the officers and, by excluding qualified candidates from out of town and compelling veteran officers to choose between their jobs and their homes, lower the caliber of the police departments, they opposed it in one city after another. Usually the rank-and-file outfits got their way. Early in the 1970s the New York PBA and other public employee groups prevailed on the state legislature to reject a bill reimposing the residency requirement. When the Los Angeles City Council approved a residency requirement in 1972, the Fire and Police Protective League and other municipal employee unions persuaded the California voters to adopt a constitutional amendment nullifying it. The Detroit POA lobbied against a motion to deprive the commissioner of his authority to waive the residency requirement for police officers. When the Detroit City Council passed it anyway in 1968, the union appealed to the courts, which upheld its contention that the requirement was within the scope of collective bargaining.[31] The campaign for the residency requirement was not yet over; but thus far it had not had much impact on the racial makeup of the big-city police.

Many Americans called on the authorities to change the entrance requirements too, a move, they insisted, that would increase the probability that blacks and other newcomers who applied would be appointed. But under intense pressure from the reform groups and rank-and-file outfits, which charged that this proposal would lower the quality of the big-city police, the authorities were extremely reluctant to do so. Thus the Massachusetts Law Reform Institute and other public and quasi-public law firms filed suit in Boston, Philadelphia, Oakland, and several other cities in the late 1960s and early 1970s. They charged that the written tests, character checks, and other entrance requirements discriminated against the blacks and other minorities and therefore violated the equal protection clause of the Fourteenth Amendment. In their defense the authorities insisted that these requirements were applied in a nondiscriminatory way and, citing prominent reformers, added that they were needed to maintain the caliber of the big-city police. But the denials were not persuasive. As Thomas A. Mela of the Law Reform Institute brought out in his examination of Arthur C. Cadegan, Jr., deputy superintendent of personnel and training of the Boston Police Department, the defendants could not produce any studies, surveys, or other evidence to support their contention that the entrance requirements were predictive of on-the-job performance.[32]

As a result, the plaintiffs won a series of major cases in the early 1970s. Judge Charles E. Wyzanski ruled in *Castro* v. *Beecher* that the written tests, which "sound as though they had been drawn from *Alice in Wonderland*," discriminated against blacks and other newcomers. He ordered the Massachusetts Civil Service Commission to stop issuing certificates of eligibility, to design a job-related and nondiscriminatory exam, and the next time around to give it only to persons who had taken the old tests. Judge John F. Pullam held in *Commonwealth of Pennsylvania* v. *O'Neill* that the character checks, whose relevance to police work had not in his opinion been demonstrated, discriminated against blacks and other minorities. He ordered the Philadelphia Police Department to revise the checks in a way that excluded irrelevant criteria, to offer applicants who had been rejected another chance, and if they were accepted, to put them high on the list of eligibles. Judge Oliver J. Carter entered a consent decree according to which the Oakland Police Department and Civil Service

Board declared that the ethnic makeup of the force should reflect the ethnic makeup of the municipality. The defendants also pledged to recruit minority candidates, develop job-related tests, validate the oral interviews, and guarantee the ethnic minorities a fair share of all new appointments.[33]

These rulings have not yet had much of an impact on the racial makeup of the big-city police. Some did not go into effect until the defendants exhausted the appellate process, a process that dragged on well into the mid-1970s in some cities. By then the fiscal situation was so grave that a few cities imposed a freeze on new appointments and others started to lay off veteran officers. In other cities the turnover was so low that even if the authorities had revised the written tests, character checks, and other entrance requirements to the courts' satisfaction, it would have taken decades before the blacks and other newcomers held their fair share of the jobs. But the rulings have already had a profound impact on the future course of the reform movement. They made it clear that by the late 1960s many Americans were no longer prepared to go along with the reform position that the best way to raise the caliber of the big-city police was to tighten the entrance requirements. They also made it clear that if the authorities could not come up with strong evidence to support this position the courts were ready to change the requirements, impose quotas, and otherwise intervene in order to enhance the access of the blacks and other newcomers.

The course of police reform aroused concern not only among many lower- and lower-middle-class blacks but also among many upper-middle- and upper-class whites, who had formed the basis of the reform coalition since the turn of the century. A few of them even expressed this concern in ways that ran counter to the conventional wisdom of the reform movement. The West 105th Street Block Association, a group of academics, professionals, and other white-collar workers, was so disturbed by the rising rate of violent crime that it hired a guard to patrol 105th Street between Riverside Drive and West End Avenue after dark. The Los Angeles Chamber of Commerce, a mainstay of the reform campaign, was so troubled by the mounting deficits of the Los Angeles fire and police pension system that it led the opposition to a scheme to peg pension benefits to the cost of living. The District of Columbia Bar Association and the National Capital Area

Civil Liberties Union, two solid upper-middle- and upper-class organizations, were so appalled by the way the Washington police handled complaints that they called on the authorities to set up a civilian review board. And Mela of the Massachusetts Law Reform Institute, a recent graduate of the Harvard Law School whose faculty had once included Roscoe Pound and other well-known reformers, was so dismayed by the way the Boston police selected recruits that he appealed to the courts to invalidate the entrance requirements.[34]

Not all, perhaps not even most, upper-middle- and upper-class Americans approved of these activities. Some insisted that the citizens could do more to reduce the rate of violent crime by supporting the attempts to professionalize the big-city police than by resorting to community policing. Others argued that the authorities would be better advised to hold down the costs of municipal services by raising the productivity of the big-city police than by cutting the salaries, benefits, and pensions of the rank-and-file. Some opposed changes in disciplinary procedures on the grounds that they would undermine the morale of the officers, impair the efficiency of the departments, inject politics into policing, and exacerbate the crime problem. Others objected to any revisions of the entrance requirements on the grounds that they would not only lower the caliber of the big-city police but also subvert the integrity of the civil service. The outcome of these issues is not yet clear, except in the case of the civilian review boards, which are defunct. But however they are resolved, one thing is certain: during the 1960s and 1970s the course of police reform aroused so much concern among so many upper-middle- and upper-class Americans that it more or less shattered the reform coalition.

The course of police reform was only one of several reasons for the breakup of the reform coalition. Of the other reasons the most important was a marked change in the make-up of the upper-middle-class Americans. Prior to 1900 these Americans were a fairly homogeneous group. The grandsons and great grandsons of northern and western Europeans, most of them had been born in the mid-nineteenth century, brought up as Protestants, and raised in the villages and small towns of rural America. They came of age in the late nineteenth century, a time when the political machines were in their heyday, the police forces were in disrepute, and municipal corruption seemed to be the most critical domestic problem. All this changed over the next sixty or seventy years as a large number of second- and third-generation immigrants managed to climb into the upper middle class. The sons and grandsons of southern and eastern Europeans, many of these immigrants had been born after World War I, brought up as Catholics or Jews, and raised in the great cities of the Northeast, Midwest, and Pacific Coast. They came of age after World War II, by which time the political machines were on the wane, the police departments were on the mend, and racial discrimination had replaced municipal corruption as the country's most serious domestic problem.

This change severely weakened the reform coalition. For the first time a good many upper-middle-class Americans did not fully share the principal concerns of the reform movement. Too young to remember the day when the political machines had had a stranglehold on the police forces and the precinct captains had been at the beck and call of the ward bosses, they were not overly alarmed by charges of political interference. Too young to remember the day when a change in administration had meant a wholesale turnover of police officers or, as the reformers saw it, the replacement of one set of scoundrels by another, they were not overly disturbed by the attacks on the civil service. It had been so long since the departments were hard pressed to find qualified applicants and so long since the rank-and-file were hard put to make ends meet that these Americans were not moved by the grumbling about starting salaries. It had also been so long since most cities had harbored one or more red-light districts, where gambling, prostitution, and other illicit activities were protected by the local police, that they were not greatly worried about the enforcement of the vice laws.

For the first time many upper-middle-class Americans had reservations about the underlying assumptions of the reform movement too. The reformers might argue that public service was not a means of social mobility, but the big-city police were still a major source of good jobs. In view of the long history of racial discrimination perhaps it was time for the authorities to revise the entrance requirements in ways that would make these jobs more accessible to blacks and other minority groups. The reformers might insist that local control was not a source of political legitimacy, but city- and state-wide control was not an unmixed blessing. In view of the sorry record of the highway commissions, urban renewal boards, and other centralized bodies perhaps it was time for the authorities to give the neighborhoods a greater role in the governmental process. The reformers might say that ethnic life-styles were not an expression of American culture, but many law-abiding citizens were not inclined to abandon them. In view of the dismal history of the Eighteenth Amendment and other sumptuary legislation perhaps it was even time for the authorities to stop employing the criminal sanction to reinforce the conventional morality.

For the first time a good many upper-middle-class Americans were skeptical about the conventional wisdom of the reform movement too. Now that the ward bosses had little or no power over the big-city police, they wondered why the authorities should attempt to consolidate or close down precincts over the strenuous objections of the local residents. Now that most officers were appointed in their early or middle twenties, they questioned whether the authorities should allow the police to retire on a handsome pension after only twenty or twenty-five years of service. Now that the local politicians had little to say about appointments, they wondered whether the authorities should impose written tests and other entrance requirements that discriminated against blacks and other minorities. And now that the rank-and-file were well organized and their unions bargained over promotional practices, disciplinary procedures, and other issues, they questioned the point of retaining the civil service. In view of the disaffection of the upper-middle-class Americans with the course of police reform it is little wonder that the reform coalition was shattered in the 1960s and 1970s.

A function of a fundamental realignment of social classes and ethnic groups, the breakup of the reform coalition brought the second wave of police reform to a standstill by the early 1970s. Not that the reformers stopped trying. On the contrary, they worked as hard as ever. Led by Murphy and other influential figures, they called on the departments to require a college degree of all recruits, shift from two-man to one-man squad cars, and employ computers to allocate manpower. They urged the universities, foundations, and federal agencies to lend support to the schools of criminology and departments of police science that transmitted the gospel of professionalism to the next generation of law enforcement officials. They appealed to the IACP, whose members had applauded reform rhetoric at their annual meetings and whose staff had incorporated reform principles into their field surveys, to take a more active role in the reform campaign. They asked the LEAA and the Police Foundation, which were supposed to upgrade policing by encouraging innovation, experimentation, and evaluation, to underwrite concrete, though as a rule fairly conventional, reforms in one department after another.

But the reformers ran into stiff resistance. Their efforts aroused the opposition not only of many police officers, which was bad enough, but also of many upper-middle-class Americans, which was even worse. These Americans were a formidable lot. They were well educated, well off, and sophisticated; they knew their way around the courts, the legislatures, the press, and the other institutions that molded the big-city police. They were not inclined to compromise, especially on civil rights issues; nor were they easily intimidated or bought off. They also gained strength from the demand for community control, the assault on civil service, and the other attempts to dismantle the monuments of the Progressive movement. By the mid-1970s they had the reformers on the defensive. Far from moving ahead with their plans, the reformers were hard pressed to preserve the entrance requirements, disciplinary procedures, and other legacies of two generations of police reform. Whether the reformers would regain the initiative in the face of this resistance remained to be seen. But the prospects were poor, indeed so poor that it is safe to say that by the mid-1970s, or roughly eighty years after the Lexow Committee opened its hearings, the campaign for police reform had come to a standstill.

Epilogue

On July 22, 1970, the National Committee to Combat Fascism, an offshoot of the Black Panthers and the New Left, submitted a petition to the Berkeley City Council that City Manager William Hanley denounced as "a step back to the Dark Ages." It called for community control of the police. Signed by fifteen thousand voters, the petition proposed a charter amendment abolishing the Berkeley Police Department, which had long been one of the showpieces of the reform movement, and replacing it with three separate departments. One would cover the white community in the hills, the second the black community in the flatlands, and the third the student community adjacent to the University of California campus. Each department would be responsible to a police council, which would consist of one representative, elected every two years, from each of the fifteen precincts into which each of the three communities would be divided. The councils were authorized to formulate departmental policies, appoint a police commissioner, and discipline the rank-and-file, who would be required to live in the community in which they worked.[1] The petition generated a good deal of controversy in Berkeley in the months ahead. But on one point most residents would probably have agreed: the demand for community control was the most serious attempt thus far to reverse the reform movement that had gotten underway two generations earlier.

The demand for community control was an outgrowth of the black power movement. Launched in the mid-1960s, a time of widespread rioting in the ghettos, this movement strongly appealed to many blacks who were infuriated by the persistence of subordination and segregation and disappointed with the progress of the civil rights crusade. Following the lead of Malcolm X, Stokely Carmichael, and other black militants, they repudiated the integrationist or assimilationist tradition that had long guided the NAACP and the Urban League. They espoused instead the separatist or nationalist tradition that had inspired Marcus Garvey's United Negro Improvement Association in the 1920s and Elijah Muhammad's Black Muslims in the 1950s. From this tradition, which stressed that integration was irrelevant and, in view of white attitudes, impossible and that white racism was ineradicable, they derived the principles of solidarity, self-reliance, and autonomy. From these principles they drew the conclusion that the blacks should control their own communities: New York's Harlem, Chicago's South Side, south-central Los Angeles, and the other ghettos that symbolized the deep-seated racism of urban America.[2] It was in the ghettos—not, as the Garveyites contended, in an independent nation, and not, as the Muslims argued, in a separate state—that the blacks would regain their manhood and self-respect.

The advocates of community control put forth two cardinal recommendations. First, the blacks had to take over the existing ghetto businesses and, through community development corporations and other quasi-governmental organizations, set up additional ones. By so doing, they would create new jobs, reduce the cost of goods, divert the flow of capital back into the ghettos, and otherwise strengthen the economic base of the black community. Second, the blacks had to win control of the schools, courts, hospitals, welfare boards, housing authorities, police departments, and other urban institutions. Staffed by whites, responsible to white officials, and sympathetic to white values and attitudes, these institutions were the instruments by which white society maintained its sway over black America.[3] Far from serving the citizens, they oppressed them; far from educating their children, they indoctrinated them; and far from protecting their communities, they contained them. By taking over these institutions, the backers of community control claimed, the blacks could compel them to upgrade the quality of their services. They could also force these institutions to change policies in ways that would enhance the black community's access to public jobs, increase its influence in local politics, and reinforce its standing in American society.

The demand for community control posed a severe threat to the ongoing campaign for police reform. Its advocates disparaged many of the reformers' major accomplishments. They urged the authorities to reimpose the residency requirement, reduce the autonomy of the police chief, turn the disciplinary process over to elected officials, and reintegrate the police precincts and political subdivisions. The spokesmen also criticized many of the reformers' basic principles. Instead of centralization, they insisted on administrative decentralization; instead of professionalism, they pressed for citizen participation; and instead of bureaucratization, they called for political accountability. Drawing heavily on the rhetoric of the machine politicians, the advocates of community control challenged many of the reformers' fundamental assumptions. Stressing that public service was a means of social mobility, they argued that blacks and other minorities were entitled to a fair share of the positions on the force. Emphasizing that local control was a source of political legitimacy, they held that the police should be responsible to community leaders rather than to city-wide officials. Pointing out that ethnic life-styles were an expression of American culture, they contended that the police should not employ the criminal sanction to impose the conventional morality on blacks and other minorities.

The demand for community control generated a barrage of criticism. Some of it came from upper-middle-class liberals who were skeptical of the reform rhetoric, critical of the big-city police, sympathetic to blacks and other minorities, and well-disposed to their efforts to change entrance requirements and set up civilian review boards. Perhaps the most sophisticated of these critics was Jerome H. Skolnick, professor of criminology at Berkeley and author of *Justice Without Trial,* a study of the Oakland Police Department that raised doubts about the long-term impact of the reform movement. Taking care to dissociate himself from conservative critics, Skolnick pointed out that community control, as embodied in the Berkeley petition, would not necessarily work out to the benefit of the lower- and lower-middle-class blacks.[4] If the authorities appropriated funds according to population, as the charter amendment provided, the well-to-do white who lived in the safest communities would receive the same share as the poor blacks who lived in the most dangerous ones, which was a highly regressive form of resource allocation. Notwithstanding the aspirations of the black militants and their white allies, the upper-middle-class residents, who had the necessary time, energy, and know-how, would probably control the neighborhood councils in much the same way as they had previously dominated the city agencies.

But most of the criticism came from businessmen, lawyers, academics, public officials, police chiefs, and other upper-middle- and upper-class Americans who were impressed by the reform movement and committed to its principles. Apart from a vociferous right-wing minority, which regarded the Berkeley petition and other proposals like it as a part of a revolutionary conspiracy, the spearhead of a Communist takeover, these critics had three main objections to community control. First, it would inject politics into policing. Once the link between the wards and the precincts was reestablished, the departments would henceforth be at the beck and call of a legion of what James Q. Wilson, professor of government at Harvard and vice-chairman of the Police Foundation, described as "fourth-rate politicians." Second, it would lower the efficiency of the police. Once the big-city departments were divided into neighborhood forces, the police would find it difficult to attract qualified recruits, retain competent chiefs, and deal with gangsters or other criminals whose activities were not confined to a particular neighborhood. Third, it would foster a form of urban apartheid. Once the police were organized along neighborhood lines, the departments would exacerbate social cleavage, intensify communal conflict, return to a double standard of law enforcement, and otherwise promote racial and ethnic segregation.[5]

Forced on the defensive, the advocates of community control denied these charges. Community control would not inject politics into policing, they argued. Politics was already there, the politics of the chambers of commerce, real estate boards, and other business organizations that watched over the police on behalf of the upper middle and upper classes. The Berkeley petition and other proposals like it were nothing more than attempts to provide the lower and lower middle classes an opportunity to shape departmental policies and practices. Nor would community control lower the quality of policing. As the systematic harassment of law-abiding blacks, the widespread indifference to citizen complaints, and the alarming increase of street crime indicated, the big-city departments left a good deal to be desired. The neighborhood forces could hardly do worse and, if they attracted officers who were sensitive to the problems of their fellow citizens, would probably do better. Neither would community control foster urban apartheid, an insidious practice for which the upper-middle- and upper-class whites bore the principal responsibility. Rather it would strip the white society of its power over the black community and thereby give the ghetto residents more of a say over their destiny, which was the very opposite of apartheid.[6]

These denials won over Congressman Ron Dellums, former Attorney General Ramsey Clark, and many other liberals, some of whom endorsed the Berkeley petition. But most Americans remained dubious. At the urging of the mayor, city manager, police chief, and One Berkeley Community, a consortium of the city's civic and commercial associations, the Berkeley voters turned down the proposed charter amendment by a two to one majority.[7] In spite of pressure from the Black United Front and other militant groups, the authorities brushed aside similar proposals in Chicago and Washington, D.C. Hence by the mid-1970s the demand for community control of the police was on the wane. Despite its short history, this movement was revealing. It showed that many upper-middle- and upper-class Americans who were sharply divided over the civilian review board issue and the credentials controversy were willing to work together to defend the principal monuments of the reform campaign. It also proved that in the face of their strenuous opposition the critics who had brought the reform movement to a standstill in the late 1960s and early 1970s were nevertheless incapable of undoing two generations of police reform.

Matters are not likely to change much in the foreseeable future. After all, the critics are a small minority; and though they are articulate and impassioned, they do not speak for most of their fellow citizens. According to public opinion polls, most Americans think that the police are doing a pretty good job.[8] Of the rest of the citizens, few are so dissatisfied that they are inclined to support community control or, for that matter, any fundamental overhaul of the structure, personnel, and function of their police departments. They may have a change of heart in the years ahead, but the critics will have trouble exploiting it. Most Americans, regardless of how they feel about the police, still hold the Progressive assumptions about social mobility, political legitimacy, and American culture. They still believe in the Progressive principle that policing should be strictly divorced from politics, even if they do not necessarily behave accordingly. As the struggle over the Berkeley petition revealed, it will be extremely difficult for the critics to win popular support for any proposal that runs counter to these deep-seated convictions.

Not only are the critics a small minority. An assortment of frightened citizens, anxious taxpayers, liberal academics, civil libertarians, civil rights leaders, and public interest lawyers, they are also a sharply divided minority. They are concerned about different things. For some, the problem is the rising rate of crime; for others, the soaring cost of policing; for still others, the denial of equal access to public employment. The critics lack anything like a military analogy or a professional model that might draw them together. A few of them, including former Attorney General Clark, are as deeply committed to the professional model as most of the reformers.[9] The critics often disagree about proposed changes too. The civilian review boards, which were sponsored by the civil liberties and civil rights groups, were opposed by the chambers of commerce and taxpayers associations. The attack on the civil service tests and other entrance requirements split them in much the same way. The critics are also divided by class, race, and ethnicity, by political ideology, and by personal style. Even if they could agree on the problem and its solution, they could not possibly work together with anything approaching the harmony and efficacy of the first and second generations of reformers.

Nor can the critics count on the police to make things easier for them. Most departments behave in a much less scandalous way now than in the past. The rank-and-file may work at less than 100 percent efficiency; but at least they no longer kidnap political opponents, stuff ballot boxes, permit hoodlums to intimidate voters, and otherwise violate the integrity of the electoral process. The vice squads may waste a lot of time attempting to enforce the sumptuary laws; but at least they no longer frame respectable women for morals offenses in return for a cut from unscrupulous lawyers and avaricious bondsmen. The superior officers may discourage blacks and other citizens from filing complaints against the rank-and-file; but at least they no longer encourage their subordinates to employ the third degree and other reprehensible tactics against uncooperative suspects. And the police chiefs may defend civil service tests that bear little relation to on-the-job performance; but at least they no longer countenance the arrangement whereby the examiners give out advance copies to party loyalists. In other words, the critics can no longer be confident that the police officers will provide them with the sort of sensational revelations that the reformers exploited so effectively in the first two-thirds of the century.

Most departments also respond to criticism in a far more sophisticated way than in the past. They no longer threaten prospective witnesses, bribe them to leave town, or resort to the other heavy-handed measures that seriously discredited them during the Lexow and Seabury committee investigations. The departments do not welcome criticism; few public agencies do. But they have learned to live with it; and on occasion they are willing to admit their mistakes and take action to correct them. Many departments have tried to improve their complaint procedures; some have labored to recruit blacks and other minorities; and others have attempted to work more closely with the community.[10] This change in policy sharply reduces the likelihood of a fundamental reorganization of the big-city police. Besides impressing the public with the good faith and common sense of the police, it prevents specific problems from developing into general issues. It forces the critics to focus on the efficacy of the recruitment programs and the validity of the civil service tests rather than on the relationship between public bureaucracies and social mobility. It also enables the police to coopt many of the critics, to give them a stake in the status quo, and to instill in them a conviction that whatever the problem it can be resolved within the existing institutional framework.

Even if the critics overcome these handicaps, which is unlikely, they will still face two formidable obstacles. The reformers are one obstacle. For years they have been formulating, popularizing, and defending the reform principles and, in many cases, even putting these principles into practice. Now that the reform campaign has been fairly successful and most police forces have been reorganized more or less according to the reform principles, the reformers are not inclined to stand by while others try to undo their lifework. True, some have doubts about the utility of the sumptuary laws, preventive patrol, the *Uniform Crime Reports,* and other by-products of the reform movement. A few reformers even have reservations about the validity of the professional model and other features of the conventional wisdom of police reform. But most are still strongly committed to the underlying assumptions advanced by the first generation of reformers and to the principal monuments erected by the second. The reformers will in all probability launch a full-scale assault against any proposal that threatens, or even seems to threaten, these assumptions or these monuments.

The reformers are well prepared for the struggle. Even though Hoover, Wilson, Parker, and many others have retired or died, their peers and disciples dominate the law enforcement community. As of January 1977 Donald D. Pomerleau commanded the Baltimore Police Department, and Glenn King, a protégé of Quinn Tamm, ran the IACP, most of whose members are strongly attached to the conventional wisdom of the reform campaign. Clarence M. Kelley led the FBI, and Joseph D. McNamara, who had succeeded Kelley as chief in Kansas City, headed the San Jose Police Department. Patrick V. Murphy presided over the Police Foundation; Herbert T. Jenkins and Stanley R. Schrotel sat on its board, as did James Q. Wilson, probably the most forceful critic of the demand for community control. Following in the tradition of Vollmer, O.W. Wilson, and the many other chiefs who went from police departments to schools of criminology or departments of police science, Jerry V. Wilson taught at American University. And Roy C. McLaren, formerly head of the IACP's Field Services Division and now chief of police in Arlington, Virginia, was revising O.W. Wilson's classic text, *Police Administration.* So far as most of their fellow Americans are concerned, the reformers speak for the police; and as the struggle over the civilian review boards revealed, their views carry a good deal of weight.

The unions are another obstacle facing the critics. For decades the rank-and-file groups fought with the reformers, criticizing their proposals to put police officers under civil service, to get rid of judicial review of departmental discipline, to change from two-man to one-man squad cars, and to replace sworn officers with civilian employees. But they gradually came to realize that many of these reforms served or, with slight modifications, could be made to serve their own interests. To the surprise of the reformers, most of whom had vigorously resisted the unionization of the rank-and-file, these groups eventually emerged as veritable bulwarks of the reform movement, staunch defenders of many of its principal monuments. So far as they are concerned, equal access to public employment is a worthwhile goal, but not if it means abolishing civil service tests, abandoning character checks, and otherwise lowering entrance requirements. The rising cost of public services is a serious problem, but not so serious that the authorities should consider cutting the rank-and-file's salaries or reducing their pensions. And full accountability of public bureaucracies is a worthy objective, but not if it means transferring disciplinary power from departmental trial boards to civilian, or even civilian-controlled, review boards. Representatives of the rank-and-file, who are probably the principal beneficiaries of the reform movement, the unions will do their utmost to preserve these and other reform monuments.

The unions are a force to be reckoned with. Not only have they learned to hold their own at the bargaining table; they have also managed to expand the scope of bargaining. If the residency requirement is bargainable — and on an appeal from the Detroit POA the Michigan Supreme Court so ruled — it is hard to figure out what is not bargainable. The unions have learned their way around city hall too. Drawing on fifteen years of experience as city administrative officer of Los Angeles, C. Erwin Piper told a *Times* reporter in 1972 that the Los Angeles Fire and Police Protective League probably has "more political clout than any other group in city government." Los Angeles is not atypical. The unions usually get their way in Detroit, Seattle, and New York, if not in Chicago. When they do not get their way, they often appeal to Lansing, Olympia, Albany, where they have developed close ties with many state legislators who are willing to help the unions out so long as the state does not have to pay the bills. Whether, as Theodore J. Lowi has suggested, the unions will emerge as "new machines," the successors to the old-line organizations, remains to be seen.[11] But with the reformers on their side they already have more than enough power to stymie any attempt to reverse the reform movement and destroy its principal monuments.

Hence most of the reform monuments are quite safe. Despite the breakup of the upper-middle- and upper-class coalition, there is little chance that the authorities will reopen the old precincts and restore their former boundaries. Nor is there much chance that the departments will take vice control, traffic regulation, or other vital chores from the special squads and reassign them to the station houses. The civil service commissions are here to stay; so are the training academies, departmental trial boards, schools of criminology, and departments of police science. So is the IACP. The ban on rewards is probably here for the foreseeable future, and so in all likelihood are the restrictions on moonlighting. It is not likely that the departments will decentralize their record-keeping. Nor is it likely that they will once again clean the streets, feed the hungry, house the homeless, find jobs for the unemployed, or take on many other noncriminal tasks. The police unions, an unintended consequence of the reform effort, will be around for a while too. So will the grievance procedure, dues check-off, collective bargaining, impasse proceedings, sick-ins, slowdowns, strikes, and other job actions. And so, unfortunately, will the occupational paranoia of the big-city police.

But some of the reform monuments are in jeopardy. The future of the entrance requirements is very much in doubt. For about a decade the critics have pressed the authorities to revise or if necessary abolish these requirements on the grounds that they serve no purpose other than to keep blacks and other minorities out of the police forces. The reformers have denied the charge, arguing that the height restrictions, character checks, civil service tests, and other entrance requirements are essential to maintain the high caliber of the big-city police. The unions have backed the reformers. Talking about a proposal to appoint young men with criminal records as juvenile officers, John Harrington, president of the National FOP, asked the Violence Commission: "What are you going to train them to be? Pickpockets?"[12] But the police have been unable to persuade the courts that the entrance requirements are related to on-the-job performance. Hence the courts have ordered the departments to develop nondiscriminatory tests, modify the character checks, validate the oral interviews, and otherwise ensure blacks and other minorities equal

access to public employment. Thus far they have made little progress. How the courts will respond is hard to tell, especially in
view of the Supreme Court's recent decision that the written
exams are unconstitutional only if they have a "discriminatory
racial purpose."[13] But there is a fair chance that they will order
the big-city police to revise their entrance requirements in the
not-too-distant future.

The controversy over credentials is anything but clear-cut. A
revision of the entrance requirements might lower the caliber of
the big-city police. But the reformers have only posited the relationship between physical fitness, formal education, personal
conduct, and test scores, on the one hand, and on-the-job performance, on the other. They have not documented it; and in
view of the inability to come up with satisfactory performance
measures, they probably never will. Some reformers have pointed
to the dangers of undue familiarity between police and public.
But few have attempted to refute the argument that the rank-
and-file would be more sensitive to the needs of the citizens if they
belonged to the same racial and ethnic groups. A revision of the
entrance requirements might enhance equal access to police departments. But the critics have shown only that these requirements are obstacles to blacks and other minorities; they have not
demonstrated that they are the primary, let alone the only, obstacles. That there are other obstacles seems likely because surveys of the racial make-up and personnel policies of the big-city
police suggest only a weak relationship between minority representation and entrance requirements.[14] Without a clear sense of
the other obstacles it is hard to foresee the impact of changes in
civil service tests, character checks, oral interviews, and other entrance requirements.

Moreover, the fight over the residency requirement is far from
over. For a decade or so the critics have urged the authorities to
reimpose this requirement on the grounds that it would improve
the quality of law enforcement, alleviate the fiscal plight of the
city, and increase the number of black officers. The unions have
vigorously opposed the proposal, insisting that their members
have a constitutional right to live outside the city and that their
residence is no more relevant to their job than their race or their
religion. Contending that the residency requirement would drive
out many veteran officers, disqualify many first-rate candidates,

and thereby lower the caliber of the big-city police, the reformers have joined the opposition. The critics made little headway through the early 1970s. With the exception of Detroit and Los Angeles, most cities refused to reimpose the residency requirement or, if they had not abolished it in the first place, declined to enforce it. But as the fiscal squeeze grew worse, the authorities came around. Philadelphia and Chicago started to enforce their residency requirements in the mid-1970s. Boston passed an ordinance requiring all employees hired or promoted after July 1, 1976, to live in the city. And similar legislation has been proposed in New York City and Washington, D.C.[15]

According to the Supreme Court, which in 1976 ruled against a Philadelphia fireman who was dismissed for moving outside the city, the residency requirement is constitutional. Whether it is advisable is another matter. If imposed on all municipal employees and not just on police officers, the requirement might, as its sponsors argue, reinforce the tax base of the cities and thereby provide them with additional funds. But as the opposition points out, these funds would add so little to the cities' total revenue that they would have only a marginal impact on their fiscal plight. The requirement would not lower the caliber of big-city policing, but neither would it improve the quality of law enforcement. There is little evidence that police officers would work harder if they lived in cities. And there is good reason to think that, if forced to do so, they would resettle not in Bedford-Stuyvesant and south-central Los Angeles but in Forest Hills and Canoga Park. The requirement would give blacks and other minorities a competitive edge; but how much this edge is worth is hard to say. The requirement has not helped these groups much in Buffalo and Pittsburgh; nor has its abolition handicapped them much in Atlanta and Washington.[16] If reimposed, the requirement will not make much difference in New York, Detroit, and other hard-up cities that will be appointing very few recruits in the near future.

Finally, the future of the pension system is very much at issue. For nearly a decade the critics have requested the authorities to tighten the eligibility requirements on the grounds that the police and other public employee pensions are forcing many cities to the brink of bankruptcy.[17] Claiming that adequate pensions are needed to attract qualified recruits and retain experienced officers, the unions have not only defended current requirements but also demanded additional benefits. The reformers have been sharply divided. Committed to keeping up the caliber of the rank-and-file, the police chiefs have sided with the unions; and anxious to hold down the costs of public service, the business leaders have gone along with the critics. The response has been mixed. Over the objections of the Detroit POA the Cavanagh administration prevailed on the voters in 1968 to adopt a charter amendment that set a minimum age requirement of fifty-five and fixed the cost of living increase at 2 percent per year. But under pressure from the Los Angeles Fire and Police Protective League the city council refused in 1966 to go along with the city administrative officer's proposal to increase the service requirement from twenty to twenty-five years and to impose an age requirement of fifty. Although the state legislature recently revised New York City's pension systems, the fiscal implications of the revision there are not yet clear.

Pension reform is long overdue. The Minneapolis police pension system had 600 beneficiaries in 1972, or roughly three beneficiaries for every four police officers. The Los Angeles fire and police pension system had an unfunded liability of $1.2 billion in 1974, or over $100,000 for each sworn officer. For every dollar the city of Detroit spent on police salaries in 1973 it put more than fifty cents into police pensions. But pension reform is far from inevitable. Most unions will resist any effort to raise the age or service requirements, and in an attempt to hold down property taxes many citizens will oppose any proposal to put the pension system on a fully funded basis. Rather than taking the risk of antagonizing these groups, the politicians may well prefer to let the deficits mount and pass the costs on to the next generation of taxpayers. Pension reform would not have much of an impact in the near future anyway. Over the years a series of constitutional amendments and judicial decisions have redefined police and other public employee pensions in New York, California, and many other states.[18] Once regarded as gratuities or rewards, these pensions are now considered contractual obligations. They can be changed. But as a rule the changes can only be imposed on incoming employees, which will do little to reduce the current obligations, much less to pay off the unfunded liabilities.

Yet from the perspective of the mid-1970s what stands out is not so much the vulnerability of some of the reform monuments as the tenacity of most of the reform assumptions. To give one example, most Americans still assume that the primary purpose of the big-city police is to provide public service and not to enhance social mobility. Not even many critics disagree, at least not in public. The attack on the entrance requirements stressed less that blacks and other minorities are entitled to a fair share of the jobs than that these requirements are not related to on-the-job performance. The demand for the residency requirement emphasized not so much that it would give blacks and other minorities a competitive edge as that it would raise the quality of law enforcement. And the criticism of the pension systems stressed that these systems are not only aggravating the fiscal crisis but also encouraging veteran officers to retire at the mid-point of their careers. The overriding achievement of the reform movement is not the special squads, training academies, *Uniform Crime Reports,* and other tangible by-products, impressive though they may be. It is rather that two generations after the Lexow Committee investigation the Progressive assumptions about social mobility, political legitimacy, and American culture still shape the debate over the future of the big-city police.

Notes

Prologue

1. New York State, Special Committee of the Assembly Appointed to Investigate the Public Offices and Departments of the City of New York and the Counties Therein Included, *Report* (Albany, 1900), I, 961 (henceforth referred to as *Mazet Committee Investigation*); James F. Richardson, *The New York Police* (New York, 1970), ch. 9; Charles H. Parkhurst, *Our Fight with Tammany* (New York, 1895), chs. 2-3.

2. New York State, Senate Committee Appointed to Investigate the Police Department of the City of New York, *Report and Proceedings* (Albany, 1895), I, 4-14 (henceforth referred to as *Lexow Committee Investigation*); Richardson, *New York Police*, ch. 9; New York State, Assembly, Special Committee Appointed to Investigate the Local Government of the City and County of New York, *Report* (New York, 1884), 2 vols.; New York State, Senate Committee on Cities, *Testimony Taken Pursuant to Resolution Adopted January 20, 1890* (Albany, 1891), 5 vols.

3. *Lexow Committee Investigation,* I, 15, 20-25; *The Nation,* June 14, 1894, p. 441; June 28, 1894, p. 481; Sept. 13, 1894, p. 191.

4. *Lexow Committee Investigation,* I, 4; V, 5,382; *Social Economist,* July 1894, p. 9; *The Saturday Review,* Aug. 17, 1895, p. 195.

5. *Lexow Committee Investigation,* I, 16-20, 30-51.

6. Ibid., I, 59-60, 62-76.

7. Richardson, *New York Police,* pp. 240-245, 268-283; *Mazet Committee Investigation,* I, 138.

8. Atlanta *Constitution,* Feb. 13, 1895; Jan. 16-Feb. 13, 1895.

9. *Journal of the Senate of the Commonwealth of Pennsylvania, of the Session Begun at Harrisburg, on the Fifth Day of January, 1897* (Harrisburg, 1897), pp. 1,401-1,412 (henceforth referred to as *Andrews Committee Report*); Philadelphia *Public Ledger,* Nov. 11, 1895-Jan. 17, 1896.

10. Kansas City *Star,* Jan. 11-Mar. 10, 1897.

11. Baltimore *Sun,* June 8-July 13, 1897.

12. *Journal of the Senate Special Session of the Fortieth General Assembly of the State of Illinois* (Springfield, 1898), pp. 136-152 (henceforth referred to as *Berry Committee Report*); Chicago *Tribune,* Jan. 7-27, 1898.

13. Los Angeles *Herald,* Nov. 8, 1900.

14. *Journal of the Assembly During the Thirty-Fourth Session of the Legislature of the State of California* (Sacramento, 1901), pp. 625-628; San Francisco *Examiner,* Jan. 29-Feb. 17, 1901.

15. *Mazet Committee Investigation,* I, 11-15; Charles A. Johnson, *Denver's Mayor Speer* (Denver, 1969), pp. 17-26; Denver *Post,* Feb. 5-17, 1901; W.H. Patterson to Board of Police Commissioners, Oct. 15, 1901, Atlanta City Council Files, City Hall, Atlanta, Georgia; Atlanta *Constitution,* Oct. 16, 1901.

16. *Record of Proceedings of the Investigation Before His Excellency Thomas Swann, Governor of Maryland, in the Case of Samuel Hindes and Nicholas L. Wood, Commissioners of the Board of Police of the City of Baltimore, Upon Charges Preferred Against Them for Official Misconduct* (Baltimore, 1868); *Report of the Joint Committee of the General Assembly Appointed to Investigate the Police Department of the City of St. Louis* (St. Louis, 1868) (henceforth referred to as *Evans Committee Investigation*); U.S. Congress, "Testimony Taken by the Select Committee to Investigate the Board of Police Commissioners of the District of Columbia," *House Miscellaneous Documents,* 44th Cong., 2nd sess., no. 40; *Report of the Special Committee Appointed to Investigate the Official Conduct of the Members of the Board of Police Commissioners* (Boston, 1881); Milwaukee *Sentinel,* Feb. 12-17, 1885.

17. Franklin Matthews, "The Character of American Police," *The World's Work,* May 1901, p. 1,314; Frank Moss, "National Danger from Police Corruption, *The North American Review,* October 1901, p.470.

18. Thomas Anthony Reppetto, "Changing the System: Models of Municipal Police Organization" (Ph.D. diss., Harvard University, 1970); James Q. Wilson, *Varieties of Police Behavior* (Cambridge, 1968).

19. George Austin Ketcham, "Municipal Police Reform" (Ph.D. diss., University of Missouri, 1967); Richardson, *New York Police,* chs. 2-3; Roger Lane, *Policing the City* (Cambridge, 1967), chs. 3-4; James F. Richardson, *Urban Police in the United States* (Port Washington, N.Y., 1974), ch. 2; Raymond B. Fosdick, *American Police Systems* (New York, 1920), ch. 2.

20. Samuel P. Hays, "The Politics of Reform in Municipal Government in the Progressive Era," *Pacific Northwest Quarterly,* October 1964, pp. 157-169.

21. Arthur I. Waskow, "Community Control of the Police," *Trans-action,* December 1969, pp. 4-7; Stokely Carmichael and Charles V. Hamilton, *Black Power* (New York, 1967); Paul Jacobs, *Prelude to Riot* (New York, 1966); Alan A. Altshuler, *Community Control* (New York, 1970); Robert M. Fogelson, *Violence as Protest* (Garden City, N.Y., 1971), ch. 7.

1. Adjunct of the Machine

1. *Proceedings of the Third Annual Convention of the National Association of Chiefs of Police of the United States and Canada* (1896), pp. 27-31;

Ketcham, "Municipal Police Reform," chs. 4-6; Richardson, *New York Police,* chs. 4-7; Lane, *Policing the City,* chs. 5-9; Richardson, *Urban Police in the United States,* chs. 3-4; Fosdick, *American Police Systems,* chs. 2-3.

2. Fosdick, *American Police Systems,* pp. 80-96; Richardson, *New York Police,* chs. 4-7; Lane, *Policing the City,* chs. 10-11; Ketcham, "Municipal Police Reform," chs. 4-6. Cf. *The Argument of Thomas C. Amory, Against the Proposed Metropolitan Police Bill, Before the Joint Special Committee of the Legislature, Monday, March 16, 1863* (Boston, 1863); *The Argument of Charles M. Ellis, Esq., in Favor of the Metropolitan Police Bill, Before the Joint Special Committee of the Legislature, Wednesday, March 18, 1863* (Boston, 1863).

3. Bruce Smith, *Police Systems in the United States* (New York, 1949), pp. 164-190, 208-209; T.A. Critchley, *A History of Police in England and Wales, 900-1966* (London, 1967), chs. 2-4; Fosdick, *American Police Systems,* pp. 96-102.

4. Richardson, *New York Police,* pp. 64-65; Lane, *Policing the City,* pp. 103-105; Ketcham, "Municipal Police Reform," pp. 223-224; J.W. Gerard, *London and New York: Their Crime and Police* (New York, 1853), pp. 14-18; *Argument of Thomas C. Amory,* p. 13.

5. Raymond B. Fosdick, "European Police Systems," *Journal of Criminal Law and Criminology,* May 1915, p. 34; Raymond B. Fosdick, *European Police Systems* (New York, 1915), ch. 6; *History of the Police and Fire Departments of the Twin Cities* (Minneapolis, 1899), pt. 1, p. 51.

6. "Report of the Standing Committee on Police," *Transactions of the Third National Prison Reform Congress Held at Saint Louis, Missouri, May 13-16, 1874* (New York, 1874), p. 133; Fosdick, *European Police Systems,* ch. 1.

7. Richardson, *New York Police,* pp. 150-152, 226-227; de Francias Folsom, ed., *Our Police: A History of the Baltimore Force from the First Watchman to the Latest Appointee* (Baltimore, 1888), pp. 478-483; Howard O. Sprogle, *The Philadelphia Police, Past and Present* (Philadelphia, 1887), pp. 158, 219; *Evans Committee Investigation,* p. 62; Boston Common Council, *Reports of Proceedings,* Feb. 3, 1887, pp. 120-121; Nov. 21, 1889, pp. 1,089-1,091; Lane, *Policing the City,* pp. 191-195, 203; *Mazet Committee Investigation,* I, 280, 296, 1,026-1,027.

8. Wilbur Redington Miller, "The Legitimization of the London and N.Y.C. Police, 1830-1870" (Ph.D. diss., Columbia University, 1973).

9. *Mazet Committee Investigation,* I, 345.

10. Oscar Handlin, *Boston's Immigrants* (Cambridge, 1941); Albert B. Faust, *German Element in the United States* (New York, 1927); Florence Edith Janson, *Background of Swedish Immigration, 1840-1930* (Chicago, 1931); Theodore C. Blegen, *Norwegian Migration to America, 1825-1860* (Northfield, Minn., 1931); Humbert S. Nelli, *Italians in Chicago, 1880-1930* (New York, 1970); Oscar Handlin, *The Uprooted* (Boston, 1951).

11. U.S. Census Office, *Report on Crime, Pauperism, and Benevolence in the United States at the Eleventh Census, 1890* (Washington, D.C., 1895), pt.2, p.1,024; George H. Hale, *Police and Prison Cyclopaedia* (Cambridge, 1892), pp.70-158; U.S. Department of Labor, Bureau of Labor Statistics, *History of Wages in the United States from Colonial Times to 1928* (Washington, D.C.,

1934), pp.145-172; International Association of Chiefs of Police (henceforth referred to as IACP), *Eleventh Annual Session* (1904), p.30; Atlanta *Constitution,* Mar. 26, 1895; Los Angeles *Times,* Jan. 1, 1889.

12. *Evans Committee Investigation,* p. 319; Kansas City *Star,* Apr. 3-7, 1894; J.T. Headley, *Pen and Pencil Sketches of the Great Riots* (New York, 1882), chs. 5-10; Ray Allan Billington, *The Protestant Crusade, 1800-1860* (Chicago, 1964), pp.70-76, 222-234, 302-311; Philip Taft and Philip Ross, "American Labor Violence," in Hugh Davis Graham and Ted Robert Gurr, *Violence in America* (New York, 1969), pp.270-289; Fogelson, *Violence as Protest,* pp.5-6, 116-117.

13. *Journal of Proceedings of the First Branch City Council of Baltimore at the Session of 1875-76* (Baltimore, 1876), Appendix, pp. 29, 91; Cincinnati *Enquirer,* Aug. 17, 1885; Chicago *Tribune,* Nov. 6/7, 1894; *Andrews Committee Report,* pp. 1,408-1,410; *Lexow Committee Investigation,* I, 16-18.

14. David Jay Pivar, "The New Abolitionism: The Quest for Social Purity, 1876-1900" (Ph.D. diss., University of Pennsylvania, 1965), chs. 4-10; Arthur Meier Schlesinger, *The Rise of the City, 1878-1898* (New York, 1933), pp. 154-155, 334-335, 353-360; Fosdick, *American Police Systems,* pp. 46-57; Joseph R. Gusfield, *Symbolic Crusade* (Urbana, Ill., 1966), chs. 1-4; R. Christian Johnson, "Vice Reform and Visions of Socio-Economic Mobility, 1872-1900" (paper delivered at American Historical Association meeting, December 1971).

15. Anonymous letter in New York City Police Department Files, 1902-1903, Seth Low Papers, Municipal Archives, New York City; Kansas City *Star,* Jan. 22/23, 1897; Los Angeles *Times,* Nov. 8, 1900; *Berry Committee Report,* pp. 142-145.

16. *Mazet Committee Investigation,* I, 280.

17. Ketcham, "Municipal Police Reform," p. 210; *Lexow Committee Investigation,* V, 5,322-5,326; Baltimore *Sun,* June 29, 1897; Los Angeles *Times,* Nov. 8, 1900; San Francisco *Examiner,* Feb. 7, 1901; Lloyd Wendt and Herman Kogan, *Bosses in Lusty Chicago* (Bloomington, Ind., 1967), pp. 302-303.

18. Kansas City *Star,* Feb. 27-May 4, 1895; Baltimore *Sun,* June 8-July 13, 1897; Fosdick, *American Police Systems,* pp. 234-238, 256-259; Annual Reports of Cincinnati, Buffalo, Chicago, and Los Angeles police departments.

19. *Mazet Committee Investigation,* I, 343-344; *Berry Committee Report,* pp. 136-141; Philadelphia *Public Ledger,* Jan. 17, 1896; New York State, Senate, *Proceedings of the Commission to Inquire into the Courts of Inferior Criminal Jurisdiction in Cities of the First Class* (Albany, 1910), III, 2,872-2,874 (henceforth referred to as *Page Commission Investigation*); Ernest S. Griffith, *A History of American City Government: The Conspicuous Failure, 1870-1900* (New York, 1974), p. 236.

20. *Lexow Committee Investigation,* I, 567, 1,048; IV, 4,195; V, 5,325-5,326; Baltimore *Sun,* June 28, 1897; Chamber of Commerce of the State of New York, *Papers and Proceedings of Committee on the Police Problem City of New York* (New York, 1905), pp. 30-31, 80-81, 251 (henceforth referred to as *Proceedings of Committee on the Police Problem*).

21. John Landesco, *Organized Crime in Chicago* (Chicago, 1968), pp. 29-30; *Lexow Committee Investigation,* V, 5,057-5,058, 5,364-5,365, 5,601-5,602;

Mazet Committee Investigation, I, 1,013-1,014; Lyle Dorsett, *The Pendergast Machine* (New York, 1968), pp. 26-27.

22. *Mazet Committee Investigation,* III, 2,566-2,567; Philadelphia *Public Ledger,* Jan. 17, 1896.

23. Chicago *Tribune,* Mar. 29, 1895; Philadelphia *Inquirer,* Mar. 14, 1897; *Proceedings of Committee on the Police Problem,* pp. 419-424; Kansas City *Star,* July 21, 1909; *Mazet Committee Investigation,* I, 798-906; Emma Schweppe, *The Firemen's and Patrolmen's Unions in the City of New York* (New York, 1948), ch. 2; *Lexow Committee Investigation,* V, 5,319-5,320; *Andrews Committee Report,* pp. 1,408-1,410.

24. Henry Mann, ed., *Our Police: A History of the Providence Force from the First Watchman to the Latest Appointee* (Providence, 1889), p. 132; A.E. Costello, *History of the Police Department of Jersey City* (Jersey City, 1891), p. 140; Mark S. Hubbell, ed., *Our Police and Our City: The Official History of the Buffalo Police Department* (Buffalo, 1893), p. 376.

25. *Lexow Committee Investigation,* I, 438; Kansas City *Star,* Jan. 22, 1897.

26. Los Angeles *Times,* Mar. 22/31, May 16, 1889; *Lexow Committee Investigation,* I, 47, 437-438; II, 2,267, 2,299; IV, 4,036-4,037; V, 4,993-4,994; San Francisco *Examiner,* Mar. 21, 1891; Philadelphia *Public Ledger,* Dec. 19, 1895; Philadelphia *Inquirer,* May 6, 1897; *Berry Committee Report,* pp. 136-141.

27. Kansas City *Star,* Jan. 29, Feb. 2, 1897; Philadelphia *Public Ledger,* Jan. 8-10, 1896; Los Angeles *Herald,* Nov. 8, 1900; *Berry Committee Report,* pp. 136-141; New York State, Assembly, Special Committee Appointed to Investigate the Local Government of the City and County of New York, *Further Report* (Albany, 1884), pp. 2-3; New York Bureau of Municipal Research, "A Report on the School for Recruits and School for Detectives," appearing in vol. VI, pp. 4,463-4,469, of the proceedings of the special committee of the New York City Board of Aldermen that was appointed August 5, 1912 to investigate the New York City Police Department (henceforth referred to as *Curran Committee Investigation*).

28. *Lexow Committee Investigation,* II, 1,283; *Proceedings of Committee on the Police Problem,* pp. 52-53, 422-423; *Mazet Committee Investigation,* III, 2,564; Kansas City *Star,* Jan. 24, 1897; Los Angeles *Herald,* Nov. 8, 1900.

29. New York State, Assembly, *Nineteenth Report of the State Civil Service Commission* (Albany, 1902), p. 45; *Lexow Committee Investigation,* I, 47-49; V, 4,968-4,969, 4,984-4,985, 5,379-5,380.

30. Philadelphia *Public Ledger,* Dec. 14, 1895; *Andrews Committee Report,* p. 1,408; Baltimore *Sun,* July 13, 1897.

31. Chicago *Tribune,* June 20, 1897; *Berry Committee Report,* pp. 136-141; Los Angeles *Times,* Mar. 31, 1889; Kansas City *Star,* Jan. 22, 1897; Baltimore *Sun,* July 13, 1897.

32. Baltimore *Sun,* June 29, 1897; Los Angeles *Times,* Nov. 25/29, 1897.

33. Alexander R. Piper, *Report of an Investigation of the Discipline and Administration of the Police Department of the City of Chicago* (Chicago, 1904), pp. 3-15, 21-34, 42-47; *Berry Committee Report,* pp. 142-145; Balti-

more *Sun,* June 17-19, 1897; *Lexow Committee Investigation,* I, 20-45; Kansas City *Star,* Jan. 22-24, 1897; San Francisco *Examiner,* Feb. 6-12, 1901; Los Angeles *Herald,* Nov. 8, 1900; Atlanta *Constitution,* Feb. 5-9, 1895; *Andrews Committee Report,* pp. 1,402-1,405.

34. *Lexow Committee Investigation,* II, 2,286; V, 5,390-5,391; Kansas City *Star,* Jan. 22, 1897; San Francisco *Examiner,* Feb. 8, 1901; *Andrews Committee Report,* p. 1,404; Boston Common Council, *Proceedings,* Jan. 21, 1897, pp. 78-81; Walter C. Reckless, *Vice in Chicago* (Chicago, 1923), pp. 234-235; *Proceedings of the National Police Convention,* pp. 56-68, 86-97.

35. *Proceedings of Committee on the Police Problem,* pp. 129-130, 172; "Testimony Taken by the Select Committee to Investigate the Board of Police Commissioners of the District of Columbia," 59-60, 101-102; *Lexow Committee Investigation,* I, 40-41; III, 2,601, 2,708-2,713; V, 5,299-5,301; Atlanta *Constitution,* Jan. 16-17, 1895; Richardson, *New York Police,* pp. 209-210; *Fifteenth Annual Report of the Chief of Police of the City of Atlanta, Georgia, for the Year Ending December 31, 1895,* in *Annual Reports of the Committees of Council, Officers and Departments of the City of Atlanta for the Year Ending December 31, 1895,* p. 232.

36. Chicago *Tribune,* Nov. 7-8, 1894; Herbert Asbury, *The French Quarter* (Garden City, N.Y., 1938), p. 404; *Proceedings of the First Branch City Council of Baltimore,* Appendix, pp. 29, 91; Kansas City *Star,* Apr. 3-7, 1894; *Andrews Committee Report,* pp. 1,408-1,410; *Lexow Committee Investigation,* I, 16-20; II, 1,368-1,370; IV, 3,905-3,907.

37. U.S. Industrial Commission, *Report on the Chicago Labor Disputes of 1900* (Washington, D.C., 1901), pp. XXIII-XXIV, CV-CVI; Headley, *The Great Riots,* ch. 21; Richardson, *New York Police,* pp. 195-198; Henry David, *The History of the Haymarket Affair* (New York, 1963), ch. 9; Gilbert Osofsky, *Harlem: The Making of a Ghetto* (New York, 1966), pp. 46-50; Hays, "The Politics of Reform," p. 434.

38. L.B. Stowe, "The New York Police," *The Outlook,* May 4, 1907, p. 22; Memo from Fred. H.E. Ebstein, Alexander R. Piper, and William H. Kipp to Police Commissioner, Apr. 7, 1903, New York City Police Department Files, 1902-1903, Seth Low Papers.

39. *Proceedings of Committee on the Police Problem,* p. 112.

40. Los Angeles *Times,* May 16, 1889; Chicago *Tribune,* June 20, 1897.

41. Two caveats are in order. First, these proportions are probably a bit misleading because in 1890 the Census Office listed policemen together with watchmen and detectives. To what degree and in what way is impossible to say. See U.S. Census Office, *Report on Population of the United States at the Eleventh Census, 1890* (Washington, D.C., 1897), pt. 2, pp. 630-743. Second, the newcomers made up a large part of the population of most cities in 1890. But according to Christine Herzog, a former student of mine who analyzed the rosters of six police forces at the turn of the century, the first generation was more heavily represented in the departments than in the population in all but one of the cities. See U.S. Census Office, *Report on Population of the United States at the Eleventh Census, 1890* (Washington, D.C., 1895), pt. 1, pp. 524-558, 670-677.

42. *Lexow Committee Investigation,* V, 5,390-5,391.

43. *Proceedings of Committee on the Police Problem,* p. 431.

44. *Proceedings of the National Police Convention,* pp. 56-68, 86-97; *Proceedings of the Eighth Annual Convention of the Chiefs of Police of the United States and Canada* (1901), pp. 19-20; Dorsett, *The Pendergast Machine,* pp. 23-25.

45. Baltimore *Sun,* Mar. 24, 1895; Pivar, "The New Abolitionism," chs. 4-10; Alice Felt Tyler, *Freedom's Ferment* (New York, 1962), chs. 13-16.

2. The Military Analogy

1. *Lexow Committee Investigation,* III, 2,733-2,738.

2. New York *Times,* Dec. 8, 1893; *Annual Report of the N.E. Society for the Suppression of Vice, for the Year 1883-4,* pp. 7-15; *Report of the Vice Commission of Minneapolis to His Honor, James C. Haynes, Mayor* (1911), pp. 81-96; *Report of the Vice Commission Louisville, Kentucky* (Louisville, 1915), pp. 10-31; Pivar, "The New Abolitionism," chs. 4-10; Mark H. Haller, "Urban Vice and Civic Reform: Chicago in the Early Twentieth Century," in Kenneth T. Jackson and Stanley K. Schultz, eds., *Cities in American History* (New York, 1972), pp. 290-305.

3. Brand Whitlock, *On the Enforcement of Law in Cities* (Indianapolis, 1913), pp. 20-21, 59-60, 79-80; William J. Gaynor, "Lawlessness of the Police in New York," *The North American Review,* January 1903, pp 19, 20, 25; IACP, *Thirteenth Annual Session* (1906), pp. 65-66; IACP, *Proceedings of the 20th Annual Convention* (1913), pp. 106-107; Los Angeles *Times,* Dec. 2, 1923; *Proceedings of Committee on the Police Problem,* pp. 440-442; *Report of the Louisville Vice Commission,* pp. 11-12; City of Chicago, Civil Service Commission, *Final Report: Police Investigation* (1912), p. 52.

4. Hays, "The Politics of Reform," pp. 157-169; Zane L. Miller, *Boss Cox's Cincinnati* (New York, 1968), chs. 7-14; Melvin G. Holli, *Reform in Detroit* (New York, 1968), chs. 1-8; James B. Crooks, *Politics and Progress* (Baton Rouge, 1969), chs. 2-4; Jack Tager, *The Intellectual as Urban Reformer* (Cleveland, 1968), chs. 4-7; Robert M. Fogelson, *The Fragmented Metropolis: Los Angeles, 1850-1930* (Cambridge, 1967), ch. 10.

5. St. Louis *Globe-Democrat,* Mar. 13-19, 1904; Philadelphia *Inquirer,* Sept. 20-30, 1917; Chicago *Tribune,* Sept. 30, 1928; *Harper's Weekly,* Jan. 13, 1894, pp. 39-40.

6. Henry Barrett Chamberlin, "The Chicago Crime Commission—How the Business Men of Chicago Are Fighting Crime," *Journal of Criminal Law and Criminology,* November 1920, pp. 386-397; Crime Commission of Los Angeles, *Bulletin Number 1,* June 1, 1923, pp. 1-6; State of New York, *Report of the Crime Commission, 1928* (Albany, 1928), pp. 7-25, 143-250; Raymond Moley, *State Crime Commissions* (New York, 1926), pp. 7-26; Mark H. Haller, "Urban Crime and Criminal Justice: The Chicago Case," *Journal of American History,* December 1970, pp. 619-635.

7. Chamberlin, "The Chicago Crime Commission," p. 391.

8. Robert M. Cipes, *The Crime War* (New York, 1968), pp. 14-15.

9. Mark H. Haller, "Police Reform in Chicago, 1905-1935," *American Behavioral Scientist,* May-August 1970, p. 649; *Lexow Committee Investigation,* I, 14; *Andrews Committee Report,* p. 1,356; Illinois Association for Criminal Justice, *The Illinois Crime Survey* (Chicago, 1929), pp. 11-12; Cleveland Foundation, *Criminal Justice in Cleveland* (Cleveland, 1922), p. V; Missouri Association for Criminal Justice, *The Missouri Crime Survey* (New York, 1926), pp. 7-9; Edward W. Sims, "Fighting Crime in Chicago: The Chicago Crime Commission," *Journal of Criminal Law and Criminology,* May 1920, p. 22; Joseph Gerald Woods, "The Progressives and the Police: Urban Reform and the Professionalization of the Los Angeles Police" (Ph.D. diss., University of California at Los Angeles, 1973), p. 138.

10. Richardson, *New York Police,* pp. 234-235; Baltimore *Sun,* June 8, 1897; *Report of the Vice Commission of Cleveland Baptist Brotherhood* (Cleveland, 1911); Illinois General Assembly, *Report of the Senate Vice Committee* (Springfield, 1916), pp. 773-847; Atlanta *Constitution,* Sept. 30, Oct. 14, 1912; June 5, Aug. 2, 1913; Los Angeles *Times,* Dec. 5, 1925; Woods, "The Progressives and the Police," pp. 140-144.

11. Woods, "The Progressives and the Police," pp. 226-228; Chamberlin, "The Chicago Crime Commission," p. 396.

12. Missouri Association for Criminal Justice, *Missouri Crime Survey,* p. 9.

13. John G. Sprout, *"The Best Men"* (New York, 1968), pp. 253-255; Allen F. Davis, *Spearheads for Reform* (New York, 1967), pp. 48-50, 88-90; John Higham, *Strangers in the Land* (New York, 1963), pp. 191-193, 202-203, 301-324.

14. *Proceedings of Committee on the Police Problem,* p. 440; Richardson, *Urban Police in the United States,* pp. 77-83; IACP, *Fifteenth Annual Session* (1908), pp. 30-43; IACP, *Sixteenth Annual Session* (1909), pp. 28-36; Los Angeles *Times,* Dec. 2-11, 1923; Haller, "Police Reform in Chicago," pp. 651-652.

15. *Proceedings of Committee on the Police Problem,* pp. 117, 261, 317; *Lexow Committee Investigation,* I, 50-51; Chicago Civil Service Commission, *Final Report: Police Investigation,* p. 52; Crime Commission of Los Angeles, *Bulletin Number 3,* Jan. 1, 1924, pp. 1-2; Fosdick, *American Police Systems,* pp. 115-116, 149-151.

16. Civic League of St. Louis, *Home Rule Legislation* (St. Louis, 1913), p. 5; *Report of the Special Committee of Board of Aldermen of the City of New York Appointed August 5, 1912 to Investigate the Police Department* (1913), p. 25 (henceforth referred to as *Curran Committee Report*); Fosdick, *American Police Systems,* pp. 234-242, 254-259; Leonhard Felix Fuld, *Police Administration* (New York, 1909), p. 25.

17. Arthur Woods, "Police Promotions," in Clinton Rogers Woodruff, ed., *Proceedings of the Cincinnati Conference for Good City Government and the Fifteenth Annual Meeting of the National Municipal League* (1909), p. 177; William McAdoo, *Guarding a Great City* (New York, 1906), p. 50.

18. *Lexow Committee Investigation,* V, 4,630-4,631; *Proceedings of Committee on the Police Problem,* p. 428; Piper, *Investigation of the Chicago Police Department,* pp. 11-14; F.D.H., "In re:- General Conditions- Chicago Police

Department," Jan. 10, 1925 (memo in Chicago Crime Commission Files, Chicago)—cf. Arthur Woods, *Policeman and Public* (New Haven, 1919), pp. 130-131.

19. Theodore A. Bingham, "The New York Police," *Harper's Weekly,* Mar. 2, 1907, p. 301; *Proceedings of Committee on the Police Problem,* pp. 28, 48, 158-159, 174, 441; Gaynor, "Lawlessness of the Police," p. 10; *Curran Committee Investigation,* V, 3,906; VI, 4,463-4,469; *Report of the Portland Vice Commission to the Mayor and City Council of the City of Portland, Oregon* (1912), p. 114. Fosdick, *American Police Systems,* pp. 270-279; August Vollmer, "A Practical Method for Selecting Policemen," *Journal of Criminal Law and Criminology,* February 1921, p. 573; Cleveland Foundation, *Criminal Justice in Cleveland,* pp. 24-26; Missouri Association for Criminal Justice, *Missouri Crime Survey,* pp. 30-34.

20. Hoyt King, "The Chicago Policemen and the 'Underworld'," *The World Today,* May 1904, pp. 667-671.

21. *Proceedings of Committee on the Police Problem,* pp. 51-53, 94-95, 149-150; McAdoo, *Guarding a Great City,* pp. 279-280; *Page Commission Investigation,* IV, 3,207-3,208, 3,223; *Curran Committee Investigation,* V, 4,124, 4,155-4,156, 4,161-4,162; VI, 4,541-4,542, 4,546-4,548, 4,566-4,577; New York Bureau of Municipal Research, *Report of a Survey of the Government of the City and County of San Francisco* (San Francisco, 1916), pp. 190-191; *Report of the Citizens' Committee Appointed at the Cooper Union Mass Meeting August 14, 1912,* pp. 12-13; Illinois Association for Criminal Justice, *Illinois Crime Survey,* pp. 366-368; August Vollmer, "Vice and Traffic—Police Handicaps," *Southern California Law Review,* May 1928, pp. 326-331.

22. *Proceedings of Committee on the Police Problem,* pp. 51-53; McAdoo, *Guarding a Great City,* pp. 276-277, 282-283; Fuld, *Police Administration,* pp. 187-190, 193-199; Chicago City Council, *Journal of the Proceedings,* Nov. 25, 1912, p. 2,421; Illinois Association for Criminal Justice, *Illinois Crime Survey,* pp. 366-368; New York Bureau of Municipal Research, *Report of a Survey of the Department of Safety of the City and County of Denver* (Denver, 1914), p. 197.

23. Samuel Haber, *Efficiency and Uplift* (Chicago, 1964), p. 107; Fosdick, *American Police Systems,* p. 246; Woods, "Police Promotions," pp. 174-175; *Proceedings of Committee on the Police Problem,* pp. 507-508; Cleveland Foundation, *Criminal Justice in Cleveland,* p. 8.

24. Theodore Roosevelt, "Taking the New York Police Out of Politics," *The Cosmopolitan,* November 1895, p. 45; *Proceedings of Committee on the Police Problem,* pp. 48, 162, 241; *Curran Committee Investigation,* V, 3,795; U.S. Senate, Committee on the District of Columbia, *Hearings [on the] Metropolitan Police in the District of Columbia* (Washington, D.C., 1919), p. 93; McAdoo, *Guarding a Great City,* pp. 18, 32, 335-336; Frank Moss, *Abstract of Suggestions Made to the Committee of Nine for the Improvement of Conditions in Police Administration in New York* (1905), p. 2; Fuld, *Police Administration,* pp. 191, 243; New York City Police Department, *Annual Report for the Year 1919,* p. 41; "Shall the Police Strike?" *Good Government,* September 1919, p. 145; U.S. Senate Committee on the District of Columbia, *Hearings*

on the Metropolitan Police, pp. 34, 93; *Congressional Record,* LVIII, pt. 9, Appendix, p. 9,064; Joseph McGoldrick, "A Policeman's Lot," *National Municipal Review,* June 1930, p. 394.

25. John F. O'Ryan, "The Policeman as a Soldier," *Spring 3100,* January 1934, p. 9; IACP, *Proceedings 34th Convention* (1927), pp. 13, 23; IACP, *Fourteenth Annual Session* (1907), p. 95; IACP, *Proceedings of the 20th Annual Convention* (1913), p. 17; IACP, *Proceedings of the 21st Annual Convention* (1914), p. 8; IACP, *Proceedings 33rd Convention* (1926), p. 239; IACP, *Proceedings 35th Convention* (1928), p. 44; Ernest Jerome Hopkins, "The War Theory of Crime," *The New Republic,* Oct. 28, 1931, pp. 288-290.

26. *Lexow Committee Investigation,* I, 55; Fosdick, *American Police Systems,* p. 314; IACP, *Proceedings of the Twenty-Second Annual Convention* (1915), p. 79; *Page Commission Investigation,* IV, 3,255; *Proceedings of Committee on the Police Problem,* p. 458.

27. Avery D. Andrews, "The Police Systems of Europe," *The Cosmopolitan,* March 1903, pp. 495-504; William McAdoo, "The London Police from a New York Point of View," *The Century Magazine,* September 1909, pp. 649-670; Fosdick, "European Police Systems," pp. 28-38.

28. Hopkins, "War Theory of Crime Control," p. 289; Landesco, *Organized Crime in Chicago,* chs. 5-6; John Kobler, *Capone* (New York, 1971), chs. 17, 21; Oscar Handlin, *Race and Nationality in American Life* (Garden City, N.Y., 1957), pp. 99-102.

29. IACP, *Proceedings of the 20th Annual Convention* (1913), pp. 70-71, 150-151.

30. Cleveland Foundation, *Criminal Justice in Cleveland,* pp. 22-23; *Proceedings of Committee on the Police Problem,* p. 317.

31. Smedley D. Butler, "Making War on the Gangs," *The Forum,* March 1931, pp. 136-138; Fosdick, *American Police Systems,* pp. 314-315; Los Angeles City Council, *Petitions,* 1918, no. 265, Los Angeles City Council Files, Municipal Records Center, Los Angeles; Milwaukee *Sentinel,* Mar. 9, 1921.

32. August Vollmer, "Police Conditions in the United States," in National Commission on Law Observance and Enforcement, *Report on Police* (Washington, D.C., 1931), p. 52; *Proceedings of Committee on the Police Problem,* pp. 45, 86, 102, 104, 248, 509-510, 653-654; Theodore A. Bingham, "How to Give New York the Best Police Force in the World," *The North American Review,* May 1908, p. 74; Cleveland Foundation, *Criminal Justice in Cleveland,* p. 20; Illinois Association for Criminal Justice, *Illinois Crime Survey,* p. 372; Leonard V. Harrison, *Police Administration in Boston* (Cambridge, 1934), pp. 22, 112; Chicago City Council, *Proceedings,* Nov. 25, 1912, pp. 2,421-2,422; *Curran Committee Investigation,* V, 3,807; *Curran Committee Report,* pp. 6, 18; New York Bureau of Municipal Research, *Survey of the Denver Police Department,* p. 211; Rochester Bureau of Municipal Research, *A Report on a Survey of the Police Department of Rochester, N.Y.* (1921), pp. 15-16; Missouri Association for Criminal Justice, *Missouri Crime Survey,* p. 42.

33. McAdoo, *Guarding a Great City,* pp. 53-57; Lowell Thomas, *Old Gimlet Eye: The Adventures of Smedley D. Butler* (New York, 1933), pp. 267-268.

34. Richardson, *Urban Police in the United States,* pp. 62-64; "The Police in a Democracy," *The Outlook,* Jan. 13, 1915, pp. 63-64; Fosdick, *American Police Systems,* pp. 296-306; *Proceedings of Committee on the Police Problem,* pp. 639-644, 653-656; New York Bureau of Municipal Research, *Survey of the Denver Police Department,* pp. 191-192, 211-212; George H. McCaffrey, "The Boston Police Department," *Journal of Criminal Law and Criminology,* January 1912, pp. 674-675; " 'No Divided Allegiance,' Say Chiefs," *Policeman's Monthly,* Oct. 1919, pp. 8-9, 45-49; Rochester Bureau of Municipal Research, *Survey of the Rochester Police Department,* pp. 11-13; New York Bureau of Municipal Research, *Survey of the Government of San Francisco,* pp. 172-174; Crime Commission of Los Angeles, *Bulletin Number 3,* pp. 2-4; Illinois Association for Criminal Justice, *Illinois Crime Survey,* pp. 361-365; Lewis Meriam, *Principles Governing the Retirement of Public Employees* (New York, 1933), pp. 3-17.

35. For evidence of professional aspirations before 1930, see IACP, *Proceedings of the 18th Annual Convention* (1911), p. 13; IACP, *Proceedings 26th Convention* (1919), p. 109.

36. Bingham, "Best Police Force in the World," p. 710; Moss, "Abstract of Suggestions," p. 3; *Proceedings of Committee on the Police Problem,* pp. 94-95; Chicago City Council, *Proceedings,* Nov. 25, 1912, p. 2,421; *Curran Committee Investigation,* VI, 4,542, 4,549, 4,558; *Curran Committee Report,* p. 22; New York Bureau of Municipal Research, *Survey of the Denver Police Department,* p. 197; Citizens' Police Committee, *Chicago Police Problems* (Chicago, 1931), pp. 254-257; Illinois Association for Criminal Justice, *Illinois Crime Survey,* pp. 366-368; Fosdick, *American Police Systems,* p. 355; August Vollmer, "Aims and Ideals of the Police," *Journal of Criminal Law and Criminology,* August 1922, p. 254; Harrison, *Police Administration in Boston,* p. 25; McAdoo, *Guarding a Great City,* p. 243; IACP, *Proceedings 32nd Convention* (1925), p. 64; *Report of the City Council Committee on Crime of the City of Chicago* (Chicago, 1915), p. 10; Butler, "Making War on the Gangs," p. 140.

37. Arthur Woods, *Crime Prevention* (Princeton, 1918), ch. 8.

38. *Lexow Committee Investigation,* I, 14; *Andrews Committee Report,* p. 1,356; Los Angeles *Herald,* Nov. 8, 1900; Baltimore *Sun,* June 8, 1897; Haller, "Police Reform in Chicago," p. 653; Illinois General Assembly, *Report of the Senate Vice Committee,* p. 856; Sims, "Fighting Crime in Chicago," p. 22; Woods, "The Progressives and the·Police," p. 138; Cleveland Foundation, *Criminal Justice in Cleveland,* p. V; Missouri Association for Criminal Justice, *Missouri Crime Survey,* pp. 7-9; Illinois Association for Criminal Justice, *Illinois Crime Survey,* pp. 11-12; Raymond B. Fosdick, *Chronicles of a Generation* (New York, 1958), pp. 124, 132; New York Bureau of Municipal Research, *Survey of the Government of San Francisco,* p. III; F.A. Cleveland to E.B. Morgan, July 1, 1914, a letter published in New York Bureau of Municipal Research, *Survey of the Denver Police Department; Curran Committee Report,* p. 2.

39. Herbert Mitgang, *The Man Who Rode the Tiger* (Philadelphia, 1963), ch. 10.

40. Kansas City *Star,* Jan. 11, 1897; San Francisco *Examiner,* Jan. 29, 1901; Charles E. Merriam, "The Police, Crime and Politics," in Thorsten

Sellin, ed., *The Police and the Crime Problem*, vol. 146 of *The Annals*, November 1929, p. 117; *Report of the Chicago City Council Committee on Crime*, p. 7.

41. Illinois General Assembly, *Report of the Senate Vice Committee*, pp. 868-873; State of New York, *Report of the Crime Commission, 1928*, pp. 7-10.

42. *Proceedings of the Eighth Annual Convention of the Chiefs of Police of the United States and Canada* (1901), pp. 37-38; IACP, *Ninth Annual Session* (1902), p. 13; IACP, *Eleventh Annual Session* (1904), pp. 30-31; IACP, *Proceedings of the 19th Annual Convention* (1912), p. 87.

43. IACP, *Proceedings of the 20th Annual Convention* (1913), pp. 70-71, 151-152; IACP, *Proceedings of the 21st Annual Convention* (1914), p. 34; IACP, *Proceedings 33rd Convention* (1926), pp. 88-89.

3. The First Wave of Reform

1. *Lexow Committee Investigation*, I, 26, 28; II, 1,365-1,366; III, 2,477-2,478, 2,639, 2,739-2,740, 3,210; IV, 4,186-4,187, 4,325; V, 5,024-5,025.

2. Ibid., I, 16-19; *Andrews Committee Report*, pp. 1,408-1,410; Kansas City *Star*, Apr. 3-7, 1894; Chicago *Tribune*, Nov. 6-7, 1894; Sept. 30, 1928; St. Louis *Globe-Democrat*, Mar. 13-19, 1904; Philadelphia *Inquirer*, Oct. 2-5, 1917; Dorsett, *The Pendergast Machine*, chs. 1-2; Walton Bean, *Boss Ruef's San Francisco* (Berkeley, 1968), chs. 2-3, 5; Harold Zink, *City Bosses in the United States* (Durham, N.C., 1930), chs. 5, 10, 14, 17, 19-20; Robert K. Merton, *Social Theory and Social Structure* (Glencoe, Ill., 1964), pp. 71-82.

3. U.S. Senate, Subcommittee of the Committee on the District of Columbia, "Hearings on Charges of Police Inefficiency," Mar. 4, 1930, pp. 48-49, 56-58, Metropolitan Police Department Files, Washington, D.C.; Thomas, *Old Gimlet Eye*, p. 268; *Proceedings of Committee on the Police Problem*, pp. 391-394, 639-640; Chicago Crime Commission, *Bulletin Number 31*, Mar. 1, 1924, pp. 22-23; *Berry Committee Report*, pp. 136-141; *Nineteenth Report of the New York State Civil Service Commission*, pp. 43-47; Dorsett, *The Pendergast Machine*, pp. 28-31.

4. Chicago City Council, *Proceedings*, Nov. 29, 1922, p. 2,371; William L. Riordon, *Plunkitt of Tammany Hall* (New York, 1963), p. 12; Kobler, *Capone*, pp. 209, 268-269, 306-307.

5. Haller, "Police Reform in Chicago," pp. 649-650.

6. IACP, *Eleventh Annual Session* (1904), p. 32; *Proceedings of the National Police Convention*, pp. 56-68, 86-97; Francis V. Greene, *The Police Department of the City of New York* (New York, 1903), p. 47; Illinois General Assembly, *Report of the Senate Vice Committee*, p. 356; Reckless, *Vice in Chicago*, pp. 271-272; Haller, "Urban Crime and Criminal Justice," pp. 630-631; IACP, *Thirteenth Annual Session* (1906), pp. 65-66; IACP, *Proceedings of the 20th Annual Convention* (1913), pp. 99-104, 118-119.

7. IACP, *Proceedings 23d Convention* (1916), p. 40.

8. Fogelson, *The Fragmented Metropolis*, p. 213; *Curran Committee Report*, p. 1; Andy Logan, *Against the Evidence* (New York, 1970), pp. 7-17; San Francisco *Examiner*, Apr. 21-30, 1913; Landesco, *Organized Crime in Chicago*, pp. 28-29.

9. Philadelphia *Inquirer,* Sept. 20, 1917; Cincinnati *Enquirer,* Mar. 20-22, 1925; San Francisco *Examiner,* Mar. 21, 1891; Landesco, *Organized Crime in Chicago,* pp. 9-23; Kobler, *Capone,* pp. 287-292; State of New York, *Report of the Joint Legislative Committee to Investigate the Affairs of the City of New York* (Albany, 1933), pp. 52-84 (henceforth referred to as *Joint Legislative Committee Report*).

10. Fogelson, *The Fragmented Metropolis,* p. 213; Albert Howard Clodius, "The Quest for Good Government in Los Angeles, 1890-1910" (Ph.D. diss., Claremont Graduate School, 1953), ch. 4; *Curran Committee Report,* 1-2; *Curran Committee Investigation,* I-VI; Landesco, *Organized Crime in Chicago,* pp. 30-31; San Francisco *Examiner,* Apr. 25-30, May 1-22, 1913.

11. Philadelphia *Inquirer,* Feb. 4, 1905; Oct. 2-5, Nov. 3-6, 1917; Cincinnati *Enquirer,* Apr. 5-30, 1925; Chicago Civil Service Commission, *Final Report: Police Investigation,* pp. 5-54; Atlanta Board of Police Commissioners, *Minutes,* Aug. 9, 1921, 116ff, Atlanta Police Department Files, Atlanta; New York State Supreme Court, Appellate Division, *In the Matter of the Investigation of the Magistrates' Courts . . . Final Report of Samuel Seabury, Referee* (New York, 1932), pp. 80-100 (henceforth referred to as *Magistrates' Courts Investigation*).

12. Richardson, *New York Police,* pp. 240-241, 247-249; Greene, *Police Department,* pp. 50, 60; Richardson, *Urban Police in the United States,* pp. 72-74; Mitgang, *Man Who Rode the Tiger,* pp. 316-320; Lowell M. Limpus, *Honest Cop: Lewis J. Valentine* (New York, 1939), pp. 160-164, 171-174; Gerald Astor, *The New York Cops* (New York, 1971), chs. 8, 11, 15-17.

13. Fosdick, *American Police Systems,* pp. 103-109, 154-159.

14. Detroit *News,* Nov. 13-16, 1912; May 17, 1913; New York *Times,* Nov. 9, 1917; Richardson, *Urban Police in the United States,* pp. 76-77; *Proceedings of Committee on the Police Problem,* pp. 67-68, 83-84, 102-103, 584-585, 651-652; Fosdick, *American Police Systems,* pp. 259-262; Bruce Smith, "Municipal Police Administration," in Sellin, ed., *Police and Crime Problem,* pp. 10-11; Los Angeles *Times,* Mar. 7, May 19, June 18, July 1, 1924; Oct. 15-17/25/26/29, Nov. 16-21/28/29, Dec. 14/15/28-31, 1929; James E. Davis to August Vollmer, Oct. 15, Nov. 5, 26, 1929, August Vollmer Papers, Bancroft Library, University of California, Berkeley; Woods, "The Progressives and the Police," pp. 207-212, 264-269.

15. McAdoo, *Guarding a Great City,* pp. 25-28; *Proceedings of Committee on the Police Problem,* pp. 48, 125, 164; Limpus, *Honest Cop,* pp. 60-61, 103-104, 166-167; Philadelphia *Inquirer,* Jan. 17, July 4, 1924; U.S. House of Representatives, Special Police Investigation Subcommittee of the Committee on the District of Columbia, *Investigation of the Metropolitan Police Department of the District of Columbia* (Washington, D.C., 1941), pp. 88, 186-194, 266-267.

16. New York *Times,* July 19-20, 1924; Chicago Civil Service Commission, *Final Report: Police Investigation,* pp. 29-30; Chicago City Council, *Proceedings,* Nov. 18, 1912, pp. 2,418-2,419; Dec. 30, 1912, pp. 3,016-3,017.

17. Philadelphia *Inquirer,* Mar. 27-28, July 4/7/12/13/19/21, Oct. 2, 1924; Philadelphia *Evening Bulletin,* Oct. 28, Nov. 8, Dec. 9, 1924; Nov. 22, 1928; New York *Times,* Mar. 9, 1928; Thomas, *Old Gimlet Eye,* pp. 263-275;

C.K. Taylor, "Baiting a Marine," *The Outlook,* Oct. 8, 1924, pp. 199-200; John Stuart, "A Leatherneck Wallops the Small Gods," *Colliers,* Jan. 17, 1925, pp. 18ff.

18. "Butler, A 'Devil Dog' in Philadelphia," *The Literary Digest,* Jan. 26, 1924, p. 44; *Proceedings of Committee on the Police Problem,* pp. 653-654; McAdoo, *Guarding a Great City,* pp. 86-87, 248-250; Chicago Civil Service Commission, *Final Report: Police Investigation,* pp. 35-36; New York Bureau of Municipal Research, *Survey of the Denver Police Department,* pp. 211-212; Los Angeles Police Department, *Annual Report, 1924,* pp. 11-12.

19. *Curran Committee Investigation,* V, 3,902-3,903; McAdoo, *Guarding a Great City,* pp. 154-155, 243-244; Detroit *Free Press,* Nov. 10, 1912; New York *Times,* Apr. 14, Nov. 15, 1914; Landesco, *Organized Crime in Chicago,* pp. 28-29; Atlanta City Council Police Committee, *Minutes,* Nov. 14, 1923, p. 281; Woods, "The Progressives and the Police," pp. 260-261; Citizens' Police Committee, *Chicago Police Problems,* chs. 6-10; U.S. Senate, Subcommittee of the Committee on Education and Labor, *Documents Relating to Intelligence Bureau or Red Squad of Los Angeles Police Department* (Washington, D.C., 1940), pp. 23,509-23,510.

20. Philadelphia *Evening Bulletin,* Jan. 5, 1928; August Vollmer to Los Angeles Board of Police Commissioners and Los Angeles City Council, Apr. 18, 1924, Appendix F, pp. 1-4, in Los Angeles City Council, *Petitions,* 1924, no. 2840; Citizens' Police Committee, *A Reorganization Plan for the Chicago Police Department* (Chicago, 1930), pp. 1-12; Woods, "The Progressives and the Police," ch. 5; Haller, "Police Reform in Chicago," pp. 658-662.

21. Richardson, *New York Police,* pp. 176-178; Chicago *Tribune,* Mar. 21-Apr. 4, 1895; Fogelson, *The Fragmented Metropolis,* p. 212; Atlanta City Council, *Minutes,* Mar. 1, 1906, pp. 763-765, City Clerk's Office, City Hall, Atlanta; Fuld, *Police Administration,* pp. 78-79, 82-83, 306-307, 428-429; Fosdick, *American Police Systems,* pp. 270-275, 279-284; Richardson, *Urban Police in the United States,* pp. 62-64; Woods, "The Progressives and the Police," pp. 160-161.

22. Commissioners of the District of Columbia, *Minutes,* Nov. 3, 1903, pp. 301-302; Sept. 19, 1930, p. 1,116, National Archives, Washington, D.C.; Atlanta City Council, *Minutes,* Jan. 16, 1922, p. 431; Feb. 20, 1922, p. 474; Oct. 20, 1924, p. 97; Mar. 16, 1925, p. 304; J.J. Clayton to Los Angeles City Council, Oct. 24, 1915, and C.E. Snively to Los Angeles Board of Police Commissioners, Nov. 6, 1915, in Los Angeles City Council, *Petitions,* 1915, no. 3,091; Citizens' Police Committee, *Chicago Police Problems,* pp. 233-234.

23. St. Louis *Post-Dispatch,* Mar. 9, 1889; Atlanta Board of Police Commissioners, *Minutes,* Nov. 8, 1910, p. 174; City Club of Philadelphia, *Bulletin,* May 7, 1913, p. 412; *Curran Committee Investigation,* V, 3,949; IACP, *Proceedings 23d Convention* (1916), p. 66; New York City Police Department, *Annual Report for the Year 1919,* pp. 181-182; Chicago City Council, *Proceedings,* Jan. 7, 1921, pp. 1,578-1,579; Chicago *News,* July 12, 1923; Schweppe, *Firemen's and Policemen's Unions,* p. 84; Fuld, *Police Administration,* pp. 262-264; Philadelphia *Inquirer,* Jan. 31, 1924; Fosdick, *American Police Systems,* p. 284; Richardson, *Urban Police in the United States,* pp. 73-74.

24. U.S. Senate Committee on the District of Columbia, *Hearings on the*

Metropolitan Police, pp. 4-18, 26-51, 109-113; "Shall the Police Strike?" pp. 139-147; " 'No Divided Allegiance,' Say Chiefs," pp. 8ff; David Ziskind, *One Thousand Strikes of Government Employees* (New York, 1940), pp. 33-52; Louis Brownlow, *A Passion for Anonymity* (Chicago, 1958), ch. 8; Francis Russell, *A City in Terror* (New York, 1975), pp. 47-204.

25. L.J. O'Rourke, "The Use of Scientific Tests in the Selection and Promotion of Police," in Sellin, ed., *Police and Crime Problem,* pp. 147-150; Philadelphia *Inquirer,* June 29, 1924; Atlanta City Council Police Committee, *Minutes,* Jan. 21, 1929, p. 391; Fuld, *Police Administration,* pp. 80-92; Citizens' Police Committee, *Chicago Police Problems,* pp. 46-47, 50-52, 54-62; Woods, "The Progressives and the Police," pp. 198-199; Richardson, *New York Police,* p. 259.

26. New York Bureau of Municipal Research, "A Report on the Homes and Family Budgets of 100 Patrolmen," in *Curran Committee Investigation,* VI, 4,489-4,506; U.S. House of Representatives, Subcommittee of the Committee on the District of Columbia, *Investigation of Salaries of Metropolitan Police Members* (Washington, D.C., 1919), pt. 3, pp. 102-109, 122-143; "Rates of Pay of Policemen in 24 Cities," *Monthly Labor Review,* October 1919, p. 147; "Salaries in the Police Departments of Principal Cities," ibid., January 1930, pp. 118-126; William C. Beyer and Helen C. Toerring, "The Policeman's Hire," in Sellin, ed., *Police and Crime Problem,* pp. 136-143.

27. Fosdick, *American Police Systems,* pp. 277-278; Vollmer, "Police Conditions in the United States," pp. 63-64; Committee on the District of Columbia, "Removal of Restriction on Residence of Members of the Police Department," U.S. Congress, *House Reports,* 74th Cong., 1st sess., no. 855, pp. 1-2; Woods, "The Progressives and the Police," p. 198.

28. *Curran Committee Investigation,* VI, 4,446-4,483; New York *Times,* June 24, 1915; August Vollmer and Albert Schneider, "The School for Police as Planned at Berkeley," *Journal of Criminal Law and Criminology,* March 1917, pp. 877-898; Fosdick, *American Police Systems,* pp. 298-306; George T. Ragsdale, "The Police Training School," in Sellin, ed., *Police and Crime Problem,* pp. 170-176; Vollmer, "Police Conditions in the United States," pp. 70-85.

29. Boston City Council, *Proceedings,* July 18, 1892, pp. 704-708; Aug. 1, 1892, pp. 724-727; Los Angeles City Council, *Records,* Dec. 19, 1911, pp. 543-545, City Hall, Los Angeles; Roy Lubove, *The Struggle for Social Security* (Cambridge, 1968), pp. 125-127; Charles P. Neill, "Pension Funds for Municipal Employees and Railroad Pension Systems in the United States," U.S. Congress, *Senate Documents,* 61st Cong. 2d sess., no. 427, pp. 62-85; IACP, *Proceedings of the 20th Annual Convention* (1913), pp. 30-36, 48-51; U.S. Department of Labor, Bureau of Labor Statistics, *Public Service Retirement Systems* (Washington, D.C., 1929), pp. 118-125; Fuld, *Police Administration,* pp. 296-300; New York Bureau of Municipal Research, *A Report on the Police Pension Fund of the City of New York* (New York, 1914), pp. 15-19, 43-52; Municipal League of Los Angeles, *Bulletin,* Nov. 12, 1917, pp. 5-6; Citizens' Police Committee, *Chicago Police Problems,* pp. 234-236; Los Angeles Fire and Police Protective League, *History of the Department of Pensions of the City of Los Angeles* (Los Angeles, 1939), pp. 1-2.

30. Richardson, *New York Police,* pp. 265-266, 280-281.

31. *Curran Committee Investigation,* V, 3,906-3,907, 3,960-3,961, 3,980-3,981, 3,995-3,997; Illinois Association for Criminal Justice, *Illinois Crime Survey,* pp. 366-367; Butler, "Making War on the Gangs," p. 140; IACP, *Proceedings of the 19th Annual Convention* (1912), p. 106; IACP, *Proceedings of the 20th Annual Convention* (1913), pp. 52-53; IACP, *Proceedings 23d Convention* (1916), p. 60; IACP, *Proceedings 28th Convention* (1921), p. 99.

32. Illinois Association for Criminal Justice, *Illinois Crime Survey,* pp. 367-368; McAdoo, *Guarding a Great City,* pp. 239-259; IACP, *Proceedings 30th Convention* (1923), pp. 60-71; IACP, *Proceedings 32nd Convention* (1925), pp. 64-73; Citizens' Police Committee, *Chicago Police Problems,* pp. 150-166.

33. McAdoo, *Guarding a Great City,* pp. 283-284.

34. *Curran Committee Investigation,* V, 4,153-4,158.

35. Eleonore L. Hutzel, "The Policewoman," in Sellin, ed., *Police and Crime Problem,* pp. 104-114; Mary E. Hamilton, *The Policewoman* (New York, 1924), chs. 1, 3, 14; Helen D. Pigeon, "Policewomen in the United States," *Journal of Criminal Law and Criminology,* November 1927, pp. 372-377; Arthur Woods, *Crime Prevention* (Princeton, 1918), pp. 112-118; Citizens' Police Committee, *Chicago Police Problems,* pp. 176-180; "The History of the Juvenile Function, Los Angeles Police Department, 1909-1965," Los Angeles Police Department Archives, Los Angeles; Los Angeles Police Department, *Annual Report, 1924,* p. 14; Harrison, *Police Administration in Boston,* pp. 140-144; Fosdick, *American Police Systems,* pp. 377-379; Vollmer, "Police Conditions in the United States," pp. 115-116.

36. Woods, *Crime Prevention,* pp. 38-45, 118-120; IACP, *Proceedings Thirty-Sixth Convention* (1929), pp. 40-41; IACP, *Proceedings of the Twenty-Second Convention* (1915), p. 69; IACP, *Proceedings 26th Convention* (1919), p. 33.

37. Joseph D. McNamara, "An Analysis of the New York Police Drug Enforcement Strategies" (1972), p. 37; Woods, *Crime Prevention,* pp. 73-74; U.S. Senate Committee on Education and Labor, *Los Angeles Red Squad,* pp. 23,515-23,516, 23,543-23,544; State of New York, *Minutes and Testimony of the Joint Legislative Committee Appointed to Investigate the Public Service Commissions* (Albany, 1916), V, 98-122; Citizens' Police Committee, *Chicago Police Problems,* p. 27.

38. Landesco, *Organized Crime in Chicago,* pp. 28-36; Woods, "The Progressives and the Police," p. 198; Noel A. McQuown to William C. Blake, Sept. 1, 1965, San Francisco Board of Supervisors Files, City Hall, San Francisco.

39. U.S. House of Representatives, Committee on the Judiciary, *Hearings [on Bills] to Create a National Police Bureau [and] to Create a Bureau of Criminal Identification* (Washington, D.C., 1924), pp. 3-32.

4. Changes in Policing, 1890-1930

1. August Vollmer, "Police Progress in the Past Twenty-Five Years," *Journal of Criminal Law and Criminology,* May-June, 1933, pp. 161-175.

2. Lynn G. Adams, "The State Police," in Sellin, ed., *Police and Crime*

Problem, pp. 34-40; Katherine Mayo, *Justice to All* (Boston, 1920), chs. 1-3; Bruce Smith, *The State Police* (New York, 1925), chs. 2-4; Smith, *Police Systems in the United States,* pp. 164-190.

3. *Curran Committee Investigation,* III, 2,959-2,969, 2,978-2,981; Thos. P. White to Frederick T. Woodman *et al.,* Aug. 20, 1917, in Los Angeles City Council, *Petitions,* 1917, no. 2,161; U.S. Senate Committee on Education and Labor, *Los Angeles Red Squad,* pp. 23,515-23,516, 23,543-23,544; New York State, *Minutes of Committee Appointed to Investigate the Public Service Commissions,* V, 98-122; *The Nation,* July 9, 1931, pp. 31-32; *Magistrates' Courts Investigation,* pp. 82-86.

4. Butler, "Making War on the Gangs," pp. 136-139; U.S. House Judiciary Committee, *Hearings on a National Police Bureau,* pp. 3, 10-11, 18-19; Critchley, *History of Police in England and Wales,* pp. 132-133, 193-194.

5. Fosdick, *American Police Systems,* pp. 279-281; Fosdick, *European Police Systems,* pp. 182-183; *Proceedings of Committee on the Police Problem,* pp. 404-418; Schweppe, *Firemen's and Policemen's Unions,* pp. 53-56; Richardson, *The New York Police,* pp. 171-172.

6. McAdoo, *Guarding a Great City,* pp. 58-62; *Curran Committee Investigation,* IV, 3,662-3,679; Fosdick, *American Police Systems,* ch. 9; Citizens' Police Committee, *Chicago Police Problems,* ch. 6; Duncan Matheson, "The Technique of the American Detective," in Sellin, ed., *Police and Crime Problem,* pp. 214-218.

7. Los Angeles returned to the ward system in the mid-1920s. See Fogelson, *The Fragmented Metropolis,* ch. 10; Charles P. Taft, *City Government: The Cincinnati Experiment* (New York, 1933), ch. 5.

8. Philadelphia *Evening Bulletin,* Oct. 16-30, 1928; Mar. 15-16, 1929; Chicago *Tribune,* Sept. 30, Dec. 1, 1928; May 1, 1929; *Magistrates' Courts Investigation,* pp. 82-100; *Joint Legislative Committee Investigation,* pp. 52-85; Detroit *Free Press,* May 26, 1930; Woods, "The Progressives and the Police," p. 264; Dorsett, *The Pendergast Machine,* pp. 88-89.

9. Chicago Crime Commission, *Bulletin Number 22,* Feb. 10, 1922, p. 16; *Bulletin Number 27,* Feb. 8, 1923, p. 13; *Bulletin Number 31,* Mar. 1, 1924, pp. 22-23; Los Angeles *Times,* Mar. 24, Apr. 15-22, 1922; Woods, "The Progressives and the Police," pp. 128-137.

10. San Francisco *Examiner,* Apr. 21/30, May 1/2/17/20/21, 1913; *Magistrates' Courts Investigation,* pp. 82-100; *Curran Committee Report,* p. 6; Atlanta Board of Police Commissioners, *Minutes,* Aug. 9, 1921, pp. 116ff; Woods, "The Progressives and the Police," p. 264; Detroit *Free Press,* Jan. 11, May 26, 1930; U.S. Department of Justice, "[Transcript of] Investigation Concerning Law Enforcement and Crime Conditions in the Territory of Hawaii," X, Feb. 9, 1932, pp. 2,208-2,214, Library of Congress, Washington, D.C.; Limpus, *Honest Cop,* pp. 83, 132-133; Los Angeles *Times,* July 21, 1924.

11. Limpus, *Honest Cop,* p. 56.

12. Schweppe, *Firemen's and Patrolmen's Unions,* pp. 53-59, 88-89; "Policemen Organize for a Strike," *The Survey,* Dec. 22, 1917, p. 348; John McDonald, "The Chicago Patrolmen's Association," *The Chicago Patrolmen's Association Official Magazine,* August 1964, p. 44; Harold J. Scott, "The

Record of Twenty Successful Years," *The Firemen's Grapevine,* August 1943, p. 21; Philip Kenneth Kienast, "Policemen and Fire Fighter Employee Organizations" (Ph.D. diss., Michigan State University, 1972), pp. 101-104.

13. Los Angeles *Times,* Mar. 7, May 19, June 18, July 1, 1924; Woods, "The Progressives and the Police," pp. 207-212; Philadelphia *Inquirer,* Mar. 28, July 4, 1924; Thomas, *Old Gimlet Eye,* pp. 267-268; New York *Times,* Jan. 1, Mar. 9, Apr. 15, 1928; Limpus, *Honest Cop,* pp. 55-56, 61-62, 83; Landesco, *Organized Crime in Chicago,* pp. 28-29, 36.

14. Vollmer, "Police Conditions in the Unites States," p. 51; Detroit *Free Press,* Jan. 11-12, May 18-22, 1930; R. Rothman, "Detroit Elects A Liberal," *The Nation,* Oct. 15, 1930, pp. 400-401.

15. Vollmer, "Police Conditions in the United States," pp. 58-63; *Sixty-Fifth Annual Report of the Board of Police Commissioners of the City of St. Louis* (1926), p. 52; Missouri Association for Criminal Justice, *Missouri Crime Survey,* pp. 31-33; F.D.H., "In re:- General Conditions- Chicago Police Department" (memo dated Jan. 10, 1925); "In re:- Police Department" (memo dated Feb. 4, 1925), Chicago Crime Commission Files; Atlanta City Council Police Committee, *Minutes,* Jan. 11, 1934, pp. 63-64; *Magistrates' Courts Investigation,* pp. 82-100.

16. O'Rourke, "Selection and Promotion of Police," pp. 147-150; Citizens' Police Committee, *Chicago Police Problems,* pp. 51-52, 60-61; Missouri Association for Criminal Justice, *Missouri Crime Survey,* pp. 30-31; E.G. to Henry Barrett Chamberlin, Sept. 22, 1920, Chicago Crime Commission Files; State of New York, *Reports of the Joint Legislative Committee to Investigate the Affairs of the City of New York* (Albany, 1922), pp. 214-221 (henceforth referred to as *Joint Legislative Committee Investigation of 1922);* Commission of Inquiry on Public Service Personnel, *Minutes of Evidence* (New York, 1935), pp. 158, 461-462; Vollmer, "Police Conditions in the United States," p. 65.

17. Leonard D. White, *The Prestige Value of Public Employment* (Chicago, 1929), p. 41; Vollmer, "Police Conditions in the Unites States," pp. 58-63.

18. *Curran Committee Investigation,* VI, 4,461-4,463, 4,473-4,483; Citizens' Police Committee, *Chicago Police Problems,* pp. 79-82; Cleveland Foundation, *Criminal Justice in Cleveland,* pp. 34-35; Missouri Association for Criminal Justice, *Missouri Crime Survey,* pp. 39-40; Vollmer, "Police Conditions in the United States," pp. 70-72.

19. Woods, "Police Promotions," pp. 175-176; Fosdick, *American Police Systems,* pp. 279-281, 289-291; E.G. to Henry Barrett Chamberlin, Sept. 22, 1920; Cleveland Foundation, *Criminal Justice in Cleveland,* pp. 36-42; Citizens' Police Committee, *Chicago Police Problems,* pp. 63-67; Haller, "Police Reform in Chicago," pp. 657-658.

20. Donald Stone, "The Control and the Discipline of Police Forces," in Sellin, ed., *Police and Crime Problem,* pp. 63-73; Fosdick, *American Police Systems,* pp. 281-289; Cleveland Foundation, *Criminal Justice in Cleveland,* pp. 45-52; Missouri Association for Criminal Justice, *Missouri Crime Survey,* pp. 35-39; Citizens' Police Committee, *Chicago Police Problems,* pp. 70-78; Special Police Investigation Subcommittee, *Investigation of the Metropolitan Police*

Department, pp. 20-21, 84-85; Vollmer, "Police Conditions in the United States," pp. 57-58.

21. *Berry Committee Report,* pp. 141-142; Woods, "The Progressives and the Police," pp. 264-269.

22. Citizens' Police Committee, *Chicago Police Problems,* chs. 5-8; Harrison, *Police Administration,* chs. 6-7.

23. Atlanta *Constitution,* Aug. 17/20, 1921; Los Angeles *Times,* Dec. 2/5, 1923; Woods, "The Progressives and the Police," pp. 260-261.

24. Smith, *State Police,* ch. 2; Smith, *Police Systems in the United States,* pp. 164-203; Albert Langeluttig, "Federal Police," in Sellin, ed., *Police and Crime Problem,* pp. 41-54.

25. IACP, *Proceedings 26th Convention* (1919), p. 48; Alexander S. Williams to William Murray, Dec. 27, 1887, New York City Police Department Files, New York City Municipal Archives.

26. Fosdick, *American Police Systems,* p. 48; Schlesinger, *The Rise of the City,* pp. 158-159, 334-335; Pivar, "The New Abolitionism," chs. 4-10.

27. Anthony F. Vachris to George W. Wickersham, Aug. 23, 1929; Charles E. Haas to George W. Wickersham, Oct. 31, 1929; George V. Moore to George W. Wickersham, Nov. 22, 1929; Hurd J. Hurst to George W. Wickersham, Nov. 29, 1929; Otto A. Rosalsky to George W. Wickersham, Dec. 18, 1929; Henry G. Pratt to George W. Wickersham, Aug. 10, 1929; Charles B. Collingwood to George W. Wickersham, Oct. 30, 1929, Glenn C. Gillespie to George W. Wickersham, Oct. 31, 1929; Raymond I. Turney to George W. Wickersham, Nov. 19, 1929, Wickersham Commission Archives, Federal Records Center, Suitland, Md.; August Vollmer, "The Prevention and Detection of Crime as Viewed by a Police Officer," in Clyde L. King, ed., *Modern Crime: Its Prevention and Punishment* (Philadelphia, 1926), pp. 148-153 (vol. 125 of *The Annals*); John L. Elliott and Mark A. McCloskey, "Environmental Conditions and Crime," in *ibid.,* pp. 162-165; Samuel O. Wynne, "Recreation Centers as a Means of Crime Prevention," in *ibid.,* pp. 175-176; James Ford, "Improved Housing as a Means of Crime Prevention," in *ibid.,* pp. 176-180; Raymond Moley, "Politics and Crime," in *ibid.,* pp. 78-84; Woods, *Crime Prevention,* chs. 4-6; Merriam, "Police, Crime and Politics," pp. 115-116.

28. Chicago *Tribune,* Mar. 28, 1895; Philadelphia *Inquirer,* Jan. 10, 1924; Thomas, *Old Gimlet Eye,* pp. 267-268.

29. IACP, *Proceedings 23d Convention* (1916), p. 40.

30. Theodore A. Ray to George W. Wickersham, July 30, 1929; Henry G. Pratt to George W. Wickersham, Aug. 10, 1929; Ainsley C. Armstrong to George W. Wickersham, Aug. 21, 1929; Anthony F. Vachris to George W. Wickersham, Aug. 23, 1929; J.G. Laubenheimer to George W. Wickersham, Sept. 19, 1929; Jacob Graul to George W. Wickersham, Sept. 23, 1929, Wickersham Commission Archives; Vollmer, "Prevention of Crime," pp. 149-150; Ernest Jerome Hopkins, "The Lawless Arm of the Law," *Atlantic Monthly,* September 1931, p. 286; IACP, *Proceedings 26th Convention* (1919), p. 50; IACP, *Proceedings 35th Convention* (1928), p. 44; Kevin Ernest Jordan, "Ideology and the Coming of Professionalism: American Urban Police in the 1920's

and 1930's" (Ph.D. diss., Rutgers University, 1972), pp. 55-56; IACP, *Proceedings 34th Convention* (1927), pp. 180-181; Zachariah Chafee, Jr., Walter H. Pollak, and Carl S. Stern, "The Third Degree," in National Commission on Law Observance and Enforcement, *Report on Lawlessness in Law Enforcement* (Washington, D.C., 1931), pp. 173-180.

31. *Proceedings of the 7th Annual Convention of the Chiefs of Police of the United States and Canada* (1900), p. 8; IACP, *Tenth Annual Session* (1903), p. 101; IACP, *Eleventh Annual Session* (1904), pp. 34-35; IACP, *Proceedings of the 20th Annual Convention* (1913), pp. 150-151; L.J. Forbes to George W. Wickersham, Sept. 10, 1920; J.G. Laubenheimer to George W. Wickersham, Sept. 19, 1929; Jacob Graul to George W. Wickersham, Sept. 23, 1929, Wickersham Commission Archives; Hopkins, "War Theory of Crime Control," pp. 288-290.

32. The Keystone Cops and gangster films are available at the Motion Picture Division of the Library of Congress.

33. IACP, *Proceedings Fortieth Annual Convention* (1933), p. 42; Wickersham Commission Archives, Boxes 29 and 30.

34. Whitlock, *On the Enforcement of Law*, pp. 19-20, 59-60, 86-87; IACP, *Proceedings 34th Convention* (1927), p. 195; Vollmer, "Prevention of Crime," pp. 152-153; Richard Washburn Child, *Battling the Criminal* (Garden City, N. Y., 1925), pp. 155-156.

35. Chafee, Pollak, and Stern, "The Third Degree," pp. 73-92; Oswald Garrison Villard, "Official Lawlessness," *Harper's Magazine*, October 1927, pp. 605-614; Hilda Ageloff, "The Third Degree," *The New Republic*, Nov. 7, 1928, pp. 321-324; Hopkins, "Lawless Arm of the Law," pp. 279-286; Jordan, "The Coming of Professionalism," pp. 83-84; Los Angeles *Times*, Dec. 1-25, 1923; Los Angeles City Council, *Petitions*, 1932, nos. 540, 547, 867, 3,090, 3,091; 1933, nos. 499, 811, 2,741; 1934, no. 1,834.

36. Ibid., 1931, no. 8,857; Fosdick, *American Police Systems*, pp. 46-57; IACP, *Proceedings 34th Convention* (1927), p. 195; August Vollmer, *The Police and Modern Society* (Berkeley, 1936), pp. 86-87.

37. Roy Hampton to Los Angeles Police Commission, Jan. 21, 1936, in Los Angeles City Council, *Petitions*, 1936, no. 302; Atlanta *Constitution*, Aug. 20, 1921; August Vollmer, "Vice and Traffic — Police Handicaps," p. 330; August Vollmer, *The Police and Modern Society* (Berkeley, 1936), p. 137.

38. Egon Bittner, *The Functions of the Police in Modern Society* (Washington, D.C., 1970), p. 6; Richardson, *Urban Police in the United States*, pp. 110-111.

5. The Impact of Reform on Urban Society

1. Chicago City Council, *Proceedings*, Feb. 9, 1931, pp. 4,590-4,591; Citizens' Police Committee, *Chicago Police Problems*, p. 3.

2. Frank O. Lowden, "Criminal Statistics and Identification of Criminals," *Journal of Criminal Law and Criminology*, May 1928, pp. 43-48; Fosdick, *American Police Systems*, pp. 350-351; U.S. House Judiciary Committee, *Hearings on a National Police Bureau*, pp. 32-33; J. Edgar Hoover, "Criminal Identification," in Sellin, ed., *Police and Modern Crime*, pp. 208-210; Citizens' Po-

lice Committee, *Chicago Police Problems,* pp. 87-88, 112-117, 140-145, 198-201; Smith, *Police Systems in the United States,* pp. 274-277, 279-281; Vollmer, "Police Conditions in the United States," pp. 86-97; IACP, *Proceedings of the Twenty-Second Annual Convention* (1915), pp. 52-53; Woods, "The Progressives and the Police," pp. 169-170; Vollmer, "Police Progress," pp. 166-167, 169-171; Haller, "Police Reform in Chicago," pp. 660-661; Harrison, *Police Administration in Boston,* pp. 107-108, 123-124, 127-128.

3. Chicago *Tribune,* Dec. 1,1928; May 1, 1929; Philadelphia *Evening Bulletin,* Oct. 16-30, 1928; Mar. 15-16, 1929; *Joint Legislative Committee Investigation,* pp. 52-85; Cincinnati *Enquirer,* Mar. 20-22, Apr. 5-30, 1925; Woods, "The Progressives and the Police," p. 264; Charles E. Merriam, *Chicago: A More Intimate View of Urban Politics* (New York, 1929), pp. 44-47; Vollmer, "Police Conditions in the United States," pp. 58-63.

4. Kobler, *Capone,* pp. 306-307.

5. Chicago Crime Commission, *Criminal Justice,* March 1929, pp. 9-11. See also Philip H. Ennis, *Criminal Victimization in the United States,* a report prepared for the President's Commission on Law Enforcement and Administration of Justice, henceforth referred to as President's Crime Commission (Washington, D.C., 1967), pp. 41-42.

6. Clarence Darrow, "Crime and the Alarmists," *Harper's Magazine,* October 1926, pp. 541-542; Walter Lippmann, "The Underworld: A Stultified Conscience," *The Forum,* February 1931, p. 68; Washington *Post,* May 6, 1929; New York *Times,* Apr. 23, 1929; "The 'New Hoover's' War-Cry Against Crime," *The Literary Digest,* May 4, 1929, pp. 5-7. For a sober effort to find out whether or not crime was on the rise, see Ellen C. Potter, "Spectacular Aspects of Crime in Relation to the Crime Wave," in King, ed., *Modern Crime,* pp. 1-18.

7. Howard McLellan, "Our Inefficient Police," *The North American Review,* February 1929, pp. 226-228; J.P. Shalloo, *Private Police* (Philadelphia, 1933), chs. 9-13; Anthony F. Vachris to George W. Wickersham, Aug. 23, 1929; J. T. Ronald to National Commission on Law Observance and Enforcement, Nov. 1, 1929, Wickersham Commission Archives; IACP, *Proceedings 33rd Convention* (1926), pp. 88-89; IACP, *Proceedings 34th Convention* (1927), pp. 180-181; Vollmer, "Prevention of Crime," p. 149; Chafee, Pollak, and Stern, "The Third Degree," pp. 173-180.

8. William G. Shepherd, "Crime in the Home of Its Friends," *Colliers,* Dec. 5, 1925, p. 19.

9. Missouri Association for Criminal Justice, *Missouri Crime Survey,* p. 33.

10. White, *Prestige Value of Public Employment,* pp. 139-156; Commission of Inquiry on Public Service Personnel, *Minutes of Evidence,* p. 365.

11. Theodore Roosevelt, "Administering the New York Police Force," in *American Ideals and Other Essays* (New York, 1906), pp. 202-203; Richardson, *New York Police,* pp. 259-260; Census Office, *Report on Population at the Eleventh Census,* pt. 2, pp. 630-743; U. S. Bureau of the Census, *Fourteenth Census of the United States Taken in the Year 1920* (Washington D.C., 1923), IV, 1,049-1,257.

12. U. S. Bureau of the Census, *Fifteenth Census of the United States,*

1930: Population, (Washington, D.C., 1933) IV, 200, 203, 448, 804, 952, 1,132, 1,286, 1,414, 1,417; Bureau of the Census, *Fourteenth Census of the United States,* IV, 1,049-1,257.

13. Census Office, *Report on Crime, Pauperism, and Benevolence at the Eleventh Census,* pt. 2, p. 1,024; United States Department of Justice, Bureau of Investigation (hereafter referred to as the FBI), *Uniform Crime Reports* I, no. 1: 32; Cleveland Foundation, *Criminal Justice in Cleveland,* p. 25; Harrison, *Police Administration in Boston,* p. 36; Woods, "The Progressives and the Police," pp. 190-192; Joseph Pois, "The Recruitment of Police" (Ph.D. diss., University of Chicago, 1929), pp. 95-98; Mitgang, *Man Who Rode the Tiger,* pp. 188-189; "Uncle Sam's Chief 'Devil Dog' to Police Philadelphia," *The Literary Digest,* Dec. 29, 1923, p. 14.

14. F.B.I., *Uniform Crime Reports* I, no. 1: 32; New York City Police Department, Annual Report for the Year 1930, p. 7. The figures include civilian employees.

15. E. G. to Henry Barrett Chamberlin, Sept. 22, 1920, Chicago Crime Commission Files.

16. Los Angeles *Times,* Mar. 24, Apr. 15-22, 1922; Oct. 15-17/25-26/29, Nov. 16-21/28-29, Dec. 14-15/28-31, 1929; Woods, "The Progressives and the Police," pp. 128-137, 264-269; New York *Times,* Dec. 23-24, 1925; "General Butler's Dramatic Exit," *The Literary Digest,* Jan. 9, 1926, pp. 10-11; Landesco, *Organized Crime in Chicago,* p. 36; Richardson, *Urban Police in the United States,* p. 77.

17. American Civil Liberties Union, *Blue Coats and Reds* (New York, 1929), pp. 7-16; IACP, *Proceedings 26th Convention* (1919), pp. 102-105; IACP, *Proceedings 28th Convention* (1921), pp. 118-122; Jordan, "The Coming of Professionalism," pp. 42-46.

18. Kansas City *Star,* May 1, 1932.

19. Citizens' Police Committee, *Chicago Police Problems,* p. 7.

20. Gaynor, "Lawlessness of the Police," pp. 25-26; Whitlock, *On the Enforcement of Law,* pp. 19-20, 59-60, 79-80; Fosdick, *American Police Systems,* pp. 46-57; Newton D. Baker, "Law, Police and Social Problems," *The Atlantic Monthly,* July 1915, pp. 12-20. The ratios were calculated from U. S. Bureau of the Census, *Fifteenth Census of the United States, 1930: Population* (Washington, D.C., 1931), vol. I; (Washington, D.C., 1933), vol. IV.

21. Gerald E. Johnson, "The Policeman's Bed of Roses," *Harper's Magazine,* May 1931, p. 736; *Curran Committee Report,* p. 6; Cincinnati *Enquirer,* Apr. 5-30, 1925; Philadelphia *Evening Bulletin,* Oct. 2-3, 1928; Detroit *Free Press,* Oct. 27, 1916; May 26, 1930; Woods, "The Progressives and the Police," p. 264; Philadelphia *Inquirer,* Jan. 10, June 23, 1924.

22. Thomas, *Old Gimlet Eye,* p. 268; William G. Shepherd, "Why Criminals Are Not Afraid," *Collier's,* Nov. 28, 1925, p. 19; U.S. Senate Committee on the District of Columbia, "Hearings on Charges of Police Inefficiency," pp. 33-34, 49-50.

23. Joseph Mayer, "The Passing of the Red Light District," *Social Hygiene,* April 1918, pp. 197-199; Asbury, *French Quarter,* ch. 14; Herbert

Asbury, *Gem of the Prairie* (New York, 1940), ch. 9; Herbert Asbury, *The Barbary Coast* (New York, 1933), ch. 12; *Report of the Minneapolis Vice Commission,* p. 22.

24. U.S. Senate Committee on the District of Columbia, "Hearings on Charges of Police Inefficiency," pp. 9-10; *Joint Legislative Committee Investigation,* pp. 52-85; Woods, "The Progressives and the Police," p. 264; Landesco, *Organized Crime in Chicago,* pp. 41-42.

25. Kobler, *Capone,* chs. 5, 9, 11, 13, 17, 22; Landesco, *Organized Crime in Chicago,* chs. 3-6.

26. *Magistrates' Courts Investigation,* pp. 18-77; Haller, "Urban Crime and Criminal Justice," pp. 633-634; Woods, "The Progressives and the Police," p. 256; Raymond Moley, *Our Criminal Courts* (New York, 1930), pp. 29-31, 236-241. See also David B. Tyack, *The One Best System* (Cambridge, 1974), pp. 172-173.

27. Fosdick, *American Police Systems,* pp. 46-57, 259-263, 284-291; Woods, "Police Promotions," pp. 174-176; H.W. Marsh, "Civil Service and the Police," *National Municipal Review,* May 1921, pp. 286-291; Cleveland Foundation, *Criminal Justice in Cleveland,* pp. 22-23; Stone, "Discipline of Police Forces," pp. 65-68; Johnson, "The Policeman's Bed of Roses," p. 737; White, *Prestige Value of Public Employment,* pp. 142-144.

28. *Lexow Committee Investigation,* I, 438; Kansas City *Star,* May 1, 1932.

29. Gaynor, "Lawlessness of the Police," pp. 25-26; IACP, *Eleventh Annual Session* (1904), pp. 32-33; *The Literary Digest,* Dec. 29, 1923, p. 14.

30. Riordon, *Plunkitt of Tammany Hall,* pp. 90-98.

31. Haber, *Efficiency and Uplift,* chs. 4, 6; Robert Caro, *The Power Broker* (New York, 1974), ch. 28; Wallace S. Sayre and Herbert Kaufman, *Governing New York City* (New York, 1965), pp. 320-337, 594-597; Robert K. Murray, *Red Scare: A Study of National Hysteria, 1919-1920* (New York, 1964), ch. 13; James H. Timberlake, *Prohibition and the Progressive Movement, 1900-1920* (Cambridge, 1966), ch. 6; Higham, *Strangers in the Land,* ch. 11; Kenneth T. Jackson, *The Ku Klux Klan in the City, 1915-1930* (New York, 1967), chs. 3-15.

32. For an exception to the rule, see Lloyd Wendt and Herman Kogan, *Bosses in Lusty Chicago* (Bloomington, Ind., 1967), pp. 294-304.

33. Richardson, *Urban Police in the United States,* p. 77; Landesco, *Organized Crime in Chicago,* pp. 31-36; Woods, "The Progressives and the Police," pp. 128-137.

6. The Professional Model

1. New York *Times,* Sept. 9, Oct. 20, 1933; Mitgang, *Man Who Rode the Tiger,* ch. 17; Arthur Mann, *La Guardia Comes to Power, 1933* (Philadelphia, 1965), ch. 3.

2. Robert Shaplen, "Not Like Taking the Waters," *The New Yorker,* Feb. 27, 1954, p. 59; Limpus, *Honest Cop,* pp. 18-22; James A. Gazell, "O.W.

Wilson's Essential Legacy for Police Administration," *Journal of Police Science and Administration,* December 1974, p. 366; Herbert Jenkins, *Keeping the Peace* (New York, 1970), pp. 1-3.

3. Unless otherwise noted, most of the biographical information in this chapter comes from *Who's Who in America.*

4. O.W. Wilson, ed., *Parker on Police* (Springfield, Ill., 1957), p. X; Limpus, *Honest Cop,* pp. 24-26.

5. Limpus, *Honest Cop,* pp. 26, 52, 73, 99, 103, 125, 132, 160, 173.

6. V.W. Peterson to Charles W. White, July 17, 1951, Chicago Crime Commission Files.

7. Wilson, ed., *Parker on Police,* pp. 12, 26, 70, 187; National Conference of Police Associations (henceforth referred to as NCPA), *Twelfth Annual Convention* (1964), p. 86, International Conference of Police Associations (henceforth referred to as ICPA) Files, Washington, D.C.; National Advisory Commission on Civil Disorders (henceforth referred to as President's *Riot Commission), *Official Transcript of Proceedings,* Sept. 22, 1967, pp. 1,788-1,789, President's Riot Commission Archives, National Archives, Washington, D.C.

8. IACP, *The Police Yearbook* (1956), pp. 10-11; "Address by Chief William H. Parker, Los Angeles Police Department, Before the Board of the National Conference of Police Associations, Tuesday, December 5, 1961," p. 1, ICPA Files; NCPA, *Twelfth Annual Convention* (1964), pp. 79-80; Jordan, "Coming of Professionalism," ch. 1; President's Riot Commission, *Official Transcript of Proceedings,* Sept. 22, 1967, pp. 1,788-1,789.

9. IACP, *The Police Yearbook* (1940), pp. 220-230; (1952), pp. 146-150, 157-166, 173-179; (1954), pp. 189-194; (1956), p. 147; (1961), pp. 199-212; (1966), pp. 300-313; G. Douglas Gourley, "Police Public Relations," in Bruce Smith, ed., *New Goals in Police Management,* vol. 291 of *The Annals,* January 1954, pp. 135-142; Wilson, ed., *Parker on Police,* pp. 135-146; O.W. Wilson and Roy Clinton McLaren, *Police Administration* (New York, 1972), pp. 216-232.

10. Atlanta City Council Police Committee, *Minutes,* Jan. 11, 1934, pp. 63-64; Atlanta *Constitution,* Feb. 18, 1936; Dean Jennings, "Portrait of a Police Chief," *The Saturday Evening Post,* May 7, 1960, p. 89; V.W. Peterson, "Re: Chicago Police Department," three memos dated Aug. 29, 1945, Dec. 23, 1946, Jan. 28, 1947, Chicago Crime Commission Files; U. S. Senate, Special Committee to Investigate Organized Crime in Interstate Commerce, *Third Interim Report* (Washington, D.C., 1951), pp. 30-144 (henceforth referred to as *Kefauver Committee Report*); State of New York, Commission of Investigation, *An Investigation of Law Enforcement in Buffalo* (1961), pp. 55-104.

11. San Francisco *Examiner,* Mar. 17, 1937; Philadelphia County Grand Jury, *Investigation of Vice, Crime and Law Enforcement* (Sayre, Pa., 1939); *Newsweek,* Sept. 19, 1938, pp. 11-12; *Time,* May 6, 1940, p. 19; Robert H. Williams, *Vice Squad* (New York, 1973), ch. 5; Albert Deutsch, *The Trouble With Cops* (New York, 1955), pp.76-77; Philadelphia *Evening Bulletin,* Apr. 21, June 3, 1951; Feb. 15/18, Mar. 14/20, 1952; U. S. Senate, Subcommittee of the Committee on the District of Columbia, *Hearings [on] Investigation of Crime and Law Enforcement in the District of Columbia* (Washington, D.C.,

1952), pp. 27-55; Aaron Kohn, *Crime and Politics in Chicago* (Chicago, 1971), pp. 15-71; Ralph Lee Smith, *The Tarnished Badge* (New York, 1965), ch. 5; New York City, Commission to Investigate Allegations of Police Corruption and the City's Anti-Corruption Procedures, *Report* (New York, 1972), chs. 3-15 (henceforth referred to as *Knapp Commission Report*).

12. Emanuel H. Lavine, *The Third Degree* (New York, 1930), chs. 5-6, 9-11; Chafee, Pollak, and Stern, "The Third Degree," ch. 2; Woods, "The Progressives and the Police," pp. 357-362; Jerry Saul Caplan, "The CIVIC Committee in the Recall of Mayor Frank Shaw" (Masters thesis, University of California at Los Angeles, 1947), ch. 3; U. S. Senate, Committee on the District of Columbia, *Report [on] Investigation of Crime and Law Enforcement in the District of Columbia* (Washington, D.C., 1952), pp. 12-16; Deutsch, *Trouble With Cops,* pp. 9-10; Smith, *Tarnished Badge,* chs. 2, 9; Atlanta *Constitution,* Feb. 2/4, 1959.

13. For classic statements of the conventional wisdom, see International City Managers' Association (henceforth referred to as ICMA), *Municipal Police Administration* (Chicago, 1943); O.W. Wilson, *Police Administration* (New York, 1950). On Vollmer, see Gene E. Carte, "August Vollmer and the Origins of Police Professionalism" (Ph.D. diss., University of California at Berkeley, 1972). On Wilson, see Gazell, "O.W. Wilson's Essential Legacy."

14. In addition to *Municipal Police Administration* and *Police Administration,* I have based my interpretation of the reform diagnosis and prescription on many other documents, perhaps the most revealing of which are Vollmer, "Police Conditions in the United States"; Citizens' Police Committee, *Chicago Police Problems;* Vollmer, *Police and Modern Society;* Smith, *Police Systems in the United States;* Smith, ed., *New Goals in Police Management;* Donald C. Stone, "Recruitment of Policemen," IACP's *Bulletins on Police Problems,* no. 1, August 1938; August Vollmer, "Police Bureau Survey: City of Portland Oregon" (Portland, 1947); Finance Commission of the City of Boston, *The Boston Police Survey* (Boston, 1949); Institute of Public Administration, *The New York Police Survey* (New York, 1952); Bruce Smith, "Report of a Survey of the San Francisco California Police Department" (1957); Institute of Public Administration, "The Atlanta Police Survey" (1957); President's Commission on Crime in the District of Columbia, *Report on the Metropolitan Police Department* (Washington, D.C., 1965); O.W. Wilson, "Police Organization and Administration," *National Municipal Review,* December 1936, 700ff. The IACP's *Police Yearbook,* the Southern Institute for Law Enforcement's *Proceedings,* and the *Journal of Criminal Law and Criminology* are also quite revealing.

15. State of New York, *Proceedings of the Governor's Conference on Crime, the Criminal and Society* (Albany, 1935), p. 525; Stanley R. Schrotel, "Changing Patrol Methods," in Smith, ed., *New Goals in Police Management,* p. 46; Paul L. Kirk, "Progress in Criminal Investigation," in *ibid.,* p. 58; IACP, *The Police Yearbook* (1964), p. 17; IACP, *Proceedings of the Forty-Second Annual Convention* (1935), pp. 65-66, 107; Wilson, ed., *Parker on Police,* pp. 67, 100; Peace Officers' Association of the State of California, *Proceedings of the Fifteenth Annual Convention* (1935), p. 33.

16. IACP, *The Police Yearbook* (1938-1939), pp. 20-36.

17. NCPA, *Fourth Annual Convention* (1956), pp. 12-16, ICPA Files.

18. IACP, *The Police Yearbook* (1964), p. 30; (1940), pp. 72-74; (1956), pp. 177-183; (1967), pp. 33-35; Chicago *Tribune*, Apr. 17, 1961; Vollmer, *Police and Modern Society*, p. 222; Raymond Clift, "Police Training," in Smith, ed., *New Goals in Police Management*, p. 113; Don L. Kooken and Loren D. Ayres, "Police Unions and the Public Safety," in ibid., p. 153; Lear B. Reed, *Human Wolves* (Kansas City, 1941), ch. 4.

19. E. Wilson Purdy, "Administrative Action to Implement Selection and Training for Police Professionalization, *Proceedings of the First Annual Southern Institute for Law Enforcement* (1963), p. 9; Quinn Tamm, "Police Professionalization: Myth or Reality?" *Proceedings [of the] Second Annual Southern Institute for Law Enforcement* (1964), p. 1.

20. Harry Caldwell, "Police Recruiting and Selection: The Cornerstone for Professionalization," *Proceedings of the Second Annual Southern Institute for Law Enforcement*, p. 49; W.D. Booth, "Need for Professionalization," *Proceedings [of the] Third Annual Southern Institute for Law Enforcement* (1965), pp. 21-22; Paul H. Ashenhust, "The Goal: A Police Profession," *Journal of Criminal Law, Criminology and Police Science*, March-April 1959, pp. 606-607; NCPA, *Transcript [of the] Board of Directors Meeting* (1954), pp. 58-59, ICPA Files; V. W. Peterson to Charles W. White, July 17, 1951, Chicago Crime Commission Files; Kooken and Ayres, "Police Unions and the Public Safety," pp. 152-158; NCPA, *Seventh Annual Convention* (1959), p. 54.

21. National Commission on Causes and Prevention of Violence, *Transcript of Proceedings,* Oct. 30, 1968, pp. 2,226-2,227, National Commission on Causes and Prevention of Violence Archives (henceforth referred to as Violence Commission Archives), National Archives, Washington, D.C.

22. Robert W. Hodge, Paul M. Siegel, and Peter H. Rossi, "Occupational Prestige in the United States, 1925-63," *American Journal of Sociology*, November 1964, pp. 291-293.

23. Harold L. Wilensky, "The Professionalization of Everyone?" ibid., September 1964, pp. 137-158.

24. See note 14 above.

25. A.E. Leonard, "Crime Reporting as a Police Management Tool," in Smith, ed., *New Goals in Police Management*, p. 128; ICMA, *Municipal Police Administration*, p. VII; Deutsch, *Trouble with Cops*, pp. 223-224; IACP, *The Police Yearbook* (1965), p. 373; New York *Times*, July 22, 1970; *Knapp Commission Report*, p. III.

26. IACP, *The Police Yearbook* (1964), pp. 370-372.

27. *Newsweek,* May 11, 1953; *Time,* Jan. 24, 1966; Williams, *Vice Squad,* p. 104.

28. Leaving aside the IACP, which made one survey in the early 1950s and another in the early 1970s, these outfits did at least three major surveys of the Atlanta Police Department after 1930. See National Municipal League, "The Governments of Atlanta and Fulton County Georgia" (1938); Institute of Public Administration, "The Atlanta Police Survey" (1957); Public Service Administration, "Government of the City of Atlanta, Georgia" (1965). On the IPA's activities in other cities, see Shaplen, "Not Like Taking the Waters," pp. 45-51, 62-74.

29. *Kefauver Committee Report,* ch. 4; *Knapp Commission Report,* pp. II-III; President's Crime Commission, *The Challenge of Crime in a Free Society* (Washington, D.C., 1967), ch. 4.

30. Arthur Niederhoffer, *Behind the Shield* (Garden City, N.Y., 1967), pp. 16-17.

31. NCPA, *Board of Directors Meeting* (1954), pp. 57-64.

32. NCPA, *Board of Directors Meeting* (1954), pp. 16, 84-85; NCPA, *16th Annual Convention* (1964), pp. 13-14; Nelson A. Watson and James W. Sterling, *Police and Their Opinions* (Washington, D.C., 1969), pp. 55-59, 128, 150; Nelson A. Watson to James E. Stargel, Oct. 17, 1966, Metropolitan Police Department Files, Washington, D.C.; Interviews with members of the New York City Police Department, Oct. 10/14, 1968, President's Riot Commission Archives.

33. Limpus, *Honest Cop,* pp. 36-38; James F. Ahern, *Police in Trouble* (New York, 1972), p. 97. A few Chicago police officers were so disaffected that they cooperated with the Chicago Crime Commission. See V.W. Peterson, "Re: Chicago Police Department," two memos dated Feb. 5, June 30, 1943; A.W. Wright, "Re: Chicago Police Department," memo dated Oct. 5, 1945, Chicago Crime Commission Files. At least one Chicago police officer served as confidential informant for the commission. See V.W. Peterson's memo dated Apr. 4, 1952, Chicago Crime Commission Files. For some of the reasons, see Chicago *Tribune,* Oct. 24/25, 1945; May 30, June 4/6, 1946.

7. The Second Wave of Reform

1. New York *Times,* Mar. 1/14, 1931; May 12, 1932; *Magistrates' Courts Investigation,* pp. 6-8; Mitgang, *Man Who Rode the Tiger,* pp. 196-197, 206-207, 218-219, 239-240; Philadelphia County Grand Jury, *Investigation of Vice, Crime and Law Enforcement,* pp. 22-32, 76-78; San Francisco *Examiner,* Mar. 17, 1937; Woods, "The Progressives and the Police," pp. 357-362.

2. Zink, *City Bosses,* chs. 14, 19-20; Bean, *Boss Ruef's San Francisco,* ch. 21; Fogelson, *The Fragmented Metropolis,* ch. 10; Miller, *Boss Cox's Cincinnati,* chs. 5, 6; Taft, *City Management,* chs. 6-8; Dorsett, *The Pendergast Machine,* pp. 134-136; Edward C. Banfield and James Q. Wilson, *City Politics* (Cambridge, 1963), pp. 124-125; Edward C. Banfield, *Big City Politics* (New York, 1965), p. 107. Cf. Mike Royko, *Boss* (New York, 1971); Scott Christianson, "Albany's Finest Wriggle Free," *The Nation,* Dec. 3, 1973, p. 587.

3. Philadelphia County Grand Jury, *Investigation of Vice, Crime and Law Enforcement,* pp. VII-XIX, 3-5; Ed Reid, *The Shame of New York* (New York, 1953), ch. 1; Smith, *Tarnished Badge,* ch. 9.

4. James Q. Wilson, *The Amateur Democrat* (Chicago, 1966), ch. 9; Banfield and Wilson, *City Politics,* chs. 9, 11.

5. Hervey A. Juris and Peter Feuille, *Police Unionism* (Lexington, Mass., 1973), pp. 132-146.

6. Kansas City *Star,* May 1, 1932; Report of the Legislative Committee to the Los Angeles City Council, Mar. 10, 1942, in Los Angeles City Council, *Petitions,* 1942, no. 10380.

7. Chicago *News,* July 16, 1962; Chicago *American,* Feb. 1/28, 1953;

Chicago *Tribune,* Nov. 5, Dec. 6, 1954; Margaret Ann Levi, "Conflict and Collusion: Police Collective Bargaining," Technical Report (No. 07-74), prepared for the Innovative Resource Planning project at MIT's Operations Research Center (1974), p. 55.

8. Levi, "Conflict and Collusion," pp. 25-26; Theodore J. Lowi, "Machine Politics—Old and New," *The Public Interest,* Fall 1967, pp. 83-92.

9. Kansas City *Star,* Mar. 27, 1934; Dorsett, *The Pendergast Machine,* p. 122; San Francisco *Examiner,* Mar. 17, 1937; Woods, "The Progressives and the Police," pp. 405-408; Chicago *Sun-Times,* Mar. 11, 1952; Reid, *Shame of New York,* pp. 18-19; Philadelphia *Evening Bulletin,* Apr. 21, June 3, 1951.

10. Chicago *Sun-Times,* Jan. 18, 1960; Smith, *Tarnished Badge,* chs. 2, 5, 8; *Newsweek,* Jan. 24, 1966, p. 30; Philadelphia County Grand Jury, *Investigation of Vice, Crime and Law Enforcement,* pp. 107-179, 240-268; *Time,* May 6, 1940; Deutsch, *Trouble with Cops,* p. 76; Williams, *Vice Squad,* pp. 163-180; *Knapp Commission Report,* pp. 1-11; Pennsylvania Crime Commission, *Report on Police Corruption and the Quality of Law Enforcement in Philadelphia* (1974), pp. 5-26 (henceforth referred to as *Pennsylvania Crime Commission Report*).

11. Dorsett, *The Pendergast Machine,* p. 125; Reed, *Human Wolves,* pp. 177-179; *Annual Report of the Police Department of the City and County of San Francisco California* (1937), p. 8; Woods, "The Progressives and the Police," pp. 407-408; Deutsch, *Trouble with Cops,* p. 10; Shaplen, "Not Like Taking the Waters," p. 51; Philadelphia *Evening Bulletin,* Nov. 28, 1951.

12. Smith, *Tarnished Badge,* pp. 144-145, 170-173; *Newsweek,* Jan. 24, 1966, p. 30.

13. Limpus, *Honest Cop,* chs. 10-11; Woods, "The Progressives and the Police," pp. 417-419; Deutsch, *Trouble with Cops,* pp. 9-10, 204; William W. Turner, *The Police Establishment* (New York, 1968), p. 170; Smith, *Tarnished Badge,* chs. 3, 5, 9; IACP, *The Police Yearbook* (1964), p. 14.

14. Smith, *Tarnished Badge,* chs. 2, 7; Chicago *American,* July 16, 1961; Williams, *Vice Squad,* pp. 56-58.

15. San Francisco *Examiner,* Mar. 10, 1937; Atlanta *Constitution,* Oct. 21, 1941; Woods, "The Progressives and the Police," pp. 465-466; Levi, "Conflict and Collusion," pp. 25-26; Smith, *Tarnished Badge,* pp. 175-176.

16. Vollmer, "Police Conditions in the United States," p. 52; Smith, *Police Systems in the United States,* p. 226.

17. Frederika Randall, "Union Resistance to Civilians in the Boston Police Department, 1968-69," paper prepared for the Municipal Employee Union project at the Harvard-MIT Joint Center for Urban Studies (1976), pp. 13-14.

18. Smith, *Police Systems in the United States,* p. 259; Boston City Council, *Proceedings,* Jan. 29, 1962, p. 39; Chicago *Tribune,* Sept. 26, 1960; Dec. 17, 1961; John B. Layton to Walter E. Washington, Mar. 24, 1969, Metropolitan Police Department Files.

19. President's Crime Commission, *Task Force Report: The Police* (Washington, D.C., 1967), p. 191 (henceforth referred to as the *Crime Commission Report*); Wilson and McLaren, *Police Administration,* pp. 436-439; Herbert J. Miller, Jr., to Charles A. Horsky, Jan. 19, 1966; John B. Layton to Herbert J. Miller, Jr., Feb. 10, 1966, Metropolitan Police Department Files.

20. Turner, *Police Establishment,* p. 170; Wilson, ed., *Parker on Police,* p. 79; Smith, *Tarnished Badge,* pp. 34-35, 136-137; Chicago *News,* Mar. 29, 1960; Rory Judd Albert, "A Time for Reform," Technical Report (No. 12-75) prepared for the Innovative Resource Planning project at MIT's Operation Research Center (1975), p. 60; Al Scharff, "The Operating Director's Annual Report for 1965," report to Houston Crime Commission, p. 5, Metropolitan Police Department Files; President's Commission on Crime in the District of Columbia, *Report on the Metropolitan Police Department,* pp. 14-16.

21. Smith, *Police Systems in the United States,* p. 243, figure XIII; Citizens' Police Committee, *Reorganization Plan for the Chicago Police Department,* pp. 7-23; Woods, "The Progressives and the Police," pp. 174-175; *Annual Report of the San Francisco Police Department* (1937), pp. 5-6; St. Louis Governmental Research Institute, *The St. Louis Police Department—A Resurvey* (St. Louis, 1948), pp. 3-4; IACP, *The Police Yearbook* (1964), pp. 14-19.

22. Woods, "The Progressives and the Police," p. 410; IACP, *The Police Yearbook* (1964), p. 18; Smith, *Tarnished Badge,* pp. 196-201; Atlanta City Council Police Committee, *Minutes,* June 2, 1965, p. 188; June 16, 1965, p. 193; *Knapp Commission Report,* p. 206; John B. Layton to J.W. Mailliard, III, Apr. 17, 1968, Metropolitan Police Department Files.

23. Smith, *Police Systems in the United States,* p. 243, figure XIII; St. Louis Governmental Research Institute, *St. Louis Police Department,* p. 4; Woods, "The Progressives and the Police," pp. 425-426.

24. IACP, *Police Personnel Selection Survey* (Washington, D.C., 1968); "Report of Committee on Police, Sheriff and Coroner to Board of Directors," May 25, 1932, Chicago Crime Commission Files; Smith, *Police Systems in the United States,* pp. 149-150; *Crime Commission Report,* pp. 126-127, 131-133; St. Louis Governmental Research Institute, *St. Louis Police Department,* p. 5.

25. Niederhoffer, *Behind the Shield,* pp. 34-36; IACP, *Police Personnel Selection Survey;* Robert A. Lothian, "Operation of a Police Merit System," in Smith, ed., *New Goals in Police Management,* pp. 103-104; Chicago *Tribune,* Jan. 14, May 8, 1961; Jenkins, *Keeping the Peace,* pp. 164-165; *Crime Commission Report,* pp. 9, 129-130, 134; Wilson, ed., *Parker on Police,* p. 6; George W. O'Connor, "A Survey of Selection Methods," *The Police Chief,* December 1962, pp. 12-14; Dale Carson, "Recruitment and Eligibility Standards," *Proceedings of the First Annual Southern Institute for Law Enforcement* (1963), p. 88; Terry Eisenberg, Deborah Kent, and Charles R. Wall, *Police Personnel Practices in State and Local Governments* (Washington, D.C., 1973), p. 51.

26. ICMA, *The Municipal Year Book* (Chicago, 1940), pp. 430-431; ICMA, *The Municipal Year Book* (Chicago, 1960), p. 398; U. S. Bureau of the Census, *Census of Population, 1960* (Washington, D.C., 1963), I, table 124; U.S. Department of Labor, Bureau of Labor Statistics, *Salary Trends: Firemen and Policemen, 1924-1964* (Washington, D.C., 1965), pp. 1-23; Bruce Smith, Jr., "The Policeman's Hire," in Smith, ed., *New Goals in Police Management,* pp. 122-124.

27. *Crime Commission Report,* p. 142; J.E. Curry to William C. Blake, Sept. 1, 1965; Noel A. McQuown to William C. Blake, Sept. 1, 1965; Donald I. McNamara to William C. Blake, Sept. 2, 1965; M.E. Cook to William C.

Blake, Aug. 31, 1965, San Francisco Board of Supervisors Files; New York *Times,* May 2, 1960; IACP, *Police Personnel Selection Survey.*

28. Smith, *Police Systems in the United States,* p. 150; Cleveland *Plain Dealer,* Jan. 11, 1936; *Annual Report of the San Francisco Police Department* (1937), p. 6; Jenkins, *Keeping the Peace,* pp. 22-23; Reed, *Human Wolves,* p. 287; Chicago *Tribune,* Aug. 25, 1949; *Crime Commission Report,* pp. 9-10, 137-140; St. Louis Governmental Research Institute, *St. Louis Police Department,* pp. 7-8; Turner, *Police Establishment,* pp. 41-44.

29. Woods, "The Progressives and the Police," p. 410; Chicago *Sun-Times,* June 22, 1960; Walter T. Storm to Major and Superintendent (Robert J. Barrett), Nov. 19, 1948, Metropolitan Police Department Files; IACP, *Police Unions and Other Police Organizations* (Washington, D.C., 1944), pp. 11-23.

30. Chicago *Daily News,* Dec. 30, 1961; O.W. Wilson, "Towards a Better Merit System," in Smith, ed., *New Goals in Police Management,* pp. 91-92; Harold Richard Wilde, Jr., "The Process of Change in a Police Bureaucracy" (Ph.D. diss., Harvard University, 1972), pp. 234-254; Jerry V. Wilson to Chief of Police (John B. Layton), Mar. 7, 1967; John B. Layton to Patrick V. Murphy, June 21, 1968, Metropolitan Police Department Files.

31. Woods, "The Progressives and the Police," p. 337; Chicago *Tribune,* Apr. 11, 1961.

32. Woods, "The Progressives and the Police," p. 409; Deutsch, *Trouble with Cops,* p. 204; Chicago *Sun-Times,* Jan. 29, 1961; Albert, "A Time for Reform," pp. 63-64.

33. U. S. House of Representatives, Select Committee on Crime, *Hearings [on] the Improvement and Reform of Law Enforcement and Criminal Justice in the United States* (Washington, D.C., 1969), pp. 709-711; IACP, *Yearbook* (1937-1938), pp. 96-99, 110, 209; IACP, *The Police Yearbook* (1954), pp. 288-290; (1952), pp. 180-193; IACP, *Proceedings of the Fortieth Annual Convention* (1933-1934), pp. 175-178; Franklin M. Kreml, "The Specialized Traffic Division," in Smith, ed., *New Goals in Police Management,* pp. 63-72; Wilbur S. Smith, "Widening the Traffic Enforcement Front," in ibid., pp. 73-77.

34. Woods, "The Progressives and the Police," p. 432; Chicago *American,* Oct. 22, 1962; U.S. House Select Committee on Crime, *Hearings on Law Enforcement and Criminal Justice,* p. 708; Albert, "A Time for Reform," pp. 66-67; ICMA, *The Municipal Year Book* (Chicago, 1951), p. 413; ICMA, *The Municipal Year Book* (Washington, D.C., 1970), p. 450.

35. IACP, *The Police Yearbook* (1940), pp. 52-56; (1956), pp. 107-114; Frank D. Day, "The Issue of One-Man Vs. Two-Man Police Patrol Cars," *Journal of Criminal Law, Criminology and Police Science,* January/February 1965, pp. 698-706; Chicago *Tribune,* Nov. 3, 1953; Chicago *American,* Dec. 15, 1964; Chicago Police Department, "One-Man Patrol Cars" (1963), pp. 4-5; *Crime Commission Report,* pp. 54-55; Wilson, ed., *Parker on Police,* pp. 42-43; Woods, "The Progressives and the Police," p. 433; IACP, *The Police Yearbook* (1956), p. 108; Jenkins, *Keeping the Peace,* p. 170; Chicago *Sun-Times,* Oct. 22, 1962; Smith, *Tarnished Badge,* pp. 181-182.

36. IACP, *The Police Yearbook* (1953), pp. 131-136; (1955), pp. 113-114; (1961), pp. 84-94; (1964), pp. 121-127; Wilson, ed., *Parker on Police,* pp. 101-

102; Jane E. Rinck, "Supervising the Juvenile Delinquent," in Smith, ed., *New Goals in Police Management,* pp. 82-84; Jenkins, *Keeping the Peace,* ch. 5.

37. Turner, *Police Establishment,* pp. 111, 145-146; Diane Fisher, "Police Investigatory Detention Practices" (1966), report prepared for President's Crime Commission.

38. IACP, *Uniform Crime Reporting* (New York, 1929), pp. VII-XI; A.E. Leonard, "Crime Reporting as a Management Tool," pp. 127-134; Smith, *Police Systems in the United States,* pp. 291-295.

39. Citizens' Police Committee, *Chicago Police Problems,* pp. 202-205; *Annual Report of the San Francisco Police Department* (1937), pp. 5-6; St. Louis Governmental Research Institute, *St. Louis Police Department,* p. 17; John Edgar Hoover to Robert J. Barrett, Aug. 19, 1947, Metropolitan Police Departments Files; Institute of Public Administration, *The New York Police Survey* (New York, 1952), pp. 33-34; State Commission of Investigation, *Law Enforcement in Buffalo,* pp. 106-111.

40. John Edgar Hoover, "The Basis of Sound Law Enforcement," in Smith, ed., *New Goals in Police Management,* pp. 39-42; IACP, *The Police Yearbook* (1968), pp. 157-171.

8. Unionism Comes to Policing

1. IACP, *Police Unions,* pp. II, 23-25, 28-30.

2. " 'No Divided Allegiance,' Say Chiefs," pp. 8-9, 45-46, 48-49; "Shall the Police Strike?" pp. 139-140; U. S. Senate Committee on the District of Columbia, *Hearings on the Metropolitan Police,* pp. 109-113; Russell, *A·City in Terror,* pp. 25, 43-58, 73-74; U. S. House Committee on the District of Columbia, *Hearings on the Metropolitan Police,* pt. 3, pp. 102-109, 122-143; U. S. Senate Committee on the District of Columbia, *Hearings on the Metropolitan Police,* pp. 4-18.

3. Russell, *A City in Terror,* pp. 73-204; Brownlow, *A Passion for Anonymity,* ch. 8; Ziskind, *One Thousand Strikes,* pp. 33-52; Richard L. Lyons, "The Boston Police Strike of 1919," *The New England Quarterly,* June 1947, pp. 147-168.

4. IACP, *Police Unions,* pp. 3-4; J. Joseph Loewenberg, "Policemen and Firefighters," in Seymour L. Wolfbein, ed., *Emerging Sectors of Collective Bargaining* (Braintree, Mass., 1970), p. 145; Juris and Feuille, *Police Unionism,* p. 17.

5. Woods, "The Progressives and the Police," pp. 392-396; Los Angeles *Times,* Mar. 8/13, 1946; Charles S. Rhyne, *Labor Unions and Municipal Employee Law* (Washington, D.C., 1946), pp. 112-113, 310-315; St. Louis *Post-Dispatch,* Nov. 23-Dec. 19, 1945; Aug. 16-Sept. 21, 1946; *Time,* Sept. 9, 1946, p. 26; *Newsweek,* Sept. 9, 1946, pp. 37-38; IACP, *Police Unions,* pp. 4, 10-23; Andrew V. Giorgi and Donald John Tufts, "Unionization of Municipal Police Forces," *Notre Dame Lawyer,* Fall 1951, pp. 88-97.

6. On the origins and development of these outfits, see Philip Kenneth Kienast, "Policemen and Fire Fighter Employee Organizations" (Ph.D diss., Michigan State University, 1972), pp. 101-109; Donald Whitney Berney, "Law

and Order Politics" (Ph.D. diss., University of Washington, 1971), pp. 66-73, 139-146.

7. Schweppe, *Firemen's and Patrolmen's Unions,* pp. 53-57; Chicago *News,* Nov. 1, 1922; *The Survey,* Dec. 22, 1917, p. 348; Woods, "The Progressives and the Police," p. 337; Cleveland Bureau of Governmental Research, "The Cleveland Police Survey" (1945), p. 130.

8. Cleveland and Bureau of Governmental Research, "Cleveland Police Survey," 129-134.

9. Schweppe, *Firemen's and Patrolmen's Unions,* pp. 168-170; McDonald, "The Chicago Patrolmen's Association," p. 44; Bruce Smith, "What the Depression Has Done to Police Service," *Public Management,* March 1934, p. 67.

10. U.S. House Committee on the District of Columbia, *Hearings on the Metropolitan Police,* pt. 3, p. 100.

11. Bureau of Labor Statistics, *Salary Trends: Firemen and Policemen, 1924-1964,* p. 1; Chicago *American,* July 11-14, 1950; Robert V. Murray to Leroy E. Wike, Jan. 18, 1957, Metropolitan Police Department Files.

12. Chicago *American,* Mar. 11, 1953; Deutsch, *Trouble With Cops,* pp. 56-57; M.W. Aussieker, Jr., *Police Collective Bargaining* (Chicago, 1969), pp. 7-10.

13. Chicago *News,* Nov. 17, 1951.

14. Levi, "Conflict and Collusion," p. 131.

15. IACP, *Police Unions,* rev. ed. (Washington, D.C., 1958), pp. 6-15, 19-21, 31-33; Levi, "Conflict and Collusion," pp. 13-15, 34-38; Edmund P. Murray, "Should the Police Unionize?" *The Nation,* June 13, 1959, pp. 530-533.

16. Levi, "Conflict and Collusion," p. 12.

17. Ibid., pp. 28-30, 127-128; Albert, "A Time for Reform," pp. 24-26.

18. Levi, "Conflict and Collusion," p. 11.

19. Chicago *Tribune, American, News,* and *Sun-Times,* issues for November 1951, June and July 1960, February and March 1961.

20. Sterling D. Spero and John M. Capozzola, *The Urban Community and Its Unionized Bureaucracies* (New York, 1972), ch. 3; B.J. Widick, "Labor's New Brood: The Public Service Unions," *The Nation,* June 28, 1975, p. 782.

21. Levi, "Conflict and Collusion," pp. 13-15, 34-38; L.H. Whittemore, *The Man Who Ran the Subways* (New York, 1968), p. 175; Berney, "Law and Order Politics," pp. 132-134.

22. Levi, "Conflict and Collusion," pp. 30-33, 128; Juris and Feuille, *Police Unionism,* ch. 8; NCPA, *7th Annual Convention* (1959), pp. 134-135; NCPA, *12th Annual Convention* (1964), pp. 178-195; New York *Times,* Nov. 22, 1971; Turner, *The Police Establishment,* chs. 11-12. For a recent analysis of the civil liberties of police officers, see "The Policeman: Must He Be a Second-Class Citizen with Regard to His First Amendment Rights?" *New York University Law Review,* May 1971, pp. 536-559.

23. Levi, "Conflict and Collusion," chs. 2, 4-5; Curtis Brostron, "Police Employee Organizations," *The Police Chief,* December 1969, pp. 6-8.

24. IACP, *Police Unions,* p. 29; Russell, *A City in Terror,* pp. 219-223; Woods, "The Progressives and the Police," pp. 392-396.

25. Spero and Capozzola, *The Urban Community and Its Unionized Bureaucracies*, ch. 3; Jack Stieber, *Public Employee Unionism* (Washington, D.C., 1973), ch. 6.

26. U.S. Senate Committee on the District of Columbia, *Hearings on the Metropolitan Police*, p. 93; IACP, *Police Unions*, rev. ed., p. 74.

27. NCPA, *Board of Directors Meeting* (1959), pp. 58-63; Stephen P. Kennedy, "The Case Against Police Unionization," undated memorandum, p. 3, Metropolitan Police Department Files. For the background thereof, see Levi, "Conflict and Collusion," pp. 35-36.

28. Lowi, "Machine Politics—Old and New," pp. 83-92; Juris and Feuille, *Police Unionism*, pp. 159-160; Berney, "Law and Order Politics," pp. 293-298.

29. Berney, "Law and Order Politics," pp. 157-167, 179-190; Juris and Feuille, *Police Unionism*, pp. 85-88; Russell, *A City in Terror*, pp. 242-244; Levi, "Conflict and Collusion," pp. 144-155.

30. Levi, "Conflict and Collusion," pp. 34-38, 137.

31. Ibid., pp. 34-55; Raymond D. Horton, *Municipal Labor Relations in New York City* (New York, 1973), ch. 2.

32. Levi, "Conflict and Collusion," pp. 117-118, 121-158; Berney, "Law and Order Politics," pp. 158-160.

33. Albert, "A Time for Reform," pp. 24-29.

34. Levi, "Conflict and Collusion," pp. 189-192.

35. Spero and Capozzola, *The Urban Community and Its Unionized Bureaucracies*, p. 43; Berney, "Law and Order Politics," pp. 262-283; Juris and Feuille, *Police Unionism*, pp. 37-38.

36. Berney, "Law and Order Politics," pp. 282-283; Albert, "A Time for Reform," pp. 26-29; Levi, "Conflict and Collusion," pp. 134-155.

37. Juris and Feuille, *Police Unionism*, pp. 85-88; Spero and Capozzola, *The Urban Community and Its Unionized Bureaucracies*, ch. 10; Stieber, *Public Employee Unionism*, ch. 8; Harry H. Wellington and Ralph K. Winter, *The Unions and the Cities* (Washington, D.C., 1971), chs. 11-12; Berney, "Law and Order Politics," pp. 157-167, 179-190.

38. Jervus E. King to John J. Cassese, Mar. 19, 1970, Los Angeles City Council, *Petitions*, 1970, no. 148500; Juris and Feuille, *Police Unionism*, ch. 5.

39. IACP, *Police Unions*, pp. 13, 62-71; Smith, *Police Systems in the United States*, pp. 337-338; Kooken and Ayres, "Police Unions and the Public Safety," pp. 152-158; Kennedy, "The Case Against Police Unionization," pp. 1-45; IACP, *The Police Yearbook* (1953), pp. 178-184; (1964), pp. 10-11; Levi, "Conflict and Collusion," pp. 39-41.

40. Levi, "Conflict and Collusion," ch. 5. For Jenkins' views on police unions, see *Keeping the Peace*, pp. 173-175.

41. Stephen C. Halpern, "An Analysis of the Role of a Police Union and Professional Association in an Urban Police Department" (paper presented at annual meeting of the American Political Science Association, September 1973), pp. 2-6; Juris and Feuille, *Police Unionism*, ch. 5.

42. IACP, *The Police Yearbook* (1964), pp. 10-11.

43. Wilde, "The Process of Change," pp. 234-254; Peter Feuille and Hervey A. Juris, "Police Professionalization and Police Unions," Northwestern University Graduate School of Management Working Paper 74-27, p. 18; Juris and

Feuille, *Police Unionism,* pp. 86-87, 89, 132-134; Randall, "Union Resistance to Civilians," pp. 18-47; Berney, "Law and Order Politics," p. 310.

44. Judy A. Levenson, "There's No Place Like Home: A Police Union's Struggle Against the Residency Requirement in Detroit" (Masters thesis, MIT, 1976), chs. 2-4; Feuille and Juris, "Police Professionalization," pp. 14, 17; Juris and Feuille, *Police Unionism,* p. 155; Turner, *The Police Establishment,* chs. 11-12; Levi, "Conflict and Collusion," pp. 91-105, 215; Halpern, "Role of a Police Union and Professional Association," pp. 4-6.

45. Juris and Feuille, *Police Unionism,* p. 122; Carol Beth Kellermann, "Political Dynamics in Municipal Labor Relations: A Case Study of the New York City Parity Dispute" (Honors thesis, Harvard College, 1972).

46. Donald D. Pomerleau, "The Eleventh Hour!" *The Police Chief,* December 1969, p. 42; "Police Employee Organizations: Report of the IACP Special Committee on Police Employee Organizations," *The Police Chief,* December 1969, pp. 51-55; IACP, Police Foundation, and Labor Management Relations Service, *Guidelines and Papers from the National Symposium on Police Labor Relations* (Washington, D.C., 1974), pp. 3-10.

9. Changes in Policing, 1930-1970

1. Chicago *American,* June 29, 1967.

2. *Crime Commission Report,* ch. 4; Leonard, "Crime Reporting as a Police Management Tool," pp. 127-130.

3. Los Angeles *Times,* June 3, 1970; Joseph C. Goulden, "The Cops Hit the Jackpot," *The Nation,* Nov. 23, 1970, pp. 520-533; Robert Wells, "Vietnamization on Main Street," ibid., July 20, 1970, pp. 38-41; Seymour M. Hersh, "Your Friendly Neighborhood MACE," *The New York Review of Books,* Mar. 27, 1969, pp. 41-44; Garry Wills, *The Second Civil War* (New York, 1968), ch. 4; FBI, *Prevention and Control of Mobs and Riots* (Washington, D.C., 1965), sec. IV; Department of the Army, *Civil Disturbances and Disasters* (Washington, D.C., 1968), ch. 7.

4. *Crime Commission Report,* pp. 98-102, 109-112; U.S. House of Representatives, Committee on Government Operations, *Report [on] Block Grant Programs of the Law Enforcement Assistance Administration* (Washington, D.C., 1972), pp. 6-11, 87-95; Hannah Shields and Mae Churchill, "The Fraudulent War on Crime," *The Nation,* Dec. 21, 1974, pp. 648-649.

5. Reiss, *The Police and the Public,* p. 11.

6. Levi, "Conflict and Collusion," pp. 25-26; Smith, *The Tarnished Badge,* pp. 170-173; *Crime Commission Report,* p. 30; Woods, "The Progressives and the Police," ch. 10.

7. New York *Times,* Mar. 18, 1971.

8. They found much less evidence than the New York State Commission of Investigation found in Rochester a few years earlier. See the commission's "Report of an Investigation of Certain Organized Crime Activities and Problems of Law Enforcement in Rochester, New York," pp. 51-64.

9. Levi, "Conflict and Collusion," ch. 3; Juris and Feuille, *Police Union-*

ism, pp. 125-127, 133-134; Schrotel, "Changing Patrol Methods," pp. 46-53; Chicago *American,* Sept. 8, 1957; Chicago *Tribune,* Aug. 3, 1968; Wilson and McLaren, *Police Administration,* pp. 333-344.

10. Williams, *Vice Squad,* pp. 12, 31, 45-48, 56-60, 92-96, 142-144, 179-180, 221-234; Deutsch, *Trouble With Cops,* pp. 9-10, 75-84; *Knapp Commission Report,* chs. 4, 7.

11. *Crime Commission Report,* pp. 195-197; *Knapp Commission Report,* ch. 19; *Pennsylvania Crime Commission Report,* ch. 5; National Center on Police and Community Relations, School of Police Administration and Public Safety, Michigan State University, *A National Survey of Police and Community Relations,* report prepared for President's Crime Commission (Washington, D.C., 1967), pp. 218-229; Chicago *Sun-Times,* Mar. 17, 1964; New York *Times,* Dec. 16, 1968.

12. Chicago *News,* July 5, 1960; Apr. 18, 1961; Chicago *American,* Dec. 30, 1960; Chicago *Sun-Times,* Apr. 17, 1963; Smith, *Tarnished Badge,* pp. 183-184.

13. Deutsch, *Trouble With Cops,* p. 50; Virgil W. Peterson to Alan Levensohn, Aug. 26, 1953, Chicago Crime Commission Files.

14. Niederhoffer, *Behind the Shield,* pp. 36-39, 141-142; William M. Westley, *Violence and the Police* (Cambridge, 1970), p. 47; John H. McNamara, "Uncertainties in Police Work: The Relevance of Police Recruits' Backgrounds and Training," in David Bordua, ed., *The Police* (New York, 1967), pp. 193-195.

15. As early as 1935 August Vollmer had called on the authorities to set up state institutes to regulate access to policing in much the same way that professional schools regulated access to other professions, but this proposal made no headway. See Vollmer, *Police and Modern Society,* pp. 233-234. On the deficiencies of the police academies in the late 1960s, see Niederhoffer, *Behind the Shield,* pp. 41-50; *Crime Commission Report,* pp. 36-37.

16. Chicago *American,* Feb. 1, 1953; Chicago *Tribune,* Nov. 5, 1954; Chicago *News,* June 29, 1960; New York *Times,* Oct. 30, Nov. 24, 1970; Aug. 3, Nov. 22, 1971; NCPA, *12th Annual Convention* (1964), pp. 178-195; Juris and Feuille, *Police Unionism,* ch. 8.

17. *Crime Commission Report,* p. 141.

18. Juris and Feuille, *Police Unionism,* pp. 142-144; *Pennsylvania Crime Commission Report,* chs. 5-6; *Knapp Commission Report,* ch. 19.

19. For an estimate of the time lost as a result of days off, annual leaves, sick leaves, injury leaves, holidays, and training, see Wilson and McLaren, *Police Administration,* p. 696.

20. Reiss, *The Police and the Public,* p. 73.

21. George L. Kelling, Tony Pate, Duane Dieckman, and Charles E. Brown, *The Kansas City Preventive Patrol Experiment: A Summary Report* (Washington, D.C., 1974), pp. 1-5.

22. Fogelson, *Violence as Protest,* pp. 62-65; Ed Cray, *The Big Blue Line* (New York, 1967), pp. 186-191.

23. Chicago Crime Commission, *Criminal Justice,* March 1929, pp. 9-11;

Philip H. Ennis, *Criminal Victimization in the United States,* report prepared for the President's Crime Commission (Washington, D.C., 1967), pp. 41-43; New York *Times,* Apr. 15, 1974.

24. Among the few noteworthy studies on occupational prestige are George S. Counts, "The Social Status of Occupations: A Problem in Vocational Guidance," *School Review,* January 1925, pp. 16-27; Mapheus Smith, "An Empirical Scale of Prestige Status of Occupations," *American Sociological Review,* April 1943, pp. 185-194; Maethel E. Deeg and Donald G. Paterson, "Changes in the Social Status of Occupations," *Occupations,* January 1947, pp. 205-208; "Jobs and Occupations: A Popular Evaluation," *Opinion News,* Sept. 1, 1947, pp. 3-13; Hodge, Siegel, and Rossi, "Occupational Prestige in the United States," pp. 286-302.

25. *Opinion News,* Sept. 1, 1947, pp. 4-5; Counts, "Social Status of Occupations," pp. 20-21; Hodge, Siegel, and Rossi, "Occupational Prestige in the United States," pp. 209-292.

26. This pattern was brought to my attention by Gilah Gilles, a former research assistant who spotted it in Kemp R. Niver's *Motion Pictures from the Library of Congress Paper Print Collection, 1894-1912* (Berkeley, 1967). For films that show this pattern, see *The Cop and the Nurse Girl* (1898); *How the Cook Made Her Mark* (1904); *A Trick on the Cop* (1904); *While Strolling in the Park* (1904). For recent portrayals, see Donald E. Westlake, *Cops and Robbers* (New York, 1973); Joseph Wambaugh, *The New Centurions* (Boston, 1970); Dorothy Unhak, *Law and Order* (New York, 1973). For the movie versions of *Cops and Robbers* and *The New Centurions,* see the New York *Times,* Jan. 6, 1974, Aug. 4, 1972.

27. Hodge, Siegel, and Rossi, "Occupational Prestige in the United States," pp. 290-292, 302.

28. Albert J. Reiss, Jr., Otis Dudley Duncan, Paul K. Hatt, and Cecil C. North, *Occupations and Social Status* (New York, 1961), ch. 4; Hodge, Siegel, and Rossi, "Occupational Prestige in the United States," pp. 290-292.

29. IACP, *The Police Yearbook* (1952), p. 249; (1956), pp. 23-24, 389-390; (1966), pp. 314-317; (1968), pp. 259-260; ICPA, *13th Annual Convention* (1965), pp. 13-14.

30. IACP, *The Police Yearbook* (1940), pp. 378-379; (1954), p. 293; (1956), p. 378; (1961), p. 245; Kirk, "Progress in Criminal Investigation," pp. 54-62; F.L. Scott, "What the Police Administrator Expects from the University," in *Proceedings of the Third Annual Southern Institute for Law Enforcement* (1965), pp. 81-84.

31. Albert J. Reiss, Jr., "Career Orientations, Job Satisfaction, and the Assessment of Law Enforcement Problems by Police Officers," in *Studies in Crime and Law Enforcement in Major Metropolitan Areas,* report prepared for President's Crime Commission (Washington, D.C., 1967), I, section II, 71-94; McNamara, "Uncertainties in Police Work," p. 217.

32. Governor's Commission on the Los Angeles Riots, *Archives,* University of California Library, Los Angeles, XI, 16 (henceforth referred to as *McCone Commission Archives*); President's Violence Commission, *Transcript of Proceedings,* Oct. 24, 1968, pp. 1,918-1,920; IACP, *The Police Yearbook* (1961), pp. 10-11, 13, 245; William H. Parker, "Crime and the Great Society" (1965),

pp. 3-16; NCPA, *Board of Directors Meeting* (1964), pp. 216-230; Turner, *The Police Establishment,* ch. 13.

33. ICPA, "Subversive Committee Notebook," ICPA Files; ICPA, "Subversive Intervention in Law Enforcement" (1965), ICPA Files; ICPA, *16th Annual Convention* (1968), Second Resolution; Interviews with members of the New York City Police Department, Oct. 10, 1968, President's Riot Commission Archives; Juris and Feuille, *Police Unionism,* p. 25; Turner, *The Police Establishment,* chs. 11-12, 14.

34. Wilson, ed., *Parker on Police,* p. 60; President's Violence Commission, *Transcript of Proceedings,* Oct. 24, 1968, p. 1,918; NCPA, *12th Annual Convention* (1964), pp. 114-115; Interviews with members of the New York City Police Department, Oct. 10, 1968, President's Riot Commission Archives; Jordan, "The Coming of Professionalism," chs. 1-2.

35. Turner, *The Police Establishment,* ch. 1; Fogelson, *Violence as Protest,* chs. 1, 3; National Advisory Commission on Civil Disorders, *Report* (Washington, D.C., 1968), ch. 11 (henceforth referred to as *Riot Commission Report*); ICPA, *16th Annual Convention* (1968), Second Resolution; State of New Jersey, Governor's Select Commission on Civil Disorder, *Report for Action* (1968), pp. 22-37; Annual editions of FBI's *Uniform Crime Reports;* New York *Times,* Aug. 27, Nov. 19, 1970; Chicago *Tribune,* Aug. 30, 1970; Boston *Globe,* June 4, 1971; Andy Logan, "Around City Hall," *The New Yorker,* Mar. 24, 1973, pp. 76ff; U. S. Senate, Committee on the Judiciary, Subcommittee to Investigate the Administration of the Internal Security Act and Other Internal Security Laws, *Hearings [on] Assaults on Law Enforcement Officers* (Washington, D.C., 1970), pts. 1-5.

36. McNamara, "Uncertainties in Police Work," p. 218.

37. Reiss, *The Police and the Public,* pp. 57-59.

38. Robert Coles, "A Policeman Complains," *The New York Times Magazine,* June 13, 1971, p. 73.

10. The Price of Progress

1. Los Angeles *Times,* July 17-21, 1966; Woods, "The Progressives and the Police," pp. 492-493.

2. Jerome H. Skolnick, *Justice Without Trial* (New York, 1966); L.H. Whittemore, *Cop!* (New York, 1969); Jonathan Rubenstein, *City Police* (New York, 1973); V. W. Peterson, "Re: Chicago Police Department," three memos dated Aug. 29, 1945, Dec. 23, 1946, Jan. 28, 1947, Chicago Crime Commission Files; Piper, *Investigation of the Chicago Police Department,* pp. 3-15, 21-34, 42-47.

3. Fred C. Shapiro, *Whitmore* (New York, 1969); Vincent Bugliosi and Curt Gentry, *Helter Skelter* (New York, 1974); Woods, "The Progressives and the Police," pp. 248-249; Washington *Post,* Sept. 23-Oct. 23, 1929; Kansas City *Star,* Mar. 18-24, 1930.

4. Reiss, *The Police and the Public,* pp. 156-160; F.D.H., "In re:- General Conditions- Chicago Department of Police," memo dated Jan. 10, 1925, Chicago Crime Commission Files; *Lexow Committee Investigation,* I, 32-43; *Knapp Commission Report,* p. 4.

5. Smith, *Tarnished Badge*, p, 153; Philadelphia *Evening Bulletin*, Oct. 11, 1928; Woods, "The Progressives and the Police," pp. 264-265; *Magistrates' Courts Investigation*, pp. 82-100.

6. Donald J. Black and Albert J. Reiss, Jr., "Patterns of Behavior in Police and Citizen Transactions," in *Studies of Crime and Law Enforcement*, II, section I, 31-32; Fogelson, *Violence as Protest*, pp. 57, 60-62, 64-65; *Twenty-First Annual Report of the Chief of Police of the City of Atlanta, Ga.* (1901), pp. 5-6; Ernest J. Hopkins, *Our Lawless Police* (New York, 1931); Lavine, *The Third Degree*.

7. U.S. Commission on Civil Rights, *Hearings Held in Cleveland, Ohio, April 1-7, 1966* (Washington, D.C., 1966), pp. 568-572; American Civil Liberties Union of Southern California, *Day of Protest, Night of Violence: The Century City Peace March* (1967), pp. 16-33; U.S. Senate Committee on Education and Labor, *Los Angeles Red Squad*, pp. 23,514-23,516; New York *Times*, Mar. 18/22, 1934; U.S. Senate Committee on Education and Labor, *Report on the Chicago Memorial Day Incident* (Washington, D.C., 1937), pp. 18-36.

8. IACP, *Proceedings Fortieth Annual Convention* (1933), pp. 41-45.

9. *Riot Commission Report*, ch. 6; *Congressional Quarterly*, Sept. 8, 1967, pp. 1,758-1,761; U.S. Bureau of the Census, *U.S. Census of Population: 1960. Final Report PC(2)-1B. Subject Reports: Persons of Spanish Surname* (Washington, D.C., 1963), pp. 195-199, and *Final Report PC(2)-1D. Subject Reports: Puerto Ricans in the United States* (Washington, D.C., 1963), p. 102; T. Lynn Smith, "Redistribution of the Negro Population of the United States," *Journal of Negro History*, July 1966, pp. 155-173; José Hernández Alvarez, "Mexican Immigration, 1910-1950," *Journal of Inter-American Studies*, July 1966, pp. 471-496; Oscar Handlin, *The Newcomers* (Garden City, N.Y., 1959), ch. 3.

10. *Riot Commission Report*, pp. 168-169; John J. Grimes, "The Black Man in Law Enforcement: An Analysis of the Distribution of Black Men in Law Enforcement Agencies and Related Recruitment Problems" (Masters thesis, John Jay College of Criminal Justice, 1969), tables 5-6; Elliott M. Rudwick, *The Unequal Badge: Negro Policemen in the South* (Atlanta, 1962), pp. 3-12.

11. Jenkins, *Keeping the Peace*, pp. 9-10, 24-29; Atlanta City Council, *Minutes*, Nov. 17, 1947, p. 66; Dec. 1, 1947, pp. 86-87; Atlanta City Council Police Committee, *Minutes*, Nov. 26, 1948, pp. 177-179; Herbert T. Jenkins to Quinn Tamm, June 8, 1962, Atlanta Police Department Files; *Crime Commission Report*, p. 168.

12. Los Angeles *Herald-Examiner*, Dec. 21, 1964; Turner, *The Police Establishment*, p. 171; E. Franklin Jackson to Robert V. Murray, Oct. 31, 1960; Robert V. Murray to E. Franklin Jackson, Nov. 7, 1960, Metropolitan Police Department Files; Smith, *The Tarnished Badge*, pp. 186-187.

13. Levenson, "There's No Place Like Home," ch. 2.

14. *Castro v. Beecher*, 334 F.Supp. 930 (1971), 942; "Comparison of School Location and Levels of Education with Pass or Fail on Otis Lennon," Atlanta Police Department Files; *Guardians Association of New York City Police Department, Inc. v. Civil Service Commission of City of New York*, 490

F.2d. 400 (1973), Plaintiff's Brief; *Crime Commission Report,* pp. 168-169; Christine Herzog, "Tests on Trial: Racial Discrimination in Access to Public Service Employment" (Masters thesis, MIT, forthcoming).

15. *Commonwealth of Pennsylvania* v. *O'Neill,* 348 F.Supp. 1084 (1972), 1,092-1,100; "Recruitment, Assignment and Promotion of Nonwhite Police Officers," President's Riot Commission Archives.

16. Ronald Christensen, "Projected Percentage of U.S. Population With Criminal Arrest and Conviction Records," in President's Crime Commission, *Task Force Report: Science and Technology* (Washington, D.C., 1967), pp. 216-228; Fogelson, *Violence as Protest,* pp. 114-115; IACP, *Police Personnel Practices,* pp. 48-51.

17. *Riot Commission Report,* p. 169; ICMA, *The Municipal Year Book* (Chicago, 1967), pp. 453-454.

18. Handlin, *The Newcomers,* ch. 4; Osofsky, *Harlem,* chs. 5-8; Allan H. Spear, *Black Chicago: The Making of a Negro Ghetto, 1890-1920* (Chicago, 1967), chs. 1, 7; Robert C. Weaver, *The Negro Ghetto* (New York, 1948), chs. 3-7; August Meier and Elliott M. Rudwick, *From Plantation to Ghetto* (New York, 1968), ch. 6; James Q. Wilson, *Negro Politics: The Search for Leadership* (New York, 1960), pp. 21-34.

19. Hays, "The Politics of Reform," pp. 157-169.

20. Virgil W. Peterson to Alan Levensohn, Aug. 26, 1953, Chicago Crime Commission Files; *Lexow Committee Investigation,* I, 50.

21. Philadelphia County Grand Jury, *Investigation of Vice, Crime and Law Enforcement,* pp. 137-164; *Lexow Committee Investigation,* I, 47-49; *Mazet Committee Investigation,* III, 2,564; Chicago *Tribune,* May 28-June 9, 1946.

22. David Lewin, "Wage Determination in Local Government Employment" (Ph.D. diss., University of California at Los Angeles, 1971), pp. 123-125; Frank J. Thompson, "The Politics of Personnel Expenditures in Oakland: The Problems and Possibilities of Control," Working Paper (107-23) of The Urban Institute (1971), pp. 6-8; Horton, *Municipal Labor Relations,* pp. 24-28.

23. *Gardner* v. *Broderick, Police Commissioner of the City of New York,* 392 U.S. 273 (1968); *Garrity* v. *New Jersey,* 385 U.S. 493 (1967).

24. Carl Werthman and Irving Piliavin, "Gang Members and the Police," in Bordua, ed., *The Police,* pp. 57-59; St. Clair Drake and Horace R. Cayton, *Black Metropolis* (New York, 1962), II, ch. 17.

25. David W. Williams to John C. Holland, July 9, 1959; Los Angeles Board of Police Commissioners to Los Angeles City Council, Aug. 6, 1959, in Los Angeles City Council, *Petitions,* 1959, Number 89512; Woods, "The Progressives and the Police," pp. 470-471; Werthman and Piliavin, "Gang Members and the Police," pp. 56-98; *Crime Commission Report,* pp. 178-186.

26. Black and Reiss, "Police and Citizen Transactions," pp. 132-139; *McCone Commission Archives,* VIII, 8-9; Jacobs, *Prelude to Riot,* pp. 34-36; Paul Chevigny, *Police Power* (New York, 1969), ch. 1; Cray, *The Big Blue Line,* ch. 9.

27. Fogelson, *Violence as Protest,* pp. 67-68.

28. John Logue and Edwin A. Bock, *The Demotion of Deputy Chief Inspector Goldberg* (1963), Case Series: Number 78 of the Inter-University Case Program.

29. Werthman and Piliavin, "Gang Members and the Police," pp. 64, 90; Fogelson, *Violence as Protest,* pp. 61-65.

30. Wilson, *Varieties of Police Behavior,* chs. 5-7.

31. *Riot Commission Report,* p. 169; Lewin, "Wage Determination in Local Government Employment," pp. 123-125; Wilson, *Varieties of Police Behavior,* p. 190.

32. U.S. Bureau of the Census, *1967 Census of Governments: Volume 3, No. 1, Employment of Major Local Governments* (Washington, D.C., 1969); Caro, *The Power Broker;* David B. Tyack, *The One Best System* (Cambridge, 1974); Anthony M. Platt, *The Child Savers* (Chicago, 1969); Frances Fox Piven and Richard A. Cloward, *Regulating the Poor* (New York, 1971).

33. Hays, "The Politics of Reform," pp. 157-169; Fogelson, *The Fragmented Metropolis,* ch. 10; Tyack, *The One Best System,* pt. 4; Caro, *The Power Broker,* pt. 6; Martin A. Levin, "Urban Politics and Judicial Behavior," *Journal of Legal Studies,* January 1972, pp. 193-221.

34. See David J. Rothman's forthcoming book on these institutions, the sequel to *The Discovery of the Asylum* (Boston, 1971).

35. Donald C. Stone, "Can Police Effectiveness Be Measured?" *Public Management,* September 1930, pp. 466-467; IACP, *Uniform Crime Reporting,* p. 47; Smith, *Police Systems in the United States,* pp. 43-45.

36. Skolnick, *Justice Without Trial,* pp. 168-173, 176-179; New York *Times,* Apr. 15, 1974; President's Crime Commission, *The Challenge of Crime,* pp. 23-25, 262-263.

37. President's Violence Commission, *Transcript of Proceedings,* Oct. 24, 1968, p. 1,912; Reiss, *The Police and the Public,* pp. 72-76.

38. Ennis, *Criminal Victimization in the United States,* ch. 7; Albert D. Biderman, Louise A. Johnson, Jennie McIntyre, and Adrianne W. Weir, *Report on a Pilot Study in the District of Columbia on Victimization and Attitudes Toward Law Enforcement,* report prepared for President's Crime Commission (Washington, D.C., 1967), ch. 1; *New York Times,* Apr. 15, 1974.

39. Clarence E. Ridley and Herbert A. Simon, "Measuring Police Activities," *Public Management,* May 1937, p. 137.

40. Harry P. Harty, "Wrestling with Police Crime Control Productivity Measurement," in Joan L. Wolfle and John F. Heaphy, eds., *Readings on Productivity in Policing* (Washington, D.C., 1975), pp. 86-128; Ivan Allen, Jr., Foreword to Wolfle and Heaphy, eds., *Readings on Productivity,* pp. I-II.

11. Reform at a Standstill

1. President's Violence Commission, *Transcript of Proceedings,* Oct. 24, 1968, pp. 1,898-1,902.

2. Wilson and McLaren, *Police Administration,* pp. 79-86, 321-327; *Knapp Commission Report,* pp. 1-3; Jerry Wilson, *Police Report* (Boston,

1975), p. 142.

3. Benjamin Shimberg and Robert J. diGrazia, "Promotion," in O. Glenn Stahl and Richard A. Staufenberger, eds., *Police Personnel Administration* (Washington, D.C., 1974), pp. 101-124; Terry Eisenberg and James M. Murray, "Selection," in ibid., pp. 76-79; Bernard Cohen, *Minority Recruiting in the New York City Police Department*, Part II. *The Retention of Candidates* (New York, 1971), pp. 50-57.

4. Ahern, *Police in Trouble*, pp. 143-150.

5. President's Violence Commission, *Transcript of Proceedings*, Oct. 24, 1968, p. 1,902; Ahern, *Police in Trouble*, pp. 192-193; Wilson, *Police Report*, p. 198.

6. Wilson, *Police Report*, pp. 174-178; Wilson's letter to the Washington *Post*, Dec. 19, 1970.

7. Police Foundation, "News Release," Apr. 29, 1974, p. 3; President's Violence Commission, *Transcript of Proceedings*, Oct. 24, 1968, p. 1,912; Ahern, *Police in Trouble*, pp. 150-155.

8. *Pennsylvania Crime Commission Report*, p. 1; *Knapp Commission Report*, pp. 1-3; Williams, *Vice Squad*, pp. 56-62; New York *Times*, Aug. 10, 1972; Mar. 4, 1974; *Christian Science Monitor*, Mar. 19, 1974; George Bliss, "Bad Apples on the Beat," *The Nation*, Feb. 9, 1974, pp. 171-174.

9. *Newsweek*, Aug. 16, 1965, p. 20; Biderman *et al.*, *Victimization and Attitudes Toward Law Enforcement*, p. 133.

10. President's Violence Commission, *Transcript of Proceedings*, Sept. 18, 1968, pp. 17, 22; Ramsey Clark, *Crime in America* (New York), p. 9, ch. 9.

11. For reviews of these movies, see the New York *Times*, Dec. 23, 1971; Nov. 25, Dec 26, 1973.

12. New York *Times*, April 15, 1974; Ennis, *Criminal Victimization in the United States*, pp. 43-47; Biderman *et al.*, *Victimization and Attitudes Toward Law Enforcement*, pp. 153-155.

13. Dick Russell, "Police Aides—Yes! Vigilantes—No!" *Parade*, June 22, 1975, pp. 8-10; Albert J. Reiss, Jr., "Public Perceptions and Recollections about Crime, Law Enforcement, and Criminal Justice," in *Studies in Crime and Law Enforcement in Major Metropolitan Areas*, I, Section II, 102-112; *The New Yorker*, Aug. 26, 1974, p. 50.

14. Washington *Post*, May 10, 1975; Raymond D. Horton, "Economic Brief for the City of New York," brief prepared for the impasse proceeding between the city and the PBA in 1975, pp. 76, 85; ICMA, *The Municipal Year Book* (Washington, D.C., 1973), pp. 175-176.

15. Horton, "Economic Brief," pp. 109, 142; ICMA, *The Municpal Year Book* (Washington, D.C., 1975), pp. 52-53.

16. Martin E. Segal Company, "Boston Police Department: Special Report on Retirement" (1974), p. 16. On the Los Angeles fire and police pension system's cost-of-living clause, see Janet M. Corpus' forthcoming paper for the Joint Center for Urban Studies' project on Municipal Employee Unions.

17. Horton, "Economic Brief," pp. 119, 145, 147.

18. Citizens Budget Commission, *New York City's Productivity Program: The Police Department* (New York, 1973), pp. 8-24; Advisory Group on Pro-

ductivity in Law Enforcement, *Report on Opportunities for Improving Productivity in Police Services* (Washington, D.C., 1973), chs. 3-5; Washington *Post,* May 10, 1975.

19. See Judy A. Levenson's forthcoming paper on pension reform in Detroit for the Joint Center for Urban Studies' project on Municipal Employee Unions.

20. See Janet M. Corpus' forthcoming paper on salary setting in Los Angeles for the Joint Center for the Urban Studies' project on Municipal Employee Unions.

21. New York *Times,* Jan. 22, Apr. 14, 1975; Horton, "Economic Brief," sec. 7; Bureau of National Affairs, *Government Employee Relations Reporter,* May 26, 1975, sec. B, pp. 6-8; sec. E, pp. 1-5. The New York State Public Employee Relations Board has since ruled that parity is illegal on the grounds that it inhibits the bargaining process. See New York *Times,* Jan. 11, 1977.

22. U.S. Commission on Civil Rights, *Hearings Held in Detroit, Michigan, December 14-15, 1960* (Washington, D.C., 1961), pp. 379-388; U.S. Commission on Civil Rights, *Hearing [Held in] Newark, New Jersey, September 11-12, 1962* (Washington, D.C., 1963), pp. 473-483; American Civil Liberties Union, *Police Power and Citizens' Rights: The Case for an Independent Police Review Board,* pp. 8-19; Joseph D. Lohman and Gordon E. Misner, *The Police and the Community,* report prepared for President's Crime Commission (Washington, D.C., 1966), I, 167-175; II, 164-165; *Crime Commission Report,* p. 196; Harold Norris, "Arrest Without Warrant," *The Crisis,* October 1958, pp. 481-486; American Civil Liberties Union, Illinois Division, *Secret Detention by the Chicago Police* (Glencoe, Ill., 1959), pp. 22-29; *Congressional Record,* vol. 108, pt. 15, Sept. 26, 1962, pp. 20,913-20,919; *Crime Commission Report,* pp. 186-188; Anthony Lewis, *Portrait of a Decade* (New York, 1965).

23. ACLU, *Police Power and Citizens' Rights,* p. 19; National Center on Police and Community Relations, *Police and Community Relations,* pp. 192-193, 202-203, 218-219; *Crime Commission Report,* pp. 195-197; Harold Beral and Marcus Sisk, "The Administration of Complaints by Civilians Against the Police," *Harvard Law Review,* January 1964, pp. 499-519.

24. Fogelson, *Violence as Protest,* p. 72.

25. Ibid., p. 73.

26. ACLU, *Police Power and Citizens' Rights,* pp. 33-38; Lohman and Misner, *The Police and the Community,* II, 213-217; David W. Abbott, Louis H. Gold, and Edward T. Rogowsky, *Police, Politics and Race: The New York Referendum on Civilian Review* (Cambridge, 1969), pp. 5-6; National Capital Area Civil Liberties Union, "A Proposed Revision of the System for Processing Civilian Complaints Against Police Misconduct in the District of Columbia" (1964), Metropolitan Police Department Files.

27. Los Angeles *Times,* July 19, 1960; Denver *Post,* July 14, 1964; Newark *Star-Ledger,* Apr. 7, 1963; Rochester *Democrat and Chronicle,* Dec. 31, 1965; ACLU, *Police Power and Citizens' Rights,* pp. 33-38; Abbott, Gold, and Rogowsky, *Police, Politics and Race,* pp. 6-8; Turner, *The Police Establishment,* chs. 11-12; NCPA, "Subversive Intervention into Law Enforcement" (1965), pp. 1-35, ICPA Files. On the waning of the review boards, see the New York *Times,*

Feb. 10, 1975.

28. *Riot Commission Report,* p. 169. This assumes that nonwhites would have been fully represented on the police forces if the percentage of nonwhite officers had been about equal to the percentage of nonwhite residents.

29. Rudwick, *The Unequal Badge,* pp. 3-4; *Crime Commission Report,* pp. 167-168; *Riot Commission Report,* pp. 165-169; Lewis, *Portrait of a Decade,* pp. 105-108; Fogelson, *Violence as Protest,* ch. 1.

30. New York *Times,* Jan. 25, 1971; Metropolitan Police Department, Police Academy and Training Section, "Information Relative to Recruiting Conducted in the District of Columbia and Metropolitan Area for the Position of Policeman" (1964), Metropolitan Police Department Files; Richard J. Margolis, *Who Will Wear the Badge?,* report of the U.S. Commission on Civil Rights (Washington, D.C., 1971), pp. 15-24.

31. Levenson, "There's No Place Like Home," chs. 1, 3; New York *Times,* Jan. 22, Feb. 3/5, 1971; June 22, 1975; Los Angeles *Times,* Dec. 14/22, 1971; Jan. 21, 1972; Nov. 6, 1974.

32. *Penn* v. *Stumpf,* 308 F.Supp. 1238 (1970), Plaintiff's Brief; *Castro* v. *Beecher,* 334 F.Supp. 930 (1971), 934-942; *Commonwealth of Pennsylvania* v. *O'Neill,* 348 F.Supp. 1084 (1972), 1,088-1,101; *Bridgeport Guardians, Inc.* v. *Members of Bridgeport Civil Service Commission,* 345 F.Supp. 788 (1973), 783-794; *Guardians Association of New York City Police Department, Inc.* v. *Civil Service Commission of City of New York,* 490 F.2d 400 (1973), Plaintiff's Brief; Herzog, "Tests on Trial"; Deposition of Arthur C. Cadegan, Jr., taken on behalf of the plaintiffs on Oct. 19 and 20, 1970, in the case of *Castro* v. *Beecher* (United States District Court, District of Massachusetts, Civil Action No. 70-122OW), I, 77, 95-96; II, 35-36, 49-50, Massachusetts Law Reform Institute Files, Boston.

33. *Castro* v. *Beecher,* 334 F.Supp. 930 (1971), 941-946; Judge Pullam's Consent Decree, entered Apr. 10, 1973, in the United States District Court for the Eastern District of Pennsylvania in the case of *Commonwealth of Pennsylvania* v. *O'Neill* (Civil Action, No. 70-3500); Judge Carter's Consent Decree, entered Dec. 20, 1973, in the United States District Court for the Northern District of California in the case of *Penn* v. *Stumpf* (Civil Action No. C-69-239 OJC).

34. Interview with David Caplovitz, professor of sociology at the City University of New York and member of the West 105th Street Block Association, Aug. 1, 1975; Janet M. Corpus' forthcoming paper on the Los Angeles fire and police pension system for the Joint Center for Urban Studies' project on Municipal Employee Unions; ACLU, *Police Power and Citizens' Rights,* p. 37; Quaco Cloutterbuck, "Castro v. Beecher: A Study of the Legal Struggle for Equal Access to Public Employment" (Masters thesis, MIT, 1973).

Epilogue

1. Berkeley *Daily Gazette,* July 23, 1970; San Francisco *Chronicle,* July 22, 1970; New York *Times,* Aug. 14, 1970; Oakland *Tribune,* Aug. 26, 1970; "Berkeley Petition for Community Control of Police," the NCCF petition, a

copy of which was made available to me by Anthony M. Platt.

2. Fogelson, *Violence as Protest,* pp. 168-169; Carmichael and Hamilton, *Black Power,* chs. 2-3; August Meier, *Negro Protest Thought in America, 1880-1915* (Ann Arbor, 1966); Edmund David Cronon, *Black Moses* (Madison, 1955); E.U. Essien-Udom, *Black Nationalism* (Chicago, 1962); Harold Cruse, *The Crisis of the Negro Intellectual* (New York, 1967).

3. Fogelson, *Violence as Protest,* pp. 173-176; Floyd McKissick, *3/5 of a Man* (London, 1969), pp. 151-159; Carmichael and Hamilton, *Black Power,* pp. 166-167.

4. Jerome H. Skolnick, "Neighborhood Police," *The Nation,* Mar. 22, 1971, pp. 372-373.

5. Berkeley *Daily Gazette,* July 24, 1970; Wilson, *Varieties of Police Behavior,* pp. 286-290; San Francisco *Chronicle,* Aug. 27, 1970; Jan. 28, Feb. 11, 1971; Oakland *Tribune,* Oct. 15, 1970.

6. Oakland *Tribune,* Oct. 15, 1970; *Daily Californian,* Feb. 16, 1970; San Francisco *Chronicle,* Feb. 5/17, 1971; Waskow, "Community Control of the Police," pp. 4-7; Altshuler, *Community Control,* pp. 28-34, 37-44.

7. Los Angeles *Times,* Apr. 8, 1971; *The Sun Reporter,* Mar. 27, 1971.

8. James Q. Wilson, *Thinking about Crime* (New York, 1977), pp. 110-116.

9. President's Violence Commission, *Transcript of Proceedings,* Sept. 18, 1968, pp. 17, 22; Clark, *Crime in America,* ch. 9.

10. New York *Times,* May 18, 1970.

11. Los Angeles *Times,* Mar. 13, 1972; Lowi, "Machine Politics—Old and New," pp. 83-92.

12. President's Violence Commission, *Transcript of Proceedings,* Oct. 24, 1968, p. 1,941.

13. New York *Times,* June 8, 1976.

14. *Riot Commission Report,* p. 169; IACP, *Police Personnel Selection Survey.*

15. New York *Times,* June 8, 1975; Apr. 2, May 13/30, June 8, Aug. 13, Sept. 25, Nov. 22, 1976; Boston *Globe,* Mar. 25/26, Apr. 19, June 7/14, 22, July 7/14/15, 24, Aug. 21, 1976; Levenson, "There's No Place Like Home," chs. 1-2.

16. New York *Times,* Mar. 23, 1976; Levenson, "There's No Place Like Home," chs. 4-5.

17. On the growing concern over the mounting costs of police and other public employee pensions, see Los Angeles *Times,* Mar. 13, 1972; New York *Times,* Oct. 16, 1975; Mar. 11, 1976; *Wall Street Journal,* June 25, 1973; Boston *Globe,* Oct. 19, Nov. 9, Dec. 4, 1975; Jan. 2/28, May 16, 1976; *U.S. News & World Report,* July 19, 1971; *Nation's Business,* September 1971, pp. 31-33; Barbara A. Patocka, "Will Pension Costs Push America's Cities over the Brink?" *Institutional Investor,* June 1975, pp. 55ff; U.S. House Committee on Ways and Means, *Hearings . . . on the Subject of General Revenue Sharing* (Washington, D.C., 1971), p. 290.

18. U.S. Bureau of the Census, *Census of Governments, 1972: Volume 6, Topical Studies: Number 1, Employee Retirement Systems of State and Local*

Governments (Washington, D.C., 1973), p. 42; Board of Pension Commissioners, City of Los Angeles, *Annual Report [for] 1974,* p. 40; Horton, "Economic Brief," p. 144; R.D. Hursh, "Vested Right of Pensioner to Pension," in *American Law Reports, Annotated,* 2nd ser. 52: 437-481. On the legal status of public employee pensions, see Rubin G. Cohen, "Public Employee Retirement Plans — The Nature of the Employees' Rights," *University of Illinois Law Forum,* Spring 1968, pp. 32-62.

Index

127, 134-139, 253, 263; and vice, 6, 7, 8,
20-21, 29, 32, 37-39, 128-129, 139; and
police appointments, 10, 23, 27-28, 36,
69, 128, 253; and immigrants, 18-19,
36-39, 48-49, 69, 252-253, 255; and
chiefs, 22-25, 64-65, 98-101, 127, 223;
and civil service, 23, 26-27, 28, 126-127,
151; and police promotions, 23, 29-30,
69, 104, 128, 254; and police discipline,
24, 30, 69, 99-100, 128, 229-230, 255;
and rank-and-file associations, 26, 81,
199-200; and police assignments, 28-29,
69, 104, 128; relations with police, 35;
and IACP, 64-65; and squads, 127-128,
224; and second generation of reformers,
146, 150-154, 167-174, 190, 191-192,
223-224, 227, 252-255; and racial minorities, 169, 192, 252-253, 255; and
police salaries, 254-255, 261
Mackey, Harry A., 77-78, 100-101
McKelvey, W. J., 13
McLaren, Roy C., 163, 303
McNamara, Edmund L., 154, 174, 176,
177, 179
McNamara, John H., 238, 241
McNamara, Joseph D., 303
Magnum Force, 277
Malcolm X, 297
Malloy, Donald M., 98
Marijuana, 146
Martin, James J., 27, 136
Marx, Oscar B., 76
Massachusetts Civil Service Commission,
290
Massachusetts Collective Bargaining Fed-
eration, 211, 212
Massachusetts Institute of Technology, 144
Massachusetts Labor Relations Commis-
sion, 211
Massachusetts Law Reform Institute, 290,
292
Mazet Committee, 18, 54, 74
Meany, George, 203
Media. *See* Motion pictures; Newspapers;
Novels; Radio; Television
Mela, Thomas A., 290, 292
Melnick, Harold, 203
Memphis police, 180
Merriam, Charles E., 63
Merton, Robert K., 267
Mexicans: and political machine, 169; and

social mobility, 191, 248, 268, 293, 298;
and political decentralization, 192, 268;
and cultural pluralism, 192, 268; morality of, 192, 256, 258, 260; migration to
cities, 247-248, 249, 252; and police
jobs, 248, 249-251, 261, 287, 288; police
prejudice against, 257, 258; and preventive patrol, 259-260
Miami police, 148, 195
Michigan State University, 283
Michigan Supreme Court, 304
Military analogy: *v.* civilian orientation,
15-16, 55, 61, 89, 94, 220, 221-222; and
first generation of reformers, 54-61, 80-
81, 94, 96; and occupational paranoia,
113; and second generation of reformers, 154, 155, 156, 190, 194, 207, 222;
and police unions, 194, 196, 207
Milwaukee police: investigations of, 10;
immigrants in, 36-37, 123; number of
officers, 124, 125; residency requirement for, 182; benevolent association,
196, 216, 217; in unions, 213, 216, 217;
salaries of, 279; cost of, 279
Milwaukee Policemen's Protective Association (PPA), 196, 216, 217
Minneapolis police: military *v.* civilian
orientation in, 16; immigrants in, 36,
37, 123; number of officers, 124; ages
of, 180; pensions for, 308
Minneapolis Vice Commission, 132
Misner, Gordon E., 269, 271, 272, 273,
283
Missouri Association for Criminal Justice,
47, 131
Missouri Bar Association, 45, 46
Mitchel, John Purroy, 74, 100, 197
Mobility, social: and European immigrants, 36, 47, 121, 154, 191; reformers
on, 47, 90, 121, 154, 191, 262, 309; and
political machine, 69-70, 139; and racial
minorities, 191, 248, 268, 293, 298, 309.
See also Class
Monaghan, George, 201, 202, 204
Monaghan, John, 245
Moonlighting: prohibited, 80, 183, 199,
228, 305; necessity of, 198
Morality: of immigrants, 20-21, 38-39, 47,
48-49, 130, 137, 192; and cultural pluralism, 38-39, 137, 192; reformers on,
41-42, 47, 62, 192, 262; and crime pre-

New York, 170, 182, 289, 307; and
racial minorities, 249-250, 288, 289,
306, 309; and rank-and-file associations,
249, 289, 304, 306; and community con-
trol, 298; and costs of policing, 307
Responsive activity *v.* preventive activity,
17, 90, 94-95, 190-191, 220-221, 222,
241
Rex, Frederick, 117
Ridley, Clarence E., 266
Ring, Peter Smith, 250
Riots: election-day, 19; squads to control,
220, 222; race, 220, 240, 288, 297
Rizzo, Frank, 208
Rochester Locust Club, 285, 286
Rochester police, 177, 196, 213, 285, 286
Rochester Police Advisory Board, 285, 286
Rockefeller, Nelson A., 278
Rockefeller Foundation, 162
Rolph, James R., 73
Roosevelt, Franklin D., 167
Roosevelt, Theodore, 64, 141; on investi-
gative committees, 2, 5, 74, 123; and
military analogy, 54
Root, Elihu, 45
Rosenthal, Herman, 56, 72, 73
Rossi, Angelo J., 173
Roundsmen, 15
Rubenstein, Jonathan, 244
Ruef, Abraham, 168
Rutledge, William P., 145, 154, 188
Ryan, Michael, 25

St. Louis Civic League, 49
St. Louis police: 1860s probe of, 10; ethnic
composition of, 19, 36, 123, 248, 251;
number of officers, 19, 124, 125, 251;
and military analogy, 80; crime prevention by, 87; reorganization of, 178, 179;
ages of, 180; civilian personnel in, 186;
crime statistics of, 188, 233, 265; in
unions, 195; pensions for, 279
St. Paul police, 36, 123, 124, 179
St. Valentine's Day Massacre, 56, 117
Salaries of police, 19, 124, 251, 293; and
rank-and-file associations, 26, 82, 181,
194-200 *passim,* 254-255, 278, 282; and
police recruitment, 82, 103, 160, 181,
227; and professional model, 160, 199,
228-229; and political machines, 254-
255, 261; and costs of policing, 278-279,
281-282, 304

San Diego police, 279, 286
San Francisco Committee on Crime, 281
San Francisco *Examiner,* 9, 63
San Francisco police: and vice, 9-10, 32,
63, 148, 172; and political machine, 17,
28, 68, 72, 128; ethnic composition of,
19, 36, 123, 124, 248, 287; salaries of,
19, 181, 251, 279; chiefs of, 23, 175;
appointments of, 28, 128; investigations
of, 62, 63, 173; crime by, 72, 73, 99;
reorganization of, 176, 178, 179; train-
ing for, 182; civilian personnel in, 186;
Operation S, 187-188; crime statistics of,
188; POA, 217; racial prejudice among,
257, 259; and *Dirty Harry,* 276; cost of,
279; and civilian review boards, 286
San Francisco Realty Board, 62
Scandinavian-American police, 18, 37
Schieffelin, William Jay, 141
Schiff, Jacob H., 45
Schmidt, Bernard J., 174
Schmittberger, Max, 3, 25, 29
Schrotel, Stanley R., 143, 144, 154, 174,
176, 215, 216, 303
Schwab, Gustav H., 1, 2, 141
Schwarz, Fred, 239
SCMWA. *See* State, County and Munici-
pal Workers of America
Scott, Walter A., 195
Scottsboro Boys trial, 247
Seabury, Samuel, 62, 132, 141
Seabury Committee, 302; and political
machine, 74, 131, 167; and police cor-
ruption, 124, 246, 271
Seattle Civil Service Commission, 182
Seattle police, 175, 182, 200, 279, 286
Seattle Police Officers' Guild, 212, 213,
216
Seattle *Post-Intelligencer,* 175
Self-defense, citizen, 277
Self-policing, 283-284, 287
Seligman, Isaac N., 48
Senate Committee to Investigate Organ-
ized Crime in Interstate Commerce. *See*
Kefauver Committee
Serpico, 276
Service Employees International Union,
212, 214
Settlement houses, 47
Sherman, Lawrence Y., 54, 207
Shuler, R. P., 45, 48